What chimera man!
    What novelty, what monster,
What chaos, what vessel of contradiction,
    What marvel! Judge of all things,
Wretched worm; Guardian of the truth,
    Cesspit of uncertainty and error:
Glory and excrement of the universe.

— Blaise Pascal, *Thoughts*

GÖRING HERMANN

HITLER PALADIN OR PUPPET?

WOLFGANG PAUL

Translated by Helmut Bögler

Brockhampton Press

Arms and Armour Press
An imprint of the Cassell Group
Wellington House, 125 Strand, London WC2R 0BB

First English-language publication 1998.
Original German-language edition published 1983 by
Bechte Verlag, Esslingen.

British Library Cataloguing-in-Publication Data:
a catalogue record for this book is available from
the British Library.

Designed and edited by DAG Publications Ltd.
Designed by David Gibbons; edited by Michael Boxall;
printed and bound in Great Britain by
Creative Print and Design (Wales), Ebbw Vale

TRANSLATOR'S NOTE.
The text of this book contains some German terms
that are not readily translatable, some whose translation
would not equate exactly to the German meaning, and
some that have been deliberately left in German to
differentiate them from the equivalent English term.
In all such cases the German term is written in
italics followed if necessary by an explanation
in parenthesis.

This edition published 1999 by Brockhampton Press,
a member of Hodder Headline PLC Group

ISBN 1 86019 922 4

Contents

1
The Meeting at Sönke-Nissen-Koog

O n this Sunday, 6 August 1939, the hot sun was high in the blue summer sky over Sönke-Nissen-Koog near the town of Husum on the west coast of Schleswig-Holstein. The harvest was being brought in. There was peace in Europe. The Spanish civil war had ended, and with General Franco's seizure of power, the division of the continent between democratic and dictatorial forms of government had reached its pinnacle. Ever since the occupation of the remains of Czechoslovakia in mid March, Hitler's Germans seemed to have been basking in the thought of an eternal peace, and even now, at the beginning of August, this feeling remained unmarred by memories of the outbreak of the Great War 25 years before, although the writing was most certainly on the wall. With the virtually unanimous support of his people, Hitler had virtually torn up the Treaty of Versailles, and its fetters had fallen without a war.

World history, however, whose course either produces chaos or tames it, had not yet decided whether it wished to preserve the peace or decide once again by battle, as in 1914, who was to rule the world. In those days the earth had not yet been perceived as a tiny ball in the sky that could be destroyed by weapons of annihilation such as atom and hydrogen bombs.

August 1939. The 25 years that have passed since 1914 have seen the Germans recalling times of distress and times of happiness; a quarter of a century of almost continuous excitement with few periods of calm in the cacophony of impressions to which they have been subjected, or to which they have submitted themselves more or less voluntarily.

The Wilhelminian Reich and the unloved Republic have become a Greater German Reich. Bismarck's former Reich of 1871 is now the *Altreich* (Old Reich). Austria, together with its former possessions in the Sudetenland, and the territory along the River Memel, have again been annexed. All this is now called *Großdeutsches Reich* (Greater German Reich), and it includes a protectorate over Bohemia and Moravia, in which Germans rule over Czechs. The former German provinces in the east, however, which had fallen to Poland after the Great War when it was resurrected as a state, have not been returned, because Poland is capable of defending itself. Danzig (Gdansk) has remained a Free City, even under the swastika.

That the demand for the return of the lost eastern provinces could lead to a new war is conceivable to the Germans, who are now only concerned with bringing in the summer's harvest from the fields, but most believe that a repeat of the Great War is beyond all human reason. Why should Hitler put the power he possesses at risk? Great Britain, which has signed a treaty with Poland but not yet ratified it, only wants to prevent a new war, not to cause one which would throw Europe into a maelstrom of new, as yet unknown, horrors.

On this Sunday, 6 August 1939, at a moment when world history is still tame enough to let itself be led peacefully, even if the peace that reigns in Europe is fragile, a group of travellers left Hamburg in several cars to drive under the bright blue sky to Sönke-Nissen-Koog where they intended to meet Field Marshal Hermann Göring the following day.

Hermann Göring. Of this man Carl J. Burckhardt writes that he detected 'passion, a powerful appetite for life, broad, visible life, naked as in the games of childhood fantasies, like with criminals who never matured beyond the age of puberty, unrestrained to the point of evil, but not naturally malicious, no petty lust for revenge, including also intelligence, at certain moments sharp strong acts of intelligence, "the only one who can read a balance sheet", said one industrialist.' This Hermann Göring was the most powerful man in Germany after Adolf Hitler, his 'most loyal paladin'. But he was also a man of peace, who now led the 'peace party' within the upper hierarchy of the Reich, wherein was also a 'war party'.

These men who had an appointment with Göring at Sönke-Nissen-Koog were a Swede, the industrialist Birger Dahlerus from Stockholm, and some businessmen and industrialists from England: Charles MacLaren and C. F. Spencer, both directors of John Brown and Co., S. W. Rawson, a manufacturer from Sheffield, Sir Robert Renwick, Brian Mountain, A. Holden, and T. Mensforth, director of a large power company. None of them was a member of the Government or sat in Parliament, but as members of the Conservative Party they had connections to both and the political mission they were undertaking had been agreed with Foreign Secretary Lord Halifax.

Originally the conference was to have taken place in southern Sweden at Count C. A. Trolle-Wachtmeister's castle Trolle-Ljungby, 10 kilometres east of Kristianstad, but the press might have got wind of it, and it was decided that Sönke-Nissen-Koog, which lay within the totalitarian Reich, would ensure complete discretion. Göring was there by agreement with Hitler who had in mind a war with Poland but not with England or France.

For the Englishmen, Göring was the only man left in the Third Reich with whom they could speak, since Prime Minister Chamberlain had burnt all bridges to Hitler after the occupation of Prague, bridges that he had crossed several times during the Sudetenland Crisis in 1938 in an endeavour to preserve the peace.

Carl J. Burckhardt calls Göring, in contrast to Hitler, 'very Prussian'. 'He is so lively and agile that one forgets his corpulence. Göring is lying down and speaking. He lies like Tristan in the final act. But its all Wagnerian, a handsome bass with shining blue eyes, the forehead, seen in profile, bulging out, the mouth, which dominates all cartoons, strangely moulded, sunken in like that of an old woman. The whole physical being emanates a powerful will and, as with most Germans, it is put on show, exaggerated outwardly, made visible, but here this show is truly nourished by a force. There he now lies before me, happy as it would appear, with traits of a Falstaff who has come into his own, generous, very much in contrast to others even chivalrous at times, sometimes even waves of emotion emanate from the heart. In some situations there is much courage, but under the strangely feverish or suddenly blank eyes of his Führer all this collapses.'

Would this courage, which Burckhardt describes as collapsing before Hitler, now manifest itself, or would the *alter ego* of this unusual man, who had it within himself to prove himself before history, display courage even against the man to whom he owed everything that he had become, but who in turn had only become Führer and Chancellor with his support?

Or would Göring now, in this harvest time between peace and war, only want to play his Wagnerian role as a handsome bass in the diplomatic foreplay to the horrors that were to come?

As State Secretary for Foreign Affairs Freiherr von Weizsäcker later reported, during the initial days in August he had gained the impression that Hitler was looking for ways and means to get his head out of the noose, but also, that this impression had stayed with him until well past mid August. Head out of the noose? Collapse of the Thousand Year Reich after only a few years?

For England too, there was much at risk. Her decline from a world power could be accelerated by a world war. Should England stop this decline through the alliance with Germany, that she was now being offered by Hitler and Göring? With Hitler never, but maybe with Göring, who could not only oppose Hitler but even remove him? Realistically, England's pact with Poland could not be honoured in the event of war. Everybody who knew anything about it knew that.

England against Germany, now with the United States as ally but also as heir to the British Empire? On 6 August 1939 there were many reasons for the seven gentlemen from England to travel to Sönke-Nissen-Koog and meet Göring.

The koog, or polder, which had been wrested from the North Sea, lay in the country of the Angles from which the ancestors of the Anglo-Saxons had once come to the island. Above the low house with its roof displaying dormer windows, the Swedish flag was flying, the yellow Christian cross in the blue waters of the sea. Birger Dahlerus had had the flag hoisted to demonstrate the neutrality of the house to his guests. But the polder was not Swedish – it was German. Its seven farms belonged to Dahlerus' wife, Elisabeth Nissen, who had been a widow. Dahlerus was unable to bring his wife from Stockholm because she was pregnant. As hostess for the Anglo-German meeting, therefore, he brought a young and pretty German woman from Stockholm, Mary-Lies Stüve, who spoke English and had formerly worked as a housekeeper for his wife. This summer she had been visiting the Dahleruses and had brought with her Hanna, the daughter of Dr Siegfried Möller, owner of a sanatorium in Dresden for whom she had been working as housekeeper and governess since 1937. The child had to break off her summer holiday in Stockholm and return to Dresden alone by train.

Mary-Lies Stüve, illegitimate daughter of a woman from Lübeck and the French film director Jacques Feydor who was making films with Greta Garbo in Hollywood, now for a short time became hostess in the house of Elisabeth Dahlerus' brother, a man named Rabe. Shortly after the meeting at the Koog, she wrote from Dresden–Loschwitz to her aunt who had emigrated to Switzerland: 'I had the dubious pleasure of appearing there in the middle of the harvest and evicting six guests as well as the owner and his wife and all the children in order to prepare noble quarters for various guests. Apart from the fact that it was not all that easy to kick a family out of their own house, it was also not easy to prepare good quarters there. I had to call in the electrician, painter, joiner, and mechanic. With them I went through the house in order to have electric bells installed, lamps changed which were either in such a state of decay that one could poke a finger through them or so covered with fly specks that they just had to go. Tapestry hanging in tatters from the ceiling had to be pasted back on, beds tested for their comfort, mattresses partly renewed. The staircase received a carpet, the toilet was made to work and got a new seat, not because of the size (they were thinking of the corpulent Most High user from Berlin!) but because the paint would have stuck if the old seat had been repainted. And all of this three-quarters of an hour by car away from Husum! And all the things I had to buy, I even came from Hamburg with quilts and sheets. Then there was a thorough cleaning in which I had the honour to participate because of lack of staff and the harvest. On Saturday evening, 5 August, I was sitting on the stairs, everybody gone, as the only living remainder on the farm saving the cows, who were mooing in the stalls.'

When the English delegation, as had been announced to Mary-Lies Stüve, arrived two and a half hours late (Dahlerus had taken the gentlemen from England on a sightseeing tour of Hamburg and the two cars in which they came belonged to him and were being driven by his two Swedish chauffeurs), the house was spic and span, and a cook had arrived from Hamburg with Swedish glasses and food because Dahlerus wanted to entertain his guests with Swedish meals. Mary-Lies Stüve's letter goes on: 'I had the honour to be introduced to all of them and to show them their rooms. I was wearing a *Dirndl* (Bavarian costume consisting of skirt, blouse and apron), naturally a particularly cute one, and received the nicest compliments. For this I was allowed to bring them warm water for shaving, which they then no longer asked for after they had discovered that I was all alone in the house in the morning. For lack of space, the staff slept elsewhere and because they were never finished before 2 a.m. I could not order them back before 8.30 a.m.'

Nor did Birger Dahlerus sleep in the house. He stayed at a hotel, the Landwirtschaftliches Haus, in Bredstedt, 11 kilometres away. Dahlerus had taken leave of his guests fairly soon because he assumed that they would wish to retire early so as to be fit for the meeting with Göring. But the English guests did not seek their beds until the early hours, as Mary-Lies Stüve recalls, who was quite nervous at the prospect of having to welcome the second most powerful man in Germany next morning, since from her family background she was what in those days was referred to as a half-Jew. And now she was to play housekeeper at Sönke-Nissen-Koog to the man who had signed the Nuremberg (racial) laws! But since the issue now was not Aryan or non-Aryan antecedents but higher things, war or peace, a future or no future at all, she was able quickly to fall asleep in the short summer night.

She was torn from sleep early on Monday morning by a telephone call from the station-master at Bredstedt who ordered her to hoist swastika flags over Sönke-Nissen-Koog, because he had been advised of the arrival of the Field Marshal and Prussian Minister President's special train from Hamburg, and that the Field Marshal intended to leave his train at Bredstedt and visit the Koog. Since the meeting was to be kept secret, the only explanation Mary-Lies Stüve had for the exaggerated zeal of the station-master was the practice of the times, where it was normal to display flags whenever one of the great men of the Reich came to call, and Göring was the second greatest after the Führer and Chancellor. Mary-Lies Stüve assumed that Bredstedt was already drowning in a sea of flags and she told the station-master that she knew the rules and he was satisfied with that, but his zeal was responsible for a paragraph in the *Hamburger Fremdenblatt* (but only there) on 9 August: 'Yesterday morning (actually it had been the day before) Field Marshal Göring went from Bredstedt, where he had arrived in his special train, to Sönke-Nissen-Koog by car in order to visit the Rabe farm.' On 9 August the English guests were back in London.

Birger Dahlerus spent a sleepless night from Sunday to Monday 7 August: 'My thoughts were constantly revolving around the problems that lay before us, I had heard them being discussed so often, both from the German and the English side, that I believed I was quite well informed about the major problems. Would Göring be so impressed by what he heard that he would really start to think things over? Would the meeting take place in such a spirit that the English for their part would really gain confidence in Göring? And if Göring became convinced of the necessity and possibility of a peaceful solution, would he prove to be strong enough to impose his conviction on the German government? I could not sleep. I had received new and very exact details about German rearmament, which made me realise all the horrors that a new world war would bring to Europe. Because of technology and newly developed means of destruction it was inconceivable that a war could break out in Europe without causing a world-wide conflagration with unforeseeable consequences. As an unimportant citizen of a small neutral country I well knew how very little I could do as an individual. If there was anything at all I could do to avoid a catastrophe, however, I wanted to do it.'

In the light of subsequent events, these words sound thin. But no respect can be too high for an individual who at such a time – or at any time in the future before new, even more terrible conflicts erupt on this planet – attempts to stem the inexorable tide, even if only by offering a little house in a polder in an endeavour to wrest a hope for peace from the antagonists of tomorrow! If they fail, the intermediaries are devoured by history. At the time, Birger Dahlerus did not have any ambitions. He saw himself as a mere chance link between the powers upon whom it depended in August 1939 whether there would be war or peace in Europe. To a lesser degree the same could be said of Mary-Lies Stüve, a handsome, intelligent woman of 32, who made all ready in the house, was friendly to the gentlemen, and earned Göring's appreciation, which he expressed heartily when leaving. An historical witness who thought that one could come to an understanding if one talked to one another, ate and drank well, and felt comfortable.

History has no pity. How much pity does it trample underfoot! On the morning of 7 August Dahlerus had breakfast with the English guests. He saw tension and earnestness written in their faces. Again it was a bright northern summer morning, an August sky infinitely high above the flat landscape of the polder. When he got back to Bredstedt at about 8.30 a.m., Göring's special train was already standing there. He spoke first to Göring's chief adjutant, Ministerial Councillor Görnert, then to State Secretary Körner who ran the four-year-plan under Göring, and finally to the two representatives who were to take part in the meeting, General Bodenschatz, the liaison officer between Göring and Hitler, and Dr Böttger, the interpreter. As Dahlerus writes, Göring then 'gave, during a conversation in the train lasting about one hour, a presentation of his opinion of the foreign political situation and the result to which in his view the meeting should lead, namely a mutual agreement to hold an Anglo–German conference with plenipotentiaries from both governments, this naturally under the condition that the meeting today showed that such an official conference could lead to a positive result'.

When Göring, dressed in civilian clothes complete with coat and fashionable hat, and smoking a Havana cigar (obtained from Vienna), left the station with Dahlerus, who was wearing a light summer coat but no hat, they were confronted by a double line of cheering Dithmarscher (the polder lies in the district of Dithmarsch) who had learned of Göring's presence through the station-master's demand for flags. Dahlerus became somewhat irritated because everything was supposed to be strictly secret. The Bredstedt photographer, who took advantage of this opportunity, has left us some pictures showing the heavy car flying the pennant of the Commander-in-Chief of the Luftwaffe, behind arms raised in the *Hitlergruß* (the Nazi 'Heil Hitler' salute), with a serious-looking Göring standing before it, hands in his pockets, while Dahlerus and his entourage are getting into the car. Dahlerus' chauffeur partly blocks the view. Göring is leaning on a cane

The first conference in the large living-room of the Rabe house lasted from 10 o'clock to 1.30, and was followed by lunch at which, following traditional Swedish custom, Dahlerus as host welcomed the guests. A little later Göring rose, raised his glass of aquavit, drank a *skål* (the Swedish toast) to the English representatives, and ended with the suggestion that they all drink a *skål* to Peace.

Dahlerus notes: 'The atmosphere was most positive and I believe that with a continuation of the contacts in such a manner there really is a possibility of a peaceful resolution of the problems. After lunch the negotiations continued.' Dahlerus summarises the results of the conference: 'In view of the spirit of the talks today, the participants are of the opinion that a meeting of plenipotentiaries from both governments could lead to an accord and they therefore agree to recommend to their governments to hold such a conference as quickly as possible, preferably in Sweden.'

Göring had given the Englishmen his 'solemn assurance as a statesman and officer', that with their claim to Gdansk and a corridor leading to it, the Germans were not intending a policy of encirclement of Poland, and that the demand for a solution to the Gdansk problem would not be followed by claims to further territory. Dahlerus writes, 'When saying good-bye the Englishmen and Germans toasted one another'.

From Dresden Mary-Lies Stüve wrote to Switzerland: 'Everything went very much according to hopes and I am very pleased, quite apart from the fact that everything having to do with me went very well. I was warmly thanked by everybody including the Most High. I made my peace with the Rabe family again when they realised the whole thing had not been a joke and particularly that carpets, furniture, and an electric stove were to remain as a lasting souvenir.'

But this is getting ahead of the story. First Göring, who had driven to Niebüll at 6.30 p.m., had to board his special train which took him to Westerland on Sylt, and from there drive to his summer house in Wenningstedt where his wife and daughter were already staying. The following morning General Bodenschatz flew to Berchtesgaden to report to Hitler.

On Tuesday, 8 August, Dahlerus again had breakfast with the Englishmen, and gathered that they were leaning towards the idea that it would be better to have representatives from the French and Italian governments take part in the meeting between the English and German representatives. This would be bringing Munich 1938 back into play; a four-power conference with fateful consequences for a country not present. Then it had been Czechoslovakia, now it was Poland.

During their drive across the island Göring, whom Dahlerus met in Westerland the same day to discuss the matter, appeared to be satisfied with the results of the meeting and said that the suggestion of a four-power conference would be acceptable to the German Government. But he strongly emphasised that the conference could not be permitted to end in a catastrophe, and preparatory discussions would have to take place.

Such discussions, of course, would be greatly at variance with the spontaneity of the informal Anglo–German talks about war and peace at the Koog, but Dahlerus returned to the mainland by train well satisfied, and that evening in a little pub in Niebüll met the leader of the delegation, Mr Spencer, who took careful notes of what Göring had told Dahlerus. Spencer went back to the Koog and Mary-Lies Stüve noted that the guests again did not go to bed before midnight. Dahlerus went straight back to Stockholm where he arrived the following noon, 'tired but full of hope', as he writes.

These calm summer days in northern Germany were followed by bad weather, with thunderstorms every day. From Dresden, after her little excursion into world history, Mary-Lies Stüve wrote to Switzerland, 'My Swedish host is now probably in London again, he really gets about.'

In fact Dahlerus had not gone to London but was busily engaged on the telephone. On 12 August he was able to inform his English guests that the Germans had accepted the suggestion of a secret four-power conference and would prefer to have it take place in Sweden. 'Now for me an inexplicable, and as it was to prove, fateful hiatus occurred, namely a complete halt in the negotiations. The only thing I was able to learn from Spencer, who had gone to Aix-les-Bains, was that one could not count on a reply from Britain for some time to come. At the moment, a large number of the key people were on holiday as was usual at this time of year. I became more and more uneasy, but naturally was unable to do anything. In the meantime the political situation deteriorated.'

In a speech made in 1974, the US Secretary of State, Henry Kissinger, said of July 1914: 'In fact they were all on vacation at this time, because they believed it was not a serious crisis. Four weeks later they had an all-encompassing war.' History does not repeat itself, but it offers comparisons which can be made after the event, because the people who hold responsibility, the key actors in history, hardly change.

2
'So Help us God'

In order to be able to understand Göring's role and position during those days in August 1939, certain facts need to be recorded. Until then, Hitler had had himself advised on foreign affairs by Göring and Ribbentrop. These two men became rivals when Hitler insisted on finally having an *Ostprogramm* (basically a plan for the conquest and enslavement of Poland and Russia) with objectives reaching far beyond Gdansk, the Corridor, and Poland. On the Obersalzberg on 11 August 1939, he said to Carl J. Burckhardt, whom he had invited there from Gdansk (where Burckhardt was High Commissioner for the League of Nations) together with *Gauleiter* (Party district boss) Forster for a discussion of the situation, with reference to this Ostprogramm: 'I have no romantic objectives. Above all, I want nothing from the West, not today and not tomorrow. All those ideas people ascribe to me are inventions. But I must have a free hand in the East.'

Ribbentrop had foolishly assured Hitler that Britain would not honour its guarantee to Poland. But the Italian Foreign Minister Ciano had told Hitler that Poland would be the *casus belli* for Great Britain. Göring was in Wenningstedt on the island of Sylt. From his meeting with the seven Englishmen at Sönke-Nissen-Koog Hitler knew that on the British side a four-power conference in Sweden had been mooted, but no statement was forthcoming from the government in London.

The partitioning of Poland by the Hitler–Stalin Pact was not yet under discussion at this time, Hitler being hesitant about going beyond a trade agreement with the Soviet Union. 'I would again like to speak with an Englishman who knows German before it is too late,' he told Burckhardt at the tea house on the Obersalzberg on 11 August. 'Sir Neville Henderson speaks fluent German I am told,' replied the League of Nations Commissioner. 'There is no sense in that,' Hitler said. 'He is a diplomat with a carnation in his buttonhole. I would like to speak with a man such as Lord Halifax. He himself can no longer come, but how about Marshal Ironside? I hear good things about him. Could you convey that to the British?'

As Hitler knew from Göring, Lord Halifax was behind the seven Englishmen at the Koog. But according to Dahlerus, after the meeting on 7 August nothing further was heard from Lord Halifax, which is why Hitler sought to make contact via Burckhardt with the Chief of the Imperial General Staff, Field Marshal Ironside.

On the day after this conversation, 12 August, Hitler gave the order for the deployment of the *Wehrmacht* (German Armed Forces) against Poland and set 26

15

August as the date for the attack. For the time being Hitler was no longer consulting Göring who was basking in the sun on the beach at Kampen. There, as early as 1933, a notice could be seen prohibiting the taking of photographs of the Prussian Minister President. In 1934 the Reich Labour Service dug a sand castle for Göring and erected barbed wire around it.

After Ciano's visit, Ribbentrop had persuaded Hitler to conclude a treaty of non-aggression with the Soviet Union, which in his opinion was the final possibility of preventing England from interfering in a German–Polish war. Hitler now persuaded Stalin to receive Ribbentrop 'as quickly as possible'. In Moscow an Anglo–French military mission was conducting negotiations with officers of the Red Army, as yet without results. On 21 August Stalin's agreement to meet Ribbentrop on 23 August arrived at the Obersalzberg.

Hitler now ordered the commanders-in-chief of the Wehrmacht branches with their chiefs of staff, the chiefs of the *Oberkommando der Wehrmacht* (OKW, i.e., joint chiefs of the armed services) and the commanders-in-chief of the army groups and armies earmarked for mobilisation, to come to the Berghof near Berchtesgaden in civilian dress on 22 August.

Göring had returned to his house on the Obersalzberg from his vacation on the North Sea. Until now he, the Commander-in-Chief of the Luftwaffe, had had no knowledge of the forthcoming deployment in the East, which had been planned by the General Staff of the *Heer* (Army). Hitler ordered Colonel General von Brauchitsch to have his Chief of Staff General Halder give a presentation of the planned military measures to Göring and the generals assembled at the Berghof. Halder felt this presentation to be superfluous, but he came from Berlin and reported to Göring on the Obersalzberg at 10 a.m. on 22 August. From his notes for the presentation, which are preserved in his war diary, one learns that 'it is the assignment of the Führer to begin the war with surprisingly strong blows which should lead to rapid results'. Mobilisation was to be delayed until the very day of the attack. The objective was the destruction of the Polish army. In conclusion, Halder 'requested of the Luftwaffe' that it consider its deployment on the Vistula–Mlawa and the possibilities of airborne landings.

After this, at noon, Hitler met the generals at the Berghof and played his trump card. He informed them that Russia would be eliminated by means of a treaty. He did not speak of his intention to divide Poland with Stalin. As the senior officer present, Göring made the closing remarks, swearing fidelity, obedience, and unconditional allegiance to Hitler. Only after the generals had left did a meeting take place between Hitler and Göring who now knew that during his absence his rival von Ribbentrop had shunted him aside. Göring considered the Foreign Ministry to be neither willing nor capable of establishing a sufficiently close contact with the Foreign Office in London, and returned to Berlin on 22 August with the intention of again using Birger Dahlerus to re-activate this contact from his side. Hitler was probably in agreement with this.

Next morning, Wednesday 23 August, Göring called Dahlerus in Stockholm and asked him to come to Berlin immediately. As Dahlerus writes: 'he emphasised that the situation had taken a turn for the worse and that the possibilities of a peaceful solution had been greatly reduced'.

At this point it must be noted that the Luftwaffe, which Göring had been developing since 1933, was not capable of waging a serious air war against Britain. Hitler had gained a false impression from the exhibition of new aircraft types at the aircraft testing field at Rechlin on 3 July 1939. His Luftwaffe adjutant von Below had pointed out to Hitler on the drive home, that everything he had seen was still very much in the future. As Below writes, according to Hitler's statements to date, Göring, Milch, and Udet were reckoning on an armed conflict in 1943 at the earliest. So whether Göring was motivated by a desire for peace or was merely unhappily aware that his Luftwaffe was incapable of fighting a major war as yet, his immediate concern, since he now knew that the war against Poland was to begin in three days' time, was to raise the question of war or peace as dramatically as possible via his line of communication with London.

Before leaving for Berlin, Dahlerus spoke to Sweden's Prime Minister Hansson, who did not share his opinion about the gravity of the situation and refused to interrupt his vacation on the Stockholm archipelago. On Thursday 24 August Dahlerus flew to Berlin. Göring had him brought to Carinhall in the Schorfheide by car. Their meeting began at 2 p.m. As Dahlerus writes, he was given a comprehensive overview of the military and political situation. Göring did not tell him about the date of attack set for 26 August. 'Göring emphasised', Dahlerus writes, 'that the danger of a war on several fronts had been eliminated by the treaty with Russia, but underlined at the same time that the German Government still had the sincere desire to reach an agreement with Britain. He deplored the fact that the intended conference (in Sweden) had not come about and attempted in the further course of the conversation, to portray the situation as if future developments depended solely on Britain's willingness and initiative. He bade me go to London the following day and to confirm to the British Government that the German Government was desirous of reaching an agreement and that he, Göring, would bring all his authority to bear in order to achieve this objective.' But how much authority did Göring still have at this point?

He had not succeeded in dissuading Hitler from a war against Poland. He had contradicted him, but then given in when Ribbentrop had brought in the harvest from Moscow. Only after the Hitler–Stalin Pact had been concluded, did he look for a final way out via Dahlerus.

'Göring's conduct was strange, but typical for him,' writes Nicolaus von Below in his book *Hitler's Adjutant, 1937–45*. 'He cast a jealous eye on Ribbentrop's success in Moscow and criticised him for not having made enough of an effort on behalf of an Anglo–German agreement. While it is true that Göring welcomed the agreement with Russia, he feared a new danger: that Ribbentrop's influence on Hitler had again become strong. Göring and Ribbentrop just did not like each other, said Bodenschatz. I had followed the fateful influence of the personal sympathies and antipathies of the "great ones of the Reich" on political matters with a complete lack of understanding. In the situation of those days it would have been important to dissuade Hitler from employing the Wehrmacht against Poland and to open the way for new negotiations by means of a collaboration between Göring and Ribbentrop based on trust. However, both of them wanted to have the sole glory of being Hitler's closest and best adviser.'

Before Göring received Dahlerus at Carinhall on 24 August, the Field Marshal had given the Commander-in-Chief of the Army, von Brauchitsch, his agreement, not to consider a French invasion of Luxembourg as a *casus belli* against France. At the beginning of the Great War in 1914, Luxembourg had been occupied by the Germans by *coup de main* in order to anticipate a French invasion. Von Brauchitsch had therefore raised this question. Göring's agreement tipped the scales for Hitler's decision not to have Luxembourg occupied.

Before Dahlerus took the regular flight from Berlin to London on 25 August, Göring had reached him by telephone at the Hotel Esplanade and informed him that the treaty with Russia had more far-reaching consequences than could be gathered from the official communiqué. When Dahlerus met Lord Halifax at the Foreign Office that Friday he learned that he would no longer need to be involved, because the British Ambassador, Sir Neville Henderson, had just been called to the *Reichskanzlei* (Chancellery) by Hitler and therefore official channels were now being used for the negotiations. However, Dahlerus refused to be satisfied with this. During dinner with the seven gentlemen who had been his guests at the Koog it was suggested that he personally find out the situation in Berlin after the meeting with Henderson. Since the telephone connections to Germany were already closed down, Dahlerus was only able to reach Göring at about 10.20 p.m. with the help of the Foreign Office. The call was switched through to the Chancellery where Göring was at the time.

Dahlerus writes: 'Göring was very nervous and expressed his unease about the situation quite openly; yes he declared that he feared the outbreak of war at any moment. He emphasised that he was placing much hope in my trip to London and that on this Friday morning he had discussed our talk on Thursday with Hitler in great detail. I expressed my astonishment about developments and asked the reason for them. Göring's reply was somewhat unclear but slowly I began to understand what he was saying. He pointed out that it had been that very Friday afternoon that the British had signed the pact with Poland. This took place in London at the same time, for all practical purposes, that Henderson called on Hitler in Berlin and was taken by Hitler as a provocation and an explicit declaration by Britain that she did not wish for a peaceful solution.'

At 7 o'clock that evening Hitler had cancelled the attack order against Poland scheduled for the morning of 26 August. It is assumed that one of the reasons for this renewed hesitation was that Mussolini had not been prepared to honour his treaty obligations. The signing of the Anglo–Polish Pact the same day had played a special part in the cancellation. When Dahlerus called Göring at the Chancellery the decision there had been taken. At 10.30 p.m. on Hitler's order, Army adjutant Engel passed the 'cancellation of the attack' to General Halder by telephone. From Engel Halder learned: 'Führer quite shattered. Slight hope that one can negotiate Britain's agreement to demands that Poland refuses. Gdansk corridor. Henderson: Offer solution corridor question and Gdansk in London for the moment. Göring – compromise.'

It now looked as though, with the withdrawal of the attack order by Hitler, it was finally Göring's move.

Next morning Dahlerus met Lord Halifax at Downing Street. The mood in London was 'terrible', as Dahlerus writes. Several of his acquaintances 'had left London early in the morning because they reckoned on the outbreak of war at any moment'. At that time it was generally supposed that if war broke out bombing the enemy's capital would be the first warlike action to take place. Dahlerus emphasised to Lord Halifax that 'the only man in Germany who can prevent a war is Göring. I therefore made the suggestion that in a personal letter to Göring which I could deliver, Halifax should affirm England's serious intent to reach a peaceful solution and expressed the hope that such a measure could calm down the excited mood in Berlin.

'After having consulted with Chamberlain for half an hour, Lord Halifax informed me that the Prime Minister approved my suggestion and that he, Halifax, would write Göring a personal letter that I was to take with me and deliver. This letter, sent by Britain's Foreign Secretary at a time when the crisis appeared to have reached its height, is not known from any of the officially published reports. Halifax read the letter to me: in it he declares clearly, honestly and in a friendly manner, Britain's decided desire to come to an understanding with Germany.'

With this letter by Lord Halifax in his pocket, Dahlerus flew to Berlin-Tempelhof via Amsterdam on 26 August. There he was picked up by Lieutenant-Colonel Conradi of the Luftwaffe who was to drive him to Carinhall on Göring's order. When they arrived there they learned that the Field Marshal had left Carinhall at dusk. For the impending campaign against Poland he had gone to his head-quarters, which consisted of his special train that was standing near Carinhall at the little station of Friedrichswalde on the railway line Joachimsthal–Templin. There Dahlerus gave him the letter from Lord Halifax which he had to translate because Göring had no English. Dahlerus detected that 'the content made a deep impression' on Göring, who said it was of decisive importance and he therefore had to speak with Hitler about it at once. They immediately set off by car and drove through the night to the Chancellery in Berlin where Göring was told that the Führer had retired for the night.

Göring remained at the Chancellery and sent Dahlerus to the Hotel Esplanade where he always stayed when he was in Berlin. There he was picked up at midnight by two officers with the rank of Colonel with the message: 'The Führer asks you to come.' At the Chancellery, Hitler, with a 'silent Göring at his side', gave him a talk for half an hour in which he first underlined the strength of the Wehrmacht and then came to Gdansk and the Corridor. Göring tore a page out of an atlas and with a red pencil marked the Polish territory to which Germany laid claim. Hitler's talk turned into a night-time discussion lasting several hours, during which Hitler also suggested a treaty between Germany and Britain. During most of the time Göring only listened. 'Göring sat there and looked quite content,' Dahlerus writes. 'He was obviously in high spirits, even if his strictly formal and devoted conduct *vis-à-vis* his boss made me wonder and feel some-what uneasy.'

On the flight back to London (if he was tired, he slept on the floor) Dahlerus considered: 'I believe I can assume with a fair degree of certainty that for one reason or another Göring was working towards a peaceful solution. He had told me enough about the situation to make me believe that one could count on his support for measures that were intended to prevent a policy of force in the present circumstances. And Hitler? From the very first moment I felt uneasy. From the beginning of our meeting I did not like his conduct towards Göring, his closest friend and comrade from the years of struggle. That Hitler wished to dominate was understandable, but that he should demand such obsequious and subserviant conduct as Göring displayed from his closest associate was repulsive and unpleasant for me.'

It was soon to become apparent that Göring's attempts to impress Hitler by his London contact via Dahlerus would have no effect. Hitler was only toying with Göring's attempts to prevent the war, which would become a world war if Britain kept its promise to Poland, and when Hitler took the reins out of his hands at the meeting with Dahlerus Göring did not oppose him. He received Hitler's thanks on 1 September. In his speech in the Reichstag Hitler named Göring as his successor if something were to happen to him.

On the morning of 3 September Dahlerus called at Luftwaffe headquarters in Potsdam–Eiche and found that Göring was prepared to fly to London:

'And there sat the second man of the German Reich in the headquarters of the Luftwaffe near Potsdam, full of anxieties about what might come and obviously incapable of influencing even to the slightest degree the written answer to Britain's ultimatum, the most important declaration', as Dahlerus believed, 'that was ever made in the course of German history. I was boiling inside when I saw the normally so powerful man sitting completely helplessly at a folding table under some beeches and it was incomprehensible to me why, given the news, he did not immediately get into his car and drive to the Chancellery in order to speak his true mind honestly and openly – provided that he really believed what he had been saying during the past two months. Was it really possible that a man whom fate had given such a position and power as Göring had acquired, could be completely in the hands of an obvious madman, or was he playing a double game?' This powerful Göring: was he really powerful? Adolf Hitler's designated successor was sitting under beeches in the Werder park near Potsdam looking depressed and thoughtful, and waiting for something that would occur at 11.15 a.m. Several senior Luftwaffe officers approached their Commander-in-Chief who was sitting at a folding table with Birger Dahlerus, and who was prepared to board the plane that was at his disposal at Staaken airport, fly to London, negotiate with the British Government, and to participate in that government's attempt to prevent world war.

Was Göring recalling the 'Prussian officer' he had once been? How often had he insisted that he still was. But instead of a king or a kaiser, he had Hitler over him, who was anything but a Prussian or a Prussian officer. For him, Hitler was the elected king and kaiser, the German Caesar, a Charlemagne, whose foremost *Reichswürdenträger* (lit. 'Dignitary of the Reich') he, Göring, had become, the paladin – as a hero and loyal follower was formerly called in the days of Charlemagne. The term 'paladin', however, derives from 'palatin', a bondsman of the palace, a chattel of the king's.

Could the paladin now renounce his loyalty to Hitler, his self-chosen king, refusing to stand by him through thick and thin, bearing the Reich – that he would soon help to destroy – on his shoulders?

To let Britain go now, to destroy Poland and divide up the country with the Soviet Union: for Göring this meant obedience to his self-chosen King, to whom he would exclaim after the events had taken their course: 'If we lose this war, then so help us God!' Even after the expiration of their ultimatum, to which the Germans had not replied by 11 a.m. on 3 September 1939, and despite the state of war against the Reich in which she now found herself, for a further three months Britain's hopes continued to be vested in Göring, in influential conservatives, and in high-ranking officers that actual war could be avoided after all.

21

In the British view, Hitler and his anglophobe Foreign Minister had provoked the outbreak of the war. A change in this compromised leadership would have opened the way to possible negotiations with a government led by Göring and avoidance of a second world war. Chamberlain and the Foreign Office assumed that Hitler's cooperation with Stalin and the risky game of the planned attack on Poland might prompt Göring and the German generals to do away with Hitler after the Polish campaign was over.

As soon became apparent, the most important commanders on the 'Western Front', which did not yet merit such a bloody name, were dead set against an attack in the west. After the quick success in Poland, they believed that holding the Wehrmacht back was the only policy that Germany should now follow.

The British Government's calculations could have proven to be correct, if Göring had joined this faction. If Army, Luftwaffe, and naturally also the Kriegsmarine, which was far too weak to take on the British Navy, had denied themselves to Hitler, the course of world history would have been different.

About these days Emmy Göring writes, and not only as apologist for her husband: 'He returned from the Chancellery on 31 August 1939 almost as a broken man. His face was like a mask. Lost in thought, he slid into an armchair, put his head in his hands and muttered: "I tried everything, literally everything, but it happened just the same. We are at war. It will be terrible, more horrible than anybody can imagine." Later he said: "Poland is nothing. But we have to keep England out. A year ago in Munich all went well. But since then the *Wilhelmstraße* [seat of the German Foreign Ministry] obviously treated Chamberlain wrongly. He is a gentleman. But the *Wilhelmstraße* just does not know how to deal with him!" I asked how long the war would last. He answered: "Two years, five years, seven, I don't know." And he added: "I do not believe that an air force alone can ever decide a war. The decision lies with the army." We then went into my living-room. On the wall next to my desk hung Lukas Cranach's "Madonna with Child", a painting that the city of Cologne had given to our Edda as a present on her baptism. He looked at the painting for a long time. "Beautiful, isn't it?" I nodded. He then turned away. "From now on there will be no beauty, no joy, and no happiness any more."'

That was Göring. He lacked the toughness which was ascribed to him, who was referred to as 'the iron one' within the Luftwaffe. Toughness, which a statesman needs together with adaptability, was not given to him when he stood alone. He was only tough on Hitler's behalf.

On 4 September the British Ambassador Sir Neville Henderson made his farewell visit to the Görings at Carinhall. 'I presume you will not attack my house in England with your Luftwaffe,' Henderson said, whereupon Göring replied: 'If English bombs fall on my Carinhall, then ... '

During the fighting near Warsaw Lieutenant Eggert, with a detachment of tanks, found himself near a hunting lodge on the Warsaw–Modlin road. He was astonished to find a photograph of Göring on a desk in the lodge, which the owner had left there. Göring had been his guest at a hunt. Poland was nothing, Göring believed at the time; he did not take a war against the Polish army seriously. But England!

He was now 46 years old and had another seven years to live. In his last conversation with Werner Bross, the assistant of his defence counsel Dr Otto Stahmer, shortly before his end in the prison at Nuremberg, he would again speak about the English who had faced Germany as old Cato had faced Carthage, which had to be destroyed by Rome and finally was. Bross interjected: 'But was not England the one power which was prepared to come to an agreement with Germany under certain conditions, even after the Polish campaign?' 'No,' Göring replied, 'not England, only Chamberlain. Because at the time, Churchill already had Roosevelt's personal assurance of American support in his pocket, and Churchill wanted to destroy Germany completely. In this however, he deceived himself regarding Russia's strength. But the Englishman is enough of a practical politician to adjust to the present situation. He has eliminated Germany in any case, and against the too powerful Russians he will just cling to the Americans for better or for worse.'

After Hitler's suicide and shortly before his own, did he again think of the opportunity that had been offered him in 1939? Could a German Government under Hermann Göring together with a British Government under Chamberlain have prevented the Second World War, if both governments had trampled out the brush fire while there was still time?

Werner Bross writes: 'After we had continued to discuss the political and economic situation in Germany for a while longer, and I had drawn attention to the general feeling of hopelessness, Göring said, while getting up: "It is probably best to travel on, because life in Germany has nothing left to offer. It is over." He threw his coat over his shoulder, put on his cap, nodded to me a final time, and slowly disappeared with measured steps down the long corridor.' Did he also disappear from history?

In His anger, God allowed not only good people to exist, but also bad people. Can therefore not a good man also be a bad man, or a bad one also a good one? Did such a strange mixture exist in Göring, such a dual nature that posed conundrums whose solutions appear to be so simple but lead into a labyrinth of human existence such as only the twentieth century has produced?

3
Origins and Education

The year 1893 in which Hermann Wilhelm Göring was born on 12 January, is a peaceful year. In Berlin, General von Caprivi is Chancellor of the Reich. In England, the 'Independent Labour Party' is founded, and in China the forerunner of the Kuomintang. Gerhardt Hauptmann writes *Biberpelz* and Oscar Wilde, *Lady Windemere's Fan*. Both works are comedies. In Russia, Peter Tchaikovsky publishes his sixth symphony, the *Pathétique*, and dies. The German doctor Behring discovers a serum against diphtheria and Rudolf Diesel builds his first diesel engine. The superheated steam engine is built by W. Schmidt, and Nansen leaves for the North Pole in *Fram*. Frege founds mathematical logic, logistics, and Reinhold Koser publishes his historical biography *King Frederick the Great*.

For the second son of the German Consul-General in Haiti, Dr Heinrich Ernst Göring, by his second wife, Franziska Tiefenbrunner, some of the events dating from the year of his birth will become important to him: the diesel engine and the *Pathétique*, the story of Frederick the Great, and Nansen's North Pole expedition, and he will embark on one extravagant undertaking after another in a bid to ensure that his life will go down in history. He will be granted 53 years in which to achieve this ambition, but his flawed temperament will bring about failure in the end. Nevertheless, something of him will remain to demonstrate in the extreme the contradictory nature of the German ethos during the twentieth century.

But the background of the child's family will also determine his future, his tendency to stand out from the mass yet remain a part of it as a consequence of his mother's background.

Franziska Göring came from a family of Bavarian farmers. She is alleged to have worked in an inn before she became the second wife of Dr Göring, his first wife having died in 1879. Five children resulted from his second marriage.

The Görings stemmed from Westphalia, and in 1866 and 1870 Dr Göring had taken part in the wars as a cavalry officer. His ancestors included a *Geheimer Kriegsrat* (War Councillor) of Frederick the Great's, who rendered outstanding service to Prussia. (Author's note. On this topic, Professor Dr Decker-Hauff wrote to me, Göring's family tree was prepared for publication by Professor Dr Otto Freiherr von Dungern of Graz University. It appeared in about 1938 in the series 'Family Trees of Famous Germans'. Göring was the only prominent Nazi who came from a 'good' family. His father's grandfather had been a Prussian

Regierungspräsident (District President), his great-grandmother a Metternich zur Gracht. Göring's mother, however (and Göring suffered much from this), was a Munich beer-hall waitress of dubious descent, which is why he laid great store on the research and publication of his ancestors on his father's side. These included, alongside much lesser nobility, genealogically interesting 'dynastic bridges', i.e., legitimate descent from high nobility, which showed that in fact he was a descendant of almost all the reigning houses of the Middle Ages. Among his patrician forebears were many important families, which were publicised extensively. What Dungern had left out, however, and probably because of pressure from on high, was the descent from the Eberler (called Grünzweig) family of money-changers in Basle, who had converted from Judaism to Christianity in the fifteenth century. According to the 'Family Trees', the Eberler/Eberlin were, among others, antecedents of Zeppelin (Count Adolf von Zeppelin, inventor of the airship); of Gertrud von Le Fort (well-known novelist), the Mercks of Darmstadt and Hamburg (founders and owners of the Merck Pharmaceutical Company); Hermann Grimm (author and biographer); Jacob Burckhardt (Swiss historian); and Carl J. Burckhardt (Swiss historian, author and diplomat); and many others. These blood lines have long been known, as can be seen from the Eberlin family tree in Stählin's *Basler Wappenbuch* (Basle Coat of Arms Book) and Strohmeyer's *Merian-Ahnen* (Merian Ancestors), both in the Stuttgart State Library. It is has also long been known that Abraham von Vesoul is a stepancestor of Göring. A few years ago I discovered that the von Vesouls are also secondary ancestors of all those named above, but I have not yet published details of this.)

Landgerichtsrat (higher court judge) Dr Göring first came to Chancellor Otto von Bismarck's attention through a memorandum on colonisation, when in the early 'eighties the latter was reluctantly obliged to start thinking about a German colonisation policy for the protection of German interests overseas. Initially Bismarck had rejected any ideas or plans for colonisation because he did not wish to embroil this new Reich, whose position in central Europe was not yet stabilised, in conflicts with other colonial powers for the sake of undertakings overseas. It was only after 1881 that he had reluctantly and carefully begun to address himself to colonisation, for which he set the motto: 'protection of German pioneers, not state-owned colonies', which was all very well except that inevitably explorers and businessmen acquired land for which they expected protection from the Reich.

On 8 December 1882 the *Deutsche Kolonialverein* (German Colonial Association) had been founded, which began massive advertising. Among other things, it was interested in obtaining property overseas for German immigrants. In 1882 the Lüderitz trading company in Bremen had bought extensive property in Angra-

Pequena (later Lüderitz Bay) where there were numerous trading posts of companies from Hamburg and Bremen. Twice a month a steamer sailed there from Hamburg. When Mr Lüderitz requested the protection of the Reich for this territory sandwiched between a Portuguese colony and Cape Colony, the cautious Bismarck had inquiries made in London as to whether Britain had any claims there. Lord Granville replied that Britain claimed sovereignty only over Walvis Bay farther north and the islands off Angra-Pequena. But the British Government was of the opinion that sovereign claims by a foreign power in this region between the southern border of Portuguese territory and the border of Cape Colony would be an infringement of Britain's legitimate rights. Bismarck requested the British cabinet to substantiate this incredible claim in law. London did not reply, whereupon Bismarck had the German Consul in Cape Town officially declare that Lüderitz and his property were under German protection. The Cape Government now wanted to put the territory claimed by the Germans under its protection, something it had previously refused to do. Cape Town was only thinking of the coastal strip up to Walvis Bay, but Bismarck declared that he would not tolerate this seizure. Britain gave in and on 18 August 1884 recognised the German protectorate over Angra-Pequena, which was soon extended to include Namaqua and Damara. In early September 1884, the gunboat *Wolf* raised the German flag over the coast from the 26th Parallel to Cape Fria. Britain remained quiet, restricting herself to sovereignty over Walvis Bay.

In 1884 Bismarck sent Landgerichtsrat Göring to London in order to have him study English colonial administration. There that same year he married Franziska Tiefenbrunner.

In November 1885 Bismarck was still insisting that: 'My objective is the governing businessman, not the governing officer and the Prussian civil servant.' But it had become apparent that the consolidation of this African territory as a German colony required a Governor who would need to combine the abilities of an officer with those of a Prussian civil servant, while simultaneously conducting his office in a strictly impartial manner. The 46-year-old Dr Göring was thought suited to the role and he was sent out as the first *Minister-Resident* (Governor). After the birth of her first child, Karl Ernst, his wife Franziska followed him, bringing the baby with her.

The legal situation in the German protectorates had been regularised by a law passed on 17 April 1886, according to which all necessary directives could be issued by imperial decree. But it was not until 1 April 1890 that a colonial department was installed at the Foreign Ministry.

In order to provide his Governor and family with a measure of comfort, Bismarck gave them a coach which he had used during the Franco–German war of 1870–1. In this comfortable wagon they travelled all over the new country.

Franziska Göring accompanied her husband even into those regions where there was sporadic fighting between the military protection forces and settlers against the Hereros, the Hill Damaras, and the Namaguas. But serious hostilities did not break out until the 'nineties, after the Görings had returned to Germany, so Göring was able to do his job in peace; he was polite and tactful to the tribal chiefs and earned himself high honours. On its many trips, the Bismarck coach was accompanied by an escort of seven German colonial soldiers and 100 *Askaris* (native troops). Later on pictures of this imposing retinue were to make a deep and lasting impression on the young Hermann Göring.

Dr Göring was a friend of Cecil Rhodes, who was pursuing a gigantic objective; that of making Africa British from the Cape to Cairo, with the aid of a railway line he intended to build. Miserable German Southwest Africa, which was mostly covered by the Kalahari Desert, lay outside the scope of his plans. He could tolerate the Germans in the colony and even befriend them.

But another acquaintance the Görings made was to prove fateful for them. This was the German Jewish Dr Hermann Epenstein who had been in Africa for quite some time and had become rich through trading. He helped them to cope with the unpleasant conditions which European families faced in the country. He fell in love with Franziska and later on took her as his mistress. When Frau Göring gave birth to her second child Olga in Africa, he took care of her and soon made himself indispensable to the Görings. Later on Epenstein was raised to the nobility in Austria and from then on called himself Dr Ritter von Epenstein.

By the end of the 'eighties, after almost six years of service, the health of the Governor had begun to fail and he was forced to return to Germany. He left an established German colony which extended from Cape Fria in the north to the Orange River in the south. Walvis Bay remained in British hands. (To the present day, Göring Street in Windhoek still recalls Hermann Göring's father.)

After an extensive rest, Dr Göring reported back to the Foreign Ministry for further assignment and was sent to Haiti as Consul-General. He retained the title of Minister Resident. Out of this young Hermann Göring later construed the paternal *Ministerpräsident* when he spoke about the services his father had performed for the Reich overseas.

Towards the end of 1890 Dr Göring's wife followed him to the island with her three children – Paula was just six months old – where life was not without its dangers; the Görings' house was attacked and they had to defend themselves against horse thieves. A good rider, with a reputation for courage and daring, Frau Göring took an active part in emergencies of this kind.

When she was expecting her fourth child, she went back to Germany in order to give birth there. Dr Epenstein found her rooms in the spa town of Marienbad near Rosenheim where, on 12 January 1893, her second son, Hermann, was born.

Unwilling to subject the infant to the risks that a voyage to Haiti entailed, she entrusted him to the care of a very close friend of her mother's, a Frau Graf, at Fürth in Frankonia where he was brought up in the Graf family, having been baptised in the Protestant faith. At Fürth he acquired that Frankonian accent which was later to contrast so pleasingly with Hitler's harsh Upper Austrian-Bavarian idiom. The Prussian Hermann Göring grew up in Frankonia which was part of the Kingdom of Bavaria. And it was in Frankonia that his life was to end.

When Frau Göring and her family came back from Haiti in 1896, Dr Göring was old and sick. She became Dr Epenstein's mistress and her husband tolerated the relationship.

That which a child experiences, perceives in its environment, clings to, are factors that can determine the course of its life. Hermann Göring could be proud of his father who – if not the founder of a colony – had developed a notable administrative edifice in Africa for Bismarck and Kaiser Wilhelm II. As Consul-General in Haiti, his father had expended what physical resources remained to him after Africa. His mother had brought up the children in difficult circumstances.

He was three years old before he saw her again, who had left him in Germany as a baby; he hit her in the face with his fist!

The Göring family moved into an apartment in Fredenstraße, in the wealthy, bourgeois district of Friedenau in Berlin. They did not pay any rent because the apartment belonged to Dr Epenstein who had also settled in Berlin and had substantial property there.

In contrast to the retired Dr Göring, who had no fortune and was keeping the family on a pension, Dr Epenstein could afford anything he desired. Franziska loved luxury, and after she had become Epenstein's mistress, he took care of the Göring family. The penchant for luxury, so evident in Hermann after he had become successful, had been nurtured in the surroundings and circumstances of his youth when, though proud of his father, his idol had been the rich Dr Epenstein.

In the Lungau in Salzburg (Austria) Epenstein owned Mauterndorf Castle, which he had restored to its medieval splendour in accordance with the spirit of the time. But he also wanted a country estate in the Reich, and after the Görings' return from Haiti he purchased Veldenstein Castle near Nuremberg, which stood on the foundations of an 11th-century Frankonian fortress. At the turn of the century the Görings moved into a Biedermeier house at Veldenstein near Neuhaus, high above the River Pegnitz. It was a romantic setting, from which the huge Veldensteiner forest extended northwards along the edge of the Frankonian Jura, behind which lay the military training area of Grafenwöhr.

Dr Göring had a small room on the ground floor; Franziska's bedroom was next to that of Dr Epenstein, who had now achieved his objective. The woman he loved was living with him and her husband accepted the situation. Young Hermann was envious of the life his brother and sisters had had, their pony riding and boat trips. From them he learned how courageously his mother had confronted the problems of life in Africa and Haiti, and had to come to terms with the fact that she was a formidable woman.

He was sent to board with a teacher at the primary school in Fürth. He was not a good scholar and his aversion to schooling became apparent very early on. He hated Fürth and wanted to burn it down. He liked Veldenstein were he could roam through the deep forests and, with his playmates, fire his enthusiasm for the Boers who were at war with England at the time. As the son of a governor of German Southwest Africa, he liked the uniform of a Boer general which his father had given him. There is a stone in the Veldensteiner forest on which 'Boer General Hermann Göring' attempted to immortalise himself as a child. He is said to have been very temperamental and domineering. But after all, his family were lords of Veldenstein and he stood above his playmates.

Playing at soldiers was very common among children of the Wilhelmian Reich. Under his hat with its broad brim, in khaki shorts, young Göring looked like a Boy Scout. His fertile imagination manifested itself very early. In his play with his lead soldiers, which every boy had, he kept finding new variations. In his games, Veldenstein was beleaguered or defended, and the heroes of German history, the sagas of the knights, and above all the *Nibelungenlied* (saga of the Nibelungen, the royal house of the ancient German tribe of Burgundians with Siegfried the dragon slayer as their greatest hero, who died to a man in battle against Attila and the Huns) made a lasting impression on him. But that too was nothing extraordinary for the times.

The splendidly furnished castle of Mauterndorf with its many art treasures, where the Göring family stayed on their holidays, became the starting point for one of his passions, mountain climbing. He did not shrink from danger, believing that nothing bad could happen to him.

At the age of eleven he had to change school. His father sent him to a very strict boarding school at Ansbach to learn obedience, but without success. At this school he organised a strike with his fellows because of the bad food. He ran away and insisted that he be allowed to stay at Veldenstein.

When he was twelve his father sent him to the cadet academy at Karlsruhe. His sister Paula was attending school there, as were the daughters of Frau Graf who had taken him in as a baby. The Baden (former duchy, today part of Baden–Württemberg) grand ducal cadet Göring now wore a uniform. When he had turned sixteen he was transferred to the Central Cadet Academy at Lichterfelde which at that time was situated in the outskirts of Berlin. Here he received a level of education equating with that of a secondary school. He enjoyed the life and decided to pursue a military career.

The Lichterfelde Academy was strictly run and standards were high; a cadet passing out with honours could be certain of a career as an army officer. Hermann's record had been excellent and his final examinations brought him the highest honours that a cadet could achieve. He received high praise from Kaiser Wilhelm II, who congratulated him in person. Young Lieutenant Göring was the pride of the family. His father gave him a present of 1,000 marks, a substantial sum in those days. He used the money for a trip to northern Italy, taking with him his father's chauffeur Sepp Rusch. The money was enough for both of them. At the age of nineteen, Hermann joined the 113th Infantry Regiment 'Prince Wilhelm', which was garrisoned at Mulhouse in the Reichsland Alsace–Lorraine.

In 1913 the relationship between Franziska Göring and Dr Ritter von Epenstein (he had been elevated to the nobility in 1910) came to an end. This led to disagreements and the family moved to Munich where Dr Göring died on 6 December 1913. Had the relationship continued a little while longer, it is quite possible that Epenstein would have become Hermann Göring's stepfather, because after the death of her husband, Franziska would have been free to marry. As the stepson of a converted Jew, Hermann Göring could never have played a role in the Hitler movement and his life would have taken a different course. Lieutenant Göring wept at his father's funeral. As an officer, he was not supposed to show tears, but it happened here, and often later on as well.

The 113th Infantry Regiment was a Prussian regiment with old traditions, and Göring found himself in surroundings that he liked, but lacking a fortune he was in financial difficulties. In those days, regular officers needed a private income in order to be able to live in keeping with their station. His father was dead and, although he was Hermann's godfather, Dr Epenstein had married and could no longer be drawn upon.

The officers in the regiment considered Göring to be coarse; he was not refined enough for their taste. But he soon found a friend in Lieutenant Bruno Loerzer. He was carefree and, like Hermann, full of fun, and they got on well together. A lasting friendship began to grow. When war broke out in the summer of 1914, Lieutenant Göring was an infantry platoon leader. The mobilisation plan for the 113th however, was a humiliation for its officers. German border defences were only intended to offer delaying resistance against the expected French advance. The regiment was to give up its garrison at Mulhouse and withdraw across the Rhine, because preparations for active service could not take place a mere 40 kilometres away from the strong French fortress of Belfort. Count Schlieffen's Plan had called for a strong right wing to force the decision in France. Colonel General von Heeringen's Seventh Army, to which the 113th belonged, was to assemble east of the Rhine in the Breisgau, between Offenburg and Freiburg. The weakest German army in the west, consisting mainly of men from Baden and Alsace, it had only 156 battalions, 33 squadrons of cavalry and 700 guns.

The regiment withdrew across the Rhine on 28 July 1914.

The day before, Göring wrote a letter of farewell to his mother in Munich and to his sisters. He did not mention the imminent withdrawal to the east bank of the Rhine and he did not mention the coming war. All he wanted to do was to say thank you for his wonderful days as a child in the castles of Veldenstein and Mauterndorf, which were now lost to the Görings. His mother was very proud of this letter, and at the same time she sensed how strongly her son was moved, something which caused her astonishment. She had not expected such an emotional upheaval from him. His sisters too were surprised.

The regiment was mobilised on the right bank of the Rhine. During the first week of the war, on 8 August, the French took possession of Mulhouse, while the German field army was advancing into France via Belgium. On 7 August, Ludendorff had taken Liège by *coup de main.* Colonel General von Heeringen now intended to secure the left flank of the western armies offensively and cross the Rhine with his army. On 9 August Lieutenant Göring was ordered with his platoon to reconnoitre the strength of the French and their positions at Mulhouse. He crossed the Rhine and learned from civilians that the French were installing themselves in Mulhouse town hall and putting up posters declaring the city to be under martial law. This outraged him so much that he decided to wipe out the shame.

Although not having been ordered to proceed to Mulhouse, he took his platoon there only to find that the French had evacuated the town hall again. Göring mounted his platoon on bicycles and found a horse for himself. During a pursuit of French dragoons a short skirmish took place, during which four of the dragoons' horses were captured. Göring had the French posters in Mulhouse torn down and withdrew.

On 10 August the battle of Mulhouse, which the French had occupied again, was fought. Göring's platoon on its bicycles was to advance to the city centre and attempt to capture French General Pau who had been installed there as city commander. Göring, again on horseback, with his grenadiers on bicycles, missed this objective, because one of the grenadiers lost his nerve and fired a shot, thereby warning the French. In compensation, the platoon was able to capture several Frenchmen at Illzach the following day.

Mulhouse was back in German hands again, and in Germany the battle was celebrated as a victory. Lieutenant Göring was awarded the Iron Cross 2nd Class, the first officer of his regiment to be decorated. He had displayed bravery, even foolishness, and that disregard of danger he had shown when climbing in the Alps. His urge to act independently had also come to the fore. He was a self-willed young lieutenant.

While the strong right flank of the German army, consisting of three Army Groups, marched towards Paris in accordance with the Schlieffen Plan, only to fail in the decisive Battle of the Marne in early September, in Upper Alsace Seventh Army began its trench warfare in the Vosges, faced by General Dubail's First Army consisting of 202 battalions, 80 squadrons of cavalry and 784 guns. In the cold wet trenches Lieutenant Göring contracted a serious rheumatic illness which made him unfit for service in the infantry. He had to leave his regiment and was sent to the hospital in Freiburg in the Breisgau. There his convalescence dragged on and he feared that he would never again be able to distinguish himself in the face of the enemy. But through his friend Lieutenant Loerzer he found a way out of this situation so unpleasant for a regular Prussian officer. He became an airman.

4
Fighter Pilot

The war of 1914 became the first air war in history. The Germans started with 264 military aircraft which were divided between thirty-two *Feldfliegerabteilungen* (lit. field flying sections) of six machines each, and eight *Festungsfliegerabteilungen* (lit. fortress flying sections) of four machines each. In addition to the Rumpler Dove monoplane, the Germans had several types of biplane: Albatros, Aviatik, L.V.G. (Air Traffic Company), and D.F.W. (German Aircraft Works). Also available were fifteen manœuvrable airships which Count Zeppelin had developed.

Before the outbreak of the war, the young Dutch aircraft designer Anthony Fokker had entered German service and was soon to give the Germans air superiority. From the Morane, Hanuschke, and Boutard monoplanes he developed the Fokker monoplane with which Immelmann and Boelcke were to gain the first great air victories. For the Fokker monoplane the Swiss aeronautical engineer Schneider developed a machine-gun which was synchronised with the engine to enable the pilot to tackle the enemy head-on and shoot through the revolving propeller.

In the autumn of 1914, when the large-scale movements of the opposing armies had given way to the trench warfare that was to last for four years, it became necessary to reinforce the air force with machines capable of reconnoitring the static front and the enemy's rear areas, and spotting for their own artillery. In these small machines the observer sat behind the pilot, shouted the course to him, drew sketches and dropped them over his own lines or brought them back to improvised forward landing fields. Each Army and Army Corps had its own Feldfliegerabteilung. The pilots and observers, lonely soldiers above the battlefield, could not have realised that they were the forerunners of future generations of airmen who would make any movement on the ground dangerous, destroy whole regions and cities and tear up the sky with the bloody trails of their squadrons. There would not only be air fights man against man, but whole air battles. It would need only a few decades to turn the still chivalrous air duelling of early 1914 into a terrible weapon.

The man who was to play a very important part in this future, Hermann Göring, began his career in the air as an observer in the spring of 1915. His friend Loerzer, who had been transferred from the 113th Infantry Regiment to flying training, had visited him in the hospital in Freiburg. The training took place on an airfield at Freiburg from which could be seen the distant Vosges, on whose passes and heights the battle was raging. If, as the doctors declared, Göring could no longer take part there on his own two legs, he at least wanted to have himself flown to the front. Loerzer's enthusiastic descriptions of this new, formerly unknown weapon, a flying weapon, prompted Göring to send a brief telegram to the commander of the replacement battalion at Donaueschingen, demanding – in a highly unmilitary manner – that he be transferred to the flying school at Freiburg. His request was turned down, but he had no intention of returning to Donaueshingen after he had recuperated.

Instead, he had himself trained as an observer by Loerzer. After completing the course, Loerzer flew him to Darmstadt and from there to 25th Flying Section at Stenay, which belonged to Fifth Army commanded by Crown Prince Wilhelm. Stenay was about twenty-five miles north of Verdun .

The commander of 113th Replacement Battalion at Donaueschingen sentenced the 'fugitive' Lieutenant Göring to three weeks' arrest for having taken himself off to another formation, but this came to nothing neither Göring nor Loerzer could be found.

In the reconnaissance section at Stenay, Göring proved his worth as an observer, skilfully photographing enemy positions in the fortress belt around Verdun, and soon earning himself a good reputation. Loerzer preferred to fly at low level and Göring shot at French soldiers with his pistol. Both officers were awarded the Iron Cross 1st Class for bravery by the Crown Prince. During the reconnaissance flights, the observer had to lean far out of the machine in order to operate the heavy camera. Göring learned the Morse code so that he could send his observations directly to the German artillery batteries, and he was the first observer to man a machine-gun in flight. Among the pilots, Loerzer was called 'Emil' and Göring was his 'Franz'.

Stenay was the target for French air attacks because the Crown Prince had his headquarters there. When Crown Princess Cäcilie was visiting him one day, a French air attack took place. Göring and Loerzer felt this to be improper conduct towards the Princess. Without orders they took off and Göring allegedly shot down an enemy aircraft with his pistol. Afterwards he dropped some small bombs known as 'airmen's mice' on the French forward airfield. As the avenger of the Crown Princess's honour, Göring now became an esteemed young officer with a future among the Hohenzollerns, one who was personally connected to the family. Every Prussian officer had the right to attend Court and by chivalrous military action, Göring had gained this privilege doubly. This was to become very important to him later on.

Göring and Loerzer took part in staff meetings at the Crown Prince's headquarters. Through their reconnaissance flights they were knowledgeable about the situation at the front and in the enemy's rear area around Verdun, and their advice was sought.

But now Göring insisted on becoming a pilot. Loerzer had become a fighter pilot and Göring wanted to follow him. At Freiburg in the autumn of 1915 he obtained his pilot's licence in the shortest possible time, and in October was transferred to 5 Fighter Squadron where Loerzer was a pilot.

Here, on the northern flank of the German western front, the opponents were British and they had numerical superiority at least. Their bombers were the big, twin-engined Handley-Pages which carried automatic weapons.

During an interception patrol with two fellow officers, Göring attacked one of these lumbering bombers with his machine-gun and forced it to go down. Attacked by six British fighters, his own aircraft took hits in the fuel tank and lost a wing. He managed to land just behind the German line, but had sustained a serious hip wound. Metal splinters had to be removed from the deep gash, and without immediate medical attention he would have bled to death. Sixty bullet holes were discovered in his aircraft. He was in for a long stay in hospital.

At this time the German air force was commanded by Lieutenant-General von Hoeppner, a general staff officer from Saxony, who had been Chief of Staff in Colonel General von Hausen's Third Army at the beginning of the war and with him had taken part in the Battle of the Marne. After the retreat from the Marne the army from Saxony was disbanded and von Hoeppner was assigned the duties of Commanding General of the Air Forces. His Chief of Staff was Lieutenant-Colonel Thomsen, and his Chief of Operations Major von Oppeln-Bronikowski. Soon von Hoeppner became Commanding General Air, with Major Siegert as Inspector Flying Forces.

Among the first pilots who created the history of the German air force were Widdessen, Caspar, *Freiherr* (Baron) von Thüna, *Freiherr* von Buttlar, and Fisch. Their example spurred the efforts of young recruits such as Immelmann and Boelcke who were soon to become famous. They were followed by *Rittmeister* (captain of cavalry) Freiherr von Richthofen. 'I want to become like Boelcke,' was the expressed wish of the young fighter pilots on the Western Front.

Göring went to hospital in November 1915. His convalescence, a period of great frustration for him as he read of the aerial victories in the Army reports, was spent at Mauterndorf Castle in Austria which Dr Ritter von Epenstein had again put at the disposal of the Görings, and here the roles were reversed for the 23-year-old Göring was a now a war hero for Epenstein. During his recuperation he fell in love with Marianne Mauser, a farmer's daughter from Mauterndorf, whose parents opposed an engagement because fighter pilots were not reckoned to have long to live.

Discharged from hospital, Göring was ordered to report to the air force replacement unit at Böblingen near Stuttgart, but he was impatient to get back to the fighting. He sent the Commander-in-Chief of the Air Force a disrespectful telegram saying that he had been unable to find Böblingen in the railway schedule or on a map and had therefore returned directly to the front.

He reported back to his old friend Loerzer at Mulhouse, his former garrison town, where Loerzer had become squadron leader of 26 Fighter Squadron. The situation was desperate. The enemy air forces had been heavily increased and there was much bitter fighting. On one occasion Göring was able to save his friend's life, whose machine was being pursued by French fighters and barely managed to make an emergency landing. Soon afterwards his friend was able to save Göring from an airman's death.

On 2 November 1916, Chief of Staff Thomsen had to read the funeral oration for the air hero Boelcke, who had been killed in action: 'And therefore as a last good-bye at the grave of our loyal friend, I lay down these words that should be a solemn oath by each of our German pilots: I want to become like Boelcke! As long as these words remain our guiding star, as long as Boelcke's spirit and ability remain alive in our flying forces, so long "Dear Fatherland you may be tranquil!"' (Thomsen's quotation was a line from the song 'The Watch on the Rhine' which was very popular during Kaiser Wilhelm's day.)

In 1917 the fighter squadron was sent to the front in Flanders. Göring had received medals: the Knight's Cross of the Household Order of the Hohenzollern, the Zähringer (Margraves of Baden) Lions Order, the Karl-Friedrich Order. In May he became squadron leader of 27 Fighter Squadron which was stationed on the same airfield at Iseghem near Ypres as Loerzer's 26 Fighter Squadron. Its reputation was far from good. First Lieutenant Göring changed that. Also flying in Flanders was the new air hero, Rittmeister Manfred Freiherr von Richthofen with his 11 Fighter Squadron.

In order to increase the efficacy of the fighter weapon, the fighter squadrons were amalgamated into fighter *Geschwader* (Wings) with which the superiority of the Allied air forces were to be overcome. Richthofen was the first to be given a Geschwader, and it was to bear his name. Loerzer's and Göring's squadrons were put into a third Geschwader. Besides Richthofen, Ernst Udet was also becoming famous as a fighter pilot with one of the highest scores.

In May 1918, after his twentieth victory, Göring received the *Pour le Mérite* from Kaiser Wilhelm II. During the latter part of the war it was customary to award this highest Prussian military medal only after the twenty-fifth victory, but Loerzer had pulled strings to have Göring receive it sooner. The award was given to him as a 'pilot with battle experience'. He did not achieve 25 air victories. Many of his former pilot comrades who had known him on the air bases protested against the glorification as a fighter pilot that he received later on.

On 21 April 1918 Richthofen was shot down allegedly by the Canadian Captain Roy Brown, and Captain Reinhardt was given command of 1 Fighter

Geschwader 'Richthofen'. Göring and he test flew a new fighter aircraft from the airfield at Berlin-Adlershof in June. Göring flew first, then Reinhardt took over; the aircraft lost both wings at high altitude and Reinhardt crashed and was killed. First Lieutenant Göring was appointed commander of 1 Fighter Geschwader 'Richthofen' on 7 July. The former adjutant of the Geschwader, Karl Bodenschatz, describes the take-over in his book *Hunting in Flanders' Skies*. Göring had looked determined, when after having been introduced by Lieutenant von Wedel, he addressed the pilots in a strangely penetrating voice. Lieutenant Bodenschatz gave Göring the knotted stick with its notches that Richthofen had carried as a talisman and which Reinhardt had also possessed for a few weeks.

The Geschwader's airfield was close enough to the front line as to be within artillery range. The Allies' numerical superiority in the air was great and the Germans were flying as many as five sorties a day. On 18 July Göring shot down a Spad for his 22nd and final victory. From 26 July to 21 August he went on leave and Manfred von Richthofen's brother, Lothar Freiherr von Richthofen, deputised for him as commander.

Fighter Geschwader Richthofen suffered heavy losses. Already in July, Göring had had to report to Air Commander Seventh Army: 'Pilots and machines cannot continue to support such an effort. The English single-seaters, usually echeloned upwards in several sections, fight well in their proven manner. The French fighters, however, only seldom advance to the front and avoid any real engagement. In contrast to this, the French twin-seaters always appear in strong squadrons and close formation and carry out their bombing attacks without compunction, often at low altitudes. The twin-engined Caudrons are favoured for these attacks. Our K ammunition normally does not penetrate their armour as repeated attempts have proven.'

Within the space of nine months 1 Fighter Geschwader had shot down about 500 aircraft, but the unequal struggle was drawing to a close and the German forces were in retreat. On 8 November, the Geschwader made itself at home on an airfield at Tellancourt in Belgium, but low cloud and incessant rain made operations impossible. On 9 November preparations were made for the retreat. In Germany, revolution erupted.

On the 10th the weather was unsuitable for flying, but Göring was ordered by the Commander of Fifth Army's air forces to fly the aircraft to Darmstadt and to send the rest of the *matériel* there by land. Shortly afterwards, a counter-order was received; the aircraft were to be handed over to the Americans. Göring refused to obey this order.

On 11 November news of the Armistice reached Tellancourt. A staff officer ordered Göring to hand over his aircraft to the French at Strasbourg, but he had no intention whatsoever of obeying this order. He wanted to go to Darmstadt. He sent his adjutant Bodenschatz there with the lorries while his pilots were waiting for the weather to clear. He was worried that he would not be able to get his aircraft back to Germany if the bad weather continued, but on the morning of the 12th the fog cleared and the aircraft took off at 10 o'clock.

Some of them got to Strasburg and crash-landed there. Another group mistakenly landed at Mannheim where the airfield was in the hands of a soldiers' council which confiscated the pilots' sidearms. Göring, who had landed in Darmstadt with the majority, ordered an immediate take-off with machine-guns loaded, and his formation appeared over Mannheim. The disarmed pilots were given back their sidearms after they had threatened that their comrades in the sky would strafe the field. Göring flew back to Darmstadt with all his aircraft which were rendered unserviceable by crash-landing them.

Bodenschatz arrived and stowed the baggage in a warehouse of the Buntpapier AG in Aschaffenburg. Göring found a place to stay in the villa of the company's director. Under the date of the armistice, 11 November 1918, he noted in the war diary of Fighter Geschwader 'Richthofen' the 644 victories the wing had achieved since its formation and totalled the casualties sustained: 56 officers/pilots and six enlisted men killed; 52 officers/pilots, and seven enlisted men wounded.

The non-commissioned officers and enlisted men were sent home. The officers, who had found quarters in Aschaffenburg, met in the Stiftskeller (wine bar). The final promotions were announced; Hermann Göring became a captain. On 19 November he formally disbanded the Geschwader. Bodenschatz wrote later that Göring had given his first major speech here. He spoke of Geschwader 'Richthofen', of battles and victories, of officers who had sacrificed themselves for the Fatherland and who had now been received back home in such a humiliating manner. He condemned the soldiers who had rebelled against their officers, the 'Soldiers' Councils' which had now seized power. But he hated the idea of his officers dispersing with great sadness after they had fought gallantly for their country. 'Into an hour', Bodenschatz wrote, 'which was grey with despair all the way up to the sky, this man threw a new belief and a new hope with inspiring words. At this moment, when Germany was bled white, weary unto death, without strength, and had despairingly given up its great struggle, this man called for a new struggle. The struggle for the inner formation of the German soul.'

The men assembled there, who in the summer had received their new commander with great reticence, listened to these bold words with astonishment and emotion while outside the Stiftskeller local inhabitants and soldiers reviled them. Göring called for a final cheer for the Geschwader, after which they shattered their wine glasses against the wall. When they left the Stiftskeller, the mob tried to tear their medals off their uniforms. And so in 1918 1 Fighter Geschwader, which carried the name Richthofen, ended in a riot. Göring never forgot this scene, and his hatred of the 'Reds' dated from this event. He managed to prevent the mob from tearing off his *Pour le Mérite* and epaulettes.

On this 19 November 1918 it was not decided until late in the evening whether there would be civil war in the Reich. For two days the Majority Social Democrats (SPD) had been negotiating in Berlin with the Independents (USPD). At about 11 p.m. an agreement was reached. Several Independents joined the government of Friedrich Ebert, and civil war was avoided for the time being.

In Aschaffenburg, the prospect of revolution had manifested itself in the riot around the officers of the Richthofen Geschwader. It was not until next morning that it was learned from the newspapers that a government of soviets based on the Russian pattern no longer intended to seize power in the Reich. The entry of the Independents into the 'Council of People's Representatives', which was enlarged thereby, having previously only consisted of six Majority Socialists with Ebert, calmed the situation in the Reich for the time being. To this was added Ebert's pact with the Supreme Command of the Army of 10 November, which strengthened the position of the Majority Socialists.

Göring stayed on in Aschaffenburg for two more weeks. As a professional officer and highly decorated wing commander, the 25-year-old captain faced a bleak future. He could not conceive of remaining a regimental officer, although this had been his sole profession since graduating from the cadet corps. He had undergone no General Staff training. He suffered greatly from the wound in his thigh, for which he had to take morphine to ease the pain. The Hohenzollern, whom his father had served, had abdicated. His world had collapsed. The oath Göring had sworn to the Kaiser and King of Prussia had become meaningless. How could this proud young officer ever swear an oath of loyalty to anyone else? Compared to the demobilised officers of the army and navy, however, he did enjoy one advantage: he was a pilot and as such had mastered a new technology which had made great progress during the war. At Aschaffenburg he, with Udet and other officers, wondered whether their situation might not be quite as hopeless as they had first thought. They knew how to fly, and pilots would always be in demand, in the Reich or abroad.

Fourteen years later in the summer of 1932, when he was President of the Reichstag, he told Martin Henry Sommerfeldt who was to become his first press officer: 'When I had to send the Richthofen Geschwader home without its aircraft in 1918, I swore to the men that I would neither rest nor pause until we Germans were again permitted to fly. That I would be the Scharnhorst [Prussian General Count Scharnhorst, 1755–1813, reformer and creator of the new Prussian army during the war of liberation against Napoleon] of the German air force.'

In 1918 it was highly improbable that Göring would be able to make good the oath which he claims to have sworn at Aschaffenburg. He was not involved in the secret activities of the *Reichswehr* (German Armed Forces during the Weimar Republic) for the preparation of a future German air force. These began early on during the French and Belgian occupation of the Ruhr, and the man who initiated them was General von Seeckt who began to build up the new Reichswehr after the end of the Kapp Putsch. And nobody was thinking of a Hermann Göring in this context. The reason could have been an incident which occurred in Berlin towards the end of December 1918. Göring had gone to Berlin with Udet early in the month with a view to seeking some form of employment before returning to his mother in Munich. In Berlin a German officers' association was to be founded, which was to look after the interests of the discharged officers. After Christmas, the acting Prussian Minister of War Schéuch relinquished his office to General Walter Reinhardt who agreed to address a meeting of the association. He thought it important to convince the discharged officers that they should stay with the armed services which, at Ebert's request, were securing the government district in Berlin and other important buildings against the People's Navy Division and the Spartacists. The meeting took place in the hall of the Berlin Philharmonic Orchestra in Bernburgstraße near the Potsdamer Station. A resolution against the future uniform was to be voted on, it having been decreed that epaulette rank insignia were to be abolished in favour of blue stripes worn on the arm. The new Prussian War Minister Reinhardt appeared without epaulettes, and wearing the blue stripes. Göring, who had heard that this would be the case, went to the meeting in full uniform with all his orders and medals. After Reinhardt had declared that he did not agree with the blue stripes either, but that he asked the officers not to abandon him now, Göring asked for the floor. In full uniform, the *Pour le Mérite* around his neck, his two Iron Crosses on his breast, the captain's stars on his white epaulettes, he marched to the rostrum as the last commander of the Richthofen Geschwader. It all happened so unexpectedly and quickly that the meeting was unable to react. In a sharp, icy tone Göring shouted: 'I knew, your Excellency, that you would appear here today. But I had hoped to see you with a mourning band on your arm which would symbolise how deeply you regret that such a situation could arise. Instead of a mourning band, you are wearing the blue stripes on your sleeve. I think, your Excellency, it would suit you better, if you were to wear red stripes on your sleeve.'

Such an affront by a captain to a general (and an Excellency to boot), who as Prussian Minister of War had come to a meeting of the officers' association to ask the officers to help him, was initially received in silence. Then loud applause broke out. General Reinhardt left the hall without replying. Göring called for silence and said: 'We officers fulfilled our duty for four long years on the ground, on the water, and in the air, and we risked life and body for our fatherland. Now we have come home, and how are we treated? They spit on us and tear off our decorations. And let me tell you this, it is not the people who are to blame. The people, they are our comrades, comrades of every one of us regardless of station during four heavy years of war. No, the people are not to blame. Those who are solely to blame, are those who incite the people. Such persons who stabbed our glorious army in the back, who thought of nothing else except seizing power, and of enriching themselves at the expense of the people!' With this, Göring had taken over the term *Dolchstoßlegende** which was becoming popular during this period.

He then spoke of the day which would come, when this 'pack' would have lost its game and be driven from the country. 'Let us prepare for that day', he entreated, 'let us arm ourselves for that day, work for that day. I am sure it will come.' He then left the hall and met some of his comrades.

With this incident, Göring had broken down all the bridges which were being built for officers by the Republic. In the eyes of the more reasonable officers, who were prepared to continue to serve even under a Republic, he had made himself impossible.

Later, this emotional speech which Göring had given without being asked to do so was to be lauded as heralding the emergence of his talents as an orator. It demonstrated that he had courage, not only as a fighter pilot but also as a discharged officer. He had drawn attention to himself. He was no longer a nobody. And he had pointed to a future about which many were thinking, even if they dared not express themselves so openly in the existing revolutionary atmosphere of the capital. At the same time, it demonstrated Göring's lack of control in attacking the Prussian Minister of War and meritorious general of the old army in a manner that previously would have been considered unworthy of an officer.

Göring left Berlin and went home to his mother in Munich. The time for brave words was passed. He had to think about making a living. His 'life as a hero' was over. Like many others, the former captain joined the unemployed, he who had not learned anything except how to fly and lead troops. Flying at least was something. But who would let him fly?

* Translator's note. *Dolchstoßlegende*, literally 'legend of the stab in the back', is the term for the claim by right-wing Germans that the Army had not been defeated in battle but had only lost the war because it had been stabbed in the back by the Left at home.

5
Pilot in the North

While he was in Munich Göring resumed contact with Marianne Mauser in Mauterndorf. He would have married her but her father, a rich farmer, asked in a letter what he had to offer his daughter and all Göring could reply was 'Nothing'.

The Treaty of Versailles had not yet been signed and German aircraft were still in production. In Munich Fokker-Werke had a factory where Göring, having flown their aircraft during the war, was always welcome as the last 'Richthofen' commander. At this time the Allies had an observer team in the Bavarian capital, one of whose members was a British pilot, Captain Frank Beaumont. Late in the war, having shot down two German fighters, Beaumont had been forced to land his damaged aircraft. As a prisoner, Göring had treated him with his customary courtesy to an adversary, dined him and offered him champagne. Göring and Udet visited Beaumont and learned that he was in Munich to supervise the dismantling of the German air force. Beaumont spoke German, but in any case fighter pilots speak the same language. When, after the assassination of Minister President Eisner, a soviet-type Republic was proclaimed at Munich, Beaumont enabled Göring go into hiding among the armed formations which were assembling around Munich to liberate the city with troops under General Ritter von Epp. Göring did not play any role in this however.

After the liberation of Munich he succeeded with Beaumont's help in borrowing a Fokker DVII, an aircraft he had flown at the end of the war. Fokker-Flugzeugwerke were looking for markets for their aircraft in countries that had remained neutral, because there was no longer going to be any German aviation. In the spring of 1919 a big aeronautical exhibition was held at Copenhagen, and for the first time since 1914 aircraft of many types were presented to a public which in the Scandinavian countries at least was wealthy enough to advance civil aviation, Göring represented Fokker-Flugzeugwerke in his DVII. The young war pilot from Germany was admired. His aircraft had excellent flying characteristics. The promotion for Fokker was such a success that they gave the DVII to Göring as a present. For the exhibition an air transport service was set up between Malmö-Bulltofta and Copenhagen-Castrup, in which Swedish 'air baron' Carl Cederstöm, who had been the second pilot to fly from Copenhagen to Malmö in 1910, showed much interest. Göring made many acquaintances and decided to stay in Copenhagen with his DVII and to go into the air show and joy-riding business.

The airport at Castrup became his place of work. He charged his passengers 50 Danish crowns a time for the thrill of being flown by the veteran and last commander of the renowned Richthofen Wing, whose daring 'stunts' brought them a vicarious whiff of the air warfare they had only heard of from afar. Twenty-six years old and good-looking, Göring made a great impression, especially with the ladies in the Danish capital. He had much to catch up with, and it was pleasant to eat and drink well. He was disgusted by the way things were going in Germany and was not thinking of returning home.

For a time he lived with a married woman to whom, in 1933 – as British historian Roger Manvell discovered – he sent a signed photograph of himself with his private telephone number. In 1940 during the occupation of Denmark, a journalist made use of this when Gestapo officers searching her apartment found the photograph with Göring's signature, and immediately became very polite and disappeared.

At Copenhagen in 1919 Göring learned of the Treaty of Versailles, which French Prime Minister Clemenceau had handed to German Foreign Minister Count Brockdorff-Rantzau on 7 May, and which a 'Committee of Four' (President Wilson, Prime Ministers Lloyd George, Clemenceau and Sonnino) had spent six months preparing. Among other things it contained a prohibition 'to maintain air forces', which Göring found particularly oppressive. 'One day we will come back and write a different treaty,' he angrily shouted at a party he was attending when the newspapers published the conditions.

In this he hardly differed from other Germans who rejected it as he did. But the way he expressed his protest demonstrated that he at least had a political objective. He wanted to replace the diktat by a treaty whose terms were less harsh. At this time he was not thinking in terms of revenge, and for good reasons: a military response was out of the question after the collapse of the Reich. The treaty, which the Germans called the 'disgraceful peace', was signed in the Hall of Mirrors at the Palace of Versailles on 28 June 1919. The Hall had been chosen to humiliate the Germans historically as well, because it was here that they had founded their Second Reich in 1871.

The German national parliament in Weimar ratified the Treaty on 9 July and three days later the blockade of the Reich was ended. On 31 July the Treaty was ratified by England, on 6 October by Italy, and on 14 October by France. The USA refused ratification. Not until after the ratification documents had been exchanged in January 1920 were German prisoners of war allowed to return home. Göring could see no reason to return to Germany. Civil aviation had not been expressly forbidden, but the prospects of employment in that sphere seemed dubious in the extreme.

The conditions of the Treaty were much harsher than those imposed by the Armistice about which Erhard Milch, like Göring an air force captain, had written in his diary on 11 November 1918: '12 noon armistice. The conditions are the best basis for a future war.'

In 1920 Göring flew to Sweden. Danish friends had advised him to get a job with the airline that was being formed there. Svenska Lufttrafik AB. was interested in the German pilot, but he was not spared examinations and long discussions before they hired him, and in the interim he continued exhibition and charter flying from Stockholm in his own aircraft. He also earned money as a salesman for the Heinicken parachute which opened automatically if the pilot of a small private aircraft had to bale out.

In 1920 Göring saw Germany again when he was flying for Svenska Lufttrafik, in a seaplane and accompanied by a mechanic, to pioneer an airmail route from Warnemünde to Malmö via Copenhagen. A newspaper photograph shows him being welcomed at Malmö's industrial port of Limhamm after the inaugural flight. Wearing a leather jacket which he has unbuttoned, he stands on the jetty, legs spread, reading aloud from a paper. Gentlemen in formal dress are listening to him in joyous excitement. In 1940 an issue of the *Malmö-Chronic* included this picture as being of importance in the history of aviation.

The news from Germany that reached Göring during this first year in Sweden was a catalogue of disasters. The Allies were demanding the extradition as a 'war criminal' of the Kaiser who had fled to Holland, but Holland refused. In early 1920 the French *chargé d'affaires* in Berlin delivered to Chancellor Bauer a list of 895 persons to be handed over: German nobles and heirs to thrones, all the well-known army commanders, former Chancellor von Bethmann-Hollweg, Großadmiral Tirpitz, U-boat commanders, officers and civil servants at all levels. Foreign Minister Müller refused for the time being to compile a German counter list. The Kapp Putsch in Berlin collapsed because a general strike had been called. The strength of the new Reichswehr was set at 100,000 professional soldiers; aircraft, armour, and heavy artillery were prohibited.

Göring enjoyed life in Sweden where many people openly displayed sympathy, even compassion, towards Germany. For the starving children in the Reich, the so-called 'Swedish Feeding' was initiated, and wooden churches, the so-called 'Swedish Churches', were donated.

He was not the only ex-fighter pilot working in Sweden. Other comrades from the air force were active there, putting their experience at the disposal of Swedish industry which, having been isolated, was anxious to catch up with the latest developments. Through these ex-pilots contracts with German companies were soon negotiated, for example with Heinkel-Werke, which supplied seaplanes to Sweden from 1921 on.

In the winter of 1921 Göring became acquainted with the young Count Eric von Rosen who had taken part in a voyage of exploration and found a new adventure on his way home to his Rockelstad Castle on Lake Baven – a flight during a winter storm. At Stockholm airport he had asked Göring whether he would fly him home because he had missed the train to Sparreholm in Södermanland. It was snowing and the early dusk of the northern winter day would soon fall. Göring had a look at the map. It was not a long flight. All he needed to do, as was customary in those days, was to follow the railway line which led from Stockholm via Södertälje to Sparreholm. In a snowstorm this would be dangerous, one could lose one's way. But Göring was impressed by this Count Rosen. They put on their parachutes and climbed into the Fokker F VII. The flight became a nightmare. With difficulty Göring succeeded in maintaining airspeed, but soon – Count Rosen had no luck as an observer – they lost sight of the railway line below them and were lost above the frozen lakes and snow decked forests. Rosen was airsick and his goggles became opaque. They landed safely, but completely exhausted, on frozen Lake Baven near Rockelstad Castle.

Count Rosen's wife, Mary von Fock, welcomed them on the stairway leading to the castle. She had been very fearful when her husband had called her from Stockholm to tell her that he was flying home. A sister of Countess von Rosen's, Countess Fanny von Wilamowitz-Moellendorff, whose husband had served in the German army and been killed in action, describes Göring's encounter with the castle – and her other sister Carin – in her book *Carin Göring*, which appeared in Berlin in 1934: 'Waving happily, even if somewhat anxious, the young housewife on the steps welcomed the men and led them into the hall where a huge fire and hot drinks soon warmed their frozen limbs. How beautiful was this house! On the walls of the room which reached up to the second floor hung antique weapons and armour, beautiful paintings, and tapestries with Nordic subjects. Everywhere there were hunting trophies and souvenirs of the world-wide voyages of the intrepid explorer. At the foot of the staircase stood a gigantic bear, one of many that the host had killed with a spear according to ancient Nordic custom.

'Göring stood before the fireplace and looked into the flames. Two large swastikas of forged iron decorated the andirons on which the logs were laid. The swastika ... he felt as if he had always known it from time immemorial.' (He was probably seeing one for the first time. It was not Hitler, whom he had not yet met, who revealed the swastika to him, but Count Rosen. For him the swastika became tied to this winter evening at Rockelstad in Södermanland. It can still be seen there. It was a Nordic sun wheel, and the North had drawn him under its spell. The hospitality with the welcoming speech by the host and the toast to the guest's fatherland is part of Swedish tradition. That Göring introduced himself and did not forget his fatherland when doing so goes without saying.) 'A tall figure comes down the stairs, a woman of noble, royal bearing, the sister of the hostess, Carin.

Her deep blue eyes meet Göring's searching gaze. This woman ... Silent and full of reverence he stood there. He felt as if he had always known her.

'That evening one sat at table for a long time. The fighter pilot was able to speak freely and openly. The outrage about the fate of his fatherland, long subdued and forcefully suppressed in a foreign surrounding, broke out impetuously. The humiliation of his people, the suffering of a young generation that had fought bravely to the last, was revealed to his deeply moved audience. Flying high and falling far were commonplace for Hermann Göring, a low cast of mind, dishonour, betrayal, these were things he could not stand.

'The host raised his glass full of German wine. His words were serious but filled with conviction as he spoke of a time to come in the hopefully not too distant future, when German men would again raise Germany's honour on a mighty shield, when Germany would again be free and respected and be able to assume its noble traditions and position among the nations as an equal. Nobody who had just heard the words inspired by the love of his fatherland spoken by this, one of its sons, need despair for Germany. He wished to drink to Germany's future in which he, like the whole Swedish nation, unshakeably believed. Solemnly everyone rose from their seats and the host firmly pressed the hand of his guest.

'The company remained together long into the night. Count von Rosen took up his lute. Sentimental, proud, and joyous folksongs were sung and the guest became aware time and again how close to German emotions the strings of the Swedish soul lay. Here was a free people that still believed in Germany's freedom despite everything, here was a feeling and an intimacy in the music that wrapped itself around a German's heartstrings.

'Göring was not able to talk to Carin at length on this first evening. His soul was far too moved for this. The stormbird of the sea had finally sighted land.'

This emotional description is in accordance with the style of the times. But it does contain, besides the fulsome words, a kernel of truth that is also like a fairy-tale.

It was inevitable that Göring should subsequently be invited to stay at the castle. When he arrived there he immediately felt at home again; a castle was familiar to him, he had grown up in Veldenstein and Mauterndorf. Here he finally found what he had lost.

To the wealth he encountered there was added the presence of an apparently unattached woman who was bound to interest him. Carin von Kantzow, sister of Mary and Fanny von Fock, was five years older than he. They drank wine and sang songs to the music of a lute. The fire, the stuffed bear, the hunting trophies, for Göring everything seemed a dream come true. And – 'love at first sight'?

An important decision had been taken for the romantic young man when he came to this Swedish castle.

6
Student in Munich

Many fairy-tales and legends were woven around the marriage, on 23 February 1922, of Hermann Göring, a student at Munich University, and Carin von Kantzow, née *Freiin* (Baroness) von Fock. They stem not only from the fact that romance ended in tragedy, but also because later many secrets were dramatised into a cult by Göring after Carin's early death. The loss of the strong influence she had had on him was to be a major factor in his future political role. His many memories of her became manifest when he had acquired the money and power to be able to live as he would have wanted to live with her, but he now lacked her inner modesty as his example, and her counsel on personal and political matters was no longer there. Carin Göring had shown herself to be strikingly interested in politics. She would have felt nothing but disgust for the progressive iniquities of the National Socialist system, and she might have been able to prevent her husband from becoming enmeshed in its horrors.

So it was that the deceased Carin Göring, who had died far too young, became a cult figure, the widow of the Prussian Minister President and paladin of the Führer and Chancellor Adolf Hitler, a sort of Queen Louise (wife of King Frederick Wilhelm III and Prussian heroine because of her courageous opposition to Napoleon after Prussia was defeated in 1806) from Sweden, who lay at rest in the mausoleum in the Schorfheide.

In 1933 Countess Fanny von Wilamowitz-Moellendorff wrote about her family in Stockholm: 'Carin was the fourth and second youngest daughter of Swedish Colonel Baron Carl A. von Fock and his wife Huldine, *née* Beamish, from Ireland. The Focks were descended from an old family from Westphalia and Lower Saxony which had formerly also called itself von Brucken, from the House of Bruck or Bruggen. The Focks had gone to the Baltic with the Order of Teutonic Knights and had been invested with property there by Walter von Plettenberg. The family also owned property in Kurland, such as the village of Fockendorf named after it, which was later sold during a minority and now belongs to the Princes of Liewen.

'Johan von Fock, born in 1575, had four sons. The youngest, Gideon, was raised to the Swedish nobility by Queen Kristina of Sweden. Due to an unfortunate lack of feeling for style, the ancient coat of arms, a fallen oak with three roots and a branch growing upwards, was changed by Swedish heraldry into a fallen tree with two balls lying underneath. In Sweden the family owned vast estates in Wästergotland. Due to careless rashness and naïve gullibility it lost most of them again. The Focks were soldiers. "One does not ask after profession, one wears the King's coat," the fathers passed on to the sons.

'Carin's mother, Huldine Beamish, came from an old English family. Carin's grandmother, Mrs Beamish, for her part was again Swedish. Young Huldine was permitted to accompany her mother on frequent visits to the Swedish grandmother, a woman with vivid intellectual interests who maintained a literary and social salon in Stockholm and in her country estate Engsholm near Drottningholm. It was there that Carin's parents met.

'Huldine Beamish was married to Freiherr Carl von Fock, at the time a lieutenant in the Svea Garde, in the Skeppsholm church in Stockholm on 15 September 1880. Five daughters were born to this marriage. In 1903 the eldest, Fanny, married Count Wichard von Wilamowitz-Moellendorff in Gadow Castle, who had been appointed to the German Embassy and who fell in the war. The second, Elsa, remained unmarried. The third, Mary, married the explorer Count Eric von Rosen at Rockelstad Castle. The fourth, Carin, became the wife of Lieutenant Nils von Kantzow, and after this marriage had been amicably dissolved, the wife of Hermann Göring. The fifth sister, Lily, married the painter Lieutenant Seth Martin.'

Countess Fanny von Wilamowitz-Moellendorff states that her sister Carin, who was born on 23 October 1888, had been very sensitive from early childhood. 'She "felt" if someone was unhappy but did not say anything, she "knew" when something bad was being considered or planned, she sensed in advance what later became reality.' This sensitivity was connected with a serious heart condition which she had had from her youth.

Two years after her marriage to Nils von Kantzow, Thomas von Kantzow was born on 1 March 1912. In 1913 the family moved to Paris, because Nils had been sent to the French military academy of St-Cyr for one year by the Swedish embassy. The Kantzows returned to Stockholm shortly before the outbreak of the Great War.

Here the estrangement between Carin and Nils von Kantzow began. Sister Fanny writes: 'Carin was happy to be back again near her parents. Now a certain unrest, sign of an inner disharmony and a feeling of loneliness, became apparent more and more frequently. She went out often, kept making new acquaintanceships, found new friends, was admired and acclaimed, but still remained lonely inside. She turned more and more to her artistic interests. Important writers and artists frequented her hospitable house. Pictures of her as one of the most beautiful women in Sweden appeared in the periodicals, poems and musical compositions were dedicated to her. During these years the longing for something great, something sensed but not yet revealed, lived strongly in her soul. Without being overtly unhappy, she felt an emptiness, a loneliness. It was then that she met Hermann Göring.'

Since one has attributed 'second sight' to her, she may have sensed that she would share a fate with this German air force officer, who had charm but little else, that would lift her out of the confines of her marriage to an unimportant Swedish lieutenant. By this time both partners in marriage had long become indifferent to each other.

When he was a child Göring had been parted from his mother, for whom he later felt not much more than the required respect, and even that was clouded by Franziska Göring's 15-year love affair with Dr Ritter von Epenstein which she had pursued before the eyes of her husband and children. In his future wife he therefore also sought a mother, not having received much from his own.

Carin von Kantzow was a beautiful woman whom he could admire. The passion that was a part of his nature also existed in Carin so that they quickly understood each other. Marrying into this noble Swedish family, which had German antecedents, was bound to strengthen his sense of self-esteem. He did however make one condition: Carin would have to get a divorce. He did not want a relationship such as had existed between his mother and von Epenstein; he wanted a clear-cut situation. Carin would have been willing to live with him even without a divorce. She would have had to leave her son Thomas with her husband in any case. A *ménage à trois* such as his mother had led with his father and von Epenstein went against his sense of honour. In this he was later also to differ from other powerful people in Hitler's entourage (and from Hitler himself), whose sex lives were not at all in accordance with the norms that had been valid before 1933.

Carin's parents were not rich, but two sisters, Fanny and Mary, had made rich marriages. The marriage would not bring him much money, but at this time Göring was not concerned about that. He could not see any professional future for himself as a pilot with the small Swedish airline. In addition, Stockholm society soon began to look at Carin's enthusiasm and love for this penniless former German officer who was five years her junior as a scandal, which could not be tolerated so openly in a Swedish military family.

At this time, the Kantzows were living in a small house in Grev Karlavägen in Stockholm which Göring first entered in early 1921 when he was invited to dinner. Thomas von Kantzow recalled later: 'My father was completely taken with him and my mother did not take her eyes off him. I sensed that she had fallen in love with him.'

Richard Wagner gave Carin her cue when she enthusiastically confessed to her sister Fanny: 'We are like Tristan and Isolde'. Göring was never to escape the spell of Richard Wagner's music, and only in this was he like Hitler. The highly emotional music enthralled this wartime generation which lacked but sought the ideals which were not forthcoming from the futile struggles of the Great War. Hitler's entry into Wagner had been through *Rienzi*, the tribune of the people.

Göring discovered Wagner through *Tristan and Isolde*. What was left to him in the end was the *Götterdämmerung*.

But for the time being, in 1921, Göring was a nobody who had had the luck to gain a beautiful, intelligent, very passionate foreign wife who undertook much in Stockholm to further his cultural understanding. They visited museums and not just to admire the paintings and sculptures. Carin induced in Göring an aesthetic feeling for style which oriented itself towards the most precious and glorious. This private introduction to the art of the old masters was also to have consequences later on when Göring began to collect art treasures.

It was not enough for Göring to be a famous air force captain whose wings had been clipped and who nurtured a determination to do away with the shame of the Treaty of Versailles. The beauty he had seen as a child in the castles of Dr von Epenstein he now admired, and Carin von Kantzow had the ability to show him why it was worthy of admiration. Göring was a passionate man who believed that everything would end well for him, an 'ego-optimist' who played this role to the last.

He would meet Carin at her parents' home. In the garden of the family property, in a small chapel, they had undisturbed solitude. This Edelweiss Chapel belonged to an Edelweiss order of sisters, a tiny Christian sect such as is often found in Sweden, which Carin's grandmother Mrs Beamish had founded. In Sweden if one were seeking solitude in a church, this could only be found on a Sunday as a rule, but this chapel was also open on weekdays. No services were held there, it was only for meditation or music. The Edelweiss which had given the chapel its name was also esteemed in Sweden as a rare Alpine flower. It symbolised 'forward', synonymous with 'upwards', as Countess Fanny von Wilamowitz-Moellendorff wrote. The sect had far-reaching connections which were to prove useful to Göring later on. One of the Edelweiss sisters was Princess Marie-Elisabeth zu Wied, who was to bring many visitors from the nobility to visit the Görings in Berlin.

In January 1926 Göring wrote a letter in Swedish to his mother-in-law: 'Dearest Mama! ... Now I would also like to thank you most heartily for the beautiful moment which I was allowed to spend in the Edelweiss chapel! You cannot imagine what I felt in that wonderful atmosphere. It was so calm, so beautiful, I forgot any other sound, all worries, felt as if I were in another world. I closed my eyes and let myself be flooded by the pure celestial atmosphere with which the whole room was filled. I felt like a swimmer who takes a short rest on a solitary island in order to gain new strength before he has to plunge himself back into the racing current of life. I thanked God and sent warm prayers up to Him that He help us all in the new year so that the sun may again finally shine into our dark lives.'

Göring's dark life? Even then, five years before this letter was written, it was professionally dark. He left Carin and went back to Munich to enrol at the university; Carin had drawn his attention to the gaps in his education. The separation was also to serve as a testing period for their relationship. They wanted to put their love to the test and Göring was to make up his mind what profession he intended to follow. But Göring was hardly back in Munich with his mother before Carin came to see him. She could not stand life without him.

Göring's mother took a liking to the Swedish woman and advised her to get a divorce. In Sweden one could possibly live together without a divorce, but in Germany it was impossible. She was speaking from experience.

While Carin was in Stockholm arranging for an amicable separation from her husband – with whom she would have to leave her son Thomas – by an official divorce, Göring began his studies in history and political science. One of the lectures he attended dealt with the wars of liberation against Napoleon from 1813 to 1815.

When his marriage was finally able to take place on 23 February 1922 in Munich, Carin brought a little money to the marriage which she received regularly from her former husband. Present at the religious ceremony were Göring's mother, his sisters and brothers and Carin's eldest sister Fanny with her daughter Dagmar. Afterwards the marriage feast was held at the Park Hotel. 'The atmosphere was serious, but still beautiful and hearty,' Countess Fanny von Wilamowitz-Moellendorff writes. 'The first after-dinner speech ended with a toast to Germany, whose situation at the time was even more unsure than before. The *Deutschlandlied* was sung. Carin looked like a fairy princess. She wore a white dress and had a wreath of white roses in her hair. The carnations glowed dark red in her large bouquet, which was wrapped in ribbons of green and white (the Focks' colours) and red and white (Görings'). A young pilot, von Köckritz, brought salutations from comrades which ended with the words: "We have always maintained: Our Göring will go farther than anybody else".'

After dinner, Göring's former adjutant in the Richthofen Geschwader, Karl Bodenschatz, sang songs by Hermann Löns (German romantic composer and song-writer) accompanied by the lute. Bodenschatz was now an officer in the Reichswehr.

The Edelweiss which the bridegroom wore in his buttonhole is specifically mentioned in the accounts of the marriage.

The Görings spent their honeymoon in a hunting lodge they had rented in the German Alps at Hochkreuth (Wildbad Kreuth) on the Austrian border near Bayerisch-Zell. 'The happiest days of their lives', writes the Countess, 'Hermann and Carin Göring spent in the small hunting lodge at Hochkreuth. There, in the wonderful mountain landscape, all care, struggle, and unrest disappeared, there

51

they were like two happy children who take each day as it comes.' Photographs from 1922 show them hiking in the mountains. They kept the hunting lodge after the honeymoon was over.

Göring evinced little enthusiasm for his studies at the university, but he met people there who like him were dissatisfied with the Weimar Republic and hoped for the reinstatement of former German glory. He remained a monarchist, but he bore a grudge against a Kaiser who had abandoned his soldiers when he fled into exile at Doorn on the advice of his General Staff. Another reason why studying in Munich became irksome for Göring was that his wife remained at Hochkreuth, and during term time he was often lonely.

It is remarkable that he did not join one of the many *vaterländische* (nationalist-patriotic) formations that had sprung up in Munich and Upper Bavaria. It would have been natural to take a part there with former comrades from the war and to prepare for a future when they would be needed again. The Reichswehr was now a professional army, but there was also its militia, the 'black Reichswehr', and the vaterländische formations which had managed to equip themselves with weapons when they were formed.

Göring remained a loner, however, who could find no joy for the time being in subordinating himself to one of these formations. He was far too well-known to let himself be ordered about again like a common soldier. If he were ever to take part, it would be only if he were offered a command. But who would offer him such a command? There was no shortage of war heroes from the lost war.

At this time, Hitler was beginning to get himself much talked about in Munich. But Göring was not interested in this former corporal who was an Austrian but had served in the Bavarian army as a volunteer during the War. He had been decorated with an Iron Cross 1st Class. What was a corporal compared to the commander of Geschwader Richthofen who wore the *Pour le Mérite*? Hitler was the leader of a political party called the NSDAP, but there were many parties in Munich and even more vaterländische groups.

There was another reason for Göring's reluctance to join anywhere. Many of his comrades had fought in the *Freikorps* (lit. free corps. Armed right-wing formations, mostly former officers, who fought under self-appointed leaders against anyone they preceived as 'left', e.g., Kapp who led the Putsch named after him against the Socialist government, or others who resisted attempts by Poland to encroach on German territory.) He had remained aloof during these years. He had heard about them, but he was living in Denmark and Sweden, and while conditions in Germany pained him, he no longer desired to take an active part. Carin had seduced him into a different world from that of his comrades from the war. There was nothing of the *lansquenet* in Göring's make-up. He wanted to enjoy his life which Carin was so purposefully directing towards the beautiful and enjoyable.

If Göring had not met Hitler in November 1922, he might have played a part in international aviation. He could also have become rich, as he did become through Hitler. But the power he was to be given by Hitler could have been put into his hands by no one else.

The *Freistaat* (Free State, i.e., Republic) of Bavaria, in which a soviet-style Republic had been proclaimed in Munich and Augsburg on 7 April 1919, and overthrown on 1 May 1919 by *Freikorps* from Bavaria, Northern Germany, and Württemberg, had developed into a strong opponent of the Reich government in Berlin. Bavaria had rejected the Reich President's decrees of 29 August 1921 and 26 June 1922 for the protection of the Republic, as well as the Law for the Protection of the Republic of 24 July 1922. An agreement between Bavaria and Berlin was negotiated, but the tensions were not allayed.

In the autumn of 1922 Hitler was but one of many who were preoccupied with the thought of cleansing the Weimar Republic of the *Novemberverbrecher* (lit. November Criminals, nationalist term for the left-wing and moderate politicians who had accepted Germany's defeat in November 1918), and of reinstating a national government which would change the black-red-gold flag of the Republic back into black-white-red flag of the Monarchy. Munich was seen as a 'national citadel' guarded by nationalistic armed formations.

When Hindenburg returned from a trip through East Prussia to Hanover in the summer of 1922, he found an invitation to a hunting-party at the convent castle of Dietramszell, issued by the former Bavarian Prime Minister Ritter von Kahr – who had rejected the laws for the protection of the Republic and subsequently stepped down – by Crown Prince Rupprecht of Bavaria, and by Ludendorff. During his short stay in Munich his three hosts proposed to him that he take up residence in Munich which they described as a 'cell of order' and the starting point for 'German rebirth'. It was here that Hindenburg is alleged to have heard about Hitler for the first time. After the visit to Dietramszell, which from then on he was to visit annually for hunting, he wrote to his estate neighbour at Neudeck (East Prussia), Count von Brünneck: 'I hope that both sectors of the country (he meant Bavaria and East Prussia) will shine the light of their national convictions so strongly and continuously that it will finally penetrate the dark centre of the fatherland.' By 'dark centre' he meant Berlin, Central, and North-western Germany.

In the autumn of 1922 many violent protest rallies by the nationalist formations and parties took place in Munich, their anti-Communist nature being a reaction to experience of the period of rule by soviet-type councils.

Hitler had increased his bodyguard, the SA, to a sizeable troop which, however, was of no military value. It was lacking a man with authority who could develop it into a para-military organisation. Göring, the student, became this man. He had heard about Hitler, he regarded Berlin with disdain, but he was still in search of a political movement to join in a Munich caught up in political turmoil. In November 1922 Göring happened to be in the crowd at a protest rally. As was customary, speakers from different parties and organisations delivered speeches. In 1946 at Nuremberg, Göring stated: 'At the end of the rally, Hitler was also called to the podium. I had already heard his name once shortly before and was eager to hear what he might have to say. But Hitler refused to say anything. By pure chance I was standing quite close to him and was therefore able to hear the reasons for his refusal. Hitler said it was senseless to shout out protests into the blue without having the slightest possibility of enforcing them. That made a strong impression on me – I held exactly the same opinion.'

Subsequently Göring attended a rally of the NSDAP at which Hitler repeated what Göring had heard him say at the end of the protest rally. Next day he went to the offices of the NSDAP to speak to Hitler. They agreed that the Treaty of Versailles, this 'shame of our fatherland', had to be eliminated. What decided Göring was Hitler's invitation to re-organise his SA. He flattered the 29-year-old student by saying that he had been looking for a long time for a man as famous as the last commander of the Richthofen Geschwader. Göring was hardly interested in the NSDAP party platform, he was looking for a job that was appropriate to a former captain and now it had been offered to him. Naturally he asked for time to consider it so as to be able to discuss everything with his wife. She was in agreement. Göring bought a little house in the Munich suburb of Obermenzing which they furnished. They now had a home in Munich.

Two months after his meeting with Hitler, Göring took on the job of turning a 'horde of wild men' as Hitler had described the SA into 'a power of eleven thousand men'. 'The most important thing at the beginning', Göring reported, 'was firmly to unite the SA, to instil obedience and thereby to develop it into a dependable force which would carry out any order from me or Adolf Hitler.

'From the beginning it was my objective to recruit Party members into the SA who were young and idealistic enough to sacrifice all their free time and to give it their full strength. Secondly, I had to try to find recruits from among the workers.' At this time the para-military formations were receiving financial support.

Göring's activities as commander of the SA lasted for less than a year. He had put himself under Hitler, but in some way felt himself to be his equal. He did not accept an office in the NSDAP, considering it to be beneath him.

Countess Fanny von Wilamowitz-Moellendorff writes about the first public appearance of the new Göring SA: 'On 28 January 1923 for the first time they were called to a large rally on the Marsfeld. They marched in serried ranks and the beautiful song hallowed by so much pain, 'Wir treten an zum Beten' (We have come to pray), was given a new meaning. Hitler consecrated the flag. Afterwards they all marched through Munich's streets to the rally at the Münchner Kindl (famous brewery and beer garden). Carin went along.'

In the Reich inflation began to soar. On 22 December 1922 the total expenditures of the budget had amounted to 1 billion marks; the deficit for 1922 totalled 7.1 billion marks. In January 1923 the exchange rate for 1 dollar was 49,000 marks. The purchase of the house in Obermenzing was probably made easier by the inflation. Carin Göring had a bank account in Sweden; she had hard currency at her disposal.

In his biography of Chancellor von Schleicher, Friedrich-Karl von Plehwe wrote:

'The year 1923 became the time of the severest test and strongest nervous crisis of the Weimar Republic. Never had the Reich been as close to total collapse as it was then. One virtually insoluble situation followed upon the heels of the last, caused by interventions from outside and internal discord. It started in January with the occupation of the Ruhr by the French, to which the German side could only react by laborious and sacrificial "passive resistance".

'Then came inflation. The breakdown of the currency had already begun the year before, and now the irretrievable decline of the mark bid fair to ruin the economy totally. Towards the end of 1922 Germany had fallen behind with some reparations deliveries. These consisted of a large number of telegraph poles and a relatively small amount of coal. The French government of Poincaré had long prepared itself to seize "productive securities" and had considered the occupation of the Ruhr for this purpose.

'Therefore a surprisingly large force of two General Commands consisting of five divisions marched in on 11 January 1923. A Belgian division joined them. The Italians also took part, albeit only by a harmless gesture: they sent a commission of engineers to the Ruhr.

'The English had advised the French against such an operation. Therefore they did not move but left their troops in the part of the Rhineland they were occupying. Nor did the Americans approve the action by the French and as a sign of this, withdrew their troops which were still in a bridgehead on the Rhine.

'For one week, a wave of the strongest outrage against the French intervention arose throughout the whole Reich. Historians and all secondary literature to date unanimously underline that in its whole history the German people seldom displayed such a strong unanimity as they did in their condemnation and outrage at this event.'

It is against this background that Göring's role as commander of the SA in 1923 must be seen. Hitler had intended to have Göring create a powerful force that would also be willing to reinforce the Reichswehr if the French were to penetrate deeper into the Reich.

General von Seeckt, who commanded the Reichswehr at the time, stated that in case of a further advance towards Berlin the French would run into the armed resistance of the whole population. The occupation of the Ruhr prompted Seeckt to begin the initial preparations for the build-up of the future German air force, which the current SA commander Göring was to bring to public attention in 1934.

A photograph of Göring taken in 1923, which was widely disseminated as a postcard, shows the first commander of the SA in a shining black raincoat with officer's belt and shoulder-straps, on his left arm an armband bearing a swastika. However this was not the simple swastika armband as worn by Hitler, but had three silver braids and the swastika had an embroidered border. His steel helmet bears a large white swastika in front, just like those of the 1920 Kapp putschists of the Loewenfeld Brigade in Berlin. Beneath his chin the *Pour le Mérite* is prominent. But his stance before the camera is anything but military; both hands in his coat pockets, as in the snapshots of him as a wartime pilot. When he was a boy he had wanted to be a 'Boer general'. That had been play. Now Göring was serious. Was he not an SA general who disposed of an armed force which could compete with other vaterländische formations such as the Bund Oberland and the organisations and free corps of Rossbach and Ehrhardt? (Oberland, Rossbach, and Ehrhardt were leaders of armed nationalistic bands which, like most such organisations at the time, were named after them.)

The brown uniform had been copied from that of Rossbach's troops. The SA cap, strangely enough, reminded one of the k.u.k. Army (k for kaiserliche and k for königliche, i.e., pre 1918 Austria which was both an imperial as well as a royal monarchy, the monarch being Emperor of Austria and King of Hungary) in which Hitler had refused to serve. The swastika had been 'presented' to the NSDAP by the journalist Dietrich Eckardt.

In *Wehrkreiskommando* VII (Army District Command), i.e., Bavaria, the liaison officer to Göring's *Stürmen* (stormtroopers. For their private armies – SA and later SS – the Nazis invented new terms for military formations and ranks so as not to annoy the regular army. Most of these terms are both jaw-breakers and untranslatable.) was a certain Captain Ernst Röhm, who saw them as a militia which the Reichswehr could use if need arose. Hitler rejected this idea however.

The SA trained in the forests around Munich, and Göring recalled his days as a lieutenant in the 113th Infantry Regiment in Mulhouse. For Hitler, this Göring was a lucky break which 'destiny' had sent him. At this time Göring's political aspirations had hardly matured; he wanted power, and this he saw in the military rather than political field.

The little house in Obermenzing became a meeting-place for the men around Hitler. Carin Göring had installed herself on the second floor, and her Biedermeier furniture, the little white harmonium, Chinese embroideries, paintings and carpets made the rooms comfortable. On the ground floor was a large study with an alcove and leaded window panes. In the cellar was a fireplace before which stood large tables and farm chairs.

Here the meetings with Dietrich Eckardt, Hermann Esser, Ernst Hanfstaengl, with Amann and Rudolf Hess, took place, and also with Alfred Rosenberg. Eckardt was the publisher of the *Völkische Beobachter* (which was to become the Nazi Party organ); the Balt Rosenberg was to become his successor. Hanfstaengl came from a wealthy Munich family of publishers. Hess, a German born abroad, was a student at Munich University like Göring. Amann had been a sergeant in Hitler's regiment.

These new comrades of Göring's gave his wife food for thought; until now she had been used to a different kind of company. Hitler, who normally only joined them late at night after the discussions were over and large amounts of beer were being drunk, had great respect for Carin Göring. He admired her aristocratic bearing. Through this Hitler, her husband had found a job that he liked and Carin was grateful to him. And she believed that here in Munich she had become involved in political events of the greatest consequences that could become important for the Görings in the near future.

7
Attempted Putsch

The appeal for passive resistance which the government of Chancellor Cuno had issued on 13 January 1923 was answered with directives, arrests and harsh sentences by the occupation forces in the Ruhr. German volunteers such as Albert Leo Schlageter, who offered active resistance, and blew up bridges and railway tracks, were sentenced to death. Schlageter's execution caused mourning and outrage. West of the Rhine all the way to the Palatinate, the French attempted to lead a separatist movement in order to cut these territories off from the Reich. The Reichswehr leadership increased the manpower of their units with short-term volunteers because they feared that France's allies, the Poles, would invade Germany.

In the summer, the Cuno government resigned and on 13 August 1923 the new Chancellor, Gustav Stresemann, formed a large coalition cabinet consisting of the *Deutsche Volkspartei*, the *Zentrum*, the *Demokratische Partei*, and the SPD (German People's Party, Catholic Centre Party, Democratic Party, and the German Social Democratic Party). On 26 September Stresemann called off passive resistance in the Ruhr. Although unsuccessful at first, his intention was to reach an agreement with the French, but it was not until the summer of 1925 that they withdrew from the Ruhr.

That same day the Bavarian government transferred all executive power to former Bavarian Minister President Gustav von Kahr and appointed him *Generalstaatskommissar* (General State Commissioner) for Bavaria, with the right to deploy the Reichswehr there. With this move, the authority of the German President and the government had been called into question in Munich, and in Berlin it was feared that Bavaria intended to secede from the Reich.

Also on that day the President, acting in conjunction with the Chancellor, transferred all executive power to *Reichswehrminister* (Armed Forces Minister) Gessler according to Article 48 of the constitution. Executive power was then delegated to the local commanders of the Reichswehr, including General von Lossow, Commander of 7th Division and Chief of *Wehrkreis* (military district) VII, Bavaria. He rejected this, because von Kahr already held executive power in Bavaria.

Gessler dismissed von Lossow, but he was immediately appointed 'State Commander for Bavaria' by the Bavarian government and entrusted with the continuing command of 7th Division. Shortly before this occurred, von Lossow had refused to take action against the *Völkische Beobachter* for an article that had insulted the Commander-in-Chief of the Army, General von Seeckt.

During the summer Hitler had withdrawn to Berchtesgaden. He now returned to Munich where Göring had organised SA protection for the *Völkische Beobachter*'s premises. In Berlin they were speaking of acts of high treason in Bavaria. General von Lossow had the Reichswehr in Bavaria swear an oath of loyalty to himself personally.

In October 1923 the government of Saxony under Minister President Erich Zeigner, formed by a coalition between the KPD (German Communist Party) and the left wing of the SPD, which styled itself a 'government of republican-proletarian defence', refused to obey the directives issued by the Commander of Wehrkreis IV, General Müller, who had been granted local executive power. The Communist press in Saxony had called for 'arming the proletariat', whereupon General Müller had banned this press. On 22 October 1923 the Reichswehr marched into Saxony, and as Zeigner refused to step down, the government of Saxony was dismissed. The Social Democrats formed a new government there on 30 October.

Before this, Bavarian Generalstaatskommissar von Kahr had declared on 26 October that he would no longer conduct negotiations with the Reich government.

A Communist putsch in Hamburg in mid-October had been put down by marines after three days of street fighting between the police and the Communists.

On 6 November the Reichswehr had to intervene in Thuringia to disarm and disband armed Communist formations. Moscow, which had called the German Communists to revolt, had immediately dissociated itself again and retracted everything, which is why the weak Reichswehr was able to suppress these uprisings so quickly.

Five years had now passed since 11 November 1918. Bavaria had turned away from the Reich. All that was now missing was for it to declare its independence.

One year previously Mussolini had seized power in Italy with the march of his 'Blackshirts' on Rome. This was going through the minds of those at Göring's house in Obermenzing. Göring had suggested to General von Lossow that he seize power with a 'march on Berlin' by the Reichswehr, the Bavarian armed formations, and the SA. But von Lossow had declined. Hitler now feared that von Lossow and von Kahr would actually take Bavaria out of the Reich, and by doing so outmanoeuvre him and his adherents.

An end to inflation was in sight. In mid November the *Rentenmark* was temporarily to be introduced after the government had passed an enabling law on 13 October. At the beginning of November the exchange rate of the dollar stood at 130 billion marks. The Red uprisings had been put down. It was foreseeable that the Reich would be able to survive its worst crisis since 1918.

But what about Bavaria? It had violated the constitution and set off a conflict with the Reich. Did von Kahr, who, with General von Lossow and the chief of the state police Colonel Seisser, was the real power in Bavaria, intend to reinstate the monarchy? The current Minister President von Knillinger might also be involved, even though he was staying in the background for the time being. And what about General Ludendorff, who was under the influence of a certain Mathilde von Kemnitz who fanatically believed in 'dark powers' that had supposedly carried out the 'stab in the back' of the German army in 1918? He was in contact with Hindenburg who in the autumn had been hunting again in Dietramszell. In a letter written in October to Groener, Ludendorff's successor in Supreme Army Command, Hindenburg had declared his confidence that 'parliamentarism would soon come to an end and former discipline and order return'.

Groener advised Hindenburg not to get himself involved in the activities in Bavaria. He wrote that 'the men around Kahr are German-minded', but the Swabian Groener was after something else. The idea of a 'reinstatement of Prussian predominance in the Reich', he went on, 'would be regarded as impossible, if not as political madness, due to Bavaria's initiative and power.' He appealed to the Prussian Hindenburg that the Prussians must decide 'to regard Prussia and the Reich as one, even under a republic'.

Until the summer, Ludendorff had also frequented Göring's house in Obermenzing. In September the meetings there of the men around Hitler had to be discontinued because Carin Göring was seriously ill. At the funeral of Göring's mother she had caught a cold which developed into pneumonia. Franziska Göring, with whom Carin had developed a good relationship, had died at the end of August aged 57. She was buried in the Munich Waldfriedhof next to her husband Heinrich.

During recent years Göring's relationship with his mother had improved. He mourned her and was very much occupied with his wife's illness, so his influence on the plans being made to launch an attack in Bavaria was small. Nor was he promised any high position. Göring was the 'good soldier' who commanded his SA and would naturally lead them when the time came. The putsch which Hitler and Ludendorff were preparing was planned in Hitler's house near Berchtesgaden, in Ludendorff's country house in the village of Prinz-Ludwigs-Höhe near Munich, and in the offices of the NSDAP. Carin had not been told about any of this.

The vaterländische formations and the SA were to march into Munich and bring the Reichswehr and the state police over to their side. How they were then to get from Munich to Berlin remained unclear. But it was Hitler's intention to seize power there, as Mussolini had done in Rome. General Ludendorff was to become commander of a new national army consisting of the Reichswehr and the armed formations. But since the Reichswehr had succeeded in putting down the Communist uprisings of early October so quickly, the time factor put Hitler's planned putsch under pressure. The Stresemann government had regained authority, even if not in Bavaria. Hitler now planned the putsch for the night of 10/11 November.

Von Kahr, von Lossow, Seisser, and Minister President von Knillinger stole a march on him by convening a major rally for 8 November in the large hall of the Bürgerbräukeller (British and other historians were to call this Hitler's Beer Hall Putsch) to be attended by the leading personalities in Munich who were filled with curiosity as to von Kahr's intentions after the rupture with Berlin. Would the von Kahr, von Lossow, and Seisser triumvirate finally declare Bavaria's separation from the Reich?

Hitler had learned that the organisers had decided not to have any police in the hall because they did not wish to give the impression that they were afraid, and based his coup upon this fact. He could not appear in Munich with the *Kampfbund* (Combat Union) to which the SA belonged, because his time plan for this had been thrown by the Bürgerbräu rally. He ordered Göring to put at least one troop of SA on alert, standing-by in a lorry. Countess Fanny von Wilamowitz-Moellendorff writes: 'Carin was not feeling well. She had just survived a serious pneumonia, was coughing, and lay in bed with fever and even though, as usual, she did not talk about how she felt, there was reason for worry. Hermann Göring was constantly on the go. On the afternoon of 8 November he was only able to sit with her for a short time. "We have big plans today, this evening there is a big rally in the Bürgerbräukeller, maybe it will go on very late. Don't worry," he said to Carin. He did not need to say more, probably was not permitted to. Left alone, she still worried.' That her husband was to undertake a military action with a few SA troops did not enter her mind.

Göring's part in the 'Beer Hall Putsch' began at 8.45 p.m. when, swastika displayed on his steel helmet, he led his storm troopers into the hall where Hitler is seated at a table in the background with Max Amann, Josef Gerum, the *Völkischer Beobachter*'s managing director, Rudolf Hess and Ernst Hanfstaengl.

His bodyguard Ulrich Graf had greeted Hitler in the hall and given him a stein of beer. While doing so he told him that the SA had arrived. Hitler and his companions thereupon drew pistols from their pockets while von Kahr was speaking on the stage. The audience became uneasy and Göring climbed on a table and shouted 'Silence!' In the meantime Hitler had had Ulrich Graf clear a way to the stage from which he now fired a shot into the ceiling. Then he shouted that he would have a machine-gun set up on the balcony unless there was instant silence. He then gave a speech in which he said that von Kahr had his full confidence and would become State Administrator while he himself, with Ludendorff, von Lossow, and Seisser, would form a new government which would speak for Germany.

Karl Alexander von Müller, who was present, wrote: 'Loud acclaim broke out, no further objections were to be heard.'

While Hitler was negotiating at pistol point with von Kahr, von Lossow, and Seisser in a side room, Göring on the stage was keeping the audience calm. 'Nobody need be afraid,' he shouted. We are your friends, there is no reason for anxiety.'

It had been planned that Ludendorff would be present, but he arrived late. Since von Kahr, von Lossow, and Seisser refused to become a part of Hitler's plan, he had Rudolf Hess and Ulrich Graf keep an eye on them while he went back into the hall and lied to the assembly, telling them that a new national government had just been formed and, furthermore, that General Ludendorff would march on Berlin with the Reichswehr, the police, and the national formations as a new 'national army'. 'Tomorrow will either find a new national government in Germany, or us dead, one or the other.'

Ludendorff finally arrived, wearing all his medals. He succeeded in persuading the triumvirate in the side room to declare support for Hitler's coup in the presence of the assembly, which they did without further delay. Von Kahr was now prepared to act as regent for the monarchy, the house of Wittelsbach. Von Lossow and Seisser said that they were prepared to support Hitler if the revolt succeeded.

It was now midnight and the audience broke up and went home. With them too went von Kahr, von Lossow, and Seisser, who had given Ludendorff their word of honour that they would stick to the agreements reached.

Some of the participants were taken as hostages and put under the guard of Rudolf Hess and some SA men. Göring was happy that the Putsch had succeeded. But since he had promised his wife to be home by midnight, he got Hanfstaengl to take a message to her. By chance her sister Countess Fanny von Wilamowitz-Moellendorf was with her.

That night Hitler already saw himself as the new Chancellor. But in Berlin that night, the government was having a meeting with General von Seeckt, chaired by President Ebert! An almost unanimous decision was reached to transfer executive power from Reichswehrminister Gessler to von Seeckt, who agreed to accept it. With this, the fate of the Reich had been given into the hands of General von Seeckt until further notice. He immediately wired the Munich City Commander, Major General Ritter von Danner – who had informed him of the events in Munich – that General von Lossow should undertake whatever was necessary to put down the putsch at once, otherwise he would personally come from Berlin to Munich. Von Lossow explained to von Danner that he had only feigned agreement in order to gain time and that he had been threatened at pistol point.

Von Kahr had meanwhile taken himself off to Regensburg. Before leaving he had announcements printed which were posted in the streets of Munich on the morning of 9 November. They said that the NSDAP had been dissolved and that all agreements with Hitler were null and void. Arrest warrants were issued for the putschists. Meanwhile Captain Röhm and some of his followers had entrenched themselves at the General Comand post.

Hitler, Göring, Ludendorff, and Hess were still in the Bürgerbräukeller. Messengers they sent to von Lossow were arrested. Ludendorff suggested a plan of his own: he and Hitler, with their followers, would march to the city centre and take over the General Command post where Röhm was surrounded by Reichswehr troops. On Hitler's order, Göring mustered the SA at the Bürgerbräukeller, and had them swear allegiance to Ludendorff.

It had snowed in Munich during the night. The morning was overcast.

Göring, who now knew that the Reichswehr and the state police were hostile to the putschists, became uneasy. He did not like the idea of a march through the city, and ordered the hostages to be brought along. The organisation of the march was amateurish. The column was led by a lorry of the *Sturmtrupp Hitler* (Storm Troop Hitler) armed with a machine-gun, but with few exceptions the 3,000 marchers were unarmed.

Advance units were now sent out to discover where the enemy stood. Ludendorff, Hitler, and Göring marched in the front rank, with Ulrich Graf carrying a swastika flag before them. The state police had blocked the Ludwigsbrücke over the River Isar, but the column, now led by Göring, was allowed to pass. Before reaching Odeonsplatz, across which it intended to proceed to the General Command post, the column had to pass through the narrow Residenzstraße. At its exit, by the Feldherrnhalle, 1st Lieutenant of Police Michael *Freiherr* von Godin had deployed his squad of policemen. He had Seisser's order not to let the column march into the Odeonsplatz under any circumstances. The lorry with the SA men was no longer at the front but somewhere in the middle of the column.

When the column came to the police barricade it stopped. Hitler sent Ulrich Graf ahead who called out: 'Don't shoot, don't shoot! His Excellency General Ludendorff is coming!' Hitler shouted: 'Surrender, surrender!' Then shots rang out; Göring had given the order to open fire. Ludendorff ignored the firing. With his adjutant Major (ret.) Hans Streck, he advanced with military bearing towards the policemen, who opened ranks to let him pass. He was then arrested. Hitler, who had been walking arm-in-arm with Dr Scheubner-Richter, was pulled to the ground by his companion and dislocated his shoulder. His companion was dead.

Göring was lying in the street with bullets in his hip and thighs. SA men carried him away. In the house of the furniture dealer Ballin they turned him over to Ballin's wife who had been a nurse during the war. Ballin was a Jew. (In 1939

Göring arranged for Ballin and his family to leave the country.) The Ballins did not betray Göring to the police. After dark they contacted Professor Alwin Ritter von Ach to whose clinic he was taken on the morning of 10 November.

Three policemen and sixteen members of the NSDAP had been killed at the Feldherrnhalle.

Carin Göring, although still ill, went to the clinic on 10 November. Countess Fanny von Wilamowitz-Moellendorff who accompanied her, writes: 'White as chalk, bandaged, tormented by pain, he lay there without being able to move. The look in his eyes has changed. Never again will these eyes be able to gaze at the world with such untroubled innocence. Loyalty is not only the highest virtue in the North, it is also the paramount duty. Here something sacred had been damaged.'

To express it with less pathos: Göring was not just seriously wounded. The first shot to be fired at the Feldherrnhalle had come from a rifle which the commander of the state police 1st Lieutenant *Freiherr* von Godin had torn from the hands of one of his men who was still hesitating after he had given the order to fire. And this shot hit Göring, who was walking ahead of Hitler and Ludendorff, the *Pour le Mérite* around his neck. Göring felt himself betrayed and cheated. If he had thus far been politically naïve when he joined Hitler and took over command of the SA, from now on he would no longer be so. If he survived, of course, and that was far from certain.

8
Exile

Three days later, on 13 November 1923, Carin Göring wrote a letter from Innsbruck to Stockholm: 'You will have learned the official version through the newspapers, dear mother, but that is probably nothing but what was released by the authorities. Hermann's leg is shot to pieces, the bullet went through half a centimetre from the artery, there are lots of stone splinters and dirt in the long channel that the bullet drilled. The shot is high up on the thigh, horribly infected because all that dirt is trying to come out, therefore causing pus, fever, and pain.

'The danger of bleeding to death is not yet passed. From Munich we drove to Garmisch, Hermann still wearing the first bandage, in the car of good friends in whose villa we lived for a few days, but then it became known that he was there, demonstrations and cheers in front of the villa with crowds of people who came there. We therefore thought it best to leave, across the border to Austria, we drove there by car, were arrested at the border, policemen with loaded revolvers drove back to Garmisch with us. The authorities took his passport away, he was taken to a hospital that was surrounded by guards.

'Despite this a miracle came to our aid. Hermann was carried out, he can't walk a step, put into a car again and then, only in his nightshirt, with furs and blankets, "taken across the border" within two hours.'

Carin Göring had arranged for the abduction from the hospital in Garmisch to be carried out by policemen and SA men masquerading as policemen, but before doing so she had had to convince her husband that von Kahr, who himself had broken his word on 9 November, would not have taken seriously Göring's promise not to flee which he had given at Garmisch. Hitler had fled to Uffing where he hid with the Hanfstaengl family. He was arrested on 11 November.

Carin Göring continued: 'But we did learn something during this time, how God helps, and how many people did we learn to love. So many helped us, with great sacrifice and danger, and one can never forget this later, so I believe.

'Mama, you should not think that Hitler's cause is lost, that it has been abandoned, oh no, on the contrary, the energy is greater than ever before. And he will win, I feel it, I know it, we have not yet seen the end.'

It becomes apparent here how strongly Carin influenced her husband who was in a state of despair. Her so-called 'second sight' which was predicting a roseate future may have been biased by the stance of the people who were sympathetic to the badly wounded Göring and to her who was weakened by illness.

At the hospital Göring's first bandage was removed, the wounds were re-opened. After an operation the fever lingered on and Göring was in great pain.

Carin stayed with Dr Soppelsa at 9 Bahnhofsplatz. On 21 November she wrote a second letter to her mother: 'Hermann's wound has improved, the fever did not rise above 38°F in the last few days, but he is naturally totally exhausted by the loss of blood. Furthermore, the boundless disappointment he has experienced prevents him from sleeping.'

In her third letter, of 30 November, she says: 'Hermann is in a bad state, the pain in his leg is hardly bearable, four days ago all the wounds that were healing broke open again, much pus in the leg, he was X-rayed and one saw in the muscles lots of bullet splinters, stones from the street, etc., which caused all this. He was operated on under chloroform, but for three days he has had a high fever, fantasises, cries, dreams of street fighting, and is in indescribable pain. The whole leg is full of rubber tubes because of the pus.'

She goes on to say how much her husband is suffering not only physically but mentally — he is 'in boundless despair'. Hanfstengl and Bodenschatz had visited Göring in Innsbruck. After he returned to Germany Bodenschatz was arrested. At the beginning of December Carin learned that a warrant for her arrest had also been issued.

To alleviate Göring's pain and insomnia the doctors authorised two injections of morphine per day, but were reluctant to prolong this treatment because of the danger of addiction. (During the Second World War this danger led to morphine injections being discontinued after a short time. The author, who suffered a similar wound before Moscow in 1941, had to accept this.)

On 8 December Carin writes: 'His wound is all pus, the whole thigh. It hurts so much that he lies there and bites the pillows in two, all I hear are inarticulate sounds. Today just one month has passed since he was shot and despite the daily morphine the pain has not diminished.'

Carin moved into the hospital because she was stoned in the street by Communists and suffered a fractured toe.

On 24 December 1923 Göring was able to leave the hospital on crutches. The couple took rooms at a hotel, the Innsbrucker Hof. 'I hardly know him any longer,' she wrote: 'I had tried to make the hotel room as homely as possible but this was very hard to do with the plush furniture and the garish lighting. The Innsbruck SA had presented Hermann with a small decorated Christmas tree, every light was decorated with black-white-red ribbons. Weary unto death he tried to hobble about on his crutches. He was carried here from the hospital at about 6 p.m. I had deliberately not bought him a Christmas present, since I knew this would be hard on him as he had not been able to buy me anything because he was lying in bed.

'Towards eight o'clock I could stand it no longer, I put on a coat in order to get some fresh air. Outside there was a terrible snowstorm, but I hardly noticed it. Suddenly from an open window on the first floor I heard something wonderful, organ and violin: "Silent night, holy night", and strangely, suddenly everything inside me became calm. Naturally I cried, but was again full of confidence and calm. Returned to Hermann and was able to cheer him up and give him courage. Next day I woke up with a heavy cold and fever and have had to stay in bed since then. I probably stood in the storm too long to listen to the singing.'

On 28 December she wrote to her father: 'The entire personality is that of someone else, he hardly speaks a word, so depressed by this betrayal, so down as I would never have believed possible with him.'

The illness Carin Göring had contracted was to last for a long time and was exacerbated by heart trouble. She became an invalid and remained so until her early death. Göring blamed himself for her physical suffering; he had brought her to this and he never forgave his political opponents for the misery they had inflicted on him and his wife.

While the continuing morphine injections eased the pain in his groin and leg, he became addicted to the drug. At the age of thirty-one he became a different person, physically and psychologically. His wife watched this with horror and astonishment, but she loved him and stayed with him.

While Göring was steadily gaining weight, his wife wasted away, and those who knew her during the final years of her life remembered her as the fragile Swedish beauty with the feverishly shining eyes. Homesick, she hoped to be able to go back to Sweden in March or April. In mid-February she learned that her mother had been taken ill and was in a sanatorium. Carin's own heart condition now made it necessary to engage a nurse.

At the end of December Goring had suggested to Hitler that he give himself up to the Bavarian authorities, but Hitler wanted him to build up a National Socialist movement in Austria. Göring hoped that he would be granted an amnesty after the trials of Hitler and Ludendorff so that he could then return to Munich. He believed that while the accused would be convicted, they would then be pardoned and released.

Countess Fanny von Wilamowitz-Moellendorff writes: 'Seen from outside, the future of the Hitler movement looked very bleak after that fateful 9 November 1923. Hitler was being held in the fortress at Landsberg on the Lech, where among others Rudolf Hess, Dr Weber, and Colonel Kriebel were also being held. Göring was living as a fugitive in Italy, badly exhausted by his psychological and physical wounds. Ludendorff appeared to have washed his hands of the common cause and the others were either under arrest or under close surveillance and scattered throughout Germany. Each of them had to try to make out for himself, public meetings were forbidden, nobody had any money. Carin was still ill. Her heart had been irreparably damaged, but she could not spare herself, nor did she ever want to. Her whole life was, and increasingly so, just one great inner turmoil which, however, she was able to control and hide from view.'

In February, before Hitler came to trial, Göring wrote to his mother-in-law, Baroness von Fock, telling her that he intended to stay in Innsbruck during the trial, 'then however, if there is no possibility to return for the time being, we want to come to Sweden by boat via Italy, because living there is still cheaper and above all much nicer than here in Austria. After all, we cannot live for years in a hotel. Maybe I will also be able to find some sort of job there until the situation permits a return to Germany. Because I only want to return to a national Germany and not to this Jew republic. I love Sweden more than any other place, because I am first and foremost a *Germane* (member of the Germanic race) and the purest form of Germanism is to be found there. Furthermore I, just as much as Carin, long for you all who are so kind and good to us. For Carin's sake as well I would be happy to live there for a time so that she could finally be back with her family and friends.'

After this – remorseful – intimation of a return to Sweden with Carin, he goes on: 'Once again accept my deepest thanks and the assurance that I am boundlessly happy to also be entitled to call you mother.'

In April Hitler, Ludendorff and others were tried. Ludendorff was acquitted, but Hitler and the others were sent to prison. Afterwards Göring submitted a request for a pardon to the Bavarian government; he had actually hoped to be treated as a holder of the *Pour le Mérite* like Ludendorff and to escape without punishment, but his request was rejected.

Martial law in the Reich had been rescinded on 28 February 1924, and national elections were scheduled for 4 May. Göring had reckoned that he would have a chance to become a member of the *Reichstag* (parliament) as a candidate for the *Deutsch-Völkische Freiheitspartei* (German National People's Freedom Party) which was acting for the banned NSDAP. This was now impossible, but he held fast to the idea and was to succeed four years later. The election returns made the *Deutschnationalen* (German Nationalists) the strongest faction with 106 seats. The Freedom Party gained only a few seats.

In mid-April Carin Göring travelled to Munich. Her bank account had melted away and had barely survived the inflation. She had to sell furniture from the house in Obermenzing and the car, mainly to members of the Hitler Party. She saw Ludendorff who was now living in Solln. But the general had learned his lesson. He no longer wanted to have anything to do with Hitler who had made him look ridiculous by the attempted putsch.

She drove to Landsberg to see Hitler who two weeks earlier had begun serving his sentence of six years. (The sentence was suspended and he was released after six months.) He gave her a photograph with the dedication: 'For the revered wife of my S.A. comrade, Frau Carin Göring, in memory of the visit to Landsberg fortress on 15 April 1924 – Adolf Hitler.' Later on this photograph was placed in her room in Stockholm and in Berlin together with the Edelweiss.

In early May the Görings went to Italy. They had accepted an invitation by a hotel owner in Venice who sympathised with the National Socialists. He was German and a friend of the director of the Innsbrucker Hof, who had waived their bill when they had had to leave under pressure from the Austrian police.

In Landsberg Hitler dictated the manuscript of *Mein Kampf* to Rudolf Hess who had given himself up voluntarily. The Görings passed out of his orbit for the time being. He had learned from Carin that they wanted to return to Sweden via Italy. He wished them luck and advised them to visit Mussolini in Rome.

The Görings could now have disappeared from history. In Munich Alfred Rosenberg, unknown to Hitler, kept the fugitive Hermann Göring on the books of the (prohibited) NSDAP but as an inactive member. Later Hitler reinstated him, but after his release from prison on 29 December 1924 he did not contact the Görings.

The secret cooperation between the Reichswehr and the Red Army resulted in a German air base being established at Lipezk not far from the upper Don, at which officers of the Reichswehr were trained as pilots. The foundations of a new German air force were laid there.

Foreign Minister Stresemann oriented German foreign policy towards the West, and the good years of the Weimar Republic began. The Görings were in exile, first in Italy, then in Sweden.

Carin Göring was ill, and Hermann had become addicted to morphine. He had been deeply disappointed by his excursion into politics, and he had no professional future. One could be excused for thinking that he would never again play a part in the reshaping of his country.

9
Phoenix from the Ashes

Of the year which the Görings spent in Italy, Countess Fanny Wilamowitz-Moellendorf, the sister with whom Carin corresponded, writes: 'Almost all her letters from Italy sound cheerful and happy. The beauty of the country, the easy and lovable nature of the people, were so boundlessly beneficial after the long period of illness. However Carin was always aware how much her husband sought political activity. His health was poor as well, the pain did not ease, the pain-killing medicines prescribed by the doctors did bring relief and could not be reduced. On top of all this the constant worry about money, the impossibility of caring for the fragile woman as his heart desired. It was a difficult time, how difficult Carin's love never let her own in Sweden know.'

For a short time they stayed at a hotel on the Grand Canal in Venice recommended by the director of their hotel in Innsbruck, and were given a special daily rate of 65 instead of 100 lire per person.

'The food is excellent, lobster, soup, omelettes, chicken with salad, lamb chops with spaghetti, fruit, fruit with every lunch,' Carin wrote. 'Delightful shops, jewellery, so that one has to look the other way so as not to break out in tears about one's poverty.' They visited art shops and museums as formerly in Stockholm, but now everything was more magnificent and Carin could see how much her husband was impressed by the old paintings. They swore to make up some day for everything they now had to do without. 'Oh dearest mother, if one had millions it would not be too much. But one does not have even the barest necessities.'

Via Siena, whose art treasures they admire, they went to Rome where they found a cheap boarding-house. They lived mostly on pasta, being unable to afford meat. Göring became bloated by the steady diet of pasta; his heavy bone structure had earmarked him for obesity from birth when he had weighed 12 pounds.

They met Mussolini through the mediation of an acquaintance, Prince Philip of Hesse, who was going to marry Mafalda, the daughter of the Italian Royal Family.

Benito Mussolini received Göring, who told him about the march to the Feldherrnhalle. But no financial help was forthcoming from the Duce of Fascist Italy for this failed officer and SA leader, who had taken part in the emulation of his march on Rome.

Since the pain-killers had no effect, Göring was forced to buy the expensive morphine, which put him further into debt. He thought about committing suicide, but could not abandon his wife whom he had reduced to these terrible straits. The amnesty both of them hoped for was not granted.

'The longing to go to Sweden, to the North, was now strong, both with Hermann as well as with Carin Göring,' Countess Wilamowitz-Moellendorf writes. 'Thanks to the support of loyal friends, this journey also became possible in the spring of 1925.' (The use of the word 'also' seems to indicate that in Italy the Görings lived off the financial support of their friends and acquaintances.)

'The way (to Sweden) was long. It led via Austria, Czechoslovakia and Poland, to Gdansk. Germany was closed to them. When Hermann Göring was back on German soil again in Gdansk he fell to his knees and thanked God. In Stockholm the joy was great. Carin was more beautiful than ever, only she had a look of suffering and tension about her from the constant psychological and physical exertions that gave her family serious grounds for worry and unease.'

At last she saw her son Thomas again who was now 13 years old. Göring had brought a large supply of morphine with him from Italy. He was now giving himself four to six injections daily. A year ago it had been two.

Carin's illness grew worse. She suffered from poor circulation which caused fainting fits. Her lungs were affected, and she had a weak heart. They rented an apartment on Odengatan and lived off the money the sale of their house in Munich had brought. 'Now Göring had to find a job,' Carin's sister Fanny writes: 'and this immediately led to great difficulties. There was widespread unemployment in Sweden. A huge mass of refugees had come from the Baltic and Russia. They all hoped for work, in the worst cases for help and support from non-Social Democratic circles. For this diligent officer, however, who had been involved in a political uprising, it was hard to find any kind of civilian employment, particularly since aviation was hardly developed. There were too many applicants. Hermann Göring did his best, and that is all a man can do.'

In addition, the family no longer understood or approved of the Görings' political stance, and this led to an estrangement and the family offered no help. Only Carin's mother 'gave with both hands', as Carin's sister Fanny writes. 'However she was not able to prevent worry, need, illness, and unrest entering the Göring home. One piece of furniture after another had to be sold. Illness and poverty had become daily guests. To tell the Swedish relations how oppressive the financial situation, and how shattered his own health and psychological condition had become, this Hermann Göring's pride prevented him from doing.'

In the summer of 1925, after eighteen months of morphine addiction, the collapse came. The von Fock family arranged for Göring to be taken into Aspudeen hospital for observation. Carin's doctor had claimed that his patient was in danger from the addict. Göring went voluntarily because he knew that he was no longer in control of himself. In the hospital, during a sleepless night, he threatened a nurse who refused an injection she was not permitted to give. Carin Göring sued for custody of her son whom she wanted to keep with her, but she was unsuccessful because Nils von Kantzow was able to prove in court that Göring was a morphine addict.

On 1 September 1925, Göring was transferred to the psychiatric hospital (at that time called an asylum for the insane) at Langbro as a 'dangerous drug addict', and underwent a rigorous detoxification programme for three months, which meant that the drug was simply discontinued and he had to cope with the subsequent withdrawal symptoms without any assistance. After his release he relapsed and was twice more admitted to Langbro. After this, however, he was cured. He never again used morphine, but later on there were other drugs available.

His wound from 1923 still pained him and continued to do so until his death. The doctors who treated him called him an emotional person who was lacking in 'moral courage'. This sounds harsh if one considers how much courage was required to cope with the primitive treatment of addicts at that time. But moral courage could also have meant a form of higher courage, and after he had become a man of power events were to prove that he actually was lacking in this .

In the summer of 1926 he tried to earn money in Sweden as a parachute salesman, and then, starting in that autumn he worked also for the *Bayerische Motorenwerke* (BMW – Bavarian Motor Works), selling aircraft engines on a commission. He obtained an order from the Swedish government for twelve engines, but when the order was processed in Munich he must have been overlooked, because after his return to Germany in the autumn of 1927 he claimed a commission of 30,000 Reichsmarks from BMW which had been paid to somebody else in the meantime. It was only after he wrote a letter to the new owner of BMW, an Italian of Jewish extraction from Trieste named Camillo Castiglioni, that he received this substantial sum of money.

His wife's heart condition grew worse. She had to lie still for hours and was in great pain. He was still waiting for an amnesty. At the end of February 1925 Hitler had re-established the NSDAP, but he was prohibited from public oratory. Most of his adherents stemmed from the middle class. The workers and the well-to-do rejected him. The SA was being led by a former officer, Pfeffer von Salomon. There was no contact with Göring in Sweden.

Reichspräsident Ebert had died on 28 February 1925. On 26 April Field Marshal von Hindenburg became his successor. Following his eightieth birthday on 2 October 1927 which, as Carl von Ossietzky (German liberal journalist who was awarded the Nobel Peace Prize and later murdered by the Nazis at Dachau) wrote in the *Weltbühne*: 'became a gigantic jubilee of all of the black-white-red', with the votes of the right-wing parties and the KPD the Reichstag declared an amnesty for all persons who had gone into exile for political reasons and simultaneously set free all prisoners who had been sentenced for political offences.

Göring returned to Germany in October. He sent a telegram to Hitler in Munich asking for an appointment and was frostily received. Hitler advised his former SA commander to create a respected position in Berlin for himself, after which one would see. He had no intention of handing the SA back to him. Göring could see no prospect of office or regular income within the Party so he stayed on as a salesman for BMW, now in Berlin, and hoped for other means of augmenting his income.

In 1922 it had been a piece of luck for Hitler that the flying hero had joined the Party because he was lacking in famous names. In 1927 Hitler was anxious to gain influence in Berlin society and hoped that Göring could be helpful to this end. Hitler was still prohibited from public speaking in Prussia, and so could not appear publicly in Berlin.

For Göring something else was important. The NSDAP (*Deutsch-Völkische Freiheitspartei*) had only fourteen seats in the Reichstag. Elections were to be held in May 1928. He hoped to be put on the list of candidates, but Hitler first wanted to see how Göring would prove himself in Berlin. Carin Göring, now bedridden, had to remain in Sweden.

Göring now had a goal: he wanted to move into an apartment in Berlin and be elected to the Reichstag. In the capital he first stayed at a hotel near the Kurfürstendamm, and shared a small office in Geisbergstrasse with Victor Siebel who was later to develop the *Siebelfähre* (a flat-bottomed motorised ferry cum landing craft for the transportation of troops or heavy weapons) for the Kriegsmarine.

He met up again with Bruno Loerzer who had married money and was able to introduce him to influential people. Göring began to work for the Heinkel Company, represented the Swedish Tornblad Company which manufactured parachutes, and was able to establish contact with Deutsche Lufthansa, whose managing director was Erhard Milch. With Paul Körner, nicknamed 'Pilli', who became his partner, Göring began to build a reputation as an independent salesman in the aircraft industry. He spent Christmas 1927 with Carin in Stockholm. He was confident that he would be able to establish himself professionally in Berlin.

In January 1928, during a visit to Munich, Göring succeeded in convincing Hitler that he would be useful to the Party as a candidate in the national elections. He was given seventh place on the candidate list of the NSDAP. Besides his work, he now had to hold election rallies. He proved himself as a speaker, imitated Hitler's style and looked dashing despite his bulk. His voice had a metallic tone which was well received in northern Germany. The *Gauleiter* (district administrator) in Berlin was Dr Josef Goebbels who was an outstanding orator. Göring and Goebbels quickly became rivals.

Goebbels, the Gauleiter, was superior to the simple Party member Göring when it came to intelligence, but Göring surpassed him by far when it came to personal impact. Goebbels was a cynic; Göring a believer, who loved comfort. Goebbels loathed Jews; Göring had nothing against Jews. As a salesman for BMW he was working for a company that was owned by a Jew. To his employer Castiglioni Göring said after 1 April 1933, the day of the first boycott of Jewish stores in Berlin: 'It is an accident, pure chance, and it will not happen again. Herr Castiglioni, the best friends from my youth were Jews and they treated me well. I have no intention of doing anything against them.' Castiglioni replied: 'But Hitler is an anti-Semite.' To which Göring replied: 'I will get him to stop that, you may depend on it.'

But in his letter to Stockholm in 1924, had not Göring written of the 'Jew republic' to which he no longer wished to return? Göring's statements would continue to remain ambiguous.

Shortly before the 1928 elections, Carin finally arrived in Berlin. Göring was living at No. 16 Berchtesgadener Strasse.

On 18 May Carin wrote her mother: 'In Berlin Hermann collected me from the station. We first had coffee at the "Nordland", then by car to here where Hermann has a huge room, a corner room with a delightfully sunny balcony with blooming lilac. The whole of Berlin is in election mood, the election takes place on Sunday. They have already begun to shoot each other to death. Every day Communists with red flags with burning bibles on them (she means the Soviet emblem) range through the city and they always meet Hitler people with flags just as red and the swastika on them, and then altercations begin and there are dead and wounded. We will have to see how the elections go. Oh yes, I hope it goes well for Hermann, then we would have peace for a longer while. Hermann looks well, but has a terrible work-load. I am glad that we always have a car (Paul Körner's Mercedes) at our disposal, one of Hermann's friends has lent it to him.'

On 21 May 1928 she was able to telegraph her mother: 'Hermann elected yesterday, Mother you do understand. Your Carin.' Only twelve National Socialists had been elected to the Reichstag, Göring as number seven.

In the Reichstag he now sat in the front row on the extreme right, together with General Ritter von Epp. Goebbels too was a member of the new NSDAP faction, as were Wilhelm Frick and Gregor Strasser. Hitler had waived his seat. The twelve National Socialists had received 810,000 votes. The Reichstag consisted of 491 members, each of whom were paid 500 Reichsmarks a month and a free first-class ticket on the *Reichsbahn* (state railway).

Göring received congratulations, including a message from the former Crown Prince who still remembered him from Stenay in France. 'May your exceptional talent, your ability to express yourself, and your physical strength prove to be useful to you in your new position as a representative of the people,' the Crown

Prince telegraphed him, and was probably also thinking of the brawls which were customary in the Reichstag.

The little band around Göring was confronted by a strong Left. With 153 seats, the SPD was the strongest of the governing parties in the 'grand coalition' which Chancellor Hermann Müller formed at the end of June.

In the Reichstag Göring concentrated on traffic and transportation. Even before his election he had been given a contract as a consultant by Deutsche Lufthansa. One year after the election he received a Lufthansa cheque for 10,000 Reichsmarks from the Deutsche Bank. As David Irving writes, Lufthansa also had other members of the Reichstag under contract as consultants, such as Keil (SPD) and Dr Cremer (Deutsche Volkspartei).

The industrialist Fritz Thyssen met the Görings and was impressed by them. With his financial support they were able to rent a modern five-room apartment at No. 7 Badenschen Straße, in a well-to-do, upper middle class district. They moved in during the autumn of 1928, with the remnants of furniture from their previous home, including her harmonium which she often played. They also managed to re-purchase some pieces of furniture which, when their fortune was at its lowest, they had been obliged to sell. The building had a subterranean garage, which was rare in those days, and the Görings' guests could park there. This was very convenient because the political altercations of the times meant that cars on the streets were often endangered. The apartment house, which survived the war, also boasted a lift.

Thyssen wrote later that he had 'learned to know Carin Göring as an exceptionally charming woman, as the only woman who could influence and lead Göring'. Carin's sister Fanny writes: 'Their home gained great importance for the work and advancement of the Party, because the Führer often received different persons here – Party leaders, but also opponents with whom he wished to speak during his presence in Berlin. This was a meeting-place where everybody was able to feel comfortable. By her profound insight, her wise judgement of people, and her mild conciliatory personality, the hostess was able to contribute much to a harmonious course of the meetings and deliberations. Carin had an intuitive eye for the essential and she always recognised before anybody else where a bridge could be built, but also where any effort would be useless. Her heart condition continued to give reason for the most serious worries. The whole thing was, as she herself said, "an adventure that required the full dedication of the whole being".'

Göring's debts had to be paid off. This became possible because he was now earning more than 2,000 Reichsmarks per month, the equivalent of a Reichsminister's emolument in those days. In addition to his 500 marks as a deputy of the Reichstag, he received 800 marks plus expenses as a *Reichsredner* of the NSDAP (lit. Reich speaker. The Nazis differentiated between Party members who were important and talented enough to speak anywhere on behalf of the Party, and *Gauredner*, who could speak for the Party but only in their own district. Deutsche Lufthansa paid him 1,000 marks per month.

'This very day Hermann has his first important speech in the Reichstag,' Carin wrote to her mother on 21 February 1929. 'This evening he will speak at the Berlin University before students from all the political parties. More than half of them are already National Socialists, and I hope that he will contribute to the rest of them becoming so as well. Tomorrow he will speak in Nuremberg, and then he will leave on a ten-day trip throughout East Prussia with twelve different presentations. The whole house is full of politicians so that one would go crazy if it were not so immensely interesting at the same time.'

For the Görings the years of destitution had come to an end. Within a short space of time, with the aid of his seat in the Reichstag and the deft *savoir faire* of his wife, a fat young man of no importance, had become a socially acceptable gentleman in Berlin.

In 1929 ten years had passed since the signing of the Treaty of Versailles. Now the Dawes Plan, which had only been intended as an intermediate means of tiding the Reich over the payment of reparations, was to be replaced by a permanent agreement. This was the Young Plan, named after the American banker Owen Young, who was chairman of the group of international experts that had been working in Paris since February 1929 to ensure that the conditions of Versailles were fulfilled.

The Young Plan reduced the annual reparations demanded by the Dawes Plan, but the spread of a payment of 34.5 billion goldmarks over a period of 59 years meant that the country would be making reparations until 1989 to those of the victorious Allies that continued to claim them. This obviously outraged the Germans who found it inconceivable that future generations should be committed to paying for a war that had taken place in 1914–1918. If the Reichstag approved the agreement, the Allies were prepared to evacuate the Rhineland in 1930 instead of 1935. There was also a revision clause and a waiver of sanctions should the Germans fall behind in their payments.

The Young Plan became a political lever for the right-wing parties, Hugenberg's Deutschnationale Volkspartei and the (still minute) NSDAP, with which to manipulate majorities and gain power. A storm broke out against 'the perpetuation of the enslavement of the German nation'. In the summer of 1929 Hugenberg's Deutschnationale joined forces with Hitler's National Socialists and other groups in the 'Reich committee for a plebiscite' which drew up rolls for a plebiscite against the Young Plan. On 16 October 1929 just under 10 per cent of the electorate signed them, thus making a plebiscite possible. In this political turmoil Göring became an important figure on the national right, far beyond his small Party. Since Hitler did not have an apartment in Berlin, his visits to the capital remained sporadic.

Gauleiter Dr Goebbels caused a sensation as an agitator with his SA, which fought battles with the *Rotfrontkämpferbund* (union of the militant groups of the left-wing parties) before it was banned in May 1929. On 1 May 1929 in the eastern sector of Berlin a street battle had taken place between the SA and the Rotfront during which nineteen people were killed and 40 injured.

Hitler appeared to be determined to wrest control of the streets from the Communists. The street battles between the 'Reds' and the 'Browns' not only worried the Reichswehr but also the business community and industry. This gave Göring the opportunity, aided by his former acquaintances, to present himself as a factor of security in this tumultuous scene, something that was very much to his taste.

During a debate on civil aviation in the Reichstag in the summer of 1929 he came out against false economy. He raised the question of why there was no Minister of Aviation. With this he was also touching on a personal torment that had given him no peace since the disbandment of Jagdgeschwader Richthofen at Aschaffenburg in December 1918. As an ego-optimist he believed that he would become Minister of Aviation one day.

In 1929 German aviation achieved great successes. A Heinkel aircraft carried out the first catapult take-off from the deck of the *Bremen* on her maiden voyage to New York – during which she broke the speed record and gained the Blue Riband – and took mail to New York. The airship 'Graf Zeppelin' flew round the world for the first time. German sports pilot Wolf Hirth was the winner of an international race over 4,000 kilometres. Dornier built his Do X flying-boat which could carry 169 passengers, and ushered in the era of trans-Atlantic bulk passenger aerial transport. Hermann Oberth published *Wege zur Raumschiffahrt* (Methods of Space Travel), the first serious dissertation on the subject. Junkers designed and built the first diesel aircraft engine. At flying-schools officers seconded from the Reichswehr were being trained as pilots for the future air force.

In this resurgence of air might, Göring recognised the possibilities for a politician, and believed himself to be the man to seize them. His father had developed German Southwest Africa as a protectorate of the Reich. The son intended to serve this Reich in his own field, that of aviation, and gain power thereby. But the Party for which he sat in the Reichstag was minute. It needed help, and he must concentrate his efforts in this regard, because only through the Party could he gain the office for which he saw himself as being predestined. In this his personal ambition matched that of Hitler's to become Chancellor.

The Hugenberg–Hitler pact against the Young Plan made the NSDAP socially acceptable, because those nationalist circles that had supported Hindenburg's election in 1925 now saw themselves abandoned by the Reichspräsident who was in favour of the Young Plan. Göring 'inherited' representatives from these nationalist circles, which also included monarchists, and now became the sought-after contact.

The battle against the Young Plan saw Hitler's breakthrough into politics at high level. When Reich Foreign Minister Stresemann, who had been a proponent of the plan, suddenly died in October 1929, and the world economic crisis began after the 'Black Monday' in New York that month, the end of the Weimar Republic loomed on the horizon.

The Hugenberg–Hitler pact failed in the plebiscite on the Young Plan. Only 5.8 million voted against it, as against more than 21 million in favour. On 13 March 1930 the Young Plan was passed in the Reichstag. The Deutschnationalen, the National Socialists, and the Communists voted against.

At No. 7 Badenschen Straße in Berlin–Schöneberg, Carin and her husband had become a focal point for interesting and influential people who wanted to know what this Adolf Hitler, of whom one heard more and more, actually intended to achieve. On 28 February 1930 she reports to her mother about this. The parties she gave and the invitations the couple accepted were draining her strength. 'Neither of us would be able to stand conventional parties any longer. And we know that those places to which we are invited, we are invited because we are supposed to give something. Wieds intend to interest all of their circle of acquaintances in the Hitler movement and Hermann is inundated by questions, by queries and objections. It is a search for all sorts of mistakes and lacks on Hitler's part, or one criticises his programme, etc. And then Hermann has to explain, give answers, so that sometimes he is completely drained afterwards. But I see that the circle about us is constantly growing and that we have gained much for Hitler and his cause. Prince August Wilhelm von Hohenzollern, like Prince and Princess Wied, brings us into contact with a large number of interesting people. Yesterday we had breakfast with Prince Henckel-Donnersmarck. He is forty years old, sits in a wheelchair, the paralysis is increasing, I pity him very much. He has himself taken to all the rallies at which Hermann speaks. It almost appears as if the National Socialist movement is becoming "in", one has to take double care that this will not lead to its becoming diluted. A few days ago we had Baron Koskull to lunch. He is with the Swedish Embassy in Berlin. With him were the von Bahrs, Prince August Wilhelm and two National Socialist workers who had come from Munich and were staying with us. Later on Count Solms and his wife and the Duke of Koburg with daughter. I am attaching a card of the deceased Kaiserin and little August Wilhelm. Written on the card is "a small souvenir of happier times". He sent it to Hermann.'

Prince August Wilhelm had joined the NSDAP and the SA in 1930 and now became Göring's companion on his campaign trips.

On 22 March 1930 Carin reports to her mother that Göring is on a speaking tour in East Prussia with the Prince from the House of Hohenzollern. From there they will go all the way to Cologne, a different town each evening. All the rallies have been sold out for days, the smallest meeting-hall can take 4,000 people, the largest 25,000. 'August Wilhelm is Hitler's man through and through. He is modest, helpful, prepared to serve, diligent.'

In the summer of 1930 Carin Göring broke down and had to be taken to a sanatorium in Kreuth near Bayerisch-Zell. Her serious heart condition had been made worse by the excitements and exertions of her life in Berlin since 1928.

There can be no doubt that Carin was an idealist who believed in the Hitler movement as something good and great. But the speed with which it gained adherents gave her an eerie feeling. She feared for the purity of the movement, which she saw as being endangered. She now also saw Hitler more objectively. He was endeavouring to allay quarrels in the Party and the SA, which had come about in no small measure through the new adherents from well-to-do and monarchist inclined circles. SA leader Otto Strasser rebelled against Hitler in Berlin, calling for strikes and turmoil in industry. His social–revolutionary ideas clashed with Hitler's intention to gain power in the Reich by legal means. Göring was the exponent of the right wing of the NSDAP; Goebbels was undecided whether he should join Strasser's men who stormed offices of the NSDAP in Berlin in September 1930.

Hitler intervened. He came to Berlin and put the SA under his personal command, having dismissed Pfeffer von Salomon who had lost control over it. On Hitler's orders, Strasser was kicked out of the Party by Goebbels, the Berlin Gauleiter and Party propaganda chief, and promptly founded the *Schwarze Front* (Black Front) which claimed to be the true national revolutionary movement.

In 1930 the average annual number of unemployed rose to 3.8 million as compared to 1.9 million in 1929. The government of Social Democrat Hermann Müller resigned and Brüning became Chancellor. He reacted with emergency decrees which were signed by the Reichspräsident and which Brüning had approved in the Reichstag by shifting majorities. When approval was denied him, Hindenburg dissolved the Reichstag on 18 July 1930. New elections were scheduled for 14 September.

Erhard Milch, at this time managing director of Deutsche Lufthansa, was pleased with Göring's cleverness during the debates in the Reichstag on the aviation budget. 'It was astonishing how quickly he oversaw all situations and was able to draw the essence from theoretical presentations,' he wrote in his diary. During the election campaign Göring appeared in a brown shirt. Over his dark brown tie he wore the *Pour le Mérite*. He looked fresh and attractive. The obesity had largely disappeared again. Milch wrote that Göring always spoke of Hitler with reverence and enthusiasm but never mentioned internal Party affairs. In those days Göring's charm impressed many people.

Hitler's Party held 34,000 election rallies between mid July and mid September. Twenty-eight Parties were competing for the 577 seats in the Reichstag. The election returns on 14 September 1930 caused a sensation. From 800,000 votes in 1928, the NSDAP went to 6.4 million. It gained 107 seats and was the second strongest faction after the SPD. The KPD gained almost 4.6 million votes and increased its seats from 54 to 77. The SPD lost almost 0.6 million votes, but with 8.5 million votes remained the strongest faction.

Göring, who attributed a large part of the success of Hitler's Party to himself, now became the political representative of his Führer. Although holding no Party office, he had become Hitler's most important adviser. Hitler brought Ernst Röhm back from Bolivia and made him Chief of Staff of the SA. Hitler remained the 'Commander'. Röhm was charged with bringing the SA back into line. Göring had the assignment of preparing by diplomatic means the take-over of power by Hitler.

Immediately after the elections the trial of three young Reichswehr officers (charged with high treason for trying to induce their fellow officers to agree that in the event of an armed Nazi revolt they would not fire on the rebels) from Ulm took place before the *Reichsgericht* (supreme court) at Leipzig. Hitler was called for the defence and was given the opportunity to answer the question under oath, whether the NSDAP intended to gain power in the state by illegal means. He stated that neither he nor the SA had any intention of fighting the Army, that on the contrary they looked to it as an ally. The officers, Lieutenant Ludin, Lieutenant Scheringer, and 1st Lieutenant Wendt (he had already left the Reichswehr) were sentenced to eighteen months in prison. Their regimental commander at Ulm was Colonel Ludwig Beck who became Chief of Staff of the Army in 1933 and was the conspirators' designated successor to Hitler as Reichspräsident on 20 July 1944 (the attempt to assassinate Hitler).

After the opening session of the newly elected Reichstag on 13 October 1930, which all the NSDAP delegates attended dressed in brown shirts, the first attacks against Jews in the streets of central Berlin took place.

That evening Göring had invited guests to his home. The Görings received Hitler, Goebbels, Prince August Wilhelm of Prussia and his son, the Duke of Hesse, Prince and Princess von Wied, Niemann and his wife, photographer Hoffmann with daughter, who was Hitler's secretary, Rudolf Hess and wife, Paul Körner, Hermann Esser, Professor Schulze-Naumburg from Weimar with wife and daughter, Frick, and Ritter von Epp. New to this circle was Erhard Milch, managing director of Lufthansa and ex-air force captain of the Great War, who was much impressed by Hitler's 'modesty, friendliness, clarity, and intelligence'. Hitler had again declined to accept his seat in the Reichstag.

The Görings now had a housekeeper and cook, Cilly Wachowiak. They spent the Christmas Eve of 1930 with Goebbels, who was still single, Thomas von Kantzow, and Cilly. Goebbels arrived with presents at 8 p.m. Dinner consisted of cold cuts and fruit. Goebbels sat at the harmonium and played old Christmas carols: 'Silent Night', 'Oh du fröhliche', which were sung in Swedish and German. While the presents were being unwrapped, Carin was seized by a shivering fit. She fell off the sofa and had to be put to bed; she had a temperature of 103°F for a few days.

On Christmas Day fourteen guests arrived. Carin was in bed, but by the New Year she was back on her feet and able to go to the Wieds' party with Hermann and Goebbels.

On 5 January 1931 Hitler, Schacht, Fritz Thyssen, and other important businessmen came to dinner (pea soup with pork and Swedish apple pie with vanilla sauce). Nonentities who were looking for help also used to visit the Görings. Carin writes about a German Count Wedel and his wife who was Swedish, young people, two children, the Count without a job, the whole family living separately with various relatives, he was desperate. Göring put his name on a list of several hundred people he intended to help. Count Wedel was eventually given a position in the SA in Potsdam.

Göring wanted Carin to go to Sweden to recuperate as soon as possible, but she was unfit to travel.

At the turn of the year 1930/31 the number of unemployed passed the 4.5 million mark.

Brüning's attempts to induce Hitler to tolerate his government failed. Brüning wanted a reform of the constitution with the objective of restoring the monarchy. Hitler, who had met Brüning for the first time on 6 October 1930, refused to cooperate. He replied to Brüning he 'was not interested in measures to ease the crisis, but only on gaining a majority in constantly new elections'.

In 1931 Göring was given the assignment of attacking Chancellor Brüning. In protest against the Brüning government's lack of a majority, the deputies of the NSDAP left the Reichstag together with those of other parties.

In early January 1931 at the instigation of Colonel (ret.) Leopold von Kleist, the chamberlain of abdicated Kaiser Wilhelm II, Göring received an invitation to visit Doorn in Holland, and as a precaution Carin was also invited. The visit took place on 18/19 January. Göring was asked to come to the former Kaiser's place of exile under the pseudonym of 'Dr Döhring', which angered the Crown Prince, who called him 'my Göring'; Prince August Wilhelm was enraged that he himself had not thought to invite Göring to Doorn. In his book *Der Kaiser in Holland*, Sigurd von Ilsemann writes as an eye-witness: 'For two days House Doorn was under the ban of this visit which went off quite well ... The Kaiser was at pains to impress this man and Göring in his turn was basking in his own pride ... On both evenings the conversation lasted until 11 p.m. Besides this the Göring couple with Kleist had tea with their Majesties on two afternoons from five to seven thirty. The talk was mostly politics, but on the evening of 18 January mostly about archaeology and cultural–morphological questions ... The Kaiser deduced from everything Göring said that he would work for his return.' On the 18th (the day the Reich had been founded), Wilhelm II stood up at the dining-table and drank to the welfare of the 'coming' Reich. Göring hoped to be awarded the *Stern von Hohenzollern* (Star of Hohenzollern), a house order, but he did not receive it. However, a car to take him from Doorn to Amsterdam was paid for. In his talks at Doorn he did not commit himself to Wilhelm II as the future monarch, but only to a 'coming king in general'.

On 20/21 May 1932 Göring again went to Doorn. He was now seen as being even more important because he went by agreement with Hitler who himself was thought to be going to visit the ex-Kaiser soon in secret, but his did not come about.

In the spring of 1931 Carin Göring suffered an acute attack of heart failure. Countess Fanny von Wilamowitz-Moellendorff writes: 'She was unconscious for hours, like dead. Hermann was completely shattered. The doctors said openly that there was no longer any hope of saving her life. He knelt besides his unconscious wife and pleaded with the doctors to come back again. Injections were given, but everything appeared to be useless.'

Göring's wife did regain consciousness, however. At the end of June Göring took her to Bad Altheide in Silesia. In mid July Hitler presented Göring with a Mercedes. He said he had been able to buy it because his book *Mein Kampf* was earning him large royalties.

On 26 August 1931 the Görings began their last journey together, which took them through Germany and Austria for a fortnight. They were accompanied by Carin's sister Fanny and Paul Körner, whom they called 'Pilli'.

Countess Fanny von Wilamowitz-Moellendorff remembers: 'The voyage first led to Dresden. There the first evening was spent in the company of the Führer. When the news had spread next morning that Hitler was in the city, masses of people who waved and called "Heil" gathered in front of the Palasthotel. Carin was delighted.'

In the further course of the trip the Mercedes with its swastika flag was marvelled at. Göring had to give autographs on picture postcards bearing his portrait.

In Austria they attended the baptism of a daughter of Göring's sister Paula Huber, to which the Duchess of Koburg had also come.

The journey by car was very exhausting for Carin. She seldom left the car while under way. From the hostels at which breaks were taken she was brought drinks and food. After returning to Berlin, she received the news on 25 September 1931 of the death of her mother in Sweden. Carin broke down. With her husband she went to Sweden, but they arrived too late for the funeral. The doctors had prohibited her taking part because they feared for her life. During the night after their arrival Carin fell so seriously ill that one could only assume that she would follow her mother into death.

Göring was called back to Berlin at the beginning of October. Together with Hitler he was to be received by the Reichspräsident on the 10th. Göring wanted to stay with his wife, but she asked him to go. First came the Führer, duty, she said. Kneeling at the bedside of the invalid, Göring said good-bye.

Göring now believed that the objective had been reached. Hindenburg would arrange for a participation in the government or ask them to form a new government. But 10 October was to be a disappointment for him. Hitler made a poor impression on Hindenburg and Göring did not get a chance to speak. Afterwards Hindenburg stated that Hitler was only good enough to become Post Minister. All the same, the communiqué issued by the Palace of the Reichspräsident on 10 October 1931 made the National Socialists 'presentable at court': 'Today the Reichspräsident received Herr Adolf Hitler and Captain Hermann Göring, a deputy of the Reichstag, and had himself informed in detail about the objectives of the National Socialist movement. This was followed by a discussion of questions of internal and foreign policy.'

Hitler and Göring immediately went to Bad Harzburg for a meeting of the right-wing parties, the *Harzburger Front*. Here Hitler was only one among many and he withdrew. The *Front* became a fiasco.

On 13 October Göring was back again in the Reichstag. Brüning presented a new cabinet, which survived a vote of no confidence on 16 October.

Early in the morning of 17 October Carin Göring died in Stockholm. With his brother Karl and his friend Paul Körner, Göring went to Sweden. He found his wife laid out in the Edelweiss Chapel in the garden of the Fock house. The funeral took place on 21 October in the family tomb at the old church of Lovö near Drottningholm. Once again Göring was on his knees before the coffin was carried outside from the altar. Göring returned to Berlin immediately. Like Hitler, he had a room in the Hotel Kaiserhof on Wilhelmsplatz. The Chancellery is just across the street.

Now there would be only one goal for him – power. He had already come very close to it at the very moment when he lost that which he loved.

10

President of the Reichstag

O
n 18 September 1931, a few days before Carin Göring's death, Hitler's niece Geli Raubal died in her uncle's apartment in Prinzregentenstraße in Munich. Hitler was in love with this daughter of his step-sister Angela whose husband had been killed in the war. When the dark-haired Geli had wanted to go to Vienna in order to get away from her uncle Alf, as she called him, he had forbidden it, having learned that she was in love with another man. She shot herself with Hitler's revolver while he was away from Munich. Although a suicide, she was given a religious burial in a cemetery in Vienna. Hitler sent Röhm and Himmler as his representatives.

Now a mutual grief for something each had considered to be irreplaceable bound Hitler and Göring together. In addition, Hitler had to bear the scandal that developed around the death of his niece. Göring reproached himself for having involved his wife in his hectic life as a politician in recent years.

Goebbels married Magda Quandt, who would probably have preferred Hitler to the short sharp-tongued intellectual. The Goebbels moved into a large apartment on Reichskanzlerplatz in Berlin's West End, and it became the focal point for the people around Hitler who lived at the Kaiserhof when he was in Berlin. Formerly he had stayed at the Askanische Hof at Anhalter station.

Göring gave up the apartment at No. 7 Badenschen Straße and moved into a house at No. 34 Kaiserdamm, on the corner of Soorstraße, very close to the Goebbels' apartment. Cilly Wachowiak kept house for him. His apartment on the third floor had nine rooms, a bath, two lavatories, and a subterranean garage. The rent was 250 marks per month. (The house was destroyed during the war though the garage survived. There is now a petrol station on the site) Hitler and Göring often spent their evenings in Goebbels' apartment, and the consultations about the *Machtergreifung* (seizure of power , Nazi term for the alleged intention to gain a majority and lead the government by legal means only) in 1932 took place.

Hindenburg's term of office was coming to an end. Would the aged Reichspräsident announce his candidacy for re-election? For this he would need the right-wing parties. Chancellor Brüning was thinking about restoring the monarchy, but he did not have a majority in the Reichstag. He therefore planned to extend Hindenburg's term of office by an amendment to the constitution for which, however, he needed Hitler and Hugenberg with their Parties.

Göring's influence on the deliberations at Reichskanzlerplatz and at the Kaiserhof hotel on Wilhelmsplatz was considerable. He became Hitler's negotiator and proved to be clever at it. After Hindenburg had agreed to stand for re-election, it was Göring who convinced a reluctant Hitler to stand against him in the elections for Reichspräsident.

For Hindenburg the whole question was problematical. He had only agreed to stand in order to prevent the succession to the Presidential office from becoming a 'battle' between Left and Right, which would have led to the most serious upheavals.

Hitler did not want to stand against Hindenburg. He did not even fulfil the most important condition for a candidacy: he was not a German citizen. But in Thuringia, the Deutschnationalen together with the National Socialists formed the state government. If this government were to appoint Hitler to a position as a civil servant for life, he would automatically attain German citizenship. The attempt failed for administrative reasons. In Brunswick, however, the government, a similar coalition, appointed Hitler as a *Regierungsrat* (administrative counsellor) to the Brunswick legation in Berlin. This took place on 25 February 1932, the same day that Hitler's candidacy for the Presidential office was announced.

Then Hugenberg set up his own candidate, Theodor Duesterberg, leader of the *Stahlhelm* (literally: steel helmet, the Deutschnationale Party's equivalent to the SA). The KPD presented its chairman, Ernst Thälmann. The centre Parties and the SPD supported Hindenburg.

During the bitterly contested campaign, Göring made a strong impact as a speaker. In the Berlin Sportpalast he was borne up by waves of applause. He improvised without notes, and his metallic voice with its Franconian inflections provoked storms of approbation. His audiences at many rallies saw him as Hitler's paladin, committed only to the leader to whom he had dedicated himself.

It can be attributed to Göring that the Crown Prince endorsed Hitler's candidacy. The monarchists believed that it was only through Hitler that a monarchy could be achieved, because Hindenburg had accepted the support of the Democrats. It was Göring who brought about a split of the Right at this time, and largely thanks to him that a majority – led by important people and supported by Thyssen, Kirdorf, and other industrialists – went over to Hitler.

The remainder of the Right, however, as well as wide circles in business, continued to support and finance Hindenburg. On 13 March 1932 almost 11.4 million people voted for Hitler. While Hindenburg achieved more than 18.6 million votes, a second ballot became necessary. Duesterberg had received 2.5 million; Thälmann nearly 5 million.

The SA had made preparations to secure Hitler's victory against an uprising by the Left in Berlin, and measures resembling a *coup d'état* had been planned. But Hitler had lost the election, although he had gained many voters at a stroke. On

17 March Göring calmed the foreign press, assuring them with much charm that there had been no intention to stage a *coup d'état*.

On the second ballot only a relative majority was required, which Hindenburg achieved on 10 April with 19.4 million votes. Duesterberg had withdrawn his candidacy. Thälmann again received about 5 million. Hitler's share rose to 13.4 million.

These 13-million-plus votes could not be interpreted as a decision in favour of the NSDAP, but they did serve to lift Hitler above his own movement and gave him credence as one who could find a way out of the grave crisis. And in the eyes of the voters, at Hitler's side was Göring, two men who stood out markedly from the mass of their party.

From this time stemmed the belief of the people that Göring was something separate, something special. He himself said that he had become what he then was 'through his own power'. His popularity lay in his 'independence'. As Reichstagspräsident he was soon even to become the third man in the Weimar Republic, after Reichspräsident Hindenburg and the President of the Reichsgericht.

But before this could happen the banning of the SA took place. One of the reasons this was done was to demonstrate to the international arms reduction conference, which had been meeting in Geneva since 2 February 1932, that the Brüning government did not want the NSDAP's 400,000-strong para-military private army to be counted as part of the future strength of the Reich army. This was one of the topics of the conference, and it was foreseen that Germany would be granted a numerical increase of its army in 1932. The ban was used by the NSDAP for purposes of propaganda, and the SA men were all taken into the Party and could therefore continue their activities.

The state elections in Prussia, Württemberg, Anhalt and Hamburg on 24 April had also brought Hitler's Party a strong increase in votes. Instead of nine seats in the Prussian Diet, the NSDAP now had 162 seats.

In the Reichstag, whose debates were broadcast over the radio with a time-lag, Göring spoke bluntly. This also contributed to an increase in his popularity, because otherwise the political parties were banned from using a microphone. Only the Reichspräsident, the Chancellor, and his ministers were allowed to speak over the radio.

The fall of Reich Interior and Armed Forces Minister Groener – who had issued the decree banning the SA – on 12 May 1932 was the beginning of the end of the Brüning cabinet. Groener, who had succeeded Ludendorff to supreme command of the army, could claim the credit together with Hindenburg, for having supported the Weimar Republic militarily in its early days, when Friedrich Ebert and Wilhelm Noske had needed help against a soviet-type regime that attempted to establish itself in Berlin. In the Reichstag Göring sharply attacked Groener who made a poor showing on the rostrum and his abdication became unavoidable.

For Göring it was a big day. He had been able to chase the man who had stood closest to Hindenburg and Ludendorff from office. After this Hindenburg could no longer retain Brüning as Chancellor. General von Schleicher, Chief of the Office of the Minister in the Armed Forces Ministry recommended to Hindenburg that he appoint Franz von Papen and form a cabinet of independent ministers which should be regarded as an interim cabinet. Schleicher was prepared to take over the Armed Forces Ministry, in which he had played an important political role for many years.

All the ministers in von Papen's cabinet were former officers of the old army. Five of them – von Papen, von Schleicher, von Eltz-Rübenach, Freiherr von Gayl, Freiherr von Braun – had served in Guard regiments at Potsdam. The 'cabinet of barons' had only three ministers who were not from the nobility: Warmbold from the IG Farben concern, Krupp director Schäfer, and Gürtner, a friend of Hugenberg's, who had rendered useful legal services to Hitler in Munich, for example in connection with Geli Raubal's death.

Five of these ministers were later to retain their positions under Hitler as Chancellor: von Papen, Freiherr von Neurath, Count Schwerin-Krosigk, Freiherr von Eltz-Rübenach, and Gürtner.

It was von Schleicher and von Papen's intention to call for a new general election for the Reichstag. Under the given circumstances this new election would be to the advantage of the NSDAP which had achieved major successes in the preceding state elections. Schleicher had to reckon with this. Concerning his point of view during this period, his biographer Friedrich-Karl von Plehwe writes: 'On the occasion of the formation of the government, Reichspräsident von Hindenburg received the leaders of the parties singly on 30 and 31 May 1932. This remained a formality, since the composition of the cabinet had already been decided. The only thing of importance was, that on this occasion to his question the Reichspräsident received the answer from Hitler that he was prepared to support the new cabinet or to tolerate it, depending on further development of the situation. As conditions, however, he demanded the withdrawal of the ban on the SA, the right for his party also to be able to use the radio, and above all, new elections to the Reichstag.

'This, however, was only a repetition of the conditions that Hitler had stated in previous conversations with Schleicher and which were known to the Reichspräsident and also to the new Chancellor von Papen. The demand for new elections had to be seen as particularly threatening, because the NSDAP would once again be given the opportunity further to increase the number of its voters and the dynamics of the movement itself, by capitalising on the advantageous position of being in opposition. It is therefore understandable that one has occasionally accused von Schleicher of having made a mistake on this matter.'

There can be no question that after the elections, von Schleicher intended to draw Hitler into the responsibility of government, an undertaking that was bound to be dangerous. That Hitler would lose votes in a new election was hardly to be expected.

On 14 June the first Presidential emergency decree was issued which announced a rigorous reduction in unemployment compensation. Now any iden- tification by Hitler with this cabinet was out of the question. The NSDAP would have lost its influence on the masses. On 5 June the new Reichstag elections were scheduled for 31 July 1932. The election campaign began immediately. On 15 June the ban on the SA was withdrawn.

Göring held many rallies at which he spoke of Hitler as having been sent by God, and that the nation longed for a leader since it was incapable of ruling itself as the regime of the political parties had proven.

In order to enable Hitler to travel rapidly from place to place, Lufthansa director Milch put Junkers 52 aircraft at his disposal at a special price.

In the spring, before this election campaign – with which Göring was to be greatly occupied – began, he had met the actress Emmy Sonnemann in Weimar. She had already been noticed there by Hitler who had struck up a conversation with her. The Kaiser Café in Weimar was a place where people met to drink coffee after lunch or in late afternoon. A table was reserved for politicians and profes- sors. The actress regularly took coffee at this café with one of her girl-friends. Hitler had probably mentioned her to Göring, because when he came in with Paul Körner, he asked Frau Sonnemann whether he could sit at her table.

Emmy Sonnemann writes: 'We only talked briefly. When I intimated to him that my girl-friend had persuaded me to go for a walk, Göring asked whether he could join us. And the four of us then promenaded in the park for almost two hours. I listened attentively to Hermann Göring's stories and sensed how much he was captivating me. Suddenly his thoughts turned to his deceased wife. He spoke about her. He did so with such boundless love and such a deep sorrow that I liked him more and more with each word. Our two companions escorted me to the theatre.'

Two weeks later Göring telegraphed her from Capri, where he was resting before starting off on this election campaign that was bound to be so decisive, that he would soon come to Weimar to see her again. On arrival in Weimar he gave a speech at an election rally. With Paul Körner he then went to the Goldene Adler where Emmy Sonnemann was waiting for both of them with a girl-friend. Emmy Sonnemann writes: 'I set off on the way home with Hermann Göring alone. It was only a short walk, but during it my future life was decided.' She became Göring's mistress. At this time he was only a deputy of the Reichstag, but he was soon to become its President.

Hitler, who was still mourning Geli Raubal, had also shown interest in Emmy Sonnemann, but it seems likely that he recommended her to Göring, who did not hesitate for long. He was now thirty-nine years old.

Like Göring, Emmy had been married. She was not ethereal as Carin had been, she was sturdy, pretty, and the same age as Göring. A North German blonde from Hamburg, she had had an excellent education before gaining a reputation at the Weimar National Theatre. She completely equated to the Nordic ideal, which Göring had found once before in Carin.

With a woman to care for him again, the political turmoil into which he must now plunge was made easier for him to bear. For guests whom he received in his apartment on the Kaiserdamm he again had a hostess, although Emmy Sonnemann continued to fulfil her engagement at the National Theatre.

In Berlin, Magda Goebbels had acquired a rival.

The 'Führer sent by God' could probably have had Magda Quandt or maybe even Emmy Sonnemann, but Hitler did not want a wife. He was content with Eva Braun, whom photographer Hoffmann had found for him.

'When I went to Berlin for the first time,' Emmy wrote, 'Göring gave a big party the same evening. He had big heavy furniture, but not in the Baroque nor in a too modern style, furnishings however that at this time were slightly above his means. He confessed to me that a large part of his income and savings were being devoured by libel suits in which he was involved because in his political life he was used to attacking his opponents very sharply. An unusual person. A man who could enthuse the masses with his striking voice. A man with an unbendable will, who fought for Hitler's idea from the bottom of his heart without regard for his own health. A Prussian officer of the true mould. Strong, with a ramrod straight carriage, with an eye of steel. And yet again, in contrast, the man who clung to his deceased wife with an overwhelming love, with so much tenderness and softness, as one would never have suspected in him. He had dedicated one room in his apartment exclusively to the memory of Carin. It was a somewhat uncanny room. Her harmonium stood there. Hundreds of small objects which reminded him of her were spread out as in a museum. From every wall she looked down out of precious frames with her beautiful eyes. My most vivid memory of the guests on that first evening are of Prince Philip of Hesse, a nephew of Kaiser Wilhelm II and his brother Prince Christoph with his young wife, Princess Sophie.'

The actress was fascinated by the new environment which Göring opened up for her. This was no longer the theatre, but real life. The princes were genuine, and the politicians were acting in a real life play whose subject was real power.

Following the 'Altona Bloody Sunday' of 17 July, which left seventeen dead after the SA marched into the workers' district of Altona and was engaged in bloody street fighting by the Communists, a state of emergency was declared on the 20th in Berlin, whose commander, General von Rundstedt, was given executive power. The Reichspräsident dismissed the government of Prussia and also the leadership of the police in Berlin. Larger troop movements were not necessary. Rundstedt had the 9th Company of the (Prussian) 9th Infantry Regiment under Captain Hauffe carry out the action together with the police. Without offering resistance, the Prussian ministers and Minister President Braun surrendered their posts. With this action, later known as the *Preußenschlag* (Prussian blow), a highly political situation had been created. Since the Chancellor had now become Reich Commissar for Prussia, any future Chancellor could assume that he too would hold power in Prussia. With this, Prussia had been eliminated politically and administratively as a counterweight to the Reich, or, as the term became later, it had been *gleichgeschaltet* (streamlined – Nazi euphemism for subjugation by absorption). Simultaneously the model had been created for future *Reichsstatthalter* (Reich governors) in the other states of the Reich.

The national elections on 31 July 1932 brought the NSDAP more than the predictable gains. It doubled the number of its seats to 230 and it was now the strongest faction. With this the turn around for a Chancellor Hitler appeared to have been achieved. But Hindenburg had no intention of offering his rival in the presidential elections this post; he wanted to keep von Papen as Chancellor. He had Hitler informed by von Papen that he could become Vice-Chancellor and Göring Prussian Minister of the Interior.

For Hitler and Göring the offer was an insult, because the Führer had no intention of becoming anyone's deputy, as Göring allegedly told von Papen. Göring himself was flattered; as Prussian Minister of the Interior he would have been given control of the police, and since his return from exile in Sweden five years ago, this was the first time that anybody had offered him a position as a minister.

Hitler remained adamant in his rejection of the offer.

On 13 August he was received by Hindenburg together with Frick and Röhm. The Reichspräsident had learned of Röhm's homosexual tendencies and found him unpleasant. Hindenburg declared that he feared unrest if Hitler were to become Chancellor, but Hitler insisted in his demand for the Chancellorship and full power.

After Hitler had returned from the palace, Göring, who had not taken part in the audience, advised him not to follow Röhm's recommendation; he wanted to unleash the SA because Hitler was not being permitted to harvest the fruits of his victory in the elections. Hitler took Göring's advice and ordered him to remain in Berlin while he retired to the Obersalzberg near Berchtesgaden.

Göring's realistic appreciation of the situation shows that he was a clever tactician. He had outmanœuvred Röhm, whom he regarded as a troublesome rival for influence on Hitler, and a personal enemy. Furthermore he could now expect to be elected to the position of President of the Reichstag when it convened again on 30 August. He achieved this with the votes of the National Socialists, the Zentrum, and the *Bayerische Volkspartei* (Bavarian People's Party). In his speech of acceptance before the Reichstag he also mentioned this majority which had elected him. He said that he was in a position to form a government that would not need to depend on emergency decrees by the Reichspräsident. He promised to execute the duties of his office impartially and to observe the rules of the house.

The von Papen government did not have a parliamentary majority behind it. Göring had. He was convinced that he could now succeed in bringing Hitler to power. He had achieved much in a short time, and he thought of his father, with whom he had now become more than an equal with regard to his position in the Reich.

He convened the Reichstag for 12 September and announced that he would now pay his inaugural visit to the Reichspräsident. At Gut Neudeck (Hindenburg's estate in East Prussia), Hindenburg told him unequivocally that he saw no reason to dismiss the von Papen government. If the Reichstag were of a different opinion, it could make use of its constitutional right and pass a vote of no confidence. But even then he was determined not to abandon the von Papen government.

For Göring, Hindenburg's words could only have one meaning: he had already given von Papen the order to dissolve the Reichstag, only the date was missing from the document.

The dramatic assembly of the Reichstag on 12 September was opened by Göring who was not wearing the brown shirt but a civilian suit with a mourning band on the left sleeve. The KPD had moved a vote of no confidence, but von Papen had come to the session without the file containing the order of dissolution. The National Socialists were granted a 30-minutes' recess during which von Papen himself fetched the file from his office. However, Göring ignored the Chancellor when he asked for the floor on a point of order. He put the no confidence motion to the vote which led to a defeat for the government. Ninety-two per cent of the delegates voted in favour of the KPD's motion. Von Papen left the Reichstag. His State Secretary declared that the vote was null and void because the Reichstag had no longer been in order. Göring read out the decree of dissolution and stated that it was invalid, because the vote of no confidence had effectively dismissed the Chancellor thereby invalidating his signature on the Reichspräsident's decree.

Such a daring coup was in line with Göring's temperament, but he had to accept being told that he had ignored the rules of the house according to which von Papen should have been given the floor. This did not bother him. He had wanted to demonstrate how weak von Papen's position was, having been supported by only 42 delegates while 421 voted against him. Since Hindenburg could not condone Göring's action, the Reichstag remained dissolved. With this incident von Papen became the only Chancellor to have been denied the floor in the Reichstag.

This vote demonstrated to the general public that if an overwhelming majority of delegates had been unable to dismiss a government that enjoyed the confidence of the Reichspräsident, the Weimar Republic was done for so far as parliamentarianism was concerned. New elections were scheduled for 6 November.

Göring filled his office at the Reichstag with furniture, family portraits, and Gobelin tapestries, some of which he had inherited from his father. He was very attached to these heirlooms.

Before 13 August a secret meeting between Reich Minister of the Armed Forces von Schleicher and Hitler had taken place in Fürstenberg north of Berlin. After this meeting von Schleicher was of the opinion that Hitler should become Chancellor after all, but ran into Hindenburg's opposition and gave in.

At this time von Schleicher was a proponent of the theory of attrition. By this he meant that one should give Hitler responsibility and he would soon fail because the circumstances were against him. A second national election could also be fitted into this theory. Von Schleicher reckoned on losses of votes for the NSDAP, whose funds had been used up. In this von Schleicher, as well as the other democratic parties and the Communists, under-estimated the Hitler movement. To bring it into power would have been easy, but to kick it out again by means of a democratic vote would have run into obstacles, which lay in Hitler's person and in the men around him, of whom Göring was the most dangerous because he was the most clever political tactician.

It did not bother Göring that the NSDAP lost 34 seats in the elections on 6 November. It remained the strongest faction. The Communists increased their seats to 100, the SPD went down to 123 seats. The Deutschnationalen gained slightly, Zentrum and Bayerische Volkspartei remained stable. The splinter parties were unimportant.

Before the elections the Communist Party had called for a strike of transportation workers in Berlin on 3 November, which led to chaos in the capital. The National Socialists under Goebbels joined the strike committee, so that for the first time the extreme Left and Right were acting together. Hindenburg was so incensed at the participation by the National Socialists, that in a talk after the elections he strongly reproached Hitler. Hitler replied: 'The people are very bitter.

If I had kept my people from participating, the strike would still have taken place, but I would have lost my supporters among the workers. That would not have been of any advantage to Germany.'

One day before the elections the National Socialists withdrew from the strike committee, and the strike began to fall apart.

After the elections, Hjalmar Schacht began to collect signatures among businessmen and industrialists for a petition to the Reichspräsident. Such petitions were quite normal during the Weimar Republic, but this time the document was of a highly explosive nature. In his biography of Hindenburg Wolfgang Ruge writes: 'Among the original copies of this petition in the central archives of the DDR (former German Democratic Republic), which consisted of individual letters with one signature, the names of Schacht, von Schröder, Fritz Thyssen, the steel baron Hecker, who was the President of the Chamber of Industry and Commerce in Hanover, the Chairman of the Farmers' Association Count Kalckreuth, Director Reinhart of the Commerz-und Privatbank, the shipping magnates Woermann and Beindorff, the potash king Rosterg, the trade magnates Hellferich and Witthoeft, as well as some of the nobility stand out. The copies of the document presented during the trial of Krupp at Nuremberg show that Krupp, Siemens, Robert Bosch, Silverberg, Cuno, Haniel, other industrialists and bankers, as well as former Ministers were also prepared to sign their names to the document.' The latter group, however, did not sign. Nor did Albert Vögler of the *Vereinigte Stahlwerke* (United Steel Works) and Paul Reusch of the Haniel business, who refused their signature because they did not wish to expose themselves politically. They are alleged, however, to have assured the Reichspräsident that they too 'stood by the grounds' of the petition.

The petition stated that it was necessary to transfer the responsible leadership of a presidential cabinet composed of the best available professionally and personally qualified forces to the leader of the largest national group without committing an open breach of the constitution in order to 'achieve the strongest possible national support for the cabinet'.

Martin Henry Sommerfeldt writes about Göring in the autumn of 1932: 'Despite his corpulence he surprised one by his great physical endurance and power. He was charged with energy and sparkled with vitality. With me, he distinctly dissociated himself from the other tribunes of the Party, was proud of his former station as an officer, of his fame as the last commander of Jagdgeschwader Richthofen, and placed much value in his descent from a "good family".'

Göring was Sommerfeldt's guest at his hunting-lodge in the extensive forests of Brandenburg, about 80 kilometres from Berlin. During their conversations Göring stated that he and Dr Goebbels were rivals for their influence on Hitler.

With his coarse propaganda methods, Goebbels wanted to bring about the failure of the negotiations with Hindenburg about a participation in the government. 'Every time I have almost softened up this East Prussian hardhead [Hindenburg], Jupp [from Joseph, i.e., Goebbels] throws a wrench in the works. He exaggerates everything, but he does it deliberately. "National Bolsheviks!" the Marshal will say to me again with a stony face.'

Göring also condemned Goebbels' support of the strike by the Berlin public transport workers, and the telegram expressing sympathy which Hitler sent to the 'Potempa' murderers (SA men in Upper Silesia had killed a Communist and been sentenced to death).

Göring asked Sommerfeldt to write a book that was to be soldierly, with as little mention of politics as possible, and not to be published by any Party publishing house. Sommerfeldt came up with a 60-page essay which was published in Berlin by E. S. Mittler & Son, a military publishing house. One year later Göring banned this booklet. Sommerfeldt recognised the deep contradictions in Göring's make-up: 'Between revolutionary impetuosity that enjoys brawling and pipe-dreams of grand seigniory, between the brown shirt of the SA in the morning, and well-cut tails in the evening'. He calls him a 'bloke', but one who wanted to become a king. 'Hermann Göring's political credo consisted of the passionate desire to be at least the second man in the Reich, in order to possibly become the first some day.'

This characterisation was shared by many in those days. Hitler remained unfathomable, Göring was easy to see through. He continually emphasised that he detested the radicalism of a Goebbels. The increasing confidence in the National Socialists shown by industry and business was primarily due to Göring's influence on Hitler.

Von Papen's position as a Chancellor without a majority had become untenable after the November elections and General von Schleicher advised him and the cabinet to step down, which they did on 17 November. Hindenburg again called in the party leaders for negotiations about the formation of a new government.

Together with State Secretary Meißner, Göring had to prepare the two meetings which Hitler had with Hindenburg on 19 and 21 November. Hitler demanded that he be appointed Chancellor of a presidential government without the restrictions of certain Presidential directives, this to be accomplished by the passing of an *Ermächtigungsgesetz* (lit. enabling law, which in the final analysis would give him dictatorial power). In effect, he wanted to govern without the consent of the Reichstag or the Reichspräsident, and he wanted his authority to do so to be decreed by the President, not enacted by the Reichstag. Hindenburg rejected this out of hand.

On 23 November von Schleicher, with Hindenburg's agreement, suggested to Hitler that he have his NSDAP participate in a government led by von Schleicher. It was von Schleicher's intention to split the NSDAP, and to form a government with Gregor Strasser as Vice-Chancellor, which would have the support of the unions. Hitler flatly refused, but von Schleicher continued to negotiate with him. On 1 December he sent Lieutenant-Colonel Ott, his confidant in the Reich Armed Forces Ministry, to Weimar as his negotiator. There local elections were scheduled and the entire leadership of the NSDAP were gathered in the capital of Thuringia. Ott would propose that Hitler join a von Schleicher cabinet as Vice-Chancellor and that the NSDAP could appoint several ministers.

At Weimar that day, the leaders of the NSDAP came to a decision. Gregor Strasser, who was in favour of joining the von Schleicher cabinet and disapproved of Hitler's course of 'all or nothing' was unable to assert himself. Hitler brusquely rejected von Schleicher's proposal and warned him not to take over the government. Afterwards Göring, who did not wish to burn all the bridges to Hindenburg, told Ott that this might not be Hitler's final word on the matter. He intimated that von Schleicher could demonstrate his readiness to compromise by offering him, Göring, the appointments of Minister President of Prussia and Minister of Aviation. On 3 December Hitler agreed to this plan, to 'propose' Göring instead of Strasser. He was convinced that Göring would remain loyal to him.

On 2 December Hindenburg had refused to charge von Papen yet again with the formation of a government, after von Papen had told him that his ministers were no longer willing to take part.

Von Schleicher, who wanted to get rid of von Papen, had pointed to the dangers of a general strike which would necessitate the deployment of the Reichswehr and the police. He had brought Lieutenant Colonel Ott with him, who was waiting in the antechamber. Ott had conducted a three-day war game study at the end of November on the effects of a state of emergency. The situation postulated had been a general strike and an uprising by the KPD and the NSDAP. The study had shown that the Reichswehr would not be able to master the situation. Ott had reported this that morning to von Papen's ministers who were deeply impressed.

In his biography of von Schleicher Friedrich-Karl von Plehwes writes on this: 'The suspicion has been voiced that the war game in the Reich Armed Forces Ministry and Ott's presentation to the ministers had been staged by von Schleicher from the very beginning only as a means of undermining von Papen's position and forcing his resignation. This insinuation is already refuted by the fact that the immediate reason for conducting the game had been the Berlin transportation strike. However, the first time thought was given to this occurred earlier, namely in connection with the court case before the State Court dealing with the dismissal of the Prussian government on 20 July 1932. According to Ott's testimony, at the time he and his colleagues Marcks and Carlowitz became specifically aware that it could easily again come to an application of Article 48 of the constitution and that one had to be thoroughly prepared for this. Von Schleicher had had to be "virtually pushed" before he agreed. An intrigue against von Papen was out of the question.'

The reason Hindenburg gave for his refusal to appoint von Papen as Chancellor under these circumstances was that he, near the end of his life, could not accept the responsibility for a civil war.

On 3 December von Schleicher had completed his cabinet and became the twelfth Chancellor of the Republic of Weimar.

On 5 December the leadership of the NSDAP met at the Kaiserhof in Berlin. The Party had debts of 12 million Reichsmarks. It was decided to stay aloof from the von Schleicher cabinet. Göring went to see von Schleicher and informed him that his faction would tolerate the new government for the time being.

Von Schleicher continued to attempt to split the NSDAP. In the local elections in Thuringia, the NSDAP had lost 40 per cent of its previous votes.

At the Kaiserhof hotel on 5 and 7 December Gregor Strasser defended himself against the accusation that he wanted to take part in the government. On 8 December he resigned from all Party offices, and Hitler and Göring feared a revolt in the Party. If the Party were to split, Hitler declared, he would make an end to himself in three minutes with a pistol. Strasser left Berlin. Hitler called the leadership of the NSDAP to Berlin on 9 December and re-established the unity of the Party. These events took place during a four-day session of the Reichstag which Göring chaired.

Nobody was now interested in renewed dissolution of the Reichstag. The NSDAP and the parties of the Right and Centre were now prepared to tolerate the von Schleicher cabinet, whereas the SPD and KPD announced their opposition. On 9 December the Reichstag recessed for an indefinite period. The sub-committees continued their work.

Two days later, on 11 December, the USA, Great Britain, France, Italy, and Germany signed the agreement in Geneva which theoretically granted Germany military equality.

11
Bring on the Champagne

In January 1933, when Göring celebrated his fortieth birthday, the Weimar Republic, faced by a combined majority of National Socialists and Communists in the Reichstag, no longer had a parliamentary majority. What the German voters had surrendered by this, they did not yet realise, but it should be noted that it had been the voters who had decided and not the dictators.

What was to become of the Reich? A proletarian dictatorship with the help of the Soviet Union? An NS dictatorship under an unpredictable Adolf Hitler based on the model of Fascist Italy? A military dictatorship? A military dictatorship would not have promised stability in the long run. It was rejected by the Reichspräsident who feared civil war. Hindenburg was now eighty-five and his days were numbered. But were not the crowns lying on the ground? Could not one pick them up and reinstate the monarchy, after the Republic had failed?

Göring, who seemed to be the monarchist in the Hitler movement, was thought to be the person who could do it. The most influential man after Hitler, had he not surrounded himself with princes and nobles?

In order to be able to take over the government legally, Hitler and Göring needed the Reichspräsident. 'In looking back on the final stretch of road of the Weimar Republic,' Friedrich-Karl von Plehwe writes in his biography of von Schleicher: 'what is particularly noticeable is that the people, the parties, and all sorts of socio-political groupings no longer had a say in the matter. In the weeks of January 1933 they appeared hardly to exist any longer.'

Hitler's chancellorship was prepared in villas on the Rhine and the Spree, behind drawn curtains, in an atmosphere of secret diplomacy and mutual protestations that were later dishonoured. Göring, as President of the Reichstag, played a leading role on the legislative side. He negotiated with von Papen, whom Hindenburg had charged with attempting to form a 'national government' as the final way out of the parliamentary crisis. Did Göring now see that the crowns were there for the taking?

The only one who could put them on a head was the ageing 'substitute Kaiser' Hindenburg, who wanted to put his house in order without breaking the oath he had sworn to the constitution of Weimar. Hindenburg felt that the final service he could render the Republic would be to bind his successor to this oath now. The man who became Chancellor would have to declare his loyalty to the constitution. And this Hitler did on 4 January 1933 in the presence of von Papen at the villa of the banker von Schröder in Cologne.

This rendered pointless any further endeavour by General von Schleicher to cling to his 'across the board front' and thereby prevent Hitler from becoming Chancellor. In the negotiations which Göring, as Hitler's political agent, conducted with von Papen towards the end of the month, he was able to point to the majority which had re-elected him President of the Reichstag in November and which embraced the entire spectrum from far Right all the way to the Zentrum, the Bayerische Volkspartei, and the small *Staatspartei* (State Party). Even though in Göring's case the issue had only been the Presidency of the Reichstag, both von Papen and von Schleicher had failed to gain such a majority.

Martin Henry Sommerfeldt writes: 'The official political agents that closed the big deal *à la hausse* (in a bullish manner) were Hermann Göring for the NSDAP and Franz von Papen for the bourgeois Right. Of an importance not to be underestimated was the role played by the prelate Kaas, whose faction tipped the scales. The real importance of this division of power that had finally come about lay not so much in the coalition's programme, which basically contained equality abroad and providing jobs at home, but in the division of the power itself.' Göring considered it appropriate to confirm this to von Papen.

The elections in Lippe, which took place in early January, confirmed that the NSDAP would not remain on the road of the loser of votes. In a speech at Dresden, Göring was again able to declare publicly that the NSDAP would not participate in a government formed by von Schleicher. With this Gregor Strasser's last hope was gone, as was von Schleicher's who still wanted to split the NSDAP with Strasser's help. The SPD would have nothing to do with von Schleicher.

On 22 January Hindenburg's emissaries, his son Oskar and State Secretary Meißner, met Hitler, Göring, and Frick in the Berlin villa of von Ribbentrop, who had become a member of the NSDAP. Hitler made concessions to the Reichspräsident. He promised not to exert any influence on the appointments of the Foreign Minister or the Minister of the Armed Forces. It was already as good as assured that Hindenburg had selected von Neurath and von Blomberg for these posts. Furthermore Hitler promised that as Chancellor he would regard a Vice-Chancellor von Papen as being equal, and only report to the President in his presence. Oskar von Hindenburg insisted on von Papen also becoming Reich Commissioner for Prussia. Göring had been thinking of that office for himself, but he would be content to become Minister President of Prussia and, additionally, Reich Commissioner for Aviation in order to keep the promise he had made to his wartime comrades at the disbandment of Jagdgeschwader Richthofen in December 1918: to become a 'Scharnhorst of the air force'.

Next day, 23 January, Hindenburg rejected General von Schleicher's demand for plenipotentiary powers to dissolve the Reichstag, to declare a state of emergency, and to postpone new elections for months in breach of the constitution.

Since Hindenburg now knew that he could have a legally constituted government (Hitler/von Papen), he saw no reason to involve himself in such an adventure which to him spelled civil war – in his view, as he told von Schleicher, 'the most terrible of all wars'.

On 24 January Göring was again negotiating with von Papen. On 28 January von Schleicher was dismissed. That evening, when the Chief of Army Command General Freiherr von Hammerstein-Equord, and the Commander of Wehrkreis III, General Joachim von Stülpnagel, went to see the President in an endeavour to secure at least von Schleicher's retention as Minister of the Armed Forces in the Hitler/von Papen government, Hindenburg replied: 'I know myself what is endurable for the armed forces and in this matter I must reject any advice by the Herren Generals.' But Hugenberg and his Deutschnationalen Volkspartei were included in the government.

On that same Saturday evening, while Lufthansa managing director Milch was with guests in his apartment in Berlin-Steglitz, Göring arrived with Paul Körner to ask Milch to become his State Secretary as future Minister of Aviation. Now that Göring had finally achieved the objective on which he had set his sights in 1918, he needed a professional deputy for his task of becoming the 'Scharnhorst of the German air force'. Erhard Milch recommended two other people: Brandenburg, Chief of Civil Aviation in the Reich Transport Ministry, and Admiral Lahs. Göring rejected these proposals and gave Milch two days to consider.

The moderation Hitler displayed during these days can be credited to Göring. On 29 January an incident occurred that developed out of a rumour. The President of the *Herrenclub* (club of important businessmen in Berlin) Werner von Alvensleben, who was acting as a political informer between von Schleicher, Hitler and Göring, had said to Hitler. 'If that bunch in the Wilhelmstraße (seat of the Chancellery and the Foreign Ministry, synonymous with German foreign policy during the Reich and the Republic) are only conducting spurious negotiations with you, then the Reich Minister of the Armed Forces and the Chief of Army Command should alarm the Potsdam garrison and clear the whole pigsty out of Wilhelmstraße.' Hitler had alerted the SA and informed State Secretary Meißner in the Wilhelmstraße. But nobody even considered bringing the Potsdam garrison to Berlin. In any case, this could only have been ordered by the Chief of Army Command von Hammerstein. He had suggested to von Schleicher that this be done but the latter rejected such a solution, and the whole thing remained merely a rumour.

On the afternoon of 29 January Göring was able to tell Hitler that his appointment as Chancellor could now be definitely counted upon. Hitler was in the Goebbels' apartment at Reichskanzlerplatz. 'This is certainly Göring's happiest hour', Goebbels noted in his diary. 'During years of exhausting negotiations

Göring has prepared the ground politically and diplomatically for the Führer. His circumspection, his strength of character, and his loyalty to the Führer were genuine, strong, and admirable, and he never hesitated for a moment. Just as admirable was his nerve. He trod his way with earnestness and firmness, an unshakeable, loyal shield-bearer for the Führer.' Bombastic though these sentiments may sound, they were true.

Göring could not withhold his triumph from his mistress. He sent a car to Weimar and she arrived at his apartment on the Kaiserdamm late that evening, just as the other guests were leaving. 'We were both deadly tired. We did not speak at all about next day,' Emmy Göring writes. 'Hermann only bade me: "Go and see Adolf Hitler tomorrow morning and bring him some flowers. He will be pleased."'

On 30 January in the morning Göring called Erhard Milch and reminded him that the time for reflection was over. After talking to his friend von Stauss, Milch accepted. But he insisted on being allowed to stay on as an honorary member of the Lufthansa management board, to which Göring agreed. Milch claims that in this conversation he also asked Göring about his morphine addiction and that Göring had replied that the matter had been overcome.

Having disposed of anything that appeared to be urgent, Göring and Hitler drove to the Chancellery which was occupied by Hindenburg at this time because his palace was being refurbished. There they met the new ministers who were largely the same ones as before. The new Minister of the Armed Forces, General von Blomberg, had arrived from Geneva by train early in the morning and had immediately been sworn in by Hindenburg.

Shortly after 11.15 a.m. Hindenburg swore in the new Reich cabinet, after which Hitler briefly re-affirmed his loyalty to the constitution. Hindenburg dismissed the new ministers with the words: 'And now, gentlemen, forward with God!' This had always been his custom as a Field Marshal when he held a briefing.

The photograph that was taken of the new Reich cabinet shows Hitler seated on a sofa between von Papen and Göring. Hitler is facing von Papen, Göring is beaming and looks happy and contented. He is now a Reich Minister (without portfolio), Reich Commissioner for Aviation, and acting Prussian Minister of the Interior. With this he has received titles such as his father had held under Bismarck: Minister-Resident and Reich Commissioner. His father had also been entitled to be addressed as Your Excellency, but this title was in abeyance, there being no kaiser, king, or princes of the Reich. However, Göring was firmly reckoning that he could become much more if he remained loyal to Hitler. Would Hitler not succeed Hindenburg after he died? Or would a monarchy be reinstated as Göring's friends from the aristocracy hoped? Could not Hitler become kaiser and Göring king? The positions they intended to occupy would at least have to equate to those that kaiser and kings had formerly held, but this time entrusted to them by the people, not by the Grace of God!

After the new acting Prussian Minister of the Interior Göring had held a press conference with foreign correspondents in a government building in Unter den Linden, he went to Hitler's first cabinet meeting at 5 p.m.

At that meeting the proposal to recommend the dissolution of the Reichstag to the President the following day was discussed. The new Minister of Finance and Economy Hugenberg objected: to bring the Zentrum into the government now in order to obtain a majority in the Reichstag would mean having to make undesirable concessions. No decision was reached because time was short. The Chief of Police had given permission for a torchlight parade to be held within the restricted area around the government buildings.

Before driving to the Chancellery Göring went to his apartment to change from formal dress into his SA uniform. To Emmy he said: 'It is really a strange moment when one realises that one has made it.' But since he had to think of her safety even at this 'strange moment', he gave her his revolver to take with her to the Hotel Kaiserhof where Göring had booked a room for her. She was to watch the torchlight procession from her window.

Emmy drove to the hotel with Göring's housekeeper Cilly Wachowiak, to whom she gave the revolver because it frightened her.

In Wilhelmstraße Göring, Hitler and Rudolf Hess watched the torchlight procession from an open window in the New Chancellery, while a few metres away Hindenburg looked out on the spectacle being presented to him. With the help of Eugen Hadamovski, Goebbels had had a microphone installed in order to have a live broadcast made for the first time, which was immediately sent out by all the German radio stations. Göring used the opportunity to make a speech to the nation in which he spoke of an atmosphere that could only be compared to the enthusiasm which had prevailed in August 1914.

He chose to ignore the fact that in 1914 the nation had gone into a war that today was unmentionable. But the *Machtübernahme* (lit. take-over of power, Nazi term for Hitler's appointment as Chancellor and rather noteworthy when one considers that he had promised to act within the framework of the constitution) was the first step into a new war. Göring also said that 30 January 1933 would go down in German history – in this he was quite right – and talked about the honourable Field Marshal, the 'Leader of Germany in the Great War' at whose side now stood Adolf Hitler, 'the young Führer of Germany'. In conclusion he said that the issue now was: 'Bread and jobs for the German people, freedom and honour for the nation.'

After the procession Emmy Sonnemann and Cilly Wachowiak returned to the apartment on Kaiserdamm, but Göring did not get back until 3 o'clock in the morning. From midnight he had been celebrating Prince August Wilhelm of Prussia's birthday with the Prince. 'In those days', Emmy Göring writes, 'the ties between the National Socialists and the House of Hohenzollern were still quite close. The German Crown Prince was thinking of a re-establishment of the German monarchy and Hitler did not dissuade him from this idea for the time being.'

And so Göring celebrated 30 January 1933 with the Hohenzollern to whose circles he felt he belonged based on his ancestry and his life until now. The Prussian cadet had become Prussian Minister of the Interior, and the last commander of Jagdgeschwader Richthofen, Reich Commissioner for Aviation.

On his belated return Emmy surprised him by saying that she had to return to Weimar immediately because there was a rehearsal of *Faust* scheduled from which she, as 'Gretchen', could not be absent. He was disappointed and reproached her, saying that she knew the part so well that it was not necessary to leave him. But she left, probably also because Göring had not taken her with him to celebrate the birthday and the victory. She did not return to Berlin until three weeks later.

In early February the annual aviation festival of the German Aeroclub took place at the Kroll Opera House opposite the Reichstag. This event was a fixture in the calendar of Berlin's high society. Göring appeared there in tails like all the other gentlemen and met his comrades from the Great War, the 'rock eagles' from the Jagdgeschwader Richthofen. In his speech to the glittering assembly he repeated his oath from Aschaffenburg in 1918 that he would found the new German air force as its Scharnhorst, and promised on his honour that the first German fighter wing would again bear the name of 'Richthofen'. At this point he had to stop because emotion had so overcome him that his voice broke.

Ernst Udet, with whom Göring had later gone to revolutionary Berlin, had also been present at Aschaffenburg. When Göring's voice broke, Ernst Udet – who was no longer a friend and admirer of Göring's – whispered to his neighbour that he now forgave him everything. Then Udet took his champagne glass and shattered it on the floor. They had done the same thing at Aschaffenburg twelve years before, when at the end of their road together, Göring had ended his speech to the last survivors of his Jagdgeschwader. Twelve years from now – only eight for Udet – they themselves would lie shattered, like the champagne glasses of then and now.

12

Prussian Minister of the Interior

To erect a totalitarian regime one needs, above all, control of the police. As acting Prussian Minister of the Interior Göring was given this on 30 January 1933. He describes what happened then in *Aufbau einer Nation* (*Building of a Nation*) (1934):

'First of all I had to gain firm control of the police. Here I cleaned house rigorously. Out of 32 Chiefs of Police I fired 22. Hundreds of police officers and thousands of policemen followed a month later and were replaced by dependable SA men.'

Martin Henry Sommerfeldt, who became press secretary in the Prussian Ministry of the Interior in early February writes: 'No new Prussian government had been formed since 20 July 1932. Prussia was being ruled temporarily and, incidentally, by the Reich. Vice-Chancellor von Papen was the acting Minister President while Hermann Göring, who immediately infused this largest of all administrations within the confines of the Reich with his massive energy, was the acting Minister of the Interior. My appointment as *Oberregierungsrat* (senior director) carried von Papen's signature. I was sworn to the Prussian constitution of 1919 by the *deutschnationale* State Secretary von Bismarck. Almost all the senior and intermediate positions of this largest administration in Europe, from the ministerial officials to the district administrators and chiefs of police, were occupied by Catholics, Democrats and Social Democrats. When I joined this Ministry, to my surprise I found fewer National Socialists than I had fingers on one hand. They were Minister Göring, his assistant Körner – who did not even belong to the Ministry however – a police captain called Jakobi, whose job consisted of sitting on an old black leather couch in the Minister's antechamber and guarding his own pistol which lay on a table in front of him, and Göring's secretary Fräulein Grundtmann.'

On taking over the ministry, Göring reminded the staff that his father had been a senior civil servant who had served the Reich and that he felt himself to be his father's heir.

He had come to power legally. How he was going to exercise it was for him alone to decide. For the time being he had no intention of accepting any directives from von Papen, who was still his superior.

'As far as I am concerned', von Papen wrote, 'my fundamental mistake consisted of under-estimating the dynamic power of the "New Idea". In contrast to the need for consistency of the Bourgeoisie, which still clung to the world of the nineteenth century, it had addressed itself to the social and national instincts of the masses. The methods which the Party applied during the next year and a half were completely alien to our thinking and upbringing.'

The Prussian Ministry of the Interior now became the switchboard for the 'national revolution' in Prussia and thereby the model for the other states in the Reich. Göring immediately banned rallies by the Communist Party, dissolved the Prussian Diet, personally fired civil servants in senior positions. Rudolf Diels, head of the state security department, was made Chief of the Political Police, something entirely new, and soon to be called Secret State Police (i.e., Gestapo). Diels handed over to Göring the ministry's dossiers and secret files dealing with the leaders of the National Socialists.

Then Göring had so-called 'blacklists' compiled of opponents of the National Socialists. Anyone who had served the Weimar Republic in an outstanding position in Prussia during the *Systemzeit* (lit. time of the system) as it was derogatorily termed, was noted on these lists with whose compilation Prussia was to set an example for the entire Reich.

For Göring, this was his 'revenge for 1918', but also, given his frame of mind at the time, his succumbing to the temptations of the power that had fallen into his hands overnight. Emmy Göring wrote later: 'Something had changed inside him since 30 January 1933, the day of the Machtübernahme. Before then, during the time in political opposition, he had appeared to me to be more carefree. More often than before I now saw him brooding, completely lost in thought.'

Instead of a rubber truncheon, Prussian policemen now had to carry a pistol on their belt because, as Göring explained in his directive, one could no longer demand of the police that they club down the people. But at an election rally in Dortmund he also said: 'Every bullet that leaves the barrel of a police pistol from now on is my bullet. If one wants to call that murder, then I have murdered.'

Within a matter of days, the tactician and diplomat Göring had changed into the authoritarian Göring who announced openly that he was accepting personal responsibility for everything that would happen from now on. As if he were still in command of Jagdgeschwader Richthofen, he declared in Dortmund: 'Whoever does his duty, whoever obeys my instructions, whoever proceeds against enemies of the state in the sharpest possible manner, whoever when attacked makes use of his weapon without compunction, he can be assured of my protection.' In Prussia in future, only one person would carry the responsibility and that person was he. From now on he began to be called the 'terrible Göring' and he appeared to enjoy this.

On 20 February members of the Reich Association of German Industry, with its Chairman Krupp von Bohlen und Halbach, appeared at the Reichspräsident's office to which they had been invited by Göring. Schacht welcomed them, Hitler gave a brief talk, Göring asked them for money. He was able to collect three million marks for the campaign fund of the NSDAP.

On 22 February the auxiliary police was formed: SA and SS men in their uniforms with white armbands, armed with rifles and pistols. It is certain that fear of an uprising by the Communists played a role in this. Göring could simply not believe that the enemy from the Left would tolerate Hitler as Chancellor. He rarely left the ministry from which he now ruled Prussia. There he had his 'command post' just as he had formerly had it on the airfields of his Jagdgeschwader. 'Göring is clearing out the Augean stable,' Goebbels had noted in his diary on 15 February.

On 24 February Göring ordered the police to search the Karl-Liebknecht-House, headquarters of the KPD in Berlin. As Göring then announced in the evening, damaging material had been found there which showed that the Communists were planning an uprising. It is hardly credible that four weeks after 30 January, the Communists were still keeping such material at their party head-quarters, otherwise Göring would have had his police immediately begin investigating these plans. This did not happen, nor were official buildings in Berlin put under special guard. The SA was not put on special alert after 24 February either. The search had only been intended to intimidate Communist voters.

Göring had told his press secretary Sommerfeldt that he placed great value on being 'the Party's right wingman'. In Berlin Goebbels, still Reich propaganda chief and not yet Reich Minister of Propaganda, was the 'left wingman', whose propaganda machine determined the election campaign. On the last day before the election, Goebbels wished to have the speech by the Führer, which was to be broadcast over all German stations, resounding in the ears of every last German. He therefore demanded that Göring rescind the police directive by which radios were not allowed to be played above domestic listening level. All the Party members were to place their radios at an open window and turn the volume up to full strength. Göring flatly refused. 'The directive stays in effect,' he told Sommerfeldt. 'Berlin is noisy enough without radios.'

'Göring was still completely of a mind to continue co-operating with the bourgeois Right,' Sommerfeldt writes, 'when a totally unexpected event made him change course by ninety degrees.'

The night of 27/28 February became Göring's night – the night when the 'take-over of power' became the 'seizure of power' and a revolution from above. And it was covered by emergency decrees that had been prepared beforehand, signed by the respective ministers, and merely awaiting the signature of the Reichspräsident. Any number of excuses could have been fabricated to justify the implementation of these decrees: an attempt to assassinate Hitler, as Count Harry Kessler assumes in his diary; attacks on government buildings; uprisings in the Ruhr, and any of these could have taken place. The lists of those to be arrested had already been drawn up, the emergency decrees prepared.

The burning of the Reichstag, which on 28 February was used as a motive for the wholesale arrest and persecution of political opponents, belongs in a separate order of historical events that have become symbols, like the burning of the temple of Artemis at Ephesus, or the library in Alexandria, even the burning of the Palace of Justice in Vienna; as though the arsonist's hand has been laid not only on the building itself but on a whole era. The NSDAP was determined to be rid of any opposition once it had come to power. What was more likely than for it to commit arson as an excuse to eliminate its political opponents?

But what of Göring, the President of this Reichstag? Why should the head of the house be the one to have burned the place? Since 1932 he had had his office in the Reichstag; his old desk stood there, and a huge heavy armchair, family portraits and the two Gobelin tapestries he had inherited from his father were on the walls. Since Göring was also entitled to occupy the palace of the Reichstag President which stood across the way, but which he only used for conferences and receptions and never lived in, he could have kept his personal belongings there. And we know what high value Göring put on possessions, on the family, on the past! But everything was left in the Reichstag where it fell victim to the flames, as did the main assembly hall.

The subterranean passage which connected the palace with the Reichstag could obviously have been used by henchmen of SA *Gruppenführer* (group leader) Ernst, who was in the process of establishing his terror regime in Berlin, to set the fire, but there is no evidence for this.

A Dutchman, Marinus van der Lubbe, was caught in the act in the Reichstag. What had he set alight with tarred fire-lighters? The wooden panelling, the heavy curtains. Everything made of wood or textiles burned. The fire that resulted in the assembly hall rose all the way up to the glass cupola of the building and caused it to explode. Van der Lubbe was arrested in the Bismarck Hall in the rear of the building.

Göring, who was working in his office in the Ministry of the Interior at Unter den Linden appeared at the Reichstag half an hour after the fire had been discovered. Then Hitler came with Goebbels, with whom he had been having dinner. Later von Papen also came. Hitler is alleged to have exclaimed: 'This is a gift of God's.' Goebbels spoke of a Communist crime.

'Göring stood in the smoke-filled foyer,' Martin Henry Sommerfeldt writes, 'surrounded by officers of the fire department and police. I reported to him. The boss was quite calm and the only impression I gained was that he too was rather upset by this arson without, however, attaching too much importance to it yet. Calmly and in a few words he told me to gather information about the cause and extent of the fire from the firemen and the police and then to prepare a report for publication on the conflagration and give it to him in the ministry.'

'I then spoke briefly with the chief of the political police, Diels, who was present and who told me that Hitler, Goebbels, and von Papen had also already inspected the damage. I asked Diels about the probable authorship and he replied that one had to assume a Communist plot, but that he recommended waiting for the interrogation of the person arrested.'

From the Reichstag Göring drove to see Hitler in the Chancellery where Goebbels was also present. Here he was given authorisation 'to suppress the Communist uprising'.

When press secretary Sommerfeldt presented his draft of the official report for the 'Official Prussian Press Service' to Göring at the Ministry of the Interior at 1 a.m., he found him highly excited in contrast to his conduct in the burning Reichstag. 'The desk is covered with papers and police radio messages. Göring quickly glances through my report, shoves all the other papers aside with a jerk, bangs his fist on the table and thunders at me: "This is bullshit! This is a police report from the Alex (short for Alexanderplatz where the Berlin central police offices were located), but it is not a political communiqué!" "These are the findings which the fire department and the police made and passed on to me. It is the official material you asked me for!" His tone hurt me, he had never dared talk to me like that before. But he screams: "This is nonsense," grabs an oversized coloured pencil: "One *Zentner* (50 kg) of inflammable material? Ten, one hundred *Zenter!*" And he draws a thick 100 over my upright 1. Now I became angry: "That is impossible, Herr Minister, nobody will believe you, one man and one hundred hundredweight ..." "Nothing is impossible!," he goes on shouting. "One man? That was not one man, that was ten, twenty men! Man, don't you understand, that was the Commune! This is the signal for the Communist revolution! The torch! It's started!"'

Since Sommerfeldt insisted on staying with his version, Göring dictated his own report to his secretary Fräulein Grundtmann. While doing so, he occasionally glanced at a document. Sommerfeldt writes: 'This report assumed as proven that with the "torch" of the burning Reichstag a Communist uprising of murder and arson was to have broken out. The precautionary arrest of Communist functionaries and the ban of the "Marxist press" were announced. Glancing at me from the corner of his eye, Göring multiplied my numbers by 10.'

When Sommerfeldt then drew his attention to the fact that he would have to sign the report himself, because it was a political document and no longer an official report about the fire, Göring put his large 'G' at the foot of the last page. Sommerfeldt then took the report to the official press office where the editor Dr Fritz Heissmann tore the paper from his hands. Sommerfeldt writes: "You've come at last, we are at our wits' end." "What's the matter? The fire is almost out." "Its not the Reichstag, but the arrests, the ban on the press and so on, people abroad are going wild." "But what do people abroad know about this?" "We reported everything already two hours ago, all we are missing is the official confirmation." "Two hours ago? And where did you get the material from?" "From me," said a young man I did not know. Dr Heissmann introduced him: "Herr Alfred Ingemar Berndt, Dr Goebbels' acting representative to our office. Herr Berndt brought all the material from Dr Goebbels some time ago." That was interesting and now I also knew why the jargon in Göring's announcement had sounded so familiar to me, and what sort of a document the Minister had kept looking at while he was dictating.'

Looking back to the burning Reichstag from the field of ruins Germany had become in 1948, Sommerfeldt believes: 'Dr Joseph Goebbels, that devilishly clever brain and extremely committed radical, watched with fear the profound influence the dignified personality of the ageing Marshal was beginning to exert on Hitler's undependable character. Wherever he turned he also felt Göring's opposition, who was beginning to make himself at home within bourgeois capitalism and showing himself to be more than prepared to sacrifice all Party doctrine for the sake of a fat sinecure. With the fire, Goebbels wanted to achieve far more than a "shot in the arm" for the vacillating voters. Much as Napoleon had virtually been pushed into the Hall of Deputies by his brother on 18 Brumaire, whereby world history took a new road, so did Goebbels with his alleged "torch of an armed uprising" cast Hitler and Göring into the maelstrom of far-reaching and irrevocable decisions. And the plan of this master psychologist worked out without fail.'

There was no lack of suspicion and accusations that Göring had set fire to the Reichstag or had had a hand in it. Göring's reaction to this was full of outrage but also cynical. 'You will have come to the conclusion', he told his judges at the Nuremberg trial in 1946, 'that in the face of my death I am not taking recourse to lies. I therefore assure you that I had nothing whatever to do with the fire in the Reichstag.'

The day after the fire Hindenburg signed the emergency decrees which had already been put into operation during the night of 28 February. All civil liberties had been suspended 'for the protection of the people and the state'. And that was how it was to remain thereafter.

Within only a few days most of the leading functionaries of the KPD were found and arrested. Ernst Thälmann's hideout was discovered on 3 March. On that day Göring exclaimed at an election rally in Frankfurt-on-Main: '... Fellow Germans, my measures will not be crippled by any judicial thinking ... I don't have to worry about justice; my mission is only to destroy and exterminate, nothing more!'

He displayed a hardness which, however, appeared to hurt him from time to time. When he learned that Ernst Thälmann had been beaten by the SA, he had the leader of the KPD, which was still taking part in the elections, brought to his office, shook his hand, and said: 'My dear Thälmann, if you had come to power I would probably not have been beaten, because you would immediately have had my head struck off.' For him it was now an eye for an eye, a tooth for a tooth, and he spoke much of this, openly admitted it. He was now 'the iron one' on whom Hitler could depend, no longer the 'soldier with the heart of a child' as Goebbels had ironically called him.

The national elections on 5 March only brought the government parties a narrow majority of 288 seats for the NSDAP and 52 for Hugenberg's Deutschnationale Volkspartei. The Social Democrats only lost two seats, but the Communists lost nineteen The Zentrum, the *Deutsche Staatspartei* (German State Party), and the Christian Socialists even achieved minor gains. In the state elections held at the same time in Prussia, where Göring was acting Minister of the Interior, the Communists gained six and the Social Democrats lost twelve seats.

In Greater Berlin in the national elections in 1932, the KPD had been the strongest party with 31 per cent of the votes. The NSDAP had only received 25.9 per cent. Now, however, the NSDAP was the strongest party with 34.6 per cent, the KPD having dropped to 24.4 per cent.

'On the evening of 5 March', writes Sommerfeldt, 'Göring's whole inner circle had been invited to the private apartment on the Kaiserdamm and people thronged the splendid rooms with a feeling of certain victory. In general, one assumed an absolute majority for the NSDAP, even hoped for a two-thirds majority, but was absolutely certain this would be achieved with the help of Hugenberg. On that evening I saw the whole Göring camp gathered together. It was undeniable that in those days he still maintained his personal relationships in all directions in a generous and charming manner. At "Hermann's" one could meet poor devils in a brown shirt who were permitted to eat their fill of everything that was good and expensive. One could meet industrialist Fritz Thyssen in evening dress, Prince August Wilhelm in the uniform of an SA brigade leader. Behind a bottle of whisky sat some pilots with the blue-gold star of the *Pour le Mérite*.

'When the first returns came in over the radio I withdrew to the Minister's office with Erhard Milch. We went to work. The election results were already becoming clear when Göring suddenly came into the room with Hitler. Both were in the best of moods. Göring kept rubbing his hands, which with him was a sign that he felt good, and Hitler was laughing loudly about some joke, something that occurred only very rarely. "Please, do not let us disturb you," Hitler said in a friendly manner. "We are finished," Milch answered. "Nothing fundamental will change in the results." "And?" Hitler asked, and everybody looked at me since I had the calculations in my hand. I said that the NSDAP lacked about 50 seats for a majority. "What sort of majority?" Göring asked. "A simple majority," I replied. Hitler firmly pressed his lips together for a moment and drummed lightly on the desk with his fingers: "Hugenberg?" "About 50 seats, Herr Reichskanzler." "Please, the total result," Hitler then asked, outwardly very calm, but his fingers drummed on the desk in front of me, softly but rapidly. I read out slowly: "NSDAP 288, Hugenberg 52, *Bürgerliche* [conservative bourgeois] 33, Zentrum 73, SPD 121, Commune 81." "Thank you!" Hitler turned away with a jerk and went to the door. We could just hear: "As long as the old gentleman lives we will never get rid of that gang."'

After the elections, Erhard Milch, as deputy of the Reich Commissioner for Aviation, took up quarters in the building of the Darmstädter and National Bank in Behrenstrasse, which had become available after the bank collapsed in 1931. In the former office of Hjalmar Schacht, who had become President of the Reichs-bank, he began the build-up of a Ministry of Aviation. The conference room had been reserved for Göring, but he hardly ever put in an appearance there.

13

'Weimar is Finally Overcome'

There can be no doubt that the setting up of concentration camps, which were initially called protective custody camps, stemmed from Göring, who recalled his childhood games in the forests of Veldenstein during the Boer War, when he had played at being a 'Boer general'. His father had been Reich Commissioner for German Southwest Africa. The colony bordered on the theatre of war from which news spread throughout the world that the British had built camps in which to confine Boer prisoners. Göring had such camps installed in Prussia, and the other states of the Reich followed suit. For thousands of unfortunates these camps were to become the scene of their humiliation and abandonment for an indefinite period, while at the same time throughout the nation the concept of 'community of the people' was being invoked. Protective custody became KZ (for Konzentrationslager, i.e., concentration camp).

Göring transferred supervision of his camps to Diels whose SA, before the KZs were built, had used cellars in Berlin and elsewhere to confine arrested persons who were treated with brutality, and even murdered. As a next step the SA installed camps of its own in which to torment its enemies.

Göring had some of these camps closed down, but the fact remains that there were 'official' Prussian concentration camps, and SA and SS camps. They differed from each other only in the relative degree of contempt for humanity displayed, if there can be such a differentiation. Göring's camps and prisons in Prussia were allegedly more 'humane' than those of the SA and SS.

The power Göring had gained was great, but he had rivals, and Hitler, concerned that none of his collaborators in the seizure of power should grow too powerful, acted on the principle of giving several men an equal chance to exercise power. This practice by his Führer was to cause Göring much grief in the future, and it can be seen that out of lust for unlimited power he kept seeking further offices which, when he had attained them, he had to defend against his rivals, often losing his breath on the way. His strong ability to assert himself had its limits. Sometimes he was 'the iron one', but at other times, only 'fatso'.

And always he wanted to play the Prussian, the Prussian officer who took responsibility upon himself. In contrast to this, Hitler was un-Prussian, a Bohemian, who did, however, possess a charisma for the Germans of the time. Göring needed charismatic Hitler in order to be able to grasp and exercise power in his shadow, until his power corrupted him.

On 21 March, the 'day of Potsdam', Göring as President of the Reichstag sat behind President von Hindenburg, but was not allowed to speak. Hindenburg and Hitler delivered their addresses from a rostrum at the entrance to the burial vault of the two Prussian kings.

After his re-election on 23 March at the Kroll Opera House, where he had cried at the pilots' ball in February, Göring made up for the speech he had not been allowed to give on the 21st: 'Weimar is finally overcome. It has a deep significance that the new Reichstag has found its way back to the city in which Prussia, and with Prussia, Germany, was founded.' In his short speech he was able to recall Bismarck, who had also appeared before the Reichstag of his day on 21 March.

On this 23 March 1933, the *Ermächtigungsgesetzt* (enabling law) was passed by the Reichstag against the votes of the SPD faction. Göring had refused the elected Communist delegates their free tickets for the Reichsbahn, but they could not have used them in any case because they were either in flight, had gone underground, or been arrested. The SPD faction deliberated whether it should take part in the session at all, and then decided to do so. It wanted to differentiate itself from the Communists, just as they had done from the SPD, whom they considered to be Social Fascists. While the passage of the enabling law by the majority of the Reichstag against the votes of the SPD did not yet make Hitler a dictator while Hindenburg still lived, with it parliament had committed suicide as consequently had the Republic of Weimar.

'Silence! The Führer will call you to account,' Göring had called down from the Presidential chair to the delegates of the Left, after Otto Wels of the SPD had given a moving funeral oration for the democratic republic.

And throughout the Reich the time had now come for a calling to account and for *Gleichschaltung* (elimination of opposition), and everything that had made up the state until now fell apart like a house of cards. In March the NSDAP recorded a very strong increase in membership, and these new members were immediately termed *Märzgefallene* (lit. those who fell in March, i.e., those who jumped on the bandwagon), which described their opportunism but also their concern for their future. Civil servants, for example, had not been permitted to join the (Nazi) Party before the beginning of 1933. Now many of them were only doing what they would have done earlier had it been permitted, but many did so for fear of being sacked. After all, there were still six million unemployed.

On 13 March, 'Rose Monday' in the Rhineland, Goebbels had become *Reichsminister für Volksaufklärung und Propaganda* (Reich Minister for Public Enlightenment and Propaganda). He moved into a palace on Wilhelmstraße opposite the Chancellery. While the power that would fall into his hands in this office was not yet discernible, Göring had the feeling, which his advisers confirmed, that it was high time for him to become Minister President of Prussia, something he had desired since 1930. He had worked very hard, his health had suffered, he was overworked. He ate a lot and he gained weight, he slept poorly, he also worried about the Party, which was structured in such a way that it could readily take over all the offices of state. His Party comrades were forcing their way into office, and in so doing were raising accusations against those who occupied them. Spying and denunciation reached such a state in Prussia that Göring had to do something about it. He admonished the members of the NSDAP not to raise complaints against their superiors because such conduct was inadmissible for a civil servant. He was not prepared to tolerate it. In a second letter he announced that he had instructed all offices, including the police, to throw anonymous accusations into the waste paper basket unread. Despite this, denunciations continued and dismissals were brought about by pressure.

On 30 March 1933 the *Deutsche Allgemeine Zeitung* reported a meeting of ministers in the Chancellery held the previous day: 'The Reichskanzler then made some remarks about defence measures against Jewish horror propaganda abroad. He stated that this defence had had to be organised because otherwise it would have come spontaneously from the people and could easily have taken on undesirable forms. By organising the defence, one was keeping the whole action under control.'

The 'action' turned out to be a boycott of Jewish shops on 1 April. Before then there had been attacks on Jewish property by the SA and the SS. This was now to be 'channelled'. In the Reich the action was organised by the Gauleiter of Franconia, Julius Streicher, who had become chief of a 'central committee for the defence against Jewish horror and boycott incitement'. In Berlin it was managed by Goebbels, the Gauleiter of Greater Berlin. The boycott began at 10 a.m. and ended at closing time. Göring remained aloof from the whole matter. He did not like such 'misbehaviour'.

Shortly after 1 April Göring had invited some American correspondents to a breakfast at which Camillo Castiglioni, the owner of BMW, who was a Jew, was also present. The journalists asked Göring about the anti-Semitic demonstrations that had just taken place, whereupon Göring replied: 'It is an accident, pure chance, and it will not happen again. The best friends from my youth were Jews and they treated me well. I have no intention of doing anything against them.' Göring was also thinking of Castiglioni for whom he had sold BMW aircraft engines in Sweden. Now, as he later recounted to Ernst Heinkel, Castiglioni interjected: 'But Hitler is anti-Semitic'!' Göring then allegedly said: 'I will get him to stop that, you may depend on it.'

Goebbels, who had suggested the boycott to Hitler shortly after he took office, now had to climb down. On 7 April the *Voßsche Zeitung* reported that Goebbels had announced that 'the weapon of a defensive boycott would only become blunt if used too often. The influence of German Jews will have to be limited by totally different step-by-step measures.'

That same day the 'law governing the reintroduction of professional civil service' was issued, which was also a part of these 'step by step measures' (among other things, the law prohibited Jews from becoming or remaining civil servants).

Göring now wanted to escape from the turbulence in Berlin by taking a vacation in Italy. He felt that he had done enough for Hitler in the early months of 1933, and told him that he felt ill. Hitler turned Göring's vacation trip into an official mission, on which he would be accompanied by von Papen, who had to call on the Vatican about the matter of the Reich Concordat which had urgently to be concluded. Hitler had promised it to the Catholics if they voted for the enabling law through their deputies in the Zentrum and the Bayerische Volkspartei.

When Göring landed at Rome airport, the German Ambassador in Rome, von Hassel, handed him a telegram from Hitler, notifying him of his appointment as Minister President of Prussia. He was to assume the office on 20 April, Hitler's birthday. With this, a long-held wish had been fulfilled. Since the Preußenschlag of 1932, Hitler as Chancellor could legally dispose of this office, and he had obtained Hindenburg's agreement. The appointment smacked of something imperial. An overlord making his vassal, to whom he owed his power in the Reich, into something like a king – King of Prussia. During the drive from the airport into the city, Göring appointed his friend Paul Körner as his State Secretary.

In the evening Göring was received and congratulated by Mussolini at the Palazzo Venezia. Later Mussolini admonished him to give up all this anti-Semitism, it only harmed one's own cause. The events of 1 April had been reported to Mussolini, whose Fascist regime was not anti-Semitic. Erhard Milch, who accompanied Göring to Rome, had a Jewish father and was therefore half Jewish.

One of the main topics in the talks with Mussolini, who was joined by the Italian Minister of Aviation, General Balbo, was Göring's nascent Luftwaffe. The clandestine training of pilots that had been taking place at Lipezk in Russia was scheduled to end in 1933, and Göring reached an agreement that German fighter pilots would be trained secretly by the Italian air force, although it seems that Göring discussed this whole matter quite superficially. Adolf Galland, who went to southern Italy in the summer of 1933 to begin training as a fighter pilot, recalls that Göring had not informed the Italians about the training being done in German flying schools, and in Italy the Germans had to start again as beginners.

Erhard Milch asked Mussolini and Balbo whether they thought that Germany should build a strong bomber fleet in order to deter Germany's neighbours from interfering in its re-armament programme. Mussolini is alleged to have agreed with this idea, but Balbo advised Milch that an air force consisting of fighters and reconnaissance aircraft would be sufficient. In his book, *The Tragedy of the German Luftwaffe – From the files and memoirs of Field Marshal Milch*, David Irving writes: '"We could not do anything with that," Milch replied. "England will only keep still if we have a bomber force." In the evening he reported to Göring about his talks with the Italians. Göring agreed with his decision whole-heartedly. He appears not to have given any thought to the matter himself. "Yes, yes, do whatever you like," was his only contribution to this problem.'

Göring had other things on his mind besides the future Luftwaffe. He was back in Rome again, where he had lived with Carin in miserable circumstances. In 1924 he had been received by Mussolini with indifference as the loser in the march on the Feldherrnhalle. Now he came as a Reich Minister and Minister President of Prussia. He was no longer an impoverished refugee but on the verge of becoming rich. What goes through the mind of a man with whom fate has played such a game?

On the flight back to Munich on 20 April a catastrophe almost occurred. Over the Alps the crew and passengers almost succumbed to altitude sickness because the oxygen was used up after the Ju 52 had circled too long in order to break through the cloud cover and climb above the mountains. Göring lay moaning on the floor. The radio operator could not find the directional beam. The crew had lost its orientation. The Ju 52 crossed back and forth over the Alps three times before it reached Munich four hours after taking-off from Milan.

Milch recalls that after having congratulated Hitler on his birthday in Hitler's apartment in Munich, Göring was already able to make jokes about this flight. In his official biography published in 1940, it was Göring who flew the Ju 52 despite the lack of oxygen and he who prevented a catastrophe.

But in the wake of this flight across the Alps Göring's pains returned, and he began again to take pain-killers for the first time since his return from Sweden. And so his past caught up with him, just at the moment when all his wishes had been fulfilled. After Hitler, he was the most powerful man in the Reich. But he was ill. He weighed far more than 200 pounds and walked with a limp. He was waiting for Emmy Sonnemann to obtain an engagement at the Prussian State Theatre in Berlin so that he could have a woman by his side, available at all times, and who, after this dizzying public elevation, could help him create a private sphere in which he could be himself. As Minister President of Prussia he now also had the chance to hold court in Berlin, and to build a residence for himself in the Schorfheide in which he could finally enjoy the power that had come his way.

115

14

'What Was Once Down is Now Up'

The new Luftwaffe which was developing under Göring, initially in secret as before 1933 and later openly as the third branch of the Wehrmacht, was able to draw on the ten years of preparatory work carried out by the Ministry of the Armed Forces. The Russo–German Treaty of Rapallo in 1922 had made secret cooperation between the Reichswehr and the Red Army possible. The occupation of the Ruhr in 1923 by French and Belgian troops had also led to General von Seeckt's giving thought to the secret rebuilding of a German air force, which was then initiated in breach of the ban imposed by the Treaty of Versailles. In Russia, at Lipezk, north of Voronesh, officers and cadets of the Reichswehr, who had been released from the service *pro forma*, had been receiving pilot training in German military aircraft since 1924. The air base belonged to the Red Army, but was managed independently by German officers. In Germany, since the mid twenties, training at civil aviation schools of Reichswehr officers who had volunteered had also begun. They wore civvies, but like the officers at Lipezk, were taken back into the Reichswehr on completion of their training. All this had taken place clandestinely with the knowledge of whichever Chancellor and Finance Minister happened to be in office, regardless of party affiliation. It was the job of the Chief of the Minister's Office in the Ministry of the Armed Forces, Colonel von Schleicher, to safeguard these training courses politically.

The German aircraft industry, which was forbidden to produce military aircraft, had also been able to work secretly since 1923 at Fili near Moscow, where a satellite plant of the Junkers Company at Dessau was erected for the production of metal airframes and engines. It had been Lenin who had desired this cooperation and who accepted the political responsibility for it. There was also a Russo–German project for producing poison gas and heavy calibre artillery ammunition, and facilities for training German officers for a future armoured force. By 1933 the number of aircrew trained at Lipezk totalled 120 fighter pilots and 100 observers. Among them were many future generals of the Luftwaffe.

At home the German Air Sports Association used gliders at numerous airfields to introduce young people to the air, with a view to the future Luftwaffe. According to American sources, before 1933 the Reich Ministry of the Armed Forces would have been able to man four fighter wings and three bomber and reconnaissance wings from this clandestine air rearmament.

With this, it can be seen that a basis for the air force was already in being when Göring became Reich Commissioner for Aviation. To his deputy Erhard

Milch, he stated his objective: 'As others collect stamps, I collect aircraft. Money is no object.'

It was his intention to obtain one thousand militarily employable aircraft for his secret Luftwaffe in the shortest possible time.

This number also had a political importance: with 1,000 military aircraft Göring could provide a protective umbrella for the manpower increase of the army, which would make intervention from outside difficult. Initially his Luftwaffe was conceived as a deterrent, and for this he needed fighters. The former fighter pilot was thinking mainly in terms of the fighter arm in which he had played a part in the previous war. In direct contrast, Erhard Milch, and above all the first Chief of Staff of the Luftwaffe, General Wever, believed the creation of long-range bomber forces to be more important than an overblown fighter arm.

Future bomber pilots were being trained at the Lufthansa Aviation School under the management of Ernst Brandenburg. During the Great War he had commanded the 'England Wing' with which he had attacked London. The British had called his aircraft 'giant bombers'.

In March 1933 civil aviation, which had formerly been attached to the Ministry of Transport under *Geheimrat* Fisch, was transferred to the Reich Commissariat for Aviation. A department for air raid protection was created under Major Großkreuz. A department for training and sports was created under Christiansen, who had flown against targets from Flanders during the Great War. Bruno Loerzer, with whom Göring had once flown as an observer, became President of the German Air Sports Association. On 29 March at the testing grounds at Rechlin in Mecklenburg, Göring was shown the aircraft with which he would equip the Luftwaffe.

After his return from Rome, the Ministry of the Armed Forces had agreed to integrate its secret aviation department, which had been expanded into an aviation command staff, with the Reich Ministry of Aviation, which was given this designation by the Reichspräsident on 27 April. This meant that the future Luftwaffe would be independent. The transfer took place on 15 May 1933, and that date saw the birth of the Luftwaffe, which took its clandestine place beside the Army and the Kriegsmarine as the third branch of the Wehrmacht.

Already on 6 May, State Secretary Milch had set about the procurement of 1,000 aircraft which were to include a large number of bombers. For the time being, the passenger Ju 52 was suitable for conversion to a bomber. The officers and men who were transferred from the Reichswehr Ministry had to report for work in the new ministry in civilian clothes.

Göring gave Milch a free hand. On 19 May he assumed his new office as Minister President of Prussia. He moved from Kaiserdamm into the official residence at No. 11a Leipziger Straße, which he then had rebuilt. In the Schorfheide, the largest state-owned hunting preserve near Berlin, the Prussian Minister President had previously had the hunting-lodge Hubertusstock at his disposal, which had formerly served the Kaiser when he went hunting.

On 9 May the Reich Hunting Association, which had been *gleichgeschaltet* like all other associations and clubs, had offered Göring, who was known to be a hunter, the chairmanship. But chairmanship was not enough for him; he became the patron of German hunters. Because Prussia had the largest forested areas in the country, a Minister President who was a hunter was in a position to further hunting. 'I will place myself at your head,' he said when he was offered the honorary office. 'I will do so with the strong intention of giving German hunting the outstanding importance it deserves. I will prepare a new law governing hunting in Prussia which will be a model for the whole Reich. It is my wish that this law will again reinstate German hunting in its most honourable form, by which the Germans may be reminded of their past.' He appointed Forestry Inspector Scherping as his commissioner in the Reich Hunting Association. Hunting in Prussia was put under legal protection and badly needed conservation decrees were issued.

Also in May 1933 the Secret State Police Office, the Gestapo, was created, which the Prussian Police Chief Diels managed until it was transferred to Himmler.

For Göring, the secret *Forschungsamt* (research office), which was located in a heavily guarded building on the Lietzensee in Berlin-Charlottenburg, became an important source of information. Its job was to tap telephones and pass details of conversations to Göring and the Chancellery via State Secretary Körner.

Göring now needed a butler. It was recommended to him that he engage an SA man, but he chose a naval man, Alfred Kropp, who served him until he became a prisoner of war in 1945.

As his adjutant he took on Colonel Bodenschatz from the Reichswehr, his former adjutant in Jagdgeschwader Richthofen. Another old friend, Prince Philip of Hesse, a son-in-law of the King of Italy, was appointed District President in Kassel.

For a brief time Göring toyed with the idea of creating a new aristocracy in Prussia, similar to that of Napoleon Bonaparte, in which he could make dukes of his State Secretaries, but he was dissuaded from pursuing this dream. However, he did create the Prussian State Council whose members he selected personally and showered with privileges and salaries. These would be his 'dukes'. He also had the idea of becoming head of the Lutheran Church in Prussia, as the King of Prussia had been, with a view to settling the disputes between Lutherans and Catholics which got on his nerves.

All these fancies were of a decidedly 'royalist' bent, but as long as Hindenburg was alive there could be no possibility of indulging them.

He had become a Gargantua with an insatiable appetite for high office, yet he experienced childish joy in the power which had been given him and intended to delegate as much of the concomitant workload as possible so that he might be free to enjoy the privileges. And there was no shortage of men ready to receive important positions from his hands. It may be that, for a balanced judgement, the grosser aspects of Göring's life-style should be viewed against the times, against the surging of a renascent Germany where anything seemed possible that did not conflict with the new direction that the Party, soon to become the sole Party, intended to take. Since Hitler refused to accept medals, they were given to the second man in the Reich, Göring.

For Göring power also meant money. He had suddenly become rich, not only through salaries which appear to have been modest, but with funds to which he had access through his offices. The log cabin he had built for himself in the Schorfhelde, for example, was paid for by the Prussian state. But his most important source of new wealth were the gifts which he insisted on being given.

'It took only about one year of sovereign power', writes his former press secretary Martin Henry Sommerfeldt, 'to change Hermann Göring, the upright soldier with the heart of a child, into one of the strangest and most striking characters of the Hitler era. In a virtual *salto mortale* (somersault), he hurled himself into the other side of his dual nature within this short span of time. What until then had only appeared rarely and among the most intimate circle as the belated and playful fantasy of an immature boy, now broke out with an intensity which made his friends deeply uneasy, but for the time being only amused the public. It is in no way true that Göring paid five marks for any good joke about himself. I had invented this white lie as a means of countering Goebbels' poisonous sarcasm. In reality, anybody who dared to recount the newest Göring anecdote to the Minister President was in for trouble, but among his closest associates nobody would have been surprised any longer if he had promoted his *Unterhemd* to an *Oberhemd* (word play: unter = under and ober = upper are terms widely used in German civil service titles to designate lower and higher ranks, therefore the allegation is that Göring would have 'promoted' an undershirt to become an outer shirt simply because it was he who was wearing it).

In the spring of 1933 Emmy Sonnemann had been offered a theatrical engagement in Berlin. Her director at Weimar, Franz Ulbrich, and the dramatist Hanns Johst, both now wearing the uniform of the SS, had been given the post of manager and artistic director of the Prussian State Theatre on 1 March. Johst, who knew that she was Göring's mistress, wanted the actress from Weimar to take a role in his play *Schlageter* which was soon to have its première.

Of her arrival in Berlin, Emmy Göring writes: 'Initially I now faced icy expressions. At least many. I was made to feel that I was basically unwelcome at the

Berlin State Theatre. The oppressive, heavy atmosphere, which was only explicable by my friendship with Hermann Göring, was just too tangible. I was taken for a "protégée of the Party". And I could understand the reaction of the members of the State Theatre. It took quite some time before it became clear to me. Hermann's position as Minister President of Prussia *vis-à-vis* the Prussian State Theatre made my situation very much more difficult. They were afraid that I would tell Hermann Göring everything I heard at the theatre.'

Emmy took an apartment in Bendlerstraße where Göring visited her. He was glad to have her in Berlin, but was not yet thinking of marrying her. While overcome by the power he had acquired, he was also very much challenged by it and was being careful to keep up appearances.

At this time, Gustaf Gründgens, who had come back in April from a trip abroad, was playing 'Mephisto' in Part I of *Faust* at the State Theatre. Ulbricht and Johst informed him that he was not wanted; the role of 'Hamlet' which had been promised him by contract could not be accommodated in the newly drawn up repertory, and his contract could not be upheld. 'Mephisto' had been Gründgens' show-piece role since 1932. When Gründgens appeared in this role in May during the 'Berlin Art Weeks', the new Minister President Göring was present in the Kaiser's box at the State Theatre and was very impressed. He had heard from Emmy that Gründgens had been dropped, and that same evening he summoned him and, as Gründgens writes, declared: '... categorically, that my contract with the State Theatre would have to remain validly binding both for the State Theatre as well as for me'. Emmy wrote that Gründgens as 'Mephisto' made the deepest impression on Göring that he had ever experienced. Göring thought him a genius and made every effort to win him over so that he might serve him, as 'Mephisto' served 'Faust'.

The Prussian State Theatre, which embraced the Opera Unter den Linden, and the playhouse on the Gendarmenmarkt, came under the supervision of the Prussian Minister President. Göring had foiled Goebbels' attempt to gain control of this artistic domain when Goebbels began to subordinate all the cultural institutions in the Reich to himself after his appointment as Minister of Propaganda. The quarrel between Göring and Goebbels was to lead to an ever deepening estrangement which was to play an important role in the battles for power among Hitler's closest associates. A further factor was that Goebbels did not get along with Emmy Sonnemann. She was a loveable, warm-hearted person, though committed to the theatre where she knew how to assert herself. Goebbels had been able to hold intellectual conversations with Carin Göring, who had been a fervent believer in Hitler during the *Kampfzeit* (lit. time of struggle, i.e., before the Nazis came to power). As Göring's mistress and subsequently his wife, Emmy Sonnemann became an enemy in Goebbels' eyes.

In May 1933 Gründgens also played 'Mephisto' in Part II of *Faust* in a production put on by the Düsseldorf director, Gustav Lindemann, which had opened at the Prussian State Theatre on 21 January , and so Göring got to know the complete 'Mephisto' through Gründgens.

On 30 May 1933, the aircraft manufacturers and experts Göring had called to Berlin learned that the new government was prepared to provide substantial loans for new aircraft, engines, air bases and factories. Göring was 'flying' again and nothing could stop him. He had become master of many things, but he still lacked a military rank. When this desire of the Prussian Minister President was put before the Reichspräsident, Hindenburg asked whether the ex-captain wanted to become a major. He was told, however, that Göring would have to be made a general. Hindenburg then said hesitantly 'major general', but he had got it wrong again, because what was meant was general of a service. (In the German armed forces the rank of full General, i.e., above Major- and Lieutenant-General, but below Colonel General and General Field Marshal, carried the additive of a service, e.g., of Infantry, of Artillery, of Panzer, etc.) And so Göring became General of Infantry because he had once served in the 113th Infantry Regiment at Mulhouse. A promotion across six ranks was a novelty, but other captains who had returned from the war in 1918 had meanwhile become generals and Göring saw no reason why he should not be treated equally even though he had never served in the Reichswehr.

Soon after his promotion he visited the 4th Company of the 9th Infantry Regiment at Potsdam in his new uniform. This regiment was bound up in the tradition of the Prussian air force to which he had once belonged and many soldiers of his future Luftwaffe were to come from it.

In August, Hindenburg was presented with the Prussian state domain of Langenau 'in gratitude for Tannenberg and his services in war and peace'. Langenau was twice as large as his Neudeck estate. Hindenburg's ancestors had once acquired Langenau through marriage, but had sold it to the Prussian state at the end of the 19th century. In order to join Langenau to Neudeck in East Prussia he was also given a stretch of forest lying between the two. Following the example of Bismarck's *Sachsenwald* (Saxonian Forest), the forest was called *Preußen-wald* (Prussian Forest). These gifts have been seen as being connected to Göring's promotion to general.

On 27 August during a big celebration at the Reich monument at Tannenberg, Göring asked the veterans and the members of the Reichswehr present to give the Field Marshal a threefold 'Hurrah!' as the latter had wished, even though 'Hurrah!' was no longer customary, having been replaced by 'Heil!'. Göring had come in the uniform of a general and was wearing a steel helmet. He recalled his time as a cadet at Lichterfelde and saw himself confirmed in his belief that everything had worked out right for him even though there had been many digressions on the way. He then drove through the Preußenwald with Hindenburg. They talked of forestry, and the landowner from East Prussia was delighted that Göring intended to take this under his wing. If Hindenburg ever liked any of the Nazi leaders, it was Göring.

It is also possible that Hindenburg, who knew that his days were numbered, saw in Göring the proponent of a future monarchy that this energetic, if overly proud, man might bring about through his influence with Hitler.

Göring's visit to East Prussia had been prepared by his personal assistant Dr Gritzbach and Martin Henry Sommerfeldt. Gritzbach had been von Papen's personal assistant and had been taken over by Göring when he became Minister President of Prussia. Sommerfeldt writes of an incident in Allenstein which shows 'how Göring's metamorphosis was furthered in such a fateful manner'. Gritzbach mentioned to the mayor of Allenstein that Göring expected to be made an honorary citizen of the city. To the mayor's question, where the letter of appointment and a gift of honour were to come from at such short notice, Gritzbach replied that he would take care of all that; there was a jeweller in Berlin who always held such things in stock. All the mayor need do was to tell him how much he wished to spend. To the objection that the Chancellor would also have to be made an honorary citizen and the demand whether Gritzbach also had a present for him 'in stock', Gritzbach replied: 'whatever is ordered will be done'. Sommerfeldt immediately called Berlin and learned that nobody there knew anything about an honorary citizenship. Powerful people have lackeys on whom they depend; they simply say: What is ordered will be done.

The first honorary citizen of Allenstein had been Hindenburg, who had driven the Russians out of East Prussia in 1914.

15

First Defeats

Göring saw the power he now held in Prussia and over Prussia as being a model for the whole Reich. It was quite clear to him that this Reich would become a National Socialist led centralised state, in which the individual states would disappear. Prussia had created the Reich, now Prussia could be absorbed by the Reich.

In order to demonstrate to Hitler his concept of a Council for the Sovereign after the liquidation of the parliament of the Weimar Party Democracy, he formed the Prussian State Council which was designed to advise him as Minister President. Since he himself selected its members, he was able to surround himself with men he liked or from whom he expected something. His State Councillors enjoyed the privilege that they could only be arrested by him personally, or with his agreement, something that now counted for much. Whoever became State Councillor stood under Göring's protection. Furthermore he received an annual lump sum payment of 12,000 marks for expenses. If he lived in Berlin he received half that amount. He had an official car at his disposal. Later on, he was entitled to two adjutants from the Luftwaffe with the rank of major.

Göring was President of the State Council, which had its offices in the 'Prussian House', the former state parliament building. Next to it was his ministerial villa which had been refurbished according to his wishes.

The people who became State Councillors were State Ministers, State Secretaries, leaders of the Party, of the SA and SS, men from the church, from business, science, and the arts. For the opening of the Prussian State Council, a parade by the SA and SS was held in Leipziger Straße on 15 September 1933 which the Prussian Minister President presided over. Röhm and Himmler were also to be seen on the grandstand, but they were in the background. It was the first time that Göring had been given such a parade and it was for him alone. Hitler did not appear and Göring was able to demonstrate how much personal power he now held.

People who had problems with the Party began to appeal to him. On 13 June, for example, Vice-Admiral von Throtha, the leader of the *Großdeutsche Bund* (Greater German Association) learned from Göring that he in no way condoned the campaign Baldur von Schirach, leader of the Hitler Youth, was conducting against this nationalistic (but not Nazi) youth association. Göring had allowed the association's national convention to be switched to Prussia, at the Lüneburger Heide near Münster, when the Gauleiter of Saxony, Mutschmann, had banned the convention from being held in Saxony.

However, the strength of Göring position was suddenly called into question by an event that took place one week after the parade in Leipziger Straße. The court case which was to clear up the arson in the Reichstag began before the Reichsgericht in Leipzig. Göring and Goebbels had been called as witnesses for the prosecution. Göring had agreed to appear even though he knew that arson could only be proven against Marinus van der Lubbe. His police had arrested the other four accused in Berlin: Ernst Torgler, a member of the Reichstag faction of the KPD, and three Communists from Bulgaria, Dimitroff, Taneff, and Popoff. Georgi Dimitroff, who acted as his own defence counsel, was a member of the Communist (Third) International (Comintern); he later became Prime Minister of Bulgaria. German radio broadcast the lengthy trial live. On 4 November 1933, the 31st day of the trial, Göring, wearing a civilian jacket, riding-breeches, and black boots, was sworn in as a witness. His duel with Dimitroff, who easily provoked Göring to make a fool of himself, became a sensation for the world press. Eighty journalists were present in court.

Göring believed that his stature was such that he would have no difficulty in disposing of an opponent like Dimitroff. But when the accused, acting as his own defence counsel, cross-examined the witness Göring and quickly moved to the subject of relations between Germany and the Soviet Union, Göring lost his composure. He later regretted that he had allowed Dimitroff to get him into a corner. The Reichsgericht building in Leipzig became the Georgi Dimitroff Museum after 1945, and the courtroom in which Göring and Dimitroff faced each other in 1933 survived. For the tourists, their voices again sound from recordings of the broadcasts.

The decisive passage which provoked Göring's enraged explosion reads as follows in the original:

Dimitroff: I said, Herr President, that the investigation by the police and later also the investigation by the court were deliberately influenced by this political conviction, and only in this direction for the most part.'
Göring: Accused Dimitroff!
Dimitroff: That is why I am asking.
Göring: But even admitting this, if it let itself be influenced in this direction it was only searching for the right direction.
Dimitroff: That is your opinion, mine is quite different.
Göring: Logically, but mine is the decisive one.
President: Dimitroff!
Dimitroff: I am the accused, naturally.
President: You are only permitted to ask questions.
Dimitroff: I go even further, Herr President. Are Herr President, Herr Minister

President Göring aware, that the party with this criminal *Weltanschauung*, as he calls it, this party rules one sixth of the world? That is the Soviet Union.

Göring: Unfortunately.

Dimitroff: This Soviet Union maintains diplomatic and political and economic relations with Germany. Through its business orders hundreds of thousands of German workers get work, have got and will get. Is that known? Do you know?

Göring: I know.

Dimitroff: Good!

Göring: What goes on in Russia is no concern of mine. I only have to deal with the Communist Party in Germany and with the foreign Communist crooks who came here in order to set fire to the Reichstag.

Public gallery: Bravo!

Dimitroff: That bravo, bravo! Naturally say bravo. To wage a fight against the Communist Party of Germany is your right. It is the right of the Communist Party in Germany to live illegally and to fight your government and it will fight, that is only matter of relative strength, not a matter of right.

President: Dimitroff, I am issuing an injunction that you are not to expound Communist propaganda here.

Dimitroff: But he is making a National Socialist one!

President: That is immaterial to me. Communist propaganda will not be expounded in this courtroom, and that was a piece of it a moment ago.

Dimitroff: Herr President, in connection with my last question in any case it must now be cleared: Party and Weltanschauung. Herr Minister President Göring stated that a foreign power like the Soviet Union and in connection with this power, this country can everything what it wants to do, but in Germany, do against the Communist Party. True Weltanschauung, this Bolshevist Weltanschauung rules Soviet Union, the biggest and best country in the world. Is this known?

Göring: Now listen to me, now I will tell you what is known among the German people. The German people know [Göring's voice rises], that you are acting with impertinence here and come running here, set fire to the Reichstag and then allow yourself such impudence against the German people. I did not come here in order to let myself be accused by you. In my eyes you are a crook who should have been strung up long ago.

President: Herr Minister President!

Dimitroff: Very good!

President: Dimitroff, I said, I have already said, that you are not to expound Communist propaganda – (Dimitroff tries to continue speaking) – if you say one more word, you will be expelled again – that you are not to expound

Communist propaganda. You have now done this for the second time and you should not be surprised if the witness flares up the way he did just now. I now forbid you most stringently to do this again. You have, if you have any questions to ask at all, you have to ask purely factual questions, nothing more.

Dimitroff: I am very pleased, I am very pleased with this statement by Herr Göring.

President: Whether you are pleased or not is no matter to me.

Dimitroff: Very pleased. Herr President, I ask questions!

President: You are no longer permitted to speak.

Dimitroff: Herr President!

President: Sit down.

Dimitroff: I have the right to ask factual questions.

President: After this form of questioning I withdraw your right to speak.

Dimitroff (to Göring): Are you afraid of these questions, Herr Minister President?

Göring (shouting): You will be afraid if I get a hold of you when you leave this court, you crook you!

President: Dimitroff is expelled for a further three days. Take him out immediately.

Göring's outburst demonstrated a disregard for due process of law to the world at large. He intended to hang Dimitroff if he were acquitted. This monstrous threat which he had let himself be provoked into making damaged him even in Hitler's eyes at the time, who was not anxious to have trouble with the Soviet Union.

Goebbels, who appeared in court on 8 November, handled Dimitroff in a more elegant manner.

Dimitroff: I stand here accused by my prosecutor among other things, that by the arson in the Reichstag I intended to bring about by force a change in the German constitution. I ask the Minister for Propaganda in Germany ...

President: Now get on with it, what is the question!

Dimitroff: I ask which actual, which constitution was in force on 30 January and 27 February in Germany, which constitution?

Goebbels: The constitution that had been passed by the parliament in Weimar was in force. Whether this constitution was good or bad is completely without importance. The decisive fact was that it was legal and that it had also been accepted by the National Socialist government. We did not wish to leave it up to the Communist Party to change it, we have reserved this right for ourselves.

Dimitroff, Taneff, Popoff, and Torgler were acquitted, van der Lubbe was sentenced to death. The arson in the Reichstag was never fully cleared up.

Van der Lubbe was decapitated on 10 January 1934. Dimitroff left Germany from Königsberg on 28 February in a Russian aircraft. According to Martin Henry

Sommerfeldt, Göring intended to avenge himself by having Dimitroff killed in an accident or shot while trying to escape. Hitler's foreign press secretary Hanfstaengl, and Sommerfeldt, who was no longer working for Göring – his Minister President had suspended him from office a few days after his appearance in Leipzig – made sure that Lochner, the Berlin correspondent of the American press agency AP, and his colleague in Berlin from *The Times* of London, learned of this 'rumour', only to issue immediately an official denial to the foreign journalists, saying Göring was too much of a gentleman and soldier to give his hand to a cowardly murder behind the scenes. Sommerfeldt added that from his background and former profession as an officer, Göring was basically quite different from other party leaders. AP reported this world-wide and Göring was able to read in *The Times* that he was a perfect gentleman. He immediately issued a sharply worded denial of the rumour that he had intended to commit a crime against Dimitroff.

Göring's loss of composure in court, made worse by its being broadcast live, was to prove a severe set-back to his standing within the National Socialist leadership. Until now his sharp intelligence and ability to react quickly had been admired. He had to admit to himself that the trial had been unable to prove conclusively that the Reichstag fire had been the signal for a Communist uprising, as Hitler, and above all Goebbels, had claimed at the time, and with whom he had so quickly agreed.

His court appearance had occurred during the election campaign. On 12 November 1933 a plebiscite on the one-party system in the Reichstag was to be taken. This vote, which was not a genuine one, became necessary because on 19 October Germany had resigned from the League of Nations on the grounds that Germany had not been given full equality at the Geneva disarmament conference.

On the ballot slip there were only two alternatives – 'Yes', or 'No'. On the eve of the ballot 86-year-old Hindenburg gave his last speech on the radio:

'I and the Reich Government, united in the will to lead Germany up out of the inner turmoil and impotency of the post-war years, have appealed to the German nation to decide its own future tomorrow, and to express to the world whether it agrees with the policy we have pursued and intends to make it its own. Thanks to the courageous, determined, and forceful leadership of Chancellor Hitler and his colleagues, whom I appointed on 30 January of this year, Germany has found itself again and gained the strength to tread the road that its national honour and its future prescribe.'

Hindenburg is alleged to have expressed misgivings about the resignation from the League of Nations, but these were allayed by a telegram from Krupp who expressed the opinion that the withdrawal from Geneva 'had been prescribed by the commandment of self respect'. By the evening of the plebiscite, 95 per cent of those eligible had voted 'Yes'.

The resignation from the League of Nations coincided with an event that hurt Göring personally very much. The ribbon on a wreath which he had had laid on Carin's grave in the Lovö cemetery on 17 October, the anniversary of her death, had borne a swastika. The ribbon had been torn off by Swedish anti-Fascists and removed. A note left behind on the grave had called the ribbon 'Nazi propaganda'. Göring, who had not forgotten that in 1920 he had seen the swastika for the first time as an ornament on the fireplace of Count von Rosen's castle at Rockelstad, immediately decided to have the mortal remains of his wife brought to Germany. She was to have her final resting-place in the former hunting preserve of the Kings of Prussia, the Schorfheide. The house he intended to have built there for himself in the style of a Swedish farm house was to be called 'Carinhall' and would include a mausoleum on the high bank of one of the Brandenburg lakes. There Carin was to be laid to rest in a pewter coffin which his remains would share when the time came. On the banks of the Große Döllnsee, the government architects Tuch and Hetzelt supervised according to his plans the modification of the main building which originally had been a blockhouse. He had the Schorfheide put under environmental protection. The costs of all this were paid for by the Prussian state. That the desecration had taken place in Sweden made Göring bitter; he loved the country in which he had formerly found refuge. Now he intended to build his own Sweden near Berlin.

On 1 December 1933 the 'law for securing the unity of Party and State' made the NSDAP into the only state party. Hitler appointed Ernst Röhm and Rudolf Hess as Reich Ministers at the end of the month. Through this act the German public learned that Hitler and the Chief of Staff of the SA were on first name terms. The appointment was announced in the press together with a personal letter from Hitler to Röhm. Göring's reputation as the second man after Hitler was thereby diminished. Suddenly he was only one of several in Hitler's entourage, not his personal friend like Röhm. And Goebbels had seized unrestricted power over artists and journalists by the foundation of the *Reichskulturkammer* (Reich Cultural Office, of which one had to be a member in order to be allowed to practise one's art) and the *Schriftleitergesetz* (law governing editors, which defined who was allowed to be an editor of a newspaper).

But was not Göring the master over forests, over the air, over the secrets which his Forschungsamt uncovered for him? And had he not at least kept control of the Prussian State Opera and State Theatre? At Christmas he decreed an amnesty for prisoners in Prussian concentration camps; over these too, he still held sway.

As President of the Reichstag, after 12 November 1933 he could no longer be anything other than a secondary speaker before or after Hitler, always supposing that the Reichstag would continue to sit.

The pomp and regalia of which Göring was so fond is evident in this formal portrait.
IWM MH 6041

Above: Mauterndorf Castle in the Salzburg Lungau.

Left: Leader of Fighter Wing 1 in the summer of 1918, First Lieutenant Göring stands armed with von Richthofen's knotted stick.

Above: First Lieutenant Göring in his single-seat Fokker DVII on the Western Front in the autumn of 1918.

Right: Göring's arrival as the first air mail pilot of Svenska Lufttrafik AB at Malmö-Limhamm, Sweden, from Warnemünde via Copenhagen-Kastrup, in August 1920, thereby opening the air mail service between Germany and Sweden.

Above: The Edelweiss Chapel in the garden of the Stockholm home of the von Fock family at Grev Karlavägen. This was a place of meditation for a Christian order of sisters named after the Edelweiss.

Left: Carin Göring at Bayerisch-Zell.

Above: Prussian Minister President Göring's office in 1934 at 'Carinhall'. Situated in the Schorfheide near Berlin, it was originally a Swedish-style log-house. On the wall is an oil painting of the deceased Carin Göring.

Right: Göring with Hitler and Ernst Röhm, leader of the SA, at Berchtesgaden in 1930. IWM NYP 68052

Göring watches Hitler greet Field Marshal von Hindenburg, the German President, after Hitler's appointment as Chancellor in January 1933. IWM NYP 22578

Above: Göring at a Nazi Party rally in 1934. IWM FLM 1535

Below: Visiting Cologne in 1934. IWM HU 7172

Above: The Condor Legion marches past Göring on its return from the Spanish Civil War. IWM MH 13115

Left: Field Marshal Göring in the Eifel at the start of the campaign against France in May 1940.

Top right: Göring and his officers view the white cliffs of Dover from the French coast – so near and yet so far! IWM HU1185

Right: Addressing German pilots during the Battle of Britain. IWM MH 13382

Above: Is Göring making light of bad news as he listens to German pilots in January 1941? IWM GER 1436

Left: Visiting the Richthofen geschwader with Hitler. IWM HU 5238

Below: Göring with Hitler and Count Ciano, Mussolini's Foreign Minister. IWM K 3978

Above: Officers meeting Göring on the battlefield. IWM HU 24783

Below: Staff Sergeant Rudolf Nacke, who flew the Ju 88, is awarded the Knight's Cross by Göring on 23 July 1941 in East Prussia. In the background is personal secretary Dr Gritzbach.

Above: Pictured with Himmler and Hitler. IWM FLAM 1920

Below: Hitler has become more cheerful, Himmler seems content, but Göring remains glum. IWM FLM 1917

Above: Göring, with Foreign Minister von Ribbentrop and Hitler, during Mussolini's visit in July 1944, shortly after the unsuccessful attempt on the Führer's life. IWM AP 32756

Left: Pictured on 12 May 1945, Göring's wife sits forlornly in the house at Zellam See in Austria where the couple had been hiding. IWM EA 67235

Right: Showing the
emotion of being
captured, Göring sits
amongst the Allied
officers who found him.
IWM FRA 203511

Right: Presented at a
press conference by his
US Seventh Army
captors, Göring responds
to questioning.
IWM AP 66900

Left: The No. 1 accused enters the courtroom at Nuremberg to hear the verdict read.

Below: Hermann Göring's corpse in Nuremberg prison on 16 October 1946.

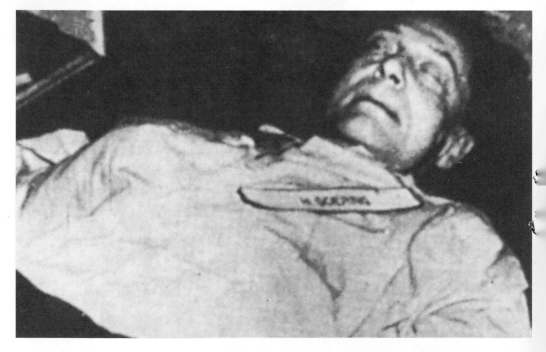

And Göring as Minister President of Prussia? He would keep the office, but the days of his power in Prussia were numbered. On 30 January 1934 the law governing the re-organisation of the Reich and the suspension of the sovereignty of the states and the state diets was to be enacted. While his office as Minister President of Prussia was to become unimportant, he would retain the sinecures. A hedonist, he needed these in order to be able to enjoy life.

He lived in a palace that had been the official residence of the Prussian Minister of Commerce. He had had it rebuilt to his own specifications. Velvet tapestries covered the walls in the smaller rooms, dark stained windows let in very little light. Heavy Renaissance furniture stood in the rooms. Göring had not forgotten the Edelweiss chapel in Stockholm which reminded him of his wife. The palace was decorated with swastikas on the ceilings, walls, and floors. Albert Speer wrote: 'It looked as if something particularly festive-tragic were going on in these apartments all the time.' Hitler had visited them and found them too sombre, and had recommended Speer who was doing some rebuilding in the Chancellery.

During the winter Göring had the apartments redone. Speer writes: 'It was a nice assignment. Money, as usual with Göring, was no object. Therefore walls were torn down in order to convert the many small rooms on the ground floor into four large rooms. The largest of these, his office, measured almost 140 square metres and was almost as large as Hitler's. Göring's furniture equated to his girth. An old Renaissance desk had gigantic dimensions, as did a desk chair, probably formerly the throne of a prince, whose back-rest towered far above his head. On the desk he had two silver lamps with oversized parchment shades together with an oversized photograph of Hitler. The original which the Führer had presented to him had not been imposing enough for him. For this purpose he had had it enlarged several times and every visitor wondered about this special honour by Hitler, since it was known in Party and governmental circles that Hitler always gave his photograph to his paladins in the same size and in a silver frame that had been specially designed for it by Frau Troost. In the hall an oversized painting was pulled up to the ceiling in order to give access to a camera concealed behind the wall. In his inconsiderate manner Göring had actually ordered "his" Prussian director of the Kaiser-Friedrich Museum to deliver the famous painting 'Diana hunting deer' by Rubens to his apartments.'

During the refurbishment Göring lived in the palace of the President of the Reichstag opposite the burned-out shell of the Reichstag. His official villa on the corner of Prinz-Albrecht-Straße and Stresemannstraße was to become the scene of an event in June 1934 that was again to change his life. It was to jolt him out of the sybaritic life into which he had withdrawn in early 1934, haunted by the terrible words 'to the gallows!' which he had shouted at Dimitroff in November. This was to turn into: 'The Führer wills it, fire!'

By now he had succeeded in having Stresemannstraße renamed Hermann-Göring Straße. There he celebrated his 41st birthday on 12 January 1934. He was given rich presents. Such presents became customary from then on and everyone tried to outdo everyone else. Hitler did not accept valuable presents or medals. In contrast, Göring took a childish joy in the precious things that flowed to him from all over the Reich. They were part of his style of life. Hitler called him a Renaissance man, and deliberately differentiated himself from Göring. But we are getting ahead of our story. Hindenburg was still alive. In early January he gave his last New Year's reception.

'He was leaning on his stick,' Martin Henry Sommerfeldt writes. 'He stood there like a monument, large and heavy. His hair was white as snow, his eyes of a very light blue, mild and old.'

'Reichskanzler Hitler stood watchfully in the background. It was of no importance that one of the men had once been a field marshal and the other a corporal; between them lay a whole world, an era of history, and the ancient was the last bridge span that reached from a past already become a legend into the present. He was the last obstruction on the way to a dictatorship.'

In his biography of Hindenburg Wolfgang Ruge writes: 'The Reichspräsident spent the winter of 1933/4 very quietly in his lonely palace. Since there was now nothing left for him to decide, there was no longer a *camarilla* (clique, private cabinet of councillors). The names of the former ideas men, Ludendorff, Groener, and Schleicher, were no longer even allowed to be mentioned in Wilhelmstraße, since they had fallen into disfavour with the Nazis. Von Papen and Oldenburg-Januschau only came to call on rare occasions. Other former confidants of the Field Marshal had become feeble and sat in their estates playing a similar role at provincial or district levels as Hindenburg. Son Oskar wandered about without a job, because the Nazis could not use any henchmen of such stunted intellect at the level he claimed for his own. The only one who still displayed any bustle was State Secretary Meißner, who was mainly concerned with keeping his position after Hindenburg's death, which could not be far off according to all human reason.'

Until now Göring had considered himself to be the link between Hindenburg and Hitler, as a Prussian intermediary who had once been a cadet just like the Field Marshal. This had been one of his strengths.

Göring remained close to the Hohenzollerns, who still maintained hopes that he would bring about a restoration of the monarchy after Hindenburg's death – in Italy Mussolini was a Fascist dictator under a king – but the former intimacy was no longer there. Göring's self-awareness had grown. After Hindenburg's death it would be Hitler who would decide what was to become of the highest office in the state. And whatever happened, Göring wanted to remain Hitler's most loyal follower.

16
To Carinhall

W hile during the winter of 1933/4 a subterranean system of air raid bunkers was being built beneath the Ehrenpforten hill above the villages of Eiche and Golm in Wildpark Werder near Potsdam, a former hunting preserve of the Kings of Prussia, to house the future command staff of the Luftwaffe if the need arose, Göring, who could always find time for his hobbies and inclinations despite his many offices, was occupied with his Prussian State Theatres. He reckoned them to be a part of his domain and jealously defended them against Minister of Propaganda Goebbels, who had become so powerful and had the final say in the area of culture and the arts. Emmy Sonnemann, who had appeared as 'Gretchen' with Gustaf Gründgens in Part I of *Faust* in 1933 and with him also in Hermann Bahr's *Das Konzert* (The Concert) was given the title of *Staatsschauspielerin* (State Actress) by Göring.

His intention was to have the most magnificant German state theatre under his control. For the moment, however, the author Hanns Johst, who belonged to the circle around Goebbels, was in his way. In December 1933 Göring issued a temporary ban on the continued performance of Johst's drama about Luther, *Propheten* (The Prophets), which Jürgen Fehling was directing.

Goebbels took this as a personal insult, and brought Johst back into his own fold, appointing him President of the *Reichsschrifttumskammer*.

The General Intendant of the Prussian State Theatre (opera and playhouse) was Heinz Tietjen. As artistic director for the playhouse on Gendarmenmarkt, Göring chose the actor by whom he was so impressed and fascinated, 'Mephisto' Gründgens. Emmy, who was surprised by this choice, voiced doubts that Gründgens would make a good artistic director, but Göring believed that an artistic talent, extraordinary to the point of genius, could be used in any area of the arts and the theatre. 'Later on', Emmy Göring writes, 'I had to admit how right he had been. Gustaf Gründgens became an exemplary artistic director. His appointment to the position in Berlin was without doubt one of Göring's finest moves. At the time it was rumoured that I had recommended Gründgens. No one knew better than Gründgens that this was not true.'

In February 1934 the actor had played Fouché in the Napoleonic drama *The Hundred Days* written by Mussolini and Forzano and directed by Ulbrich. After the première, which was intended as a homage from Göring to Mussolini, Göring offered Gründgens the directorship, which however, the latter initially declined. He asked for time to consider, because he wanted to consult his friends, Erich Ziegel and Mirjam Horwitz, in Hamburg. In his biography of Gustaf Gründgens Heinrich Goertz quotes from the sworn statement which Erich Ziegel made in 1945: 'When Gründgens was given the assignment by Göring to take over the direction of the Berlin State Theatre, he consulted at length with me and my wife about the difficulties of this problem. As I know from this conversation, what finally decided him was the conviction that in this position – Göring had promised him a free hand – he could achieve much good and prevent much harm in the artistic, but above all in the human area. He then achieved this inner programme on all occasions, in many cases with passion, energy, and wisdom.' Goertz continues: 'Erich Ziegel should know. When the former patron of expressionist drama and husband of a Jewish woman was forced out of his position at Hamburg, Gründgens hired him for the State Theatre, without demanding, and this goes without saying, that he leave his wife. The actors Wolf Trutz, Paul Bildt, Paul Henckels, and Karl Ettlinger all had Jewish wives, and nothing happened to any of them.'

The negotiations between Göring and Gründgens took four weeks. Göring promised him a free hand in all respects. Goertz writes: 'Gründgens reported directly to Göring, could count on his support on difficult questions and always had free access to him. No one among the unprepared public had expected that the National Socialists would appoint a person who was so totally different from their concept of a German artist to become the director of the most prominent theatre. But it was Göring, who had his own feeling for theatrical effects, who was solely responsible for this appointment. From the roles he had played in films, Gründgens was tainted with the odium of being neurotic, distressed, morbid, and disreputable. Göring ignored all this, or more likely it was this aura which fascinated him. The world of the National Socialists and that of Gründgens stood in opposition to each other, and yet there were points of contact, of overlap.'

With the appointment of this Gründgens, his 'Mephisto', Göring naturally also wanted to create his own theatrical image, which stood out from Hitler's Wagnerism and his preference for Bayreuth.

National Socialism had intended to be a Weltanschauung, but it became above all a theatrical event, which manifested itself not only in the temples of the Muses, but also in celebrations, festivals, and processions, which became more and more pompous up to 1939 and were to complement the bread that the people could now earn again: *circenses* in Greater Germania.

That Göring preferred plays whereas Hitler reserved musical drama and operetta to himself, appears as a division of labour, but the real reason was quite different. Göring was a person who could still be moved to tears, and in those times it was the language of the classics that could achieve this. Wagner's music did not provoke any tears from Hitler, it transferred him into a state of euphoria.

German film became Goebbels' domain where he acted as he pleased, this mass media suiting his talent for propagandistic seduction. On 9 April Gründgens called on Goebbels at his palace on Wilhelmsplatz and reached an agreement with him to produce 'activist and representative' theatre. Like Goebbels, Gründgens stated that there was no art without objective, but this verbal kowtow before the minister who controlled the press had no practical importance. Gründgens now belonged to Göring's sphere of power and also to his court. The new artistic director, initially on a six months' probation period at his own request, began to collect the best of the German acting élite at the State Theatre.

At the beginning of the 1934–5 season he gave Emmy Sonnemann the role of Minna von Barnhelm in Lessing's Saxo-Prussian comedy, which he directed and in which he played Riccaut de la Marinière.

Göring's statement, 'I decide who is a Jew', which now became known and was to become proverbial, has a story attached to it. In October 1933, Theo Chroneiß, an SA leader who had Göring's ear, raised the suspicion that Erhard Milch was a half-Jew. It was discovered that Milch's father, who was long dead, had been Jewish. His mother was therefore induced to state that Erhard's birth had been the result of an infidelity with an Aryan. In this way Göring was able to keep his deputy for the build-up of the Luftwaffe, who at the time was seen to be the actual Minister of Aviation.

The rivalry between Göring and Milch, which began later, had nothing to do with Milch's descent. It arose from factual disagreements and matters of competence. At the end of March 1934, Hindenburg promoted Milch from colonel to major-general. He led the secret building programme of the Luftwaffe which, like the building of the autobahns, was to become one of the largest job-creation programmes. The infrastructure of a new branch of the armed services had to be created overnight. Deutsche Lufthansa acted as a cover for the construction of airfields and bases and was given aircraft that were designed for military employment. In the 1934/35 budget, more than one billion Marks were provided for the implementation of this programme. The British and French saw through this deception but their governments did nothing about it.

At the end of January 1934 a 10-year treaty of non-aggression was agreed between Germany and Poland. With this the eastern border had been relieved from pressure, but Göring also gained something by it. He was able to take hunting trips to Poland, to which he was invited by the authoritarian Pilsudski government. As *Reichsjägermeister* (Reich Master of the Hunt), for whom a new ministry was created in early 1934, he was drawn to the hunting preserves in eastern Poland where he hoped to find bears

His Reich Ministry of Aviation became the place of work for active and reserve officers who saw greater possibilities of promotion in the Luftwaffe but were also fascinated by flying. All officers who transferred in or were newly employed had to learn to fly if they were earmarked for senior positions.

At this time the foundations for an air intelligence service were also laid, which remained outside the flying units, in other words was given tactical independence. General Wever, the Luftwaffe's Chief of Staff had insisted on this.

In March 1934 Göring lost his position as Prussian Minister of the Interior. The ministry was integrated into the Reich Ministry of the Interior, in which Himmler was put in charge of the Prussian Gestapo which Göring had founded. With this, not only the Gestapo, but also the Prussian concentration camps fell into Himmler's hands. Göring appeared at the ceremony of the transfer of office in a light blue air force uniform. At his belt he wore a long Germanic sword, the 'aviator's sword'. The light blue uniform was reserved for the members of the German Air Sports Association. Flying personnel wore two aiguillettes, ground crews one.

From the Prussian state police, which was quartered in barracks, Göring formed a 'state group' which was responsible for personal protection. The mass of the police was then integrated into the new regiments of the Army or the Air Force.

At the same time the other Prussian ministries were also amalgamated with the appropriate Reich ministries, with the exception of the Ministry of Finance which remained under the control of the Minister President. The reason given for this exception was the far-reaching administrative duties of finance in Prussia, but with it Göring did not lose the source of his personal expenditure which the state had to pay for. Prussia now maintained only a rump government under its own law, consisting of the Minister President and the Minister of Finance.

Göring explained these measures which curtailed his power and had been decreed by Hitler with the words: 'It does not matter whether Prussia disappears from the map in the near future, if only the famous Prussianism and Prussian morality remain as a mighty expression of the spirit of the Reich. States may come and go, but the people remain.'

The ordinary police stayed Prussian for the time being; Himmler did not get his hands on them until 1936. Nor did Göring pass over to Himmler the Forschungsamt, from which he received his daily morning reading material. The more important matters, and this could cover much, were presented to him in a briefcase. The telephones of ambassadors, SA leaders, ministers, and above all of people suspected of being opposed to the new state, were all bugged by the Forschungsamt, including even General von Schleicher's telephone. The Forschungsamt used the most modern technology and the victims were unaware of the bugging. Göring passed the information to Hitler, and was able to feel like Harun al Rashid, who learned everything that went on in his empire. This omnipotence made him a powerful figure, even without the backing of the Gestapo.

But there was still Hindenburg. In April 1934, the Reichspräsident had to consult Professor Sauerbruch about a bladder complaint caused by old age. Those who were informed about the state of his health began to take his approaching death into their calculations. Once again the Reichswehr, now renamed Reichsheer (Reich Army) was given a key role. But it had become the object of the attentions of Reich Minister and Chief of Staff of the SA, Ernst Röhm, who was seeking to establish a militia-like Reich defence force in which his SA and the Army could be united. The concept of a militia had been developed at the Geneva disarmament conference before 1933.

If Hitler wanted to succeed Hindenburg as Head of State, he had to assure himself of the support of the Reichsheer while he was still Chancellor. Göring's Luftwaffe did not yet exist officially as a branch of the armed forces. Reich Armed Forces Minister Colonel General von Blomberg and his Chief of the Office of the Minister, General von Reichenau, were prepared to recognise Hitler as Head of State. The price they demanded for this was the promise that the Wehrmacht would remain the only armed force. With this, the conflict with SA Chief of Staff Röhm, an intimate friend of Hitler, was set in train. Röhm had developed the SA into a paramilitary formation led by regional commanders who were locally powerful and completely dependent upon him. The SA was still waiting for the 'second revolution', which was to be a 'socialist' one. At the same time the monarchists were attempting to influence Hindenburg so that on his death the monarchy could be re-established in a new form. The monarchists were not opposed to Hitler as Chancellor, but they wanted to prevent his becoming Head of State as well, because this would have made his dictatorship unassailable.

These various pretensions to power were to provide the cause for the decisive events which occurred in June 1934. And Göring, the man who was to play a key role in them, was fed by the Forschungsamt with a hodge-podge of rumour, half-truths, and misinformation.

The Prussian Prince August Wilhelm, brother of the Crown Prince, whom the monarchists did not consider to be qualified to become Head of State, was given a supporting part. He was mentioned for the position of *Reichsverweser* (Regent of the Reich) after Hindenburg's death, something which struck this friend of Göring's and Röhm's as utterly fantastic. He even discussed it with Röhm, and had received from him the sword of honour of the SA with the engraving 'Everything for Germany'.

At Berlin's Herrenclub in early June 1934, Werner von Alvensleben was talking about a new cabinet list, on which under a Regent Prince, August Wilhelm of Prussia, the names of Hitler as Chancellor, General von Schleicher as Vice-Chancellor, Röhm as Armed Forces Minister, and Gregor Strasser as Economics Minister were being touted. Göring's name was missing.

Von Papen had been urging Hindenburg to leave a political testament in addition to his personal will, in order to regulate his succession, and Hindenburg gave von Papen the task of drafting it.

On 11 May 1934, before leaving Berlin for his Neudeck estate, which he visited annually in the summer, Hindenburg wrote it out from von Papen's draft. His son Oskar was present as a witness. The testament consisted of two parts, an appeal to the German nation and a letter to Chancellor Hitler. The appeal, which consisted mainly of verbatim quotes from Hindenburg's memoirs which Mertz von Quirnheim had written down after the Great War, concluded: 'My Kanzler Adolf Hitler and his movement have taken a decisive step of historical importance towards the great objective of leading the German nation to inner unity above and beyond all differences of status and class. I leave my German nation in the firm hope, that what I longed for in 1919 and which in a slow process of maturing led to 30 January 1933, will ripen to a full fulfilment and culmination of our nation.' The testament was entrusted to von Papen.

The letter to Hitler was never published. After the Second World War a version became known which, it is alleged, contained the words 'It is ... my will that after my death Germany will again be given a monarchist form of government.' But the authenticity of this has never been verified.

In early June Hindenburg was again back in Neudeck.

At this time Göring's blockhouse hunting lodge in the Schorfheide, 'Carinhall', and the mausoleum for his deceased wife had been finished. The preserve in which both buildings had been constructed on the Große Döllnsee and the Rarangsee enclosed 210,000 acres of forest. At the beginning of the 18th century the huge stand of old oaks had been reduced; Prussia had needed money and the timber had been sold.

The name 'Schorfheide' comes from 'schürfen' (to scrape). Before the potato was introduced into Prussia acorns served as fodder for pigs. In the spring and summer the farmers drove their pigs into the oak forest, in the autumn the acorns were collected. The farmers 'scraped' them and fed them to the breeding sows during the winter in the hope of producing healthy litters.

In this enormous forest, which had been fenced in, Göring had his Carinhall which was to commemorate the beautiful and intelligent Swedish woman who had shared his life in difficult times. Here he intended to live a withdrawn life, but also to receive visitors from abroad. Hitler did not want a country estate near Berlin. His was on the Obersalzberg near Berchtesgaden.

Initially Göring's estate was his 'Waldhof', as he called it, built in the style of a Swedish summer house, with a large hall which reminded him of the hall in Rockelstad Castle where he had met Carin von Kantzow in 1920. Instead of a stuffed bear, which he had admired there, here were bearskins on the floor. On one wall was a large open fireplace. A huge chair with Göring's coat of arms – an armoured fist with an oak wreath – stood by the window. Giant candles rose to the ceiling from the wooden farm table. Hunting trophies hung from the walls. A large tiled stove with bench completed the furnishings of the living hall. Attached to it was a small office with a painting by Rubens and a portrait, framed in edelweiss, of Carin, against a background of the Bavarian Alps. The house became the centre-piece of a huge estate on which construction continued, even during the war.

The house stood in the northern part of the Schorfheide on the south bank of the elongated Große Döllnsee. The subterranean mausoleum was on the small Rarangsee nearby. (Much later the Chairman of the State Council of the German Democratic Republic had a large, closely guarded preserve with guest houses on the northern bank of the Große Döllnsee.) The estate was reached after a 70-kilo-metre drive from Berlin via Wandlitz to Groß-Schönebeck, leading towards Prenzlau. A newly constructed side road branched off from this road. North of Groß-Schönebeck the main road had been blocked. After passing a check-point, Göring's guests were permitted to drive into the preserve and reached the estate after a drive of twelve kilometres.

In 1936 the preserve was converted to the 'Schorfheide Foundation', which embraced eight forestry districts comprising more than 200,000 acres. The most picturesque part lay to the east of the Werbellinsee and the Werbellin canal, and had been opened to hikers by the forestry administration, whereas to the west of the lake and the canal there was a strict injunction to use only public roads. The hiker's guide book of 1940, *1,000 Trails around Berlin*, states: 'Since the days of the Askanier (noble family which held land in Brandenburg from the early 12th century), the preferred hunting-ground of the Brandenburg princes, the Schorfheide is still very rich in game today. *Reichsforstmeister* Göring has had a large forest area fenced in south-west of the Werbellinsee and stocked with bison. In the display area (game reserves 11 and 12) one can view the animals (open in summer 10 a.m. to 6 p.m.; winter 1 p.m. to 4 p.m., entry fee 20 Pfennige). In an adjoining preserve elk are being kept, and in other areas of the Schorfheide the forestry administration is attempting to acclimatise wild sheep.'

Carinhall stood on the central point of the south bank of the Große Döllnsee. Just south of the house was the north bank of the Rarangsee, so that the estate was enclosed by two lakes. The mausoleum was on the opposite bank of the Rarangsee, and Göring could reach it by boat.

'This Germanic house,' writes Martin Henry Sommerfeldt in the epilogue of his 1934 book on Carin Göring, which Countess Fanny von Wilamowitz-Moel-lendorf published, 'above which spreads a reed roof in benediction, whose walls of heavy logs shut out all the rigours and unrest of frantic life, and whose bright rooms are filled by the pure Nordic spirit in every line and every piece, this "Carinhall" breaths the living presence of Carin Göring.'

For the inauguration of Carinhall on 10 June 1934, Göring had invited 40 guests whom he welcomed on the south side of the Schorfheide in order to show them the fauna and forestry. He also wanted to show them the bison he had had released, but the attempt to get a bull to mate with a cow failed, as the British Ambassador Sir Eric Phipps wrote to his Foreign Secretary in London.

Göring drove off in a racing car ahead of his guests, so as to be able to greet them again at his Waldhof in a new set of clothes. Over a white flannel shirt he wore a green leather jacket with white trousers and tennis shoes. In his belt was a long hunting-knife. This unusual get-up, based on a Swedish pattern, had been designed for him by Carin. For a walking-stick he carried a 'long object like a harpoon', as the Ambassador reported with amusement. He leaned on it because his leg wound from the Feldherrnhalle was still causing him pain. He introduced Emmy Sonnemann as his private secretary. The guests were shown the mausoleum, whose walls were 1.8 metres thick. The Ambassador called it 'the most artistic building' that he had ever seen.

In mid June Hitler visited Mussolini in Venice. After his return, the entombment of Carin Göring in the Schorfheide took place. The pewter coffin arrived in a railway car via ferry from Trelleborg to Sassnitz, and then via Eberswalde through Mecklenburg and Uckermark. The towns along the way were beflagged in mourning and there were women and children standing at all the stations.

The return of the deceased recalled the solemnities that had attended the return of the deceased Queen Louise to Berlin in 1810. These had been copied, including the people standing on the sidelines, the funeral music and the final ceremony, which Hitler attended together with the von Focks and von Rosens, and Thomas von Kantzow, Göring's step-son. Emmy Sonnemann was present as well and from then on took charge of Thomas von Kantzow who immediately showed her respect. Himmler also attended the ceremony, although he arrived late. On the drive through the Schorfheide, so he claimed, a bullet had shattered his windscreen, but it could also have been a stone. He had not heard any shot. Hitler immediately ordered the disbandment of Göring's SA guard which was replaced by state police. Before this the coffin had been lowered into the tomb. Hunting-horns and trumpets were sounded. Göring and Hitler descended the steps and spent time beside the coffin. All this took place on 19 June 1934.

Two days previously, Vice-Chancellor von Papen had given a speech at Marburg University which his colleague, the lawyer Dr Edgar Jung, had written. In this speech he lamented the Byzantism which was spreading out of control, denied the monopoly on Nationalism the NSDAP claimed for itself, described the attacks on the churches as a serious mistake, and warned of locking Germany into a ghetto and separating it from Europe. He spoke of a new class war against intellect, of the muzzling of the press, of terror. He decried the 'constant revolution from below' and spoke of 'the German people's finely developed sense of violence and injustice'. 'What is dangerous is the reaction against force. As an old soldier I know that strict discipline must be complemented by certain freedoms. The application of military discipline to the whole of a nation's life must therefore be kept within certain limits that do not contradict human nature.'

The author of the speech, Dr Jung, was arrested immediately, and its dissemination by the Vice-Chancellor was banned by Goebbels. Hitler sent Funk, the State Secretary in the Propaganda Ministry, to Hindenburg in East Prussia to inform him about the conflict between the Chancellor and his Vice-Chancellor. Hindenburg immediately dropped von Papen, saying, 'If he has no discipline, then he will just have to suffer the consequences of this.'

The courageous speech by von Papen, which he had made before Catholics as a Catholic, was seen by Göring in connection with the reports he received from the Forschungsamt. The day after the funeral in the Schorfheide he spoke to the Prussian State Council of a certain unrest, of rumours of a 'second revolution'. 'The first revolution was begun by the Führer and concluded by the Führer. If the Führer wants a second revolution he will always find us ready for this. If he does not wish it, we are ready to proceed against anybody who attempts to oppose the will of the Führer.'

He had only a few days remaining on which he could boast that he had never spilled blood, except as a soldier during the Great War.

17

The Bloodbath

In the battle for power which was decided in Hitler's favour by the blood-bath of 30 June 1934, Göring had placed himself at the side of his Führer very early on. He had personal reasons for doing so. Among the SA leadership in Berlin, as he learned through his Forschungsamt, he was known as 'the fat pig', who 'had to be done away with'. To his fear for his life and position was added statecraft, as he had been brought up to understand it. Since the leadership of the Reichswehr openly took sides with Hitler, who had promised that it would remain the only 'armed force in the nation' – and confirmed this in the *Professional Conduct of the German Soldier* issued on 4 June 1934 – the chances were very high that an armed uprising by the SA would be defeated. A pact between the 'Reactionaries' and the socialist inclined SA leadership was to be broken up even before Hindenburg's demise.

When Göring returned from the Schorfheide, a list of men who were to be liquidated or arrested was already lying in his State Secretary Körner's safe. On 10 June the *Völkische Beobachter* had published an order by Chief of Staff Röhm, which concluded: 'If the enemies of the SA entertain the hope that the SA will not, or only in part return under arms after its holidays, we shall briefly let them enjoy this hope. They will be given the appropriate answer at the time and in the form deemed necessary. The SA is and will remain the fate of Germany.' The SA's vacation ended on 30 June.On 24 June Colonel General von Fritsch ordered 'preparations for defence as discreetly as possible' because of an imminent attack by the SA. The relative numerical strength of Reichswehr to SA was 1:6. Röhm's reaction to the Army's defensive preparations, which had become known to the SA leaders – some of them had alerted their units – was the convening of a leadership conference at Bad Wiessee where he was on holiday.

Although Hitler was away on trips in western Germany during these last days of June, Göring kept him up to date on the latest Forschungsamt telephone taps. He also met Göring briefly at the wedding of the Berlin SA leader Max Ernst, who had been Göring's radical opponent in the capital since the seizure of power, and agreed that Hitler would strike in Bavaria and Göring in Berlin and Prussia. Since the Reichswehr had been ordered merely to 'stand at arms ready', the only forces available for the action planned were the SS and the police. Himmler and Heydrich were in Berlin. Göring's state police group which, together with the SS, had taken over his personal protection, was earmarked to proceed against the alleged SA conspirators.

Röhm had no intention of attempting an SA Putsch on 30 June 1934.

On the morning of the 29th, a declaration of loyalty to Hitler by Armed Forces Minister von Blomberg appeared in the *Völkische Beobachter*, beginning with the words: 'The role of the Wehrmacht is unequivocal and clear. It serves the state, which it affirms from an innermost conviction, and it stands by this leadership, which gave it back its most distinguished right to be not only the sole bearer of arms, but to be recognised by the people and the state as the bearer of their unlimited confidence.' Next day, 30 June, Hitler struck in Bavaria, Göring in Berlin and, in addition, Himmler and Heydrich had 'liquidations' carried out.

In Berlin police and SS closed off the governmental district. Göring directed the action from his official villa, after having paid a call on the Berlin SA headquarters building in Wilhelmstraße with his police escort and ordered arrests there. Many weapons were discovered. On this day the villa was the seat of an executive council under Göring and simultaneously the 'refuge' for endangered persons of various political shades.

Erhard Milch, who had been ordered to the villa for deployment with Berlin formations of the still secret Luftwaffe, reports on the meeting of the executive council, which consisted of Göring, Himmler and (General) von Reichenau, with (State Secretary) Körner as observer and keeper of the minutes; they were assembled in a small room. When he came in Himmler was reading aloud a list of names. According to Milch, as each name was read out Göring and von Reichenau either nodded or shook their heads. If there was agreement, Himmler passed the name to Körner with the words: 'report instructions carried out'.

Milch speaks of a 'sinister conclave' to which he became an eye-witness. Since so many senior people of the Reich were gathered here, he knew that the defence of the Reich against insurgents was not being played out as an exercise or a war-game, but as an actual fact.

The seeming unreality of the day is expressed in many reports, but in fact it was all too real. The executions took place in the police barracks at Lichterfelde, where as a cadet Göring had been educated to become a Prussian officer. SA *Gruppenführer* (Group Leader, equivalent rank to Colonel in the Army) Ernst, whose wedding Göring and Hitler had attended shortly before, was among those shot there. At the executions in Munich, the command to fire was: 'The Führer wills it, fire!'

In addition to these executions there were outright murders, which were committed by Himmler and Heydrich's SS.

On the 'Reich list of undesirable persons', who were now exterminated like weeds, the names of the two Reichswehr Generals von Bredow and von Schleicher were included. In his biography of von Schleicher which Friedrich-Karl von Plehwe wrote in 1983, he says: 'Naturally Hitler had good reasons for entertaining a lust for revenge against his old opponent Schleicher. But it is quite certain that Göring also had a personal interest in paying off an old score. There is also the version that it was Himmler who gave the order to shoot Schleicher and that it was his people who did the deed. For this the fact may speak that during the early afternoon of 30 June another armed group appeared in Schleicher's house to arrest the General, but found him already dead. Since after his capture Göring often stated that he had only wanted to have Schleicher "arrested", it could be true that the killer gang came from Himmler and the second group from Göring.' However this is contradicted by Erhard Milch's eye-witness report from the villa. The second group consisted of Gestapo men as was conclusively proven. Von Schleicher's wife was also slain.

When Hitler returned to Berlin from Munich on the evening of the bloodbath, he was welcomed at Tempelhof airport by Göring and many high functionaries, and in addition to an SS formation, by two companies of the future Luftwaffe, who had formed up in the uniform of the German Air Sports Association with aiguillettes on both shoulders. They presented arms. Hitler asked Göring what men these were and received the answer that this was the new Luftwaffe. Milch had entrusted the two companies with the security of the airport.

The murders were retroactively sanctioned and justified by a Reich law as having been 'legal'. The official death list contains 83 names, but it is certainly not complete. Among those shot were Gregor Strasser, Edgar Jung, Ministerial Councillor Klausner and others who had nothing whatever to do with Röhm and the SA. While in prison at Nuremberg awaiting trial, Göring dictated his version of the affair to Werner Bross:

'In order to prevent further mistakes, which had unfortunately occurred in northern Germany in connection with the suppression of the revolt – albeit not to such a great extent as in southern Germany – I obtained the order to stop from Hitler on the Sunday of 1 July following the putsch. With this I wanted to prevent subordinate formations continuing to commit excesses and thereby getting out of hand. Those responsible for the excesses remained unpunished based on the Führer's decree concerning the national state of emergency during the Röhm putsch.'

Göring, who had been lord of life and death, had had some destroyed and others saved. The latter included Vice-Chancellor von Papen and Prince August Wilhelm, whom he had called to Berlin from Cologne by telephone during the night of 30 June in order to put him under his personal protection in the ministerial villa. 'One does not shoot a Hohenzollern,' Göring is alleged to have remarked.

On Monday, 2 July, he received a telegram of thanks from Hindenburg on the occasion of 'the successfully conducted action against the traitors' as the Reichspräsident described the blood-bath.

Was Göring proud of his action, by which a putsch, which was no Putsch, had been suppressed in northern Germany? In July, he sought distraction from thoughts of the massacre in which he had played a leading role, by preoccupying himself with his Luftwaffe. He approved a programme which foresaw the production of 4,021 aircraft by September 1935. These were to consist of 822 bombers of the types Ju 52, Do 11 and 13, as well as fighter aircraft and trainers. Hitler, however, was not satisfied with this number. After the Austrian Chancellor Dollfuß had been murdered in Vienna by Austrian SS men during an attempted putsch on 25 July, Hitler – who was attending the Wagner Festival at Bayreuth – called Göring, Milch and General Wever, Chief of Staff of the clandestine Luftwaffe, to the festival town. Mussolini had deployed troops in the Brenner Pass. Hitler demanded an increase in the Luftwaffe's aircraft construction programme because he was worried that the Western Powers might intervene to prevent re-armament. Milch spoke out against this demand, and was reproached by Göring for daring to contradict Hitler. Milch was against a 'propaganda air force', such as Göring envisaged, as a means of deterrence.

To demonstrate abroad that he had nothing to do with the putsch in Vienna, on 26 July Hitler appointed Franz von Papen, who had lost his post as Vice-Chancellor, to be special ambassador in Vienna. Hindenburg signed the document of appointment on 28 July .

On 1 August Hitler came to the deathbed of the Reichspräsident in Gut Neudeck. The semi-conscious Hindenburg is alleged to have addressed him as 'Your Majesty'. Afterwards Hitler said that the dying Field Marshal had reported his absence from duty like a soldier.

On this day a law was passed concerning 'the abolishment of the position of Reichspräsident', and it was published on 2 August. That morning Hindenburg had died. As 'Führer and Chancellor' Hitler was now Head of State and Head of the Government in one.

In the afternoon of 2 August 1934 the soldiers were sworn-in on their parade grounds. The new oath had been written by General von Reichenau and approved by Field Marshal von Blomberg. In the Reich Ministry of Aviation Göring recited it aloud to his colleagues of the nascent Luftwaffe. He was moved, close to tears, when he drew his pilot's sword from its sheath and swore on this sword: 'By God above I swear this holy oath, that I will render unconditional obedience to the Führer of the German Reich and people, and Supreme Commander of the Wehrmacht, Adolf Hitler, and be prepared as a brave soldier to risk my life for this oath at any time.'

No one refused to swear the oath, whose wording nevertheless took the officers and soldiers of the Wehrmacht by surprise. It was only now that Hitler had reached his goal. The Wehrmacht stood under his personal command. He was finally dictator. The seizure of power which had begun on 30 January 1933 was completed on 2 August 1934. On 19 August he had his rule confirmed in a plebiscite: 90 per cent of the electorate voted 'Yes'.

In his Berghof near Berchtesgaden on 22 August, in Göring's presence, the dictator approved an arms budget of 10.5 billion marks over the next four years.

During these summer months, Gustaf Gründgens and Emmy Sonnemann played guest roles in Hermann Bahr's comedy *The Concert* at the Munich Studio Theatre. Towards the end of August Göring came to fetch the actress in his Mercedes, to take her to the Obersalzberg; they intended to hike to Göring's lodge, 2,000 metres up. Near Rosenheim, the city of his birth, Göring's Mercedes collided with another car at high speed during an attempt to pass. The Mercedes lost a wheel, the steering wheel broke several of his ribs, and Emmy Sonnemann suffered a head injury.

At the end of August Göring told Milch that he had asked Hitler to make Milch the new Minister of Aviation if anything were to happen to him. In the Reich Göring was now really the second man after Hitler, who had taken final leave of the deceased Hindenburg on 8 August at the Tannenberg monument with the words: 'Dead Commander, enter now into Valhalla!' But Hindenburg had died a Christian and his family and friends rejected this consignment to Valhalla.

Like Hitler, Göring feared assassination. In December Hitler named him as his successor if he were to be murdered. Göring had already taken care of the succession in his office with the nomination of Milch at the end of August.

At the Prussian State Theatre in Berlin the new season began with *Minna von Barnhelm*, in which Emmy took the lead role. Soon afterwards a new production of *King Lear* opened in which Gründgens presented his new ensemble of famous names. Göring sat in the Kaiser's box and applauded enthusiastically. The *Völkische Beobachter* described the première as being a 'homage to the attending Minister President'. King Lear was played by Werner Krauß.

> 'Let the great gods,
>> That keep this dreadful pother o'er our heads,
> Find out their enemies now. Tremble, thou wretch,
>> That hast within thee undivulged crimes,
> Unwhipp'd of justice: hide thee, thou bloody hand;
>> Thou perjur'd, and thou simular of virtue
> That art incestuous: caitiff, to pieces shake,
>> That under covert and convenient seeming

Hast practis'd on man's life: close pent-up guilts,
Rive your concealing continents, and cry
These dreadful summoners grace. – I am a man
More sinn'd against than sinning.'

This moved Göring, but in which sense?

Now Ritter von Epenstein, Göring's godfather, who had been like a father to him, died at Mauterndorf Castle in Austria.

18
The Wedding Feast

The build-up of the new German air force had not gone unnoticed abroad, but the deception had been so perfect that the most varied speculations as to its numerical strength were being made. Early in 1935, in order to get Hitler and Göring to disclose the true strength, Great Britain and France proposed an air treaty with the Reich.

In January Erhard Milch laid the cornerstone for the new Reich Ministry of Aviation in Leipziger Straße, and the building was completed the following year. It stood on the site of the old Royal Prussian War Ministry which had been torn down.

In mid February Hitler agreed to the suggestion of the two Western Powers. Simultaneously he set 1 March as the day for the unmasking of the Reichsluftwaffe as an independent arm of the Wehrmacht. Göring drove to Berlin from the Obersalzberg, but interrupted his journey in Schleißheim near Munich, where the former branch of the German commercial pilot school had become the first, still secret, fighter pilot school.

'In February 1935 there was much excitement,' writes Adolf Galland in his book *The First and the Last*. 'Göring had announced his visit for an inspection. Everything worked perfectly. Afterwards he addressed us in Mittenheim Castle. He gave us a convincing overview of the development of German aviation during the last two years. Astonishing things had been achieved in this short time. Starting from nothing, the generously conceived – even if still veiled – foundation of the Luftwaffe had been created. On it an imposing edifice was soon to arise. Göring intimated that the time of secrecy would soon be over. He had also brought along a model of the uniform we would soon be wearing. *Rittmeister* (Captain) Bolle acted as a sort of military mannequin. For the first time in the history of the German armed forces a tie and collar were to be worn with the uniform. The effect was sensational. And in the Army, we flyers immediately had our nicknames: "tie soldiers".'

Back in Berlin, Göring, together with Milch, subsequently informed the *Reichs-* and *Gauleiter* of the Party about impending developments.

On a February morning, he surprised Emmy Sonnemann with the suggestion: 'Would you like to marry me at Easter? The Führer will be our best man.' Emmy Sonnemann read the proposal on a note he had handed her. She replied: 'Yes, I would.' Göring had set the wedding date, 7 April, after the planned unveiling of the Luftwaffe. But because 7 April was the anniversary of the death of the last

Kaiserin, the wedding was postponed so that Prince August Wilhelm would be able to attend.

The 'unveiling' of the Luftwaffe was to be carried out by Göring 'bit by bit'. The number of aircraft had still to remain secret. 'On 10 March 1935,' writes Paul Deichmann, who at the time was an official in the *Luftkommandoamt* (Air Command Office) of the Reich Ministry of Aviation, the secret General Staff of the Luftwaffe, under General Wever, 'Hermann Göring let the cat out of the bag, and informed the English journalist Ward Price that Germany now had an air force. To the Englishman's question as to how strong this air force was, Göring replied that he could not disclose exact numbers, but since Germany's location in central Europe made it more vulnerable to attacks from the air than any other nation, he had made the Luftwaffe so strong that it could take on any other European air force. This was a wild exaggeration. Fully equipped and ready for combat, there were at the time three and a half fighter groups, two bomber groups, and five reconnaissance squadrons. Each group had thirty, each squadron nine aircraft. In total in 1935 there were 251 fighters, 822 bombers, 51 dive-bombers, and 590 reconnaissance aircraft. In case of mobilisation, the number of formations could probably be slightly more than doubled. The aircraft types, which had mostly been developed already during the time of the Reichswehr, did however by and large correspond to the standards of foreign air forces as far as airframes were concerned, with the exception of the Ju 52, which made up half of the bomber force and could not even be classed as an auxiliary bomber, because any fighter could shoot it down. Our biggest weaknesses were the aircraft engines. We did not have any engines that could produce more than 600hp at cruising speed or 750hp at short-term emergency speed. And we did not have any engine with a supercharger, so that at high altitudes performance fell off markedly. In contrast to this, at this time the French and the British had engines with up to 1,000 hp, some of them with superchargers.

'As far as numbers were concerned, the French air force and the Royal Air Force were also still superior to us at this time. Until 1936 the Luftwaffe was only a risk factor for a single antagonist. It would not have been able to withstand a coalition by the League of Nations or an attack by the 'small Entente' (France, Poland, Czechoslovakia, Roumania).

'Göring's boastful interview was a feeler put out with Hitler's agreement. How would the signatory powers react to this openly admitted breach of the Versailles Treaty? They did not react at all, and six days later, on Saturday 16 March 1935, the Reich government announced the re-introduction of conscription and the increase of the army to 36 divisions, in other words to a peace-time strength of 500,000 men.'

On 28 March at Döberitz, the newly appointed General of the Air Force Hermann Göring, with Milch, now promoted to Lieutenant-General, at his side, was able to put on a fly-past for Hitler of his new Fighter Wing Richthofen, which was now given the number 2, number 1 being reserved for the original Wing from the Great War. The aircraft were Heinkel He 51 biplanes.

This was the first formation of the new Luftwaffe in the Berlin area. Göring had kept his word. He had got 'his' Fighter Wing and it was the first Luftwaffe formation to appear in public.

As Commander-in-Chief of the Luftwaffe, Göring was contemplating having Hitler appoint him 'Air Marshal' after the British fashion, but Hitler refused. It was not a German term and, furthermore, Göring could not hold office as a 'Marshal' while the C-in-Cs of the Army and the Kriegsmarine were only a General and an Admiral. He had been made their equal in rank and his promotion to Colonel General was soon to come through, as was that of Freiherr von Fritsch, Commander-in-Chief of the Army.

Emmy Sonnemann now had to bid farewell to the stage. The wedding was set for 10 April. She was given a send-off by Gustaf Gründgens and her colleagues after the final curtain had fallen on *Minna von Barnhelm*. 'On the day before the *Polterabend*,' (German custom of having a party on the eve of a wedding at which glass and crockery are smashed to ensure good luck for the happy couple) Emmy Göring writes, 'we could see the reaction the announcement of the intended wedding had already produced. The presents already received filled two large rooms. From all countries, from official as well as private sources, splendid treasures had come. To give only a few examples: from the Tsar (*sic*) of Bulgaria the highest Bulgarian decoration for Hermann, for me a wonderful sapphire bracelet; from the city of Hamburg a silver sailing-boat, just like the one I had often admired in the town hall as a child during school outings. IG Farben sent several marvellous examples from their first production of synthetic precious stones. And countless people sent piles of various handicrafts. The Polterabend began with a performance by the State Opera of Richard Strauss' *Die ägyptische Helena*, for invited guests only. Afterwards there was a tattoo in our honour on the square in front of the Opera which the Luftwaffe presented. That night for the first time, an armed soldier sat outside my bedroom. He was sleeping so peacefully that I was afraid of waking him up when I went into my room. Early next morning Hermann came to Bendlerstraße to collect me. Together we drove to the Chancellery, where Hitler greeted me with a bouquet of orchids. On the way to city hall, he and we were cheered by a large crowd of people.'

For actress Emmy Sonnemann this 'royal' wedding was both a farewell and a fairy-tale in which she played the leading role. Not since the time of the Hohenzollerns, had Berliners seen a wedding attended by such pomp, and they were astonished. It was *Kaiserwetter* (lit. emperor's weather, German term for glorious sunshine such as a Kaiser is entitled to expect) and the Prussian sky shone down on a new upper class that was to govern the country. Hitler, now Head of State, shy in his brown Party uniform, stayed in the background. The beaming 42-year-old General Göring and the actress from Hamburg, who was the same age, were the focal-point for the homage which the crowds expressed spontaneously. The Berliners once again had a prince, a king. During the drive to the cathedral in the Lustgarten, a squadron of the Richthofen Wing flew over the cavalcade of cars. One of the pilots was Mölders.

The marriage ceremony was performed by Reich Bishop Müller, a former military district chaplain whom the 'German Christians' had had appointed to this new office. He gave the bride and groom a quotation from the Bible which they had both received at their confirmation: 'Be loyal unto death and I will give you the crown of life.' Viorica Ursuleac and Heinrich Schlusnus sang. The organ thundered. As the pair came out on to the steps of the cathedral, a pair of storks flew over the Lustgarten which caused the cheers of the crowd to redouble.

In the Kaiserhof the wedding table had been set for 320 guests. At it sat Hitler, but also Göring's servant Kropp, the relatives of the bride and groom, princes and princesses, field marshals and young officers from the Luftwaffe. Hitler's partner was Countess Rosen from Rockelstad; Prince Wied was with Magda Goebbels; Prussian Minister of Finance Popitz escorted the wife of Church Minister Kerrl; State Councillor Thyssen the wife of Rudolf Hess; Goebbels the wife of Minister of Education Rust; Himmler the wife of Hamburg's Lord Mayor Krogman. Chief Forester von Keudell was with Winifred Wagner; Heydrich with the wife of Robert Ley; Major General Wever with Frau Kesselring; Streicher with Frau Bouhler; Schacht with Frau Frick, Prince Philip of Hesse and Countess Fanny von Wilamowitz-Moellendorf; General Freiherr von Fritsch and Frau Sahm, wife of Berlin's Lord Mayor who had conducted the civil ceremony. Lieutenant-Colonel Student sat next to the actress Elsa Wagner; Admiral Raeder next to the wife of Ambassador von Dirksen; Gründgens was with Frau Tengelmann; Werner Krauß with the wife of Bruno Loerzer.

'Our relatives, friends, and closest colleagues, as well as all those who were dear to us had been invited,' Emmy Göring writes. Both witnesses, Hitler and Church Minister Kerrl, gave the first speeches. Hitler had to admit that he was a poor after-dinner speaker. Blomberg and Krogmann spoke next, and last of all Göring's Swedish brother-in-law, Count Erik von Rosen. During dinner Hitler told Emmy that she was now the 'first lady of the German Reich', and that meant that she had to take on responsibilities.

'The first impression I gained of my dignity,' she writes, 'was that for broad segments of the population I had become the "authority" on whom one could unload one's problems and worries. Besides the voluminous "fan mail" I received requests that frequently caused me problems with many a department of the Reich government, yes, which even led to serious conflicts. As much as we tried to keep our Carinhall free of all too many invasions by guests, we were nevertheless obliged to play host for the Reich and receive Hitler's most personal guests here as well, and not only in the official apartments at Leipziger Platz.'

Prince August Wilhelm was at table next to Frau Thyssen, but he had been so placed that he could not be seen by Hitler, who had become Hindenburg's successor in place of the Hohenzollern Prince. Far removed from Hitler sat 1st Lieutenant von Below, who was soon to become Hitler's adjutant to the Luftwaffe.

The wedding table did not demonstrate a mutual future fate of the people who seemed to belong together here. It was like a Shakespearian tragedy, which begins with a feast at the court of some king and ends in blood. For the moment it was an amalgamation of the most diverse elements that would soon fall apart again.

From the Kaiserhof the Görings drove to Carinhall with only a few friends. The 'groom went to visit Carin's tomb in the mausoleum and stayed there for one hour. This was not only a gesture towards the Swedish relatives who had come, among them his step-son Thomas von Kantzow. Göring could not forget Carin, but he also loved his second wife, with whom he now set off via Wiesbaden for a honeymoon in Dubrovnik in Yugoslavia.

He was to take many more trips abroad, because he was now Hitler's most suitable ambassador, and his wife knew how to play her part. To foreigners Hitler remained an enigma, but Göring gave the impression that one could get along with him. Chief interpreter Schmidt of the Foreign Ministry, who was to accompany Göring on these trips, discovered that he liked to play the simple country boy and knew how to conceal the fact that he was a very skilful diplomat.

While the Görings were away on their honeymoon, an important success in foreign relations was maturing: the Anglo–German Naval Treaty of 1935 whereby it was agreed that Germany could build up her naval strength to 35 per cent of that of the Royal Navy (excluding submarines). The treaty was signed in June by special ambassador von Ribbentrop in London.

Göring was taking care of the Balkans, but also of Italy and above all Poland. He frequently went there to hunt and invited Polish ministers and the ambassador in Berlin to go hunting in Rominten (East Prussia) and in the Schorfheide.

After his honeymoon, Göring visited the capital cities of Belgrade, Sofia, and Budapest in May 1935. The second most powerful man of the German Reich was received like a head of state who could conduct important political negotiations.

During his absence Goebbels, the man among Hitler's paladins who hated the Jews, received his chance. He wanted to separate German Jews from the 'Aryans' once and for all. This led to the passing of the Nuremberg Racial Laws by the Reichstag which had been convened in that city on the occasion of the 'Party Rally of Profession', as the annual September meeting had been designated this time. As President of the Reichstag, Göring was required to read out the wording of these laws which were unique in German history. As the newsreels show, he undertook the task with the routine of a registrar who, in this instance however, was not joining together, but sundering 'for all time to come'. The words from the text of the law, in which Jews were prohibited from marrying anyone of German blood, or having sexual relations with them, came from the mouth of a man who claimed, that he himself would decide who was or was not Jewish, and whose mother had lived with a Jew for fifteen years in a condition which was now being called 'racial disgrace'. From now on only 'true' Germans could be 'citizens of the Reich' and German Jews were deprived of their citizenship. Göring's promises to Jewish friends and acquaintances that he would intervene with Hitler against anti-Semitism, had turned out to be just so much hot air.

In October Mussolini began his war against Abyssinia. The British permitted his troop transports to pass through the Suez Canal which they controlled. The ineffective sanctions imposed by the League of Nations resulted only in pushing the Italian dictator closer to Hitler.

The new Luftwaffe now had a fighting strength of 1,800 aircraft, but in view of the seriousness of the external political situation, Göring demanded a further increase in capacity.

On 1 November 1935 he inaugurated the Air War Academy in Berlin-Gatow. The Luftwaffe Chief of Staff, General Wever, made a trend-setting speech in which he paid tribute to the fighter pilots of the Great War – he mentioned Manfred von Richthofen – but described the bomber fleet as the decisive factor in a future air war: 'Only that nation with strong bomber fleets at its disposal can expect decisive actions by its air force.' Wever demanded long-range four-engined bombers, whose prototypes were the Dornier Do 19 and the Junkers Ju 89, which had begun test flights in 1936.

Wever had no time for Göring's fighter pilot romanticism of the open cockpit. He was an adherent of the concepts of the Italian military theoretician General Douhet, as were his opposite numbers in France, Italy, Britain and the USA. Göring saw the air force as a weapon of deterrence, which was to be employed in defence after an attack by an enemy. 'Without my express order,' Göring wrote in the contribution by the Luftwaffe to an overall strategic study of the Wehrmacht of 18 November 1935, 'the Reich frontier may therefore neither be crossed nor flown over. An advance into the demilitarised zone, or flying over it, will only be permitted when an enemy border violation with an evident hostile intent has preceded it.'

Thus ended the year 1935, which saw Göring at the zenith of his power. In the autumn, France and Czechoslovakia had concluded a military alliance with the Soviet Union. This was a breach of the Locarno Pact and Hitler believed that he was no longer bound by it. He was thinking in terms of a military occupation of the demilitarised Rhineland.

19

Even More Power

When Göring's former squadron comrade Ernst Udet was appointed to the position of Inspector of Fighter and Dive-Bomber Aircraft on 1 January 1936, the Luftwaffe was given an aircraft for the conduct of a future air war in the realm of tactics, not strategy. The Ju 87, built by Junkers at his satellite plant in Sweden after an American aircraft design called 'Helldiver', was a weapon of support for the army, above all for the new Panzer forces which were being developed by Guderian and his colleagues at the same time as the Stuka. Udet, who had been a consultant to the Ministry of Aviation since 1934, had impressed Göring very much with the Stuka. The idea of a strategic bomber fleet, such as General Wever was after, displeased Göring. When in 1935 he had inspected a model of the fuselage of the Ju 89 – a four-engined long-range bomber – at the Junkers plant in Dessau, he had asked the Chief of the Technical Office, Colonel Wimmers, what the hell it was for. The new aircraft was ten times as large and heavy as the biplane Göring had flown in the Great War.

General Wever too, saw the Stuka as an important weapon for the Luftwaffe, but one that would obviate the need for the bomber fleet to intervene in ground fighting.

'A man stepped forward', writes Paul Deichmann, 'who was to have a decisive influence on the development of the Luftwaffe. With 62 kills, Ernst Udet had been the most successful fighter pilot of the Great War after Manfred von Richthofen (80 kills). He detested Douhet's theory. For him air fighting was a chivalrous battle, man against man, fighter against fighter. While bombers were probably necessary, the thought that a future air force should operate in close formation like the Frederickian Guard, was just not his cup of tea.'

For the time being, such rivalries remained unimportant. Hitler decided to occupy the demilitarised zone of the Rhineland, and the risk was taken on 7 March 1936. This came as a complete surprise to the leadership of the Luftwaffe, as it did to the rest of the Wehrmacht which was still in the process of being built.

Hitler used the ratification of the Franco–Soviet pact as his justification. The coup succeeded. David Irving writes about the role of the Luftwaffe: 'Milch found a simple solution. Since only one fighter group could be spared, this was distributed on airfields in Cologne and Düsseldorf. One Stuka group was also transferred that day to the Rhineland and to airfields at Frankfurt and

Mannheim. The fighters each had 1,000 rounds on board, but the machine-guns had not yet been aligned. With this small ensemble, the Luftwaffe put on a huge show.'

Göring's weapon of deterrence had fulfilled its task. Deterrence also means being able to bluff, and Göring had demonstrated this here. After the coup, in order to deceive the world about the strength of the Luftwaffe, he had pilot schools and administrative offices given military-tactical numbers, so that they might be taken for squadrons, groups, or wings.

'Foreign military attachés were willingly taken through air bases and aircraft factories,' Paul Deichmann writes. 'What was shown them was really quite impressive. But everywhere there was a hall into which they were not allowed to enter, because allegedly that was where the newest still secret developments were being kept. Sometimes this was true, but sometimes the halls were just empty. With prototypes, which were equipped with specially tuned engines that were not available in series, world records were flown. By forged photographs the impression was created that these aircraft were already in series production and had been issued to the troops.

'These manœuvres of deception only had a base in reality in so far as during this period of risk, aircraft models were maturing within the German aircraft industry that were soon to make our air force the most modern in the world. When the first prototypes of this new generation appeared in the sky in 1935, we had a lead in development of about two years.'

Irving writes (based on Milch's diary): 'In the research facilities at Rechlin, in March 1936, test pilots were already flying prototypes of the Messerschmitt fighter Me 109, the twin-engined Messerschmitt fighter Me 110, the dive-bombers Ju 87 and He 123, as well as the medium-range bombers Do 17, Ju 86 and He 111. Even an early version of the Ju 88 was already under development.'

From May 1936 Ernst Heinkel, whose aircraft factory was at Marienehe near Rostock, was building a new aircraft plant at Oranienburg at the expense of the Ministry of Aviation for the production of his He 111, the standard bomber. One hundred aircraft of this type were to be produced there per month.

In May 1936 the first Luftwaffe directive for the conduct of air war (Ldv 16) was issued, which said: 'Attacks on cities for the purpose of exercising terror against the population are to be rejected out of principle.' General Wever, who had had this directive prepared and had signed it, crashed and was killed on 3 June 1936 near Dresden in an He 70 which was being used as a courier aircraft. His mechanic had forgotten to release a small lever before take-off, which blocked the hand-wheel by which the side rudders were controlled. When

Wever discovered the blockage shortly after take-off, he could not find the lever. 'Only a very few learned', Ernst Heinkel writes, 'that the fate of this man, and with it also a large part of the fate of the Luftwaffe had hung upon the adjustment of a minute lever.'

Edward Jablonski, in *Air War*, an American history of the air war 1939–45, writes: 'The Battle of Britain, and possibly the result of the European part of the Second World War, were anticipated on 3 June 1936 by the crash of a small aircraft in the vicinity of Dresden. In later years Dresden was to claim immortality as the site of a greater tragedy than the death of a German general and his mechanic. But both the small tragedy and the large one would go down in history one day. With General Wever's crash the concept of an operational bomber weapon also fell, which might have given the Luftwaffe the victory over the Royal Air Force in 1940.'

While these are quite bombastic words from the USA, they do contain a kernel of truth and also reality. As the successor to Wever, Göring appointed General Kesselring, who immediately gave up the concept of the four-engined long-range bomber, and Udet took over the Technical Office from Colonel Wimmer, which was responsible for the entire Luftwaffe. There was now no longer room for a strategic air force, such as was developed during the Second World War by the British and the Americans.

Kesselring and Udet's intentions chimed with those of Göring, who wished to hold on to his air force of deterrence. He did not want to see his Luftwaffe embroiled in a war against Britain, which for him was to be avoided at all costs. For military confrontations in Central Europe, the air force that was now being developed by Kesselring and Udet according to his intentions was sufficient.
In the meantime he had taken over a new position which brought him powers beyond his wildest dreams.

On 27 March, a plebiscite revealed that 98.5 per cent of the electorate had approved Hitler's coup in the Rhineland. This was the highest percentage that Hitler had achieved to date, but since there was no obvious reason why the voters should have voted against a return of the Rhineland under the military sovereignty of the Reich at this time, the success was not exceptional. However Hitler believed that the accord between his will and actions and the German nation had now become total, and concluded that it could be put to ever greater tests.

The armaments industry, which was under the control of Minister of Economics Schacht, had run into problems, because each branch of the Wehrmacht laid claim to such quantities of raw materials that these could no longer be acquired by normal means. So Hitler appointed the one man of his immediate entourage who could read a balance sheet to become 'dictator of raw material', who was to control exchange rates, foreign currency and raw material imports, or, if these could not be afforded, the acquisition of synthetic alternatives.

Göring took over this job on 27 April. Since his nephew, Herbert Göring, was an official with the Reichsbank, he was able to have himself advised '*en famille*'.

But he was also the man to teach the Germans how to live with unpopular decisions. His radio broadcast when he had stated 'Guns will make us powerful; butter will only make us fat', had been received with acclaim. For the Germans, Hermann had made another one of his jokes, but they were soon to discover that it had been meant seriously.

Schacht, who was now restricted in his authority as Minister of Economics, had – like von Blomberg – favoured appointing Göring, who had the reputation of being the strong man.

The Olympic Games, which were to be held in Berlin, were in the offing. Many invitations to foreign guests were sent out, but Charles Lindbergh, who arrived at the end of July, came at the request of Major Truman Smith, the US Air Attaché in Berlin. The Major intended bringing Lindbergh into contact with the Luftwaffe leadership, hoping thereby to get better information than had been obtainable so far. Göring welcomed Lindbergh's visit, and invited him to take part in the opening of the games. This man who had achieved fame with his trans-Atlantic flight, entered his name in the Golden Book of the City of Berlin. He drove to the former Crown Prince in Potsdam to have tea at the Cecilienhof palace. Fighter Wing Richthofen invited him to lunch at Döberitz, where he proposed a toast to the bomber aircraft which were becoming slower and the fighter aircraft which should multiply faster. On 28 July he was Göring's luncheon guest at the ministerial villa. Beforehand and afterwards he was shown aircraft factories and Luftwaffe installations. The American press covered all this extensively.

During these last days of July Göring was not only occupied with gaining Lindbergh as a friend of Germany and of his Luftwaffe, in which he was successful. In mid July the Spanish civil war had broken out. General Franco, who had initiated the war from Spanish Morocco, sent an officer to Berlin to obtain Ju 52s from Hitler for the transport of his Moroccan troops, whose route to the mainland by sea had been closed off by the Spanish navy. Hitler, who was in Bayreuth attending the Wagner Festival, gave his assent to this. At Bayreuth, Göring told Generals Milch and Stumpf that German intervention in the Spanish civil war should stop short of combat. On 27 July the first Ju 52 took off from Tempelhof for Spanish Morocco. On 31 July a freighter with six He 51s and 86 volunteers from the Luftwaffe sailed for Cadiz.

On 28 July Göring had invited Lindbergh, who was strongly impressed by the new Germany – in contrast to this, he had observed apathy in the USA, indifference in England, and decadence in France – for a second visit to Germany. As Göring's guest, Lindbergh was in the Luftwaffe's box for the opening ceremony in the Olympic Stadium. There also was the American swimmer Eleanor Holm, whom Avery Brundage had kicked out of the team during the crossing from America because she had dared to drink champagne with some journalists. Emmy Göring had invited her to the Luftwaffe box.

When Lindbergh, who left to attend a congress in Copenhagen, returned to London, Harold Nicolson noted in his diary: 'He admires Nazi Germany for its energy, masculinity, spirit, organisation, architecture, planning, and strength. He claims it has the largest air force in the world with which it can destroy any other country. He declares the future will bring a conflict between Fascism and Communism, and he believes that if Great Britain were to support decadent France and Red Russia against Germany in this, it would bring about the end of European civilisation.'

Göring watched the games in civilian clothes, but for the big party which he gave at his villa and park in Leipziger Straße, he appeared in Bavarian costume: leather shorts, shirt, edelweiss on his hat. A Bavarian brass band played dance music. The party lasted until the early hours, which was when his step-son, Thomas von Kantzow, saw the couple sitting beside the heated swimming-pool which had been installed in the recently refurbished villa. In the water, a naked, lonely, beautiful swimmer, Eleanor Holm, swam her rounds. During the party Udet had flown aerobatics over the park; now it was ending for the Görings with a sensual, aesthetic picture.

In his memoirs, the creator of the German Panzer weapon, Heinz Guderian, writes about Göring: 'He was a ruthless, abundantly informal man, who initially developed a remarkable drive, but after having lifted the young German air force from the baptismal font, he succumbed to the temptations of the newly acquired power, gave himself over to feudal airs and graces, collected medals, precious stones, and antiques, and turned to the joys of the table.' The turning-point Guderian refers to could have occurred in the summer of 1936, but he suggests that only now could Göring display openly the acquisitive desires that had been part and parcel of his nature from the start.

On 24 August, shortly after the end of the Olympic Games, conscription to the armed services was introduced, initially for a two-year period of service.

On 30 October von Blomberg and Göring were informed by Milch that Hitler had approved unrestricted intervention in the Spanish Civil War by the Luftwaffe. When Milch suggested to Göring that he send off the first bomber group of 'Legion Condor' on 6 November from the Greifswald air base, the

Commander-in-Chief of the Luftwaffe sent Milch in his stead. Until now he had left everything to do with the entanglement of the Luftwaffe in the Spanish Civil War to his deputy. He did not like the idea at all, feeling that it might provoke conflict with Great Britain. but he was obedient to Hitler.

He had reckoned that the Germans could be kept free of military commitments until 1941, and made his plans accordingly. In early December, when he again alluded to this time span during a meeting with the chiefs of his departments, he said: 'We can not yet know whether there might not be entanglements beforehand, we are already at war, only there is no shooting yet. The overall situation is very serious. Russia wants war. England is rearming very heavily.'

He ordered an even stronger build-up of the Luftwaffe. To achieve this, resources from the armaments industry were required, which he could provide, because on 18 October Hitler had appointed him *Beauftragter* (person responsible) for the four-year plan, of which Hitler had said at the national Party convention in Nuremberg in September: 'In four years Germany must become independent of all imports which can be substituted for by our diligence and activities in the chemical, machine, and power industries.'

The written authorisation Göring received gave him full authority to issue decrees and laws. He was empowered to make use of any German authority of the State and the Party. He had become omnipotent. As Beauftragter of the four-year plan, between 1937 and 1941 he had absolute power of attorney over the state and the economy in order to make Germany self-sufficient.

On 28 October in the Berlin Sportpalast, Göring called upon the people to help him. On 29 October he allowed himself and his wife to be feted at the State Theatre, and soon afterwards stood on the street with the collection box for the *Winterhilfswerk* (lit. winter aid works, Nazi euphemism for an annual campaign to get the population to donate money under the guise that it would be spent for the needy in winter), in which copper, silver, and gold coins were collected. 'Hermann needs small change,' passers-by quipped.

In the beginning, the working staff Göring installed was small. Paul Körner became his State Secretary and deputy and normally chaired the weekly meetings. The model for the four-year plan, whose details Hitler had worked out during the summer, were the five-year plans in the Soviet Union.

With the take-over of the new office, which did not have a Ministry, but which could dispose of all the Ministries, a personal source also opened up for Göring, which was to lead him into temptation more and more frequently: the right to dispose of all the foreign currency in the Reichsbank. Now it had become possible for him to fulfil wishes which equated to his feudal style of life.

The omnipotence Hitler had conferred on him was irresistibly tempting for a man whom no one could control any longer, except Hitler, who had no intention of doing so. Göring – according to Hitler – was a Renaissance man. After the Röhm affair, Hitler no longer wanted to interfere in the private lives of his paladins.

On 30 January 1937 Hitler made a speech in the Reichstag in which he proclaimed Germany's desire for peace in Europe and the rest of the world. He added that the four-year plan would certainly not contribute to isolating Germany from the rest of the world. These words camouflaged what was really being planned.

Göring actually did hope to have four years of grace, but the war began two years before he expected.

Göring's motto now was: 'For the life and safety of the German nation.' He never tired of saying it.

20

The Heir

I nevitably, the Spanish Civil War drew Fascist Italy closer to National Socialist Germany, but between them stood the question of Austria on which the final word had not yet been spoken. In mid January 1937 the Görings went to Rome on a state visit which provided the opportunity to talk to Mussolini about Austria. But Göring's good relationship with the Duce could no nothing to budge Mussolini's continued insistence on Austrian independence. In 1936 Mussolini had been able to conclude his war in Abyssinia victoriously; the King of Italy had become Emperor of Abyssinia, and Mussolini's self-esteem was now boundless.

From Rome the Görings went to Capri for a few days. There they visited the Swedish doctor Axel Munthe who was thinking of selling his museum-like villa 'San Michele'. Göring expressed a lively interest in the villa, but he was not yet in a position where he could afford the half a million Swedish crowns Munthe was asking for it. Carinhall was still being extended, he had a country house on the Obersalzberg, his Reich hunting-lodge lay in the Rominter Heide, the ministerial villa in Berlin had been refurbished in 1936. Although these properties were maintained at the state's expense, Göring's personal wealth was not yet such that he could purchase a foreign property from his own pocket.

In the following November Munthe was to write to Göring, again offering to sell the villa. The reasons being his increasing blindness and his preference to sell his home, which had become famous through his book *The Story of San Michele*, to Göring rather than to some American millionaire. Because of Germany's tight foreign currency situation, Göring again would be unable to accept the offer. His omnipotence, which his appointment as Beauftragter for the four-year plan had brought him, had reached its limits.

In February 1937 Udet, as Chief of the Technical Office, reported to Göring that the aircraft building programme would be seriously delayed, the allotment of iron and steel having been sharply reduced. Göring took a decision that was to have a far-reaching effect on the Luftwaffe: the four-engined long-range bombers, Do 19 and Ju 89, were stricken from the development programme. Kesselring and Udet were opposed to them and Göring followed their advice. Originally, the long-range bombers had been scheduled for completion in 1939. While Germany was surrendering this weapon, the first Boeing four-engined Y1B-17 bombers, which the newspapers called 'Flying Fortresses', were being flown in the USA.

Paul Deichmann writes: 'I learned of this by chance in mid April 1937. I reported to Göring at Carinhall and found Milch already there.' An altercation between Milch and Deichmann occurred, to which Göring only listened. 'From time to time he nodded in agreement to Milch's arguments. He also nodded when Milch said that this was now the end of the matter. The four-engined bomber was superfluous. Bomber production would first be concentrated on the twin-engined He 111 and then on the fast bomber Ju 88, which was being tested at that time. Göring again nodded assent. I raised the demand to at least continue to test the four-engined prototypes and to develop them further with more powerful engines. The answer was neither "yes" nor "no". In prison in Landsberg on the Lech (after the war) Milch gave me another reason for the cancellation of the four-engined planes. At the time Göring had said: "The Führer will only ever ask me, how many bombers do you have? He will never ask me how big they are. For one four-engined job I can build two and a half medium bombers." To my great astonishment I learned after the war that the initiative to cancel the long-range bombers had come from my boss Lieutenant-General Kesselring. Neither Göring nor Milch had so much as hinted at this during my presentation. That the Chief of the General Staff had omitted to consult with his operations department on such a decision or at least to inform it, was not only a breach of regulations, it shows that at the time he was not aware of the importance of long-term strategic planning.'

But who was thinking of a world war at that time? Göring was developing the Luftwaffe with a view to a possible war that would be restricted to Europe. He desired an alliance with Britain whom he could not visualise as a future opponent.

In April he was back in Italy again in an endeavour to find out what Mussolini had agreed with the Austrian Chancellor Schuschnigg. His wife meanwhile went to stay at a spa which Mussolini had recommended for her sciatica.

On 12 May Göring was supposed to represent the German Reich at the coronation of King George VI in London. But in the Commons the Labour MP Ellen Wilkinson had called him 'the man with the blood-stained boots', by which she was referring to the bombing of Guernica on 26 April by the He 111s of 'Legion Condor', so Field Marshal Blomberg went instead. Göring flew to London privately, but Ribbentrop kept the visit a secret and took care that Göring flew back home again next morning. Göring never forgave Ribbentrop for this humiliation.

The exchange of visitors and information between the Luftwaffe and the Royal Air Force, which had begun in 1936, had been going on at very high level, prompted by the hope of both Göring and Hitler that an accord with Britain could be attained. In May the new British Prime Minister Chamberlain sent Sir Neville Henderson as Ambassador to Berlin; he soon became friendly with Göring. Göring never left him in any doubt that he was the natural successor to Hitler, and Henderson gained the impression that this man, if one excluded

Hitler, was the only Party leader whom the German people really respected. He praised Göring's quick comprehension and considered him to be a man with whom one could talk openly, who was able to take things in his stride without being easily insulted, and one who could not hurt somebody else inadvertently. Göring had other contacts in Britain. Former Air Minister Lord Londonderry had been his hunting-guest since 1936. Göring told him no power on earth would be able to undertake anything against an Anglo–German alliance.

It now became necessary to re-organise the Reich Ministry of Aviation. The build-up of the Luftwaffe had reached a stage where ministerial bureaucracy and its representatives could be split off from the military sector. This meant a reduction in Milch's powers, who, as Göring's deputy, had to all intents and purposes run the ministry himself. By an order of 1 June 1937 Göring made himself Commander-in-Chief of the Luftwaffe, to whom the State Secretary and the Chief of Staff both reported directly as equals. General Stumpff became the new Chief of Staff. Some time later the Personnel Department under Ritter von Greim and the Technical Department under Udet were taken out of the area of responsibility of the State Secretary and put directly under Göring. From now on, Milch, Stumpff, von Greim, and Udet were equals. Milch, who was infuriated by this, wrote in his diary: 'It quickly became apparent that my fears about a rupture in the continuity of our work were all too justified. Göring only intervened sporadically and then on unimportant matters. He only spoke about the problems with the department head, did not consult anybody, did not tolerate any questions, let alone contradictions, never involved those most directly concerned, got carried away, so that one subject just led to another, moaned about those not present, and idolised himself. He kept taking notes, mostly in a different book each time, without one ever being able to discover what this work was for, because he kept forgetting or distorting what had gone on before.'

After the war, Milch described the reorganisation of the Luftwaffe in 1937 as the primary and most important reason for its defeat. This may be going too far. But the example of Udet was to show that it had been wrong to leave him and his important Technical Department without constant supervision, which Milch considered to be bitterly necessary particularly with this friend of Göring's.

Göring was incapable of exercising this supervision because he had too many other things to do. On 21 June, in a speech before the International Chamber of Commerce in Berlin, he said that a self-sufficient German economy would not harm world economy; German research and inventions that were now being made would benefit the whole world one day.

In July Göring founded the *Reichswerke Hermann Göring* at Salzgitter (Reich Works, a large conglomerate producing iron, steel, and heavy machinery, from which the present day Salzgitter AG developed), whereby he delightedly recalled one of his ancestors who had established Prussian manufacturing facilities as a Geheime Kriegsrat under Frederick the Great. There were iron ore deposits at Salzgitter that were to be smelted on the spot. At the same time he was given responsibility for the entire German iron and steel industry.

By now Schacht, urging restraint, was no longer prepared to tolerate Göring's interference in his economic policies. On 1 November 1937 he resigned as Minister of Economics, but stayed on as President of the Reichsbank and Minister without portfolio. Göring thereupon took over his chair at the Ministry of Economics. 'How on earth can a man gain insights into great matters if he sits in such a small room,' he allegedly exclaimed when he came into Schacht's office. That was the end of the friendship with Schacht, which had begun before 1933. Göring had always shown respect for the great abilities of Schacht, who had succeeded in financing the rearmament programme.

Throughout 1937 Göring had subjected himself to cures to lose weight which weakened him. In the Frankfurt clinic of Professor Kahles he had himself regularly treated for his addiction to pills. After each reducing diet, his body quickly became obese again, he became nervous and lost his sprightliness, which he had been able to retain until then despite his physical complaints. He began to dress more and more wilfully and applied perfume to cover his attacks of sweating. This was remarked on by his subordinates. He also began to apply make-up in order to appear fresher than he actually was.

The Görings had many people who admired them or flattered them, but hardly any real friends. Göring could not stand the other Party leaders and kept away from them. He was different from them, and he was Hitler's heir.

During this time Göring believed that nobody could contest his inheritance. Hitler did not take any important political or military decision without consulting him beforehand, as Nicolaus von Below writes in his book *As Hitler's Adjutant 1937–45*. The 29-year-old von Below from Fighter Wing Richthofen No. 2, had become Hitler's adjutant to the Luftwaffe in June 1937. Göring's personal liaison officer to Hitler, however, continued to be his chief adjutant Colonel Bodenschatz. Von Below noted how Göring distanced himself whenever he came to the Chancellery: 'Göring's appearance announced itself from afar. From the street some shouted Heil!s could be heard, then the parading of the guard, commands and presentation of arms, the sounds of the cars coming to a halt in front of the entrance and the heel-clicking of the SS guards. Göring entered the hall. All those present greeted him with the *deutsche Gruß* (the 'Heil Hitler!' salute, which had become mandatory in Nazi Germany). He himself, as I was able to observe many times later on, jovially returned the greetings in all directions, but hardly gave anybody his hand unless there was a Reich Minister or a Reich Leader of the Party among those present.'

Emmy Göring writes: 'Except during the big official receptions at the Chancellery, or on the occasion of entertaining foreign visitors at Carinhall, when we also met Ministers and Party leaders, we had very little close contacts with the latter. Exceptions were Church Minister Kerrl and his family, Reich Leader Bouhler and his wife, and Baldur von Schirach and his wife Henriette. In any case, there were no personal ties of friendship with others.'

After visits by Mussolini in September and the Duke of Windsor with his wife in October, Emmy Göring was convinced that she herself could contribute something in representing the Reich. Göring told her that he wished the Duke had become King of England, but that he had had to renounce the throne.

Originally, ten years had been envisaged for the build-up of the Wehrmacht, which was to have been completed in 1944. But on 5 November 1937, during a meeting behind locked doors at the Chancellery, Hitler surprised the Reich War Minister, the Commanders-in-Chief of the three branches of the Wehrmacht, and Foreign Minister von Neurath, by disclosing a verbal will in case of his demise. He modified the planning of the build-up of the Wehrmacht and spoke of using force to decide the *Raumfrage* (lit. space question, i.e., Hitler's constant preoccupation with the idea that Germany needed more territory so that the German – master – race could multiply), because opponents would have become superior economically and numerically to the German armed forces by 1943–5. Therefore the greatest possible gain, using the smallest possible stakes, must be achieved beforehand. Hitler was thinking of proceeding against Czechoslovakia and Austria, and he named the summer of 1938 for this. In the ensuing discussion, which Hitler's adjutant to the Wehrmacht, Colonel Hoßbach, recorded in his minutes just as he did Hitler's remarks, Göring supported his Führer. Generals von Blomberg and von Fritsch had reservations, Foreign Minister von Neurath warned of diplomatic–political entanglements, and Admiral Raeder stayed in the background. Hitler's health was poor and he feared that he might die before he had settled the Raumfrage. That Göring, his heir, took his side on the matter he considered only natural. He hoped to overcome opposition by others and in this he was soon to succeed with Göring's help.

Two external events may have driven Hitler to take the bull by the horns. On 5 October America's President Roosevelt had given his 'quarantine' speech in which he had said that 90 per cent of the world population was being threatened by 10 per cent, among which he numbered Italy, Japan, and Germany. At the end of October Milch and Udet had been guests of the Royal Air Force in England. On 1 November Hitler received them and heard that the potential of the Royal Air Force to arm was constantly increasing; that 'shadow factories' were being established, and Churchill, who had no official position, should not be under-estimated. Hitler assured Milch and Udet that he would never proceed against Britain.

Göring was not present on this occasion, but at the end of October Hitler had held conversations with him and Hess during which he had probably not withheld his thoughts, which therefore did not come as a surprise to Göring on 5 November. Schacht had been disempowered on 1 November.

How did it come about that Göring, the Anglophile, now supported Hitler? He had his assurance that he did not intend to proceed against England, and this was sufficient to allow him to support the adventurous policy which Hitler had decided upon. As Beauftragter of the four-year plan, he knew that the financial and economic situation of the Reich was deteriorating. The Raumfrage had therefore to be solved in order to ease the tight situation *vis-à-vis* raw material supply.

The new objectives were Austria and Czechoslovakia. There was no mention yet of Poland or Russia, as von Below recalls, who had access to the Hoßbach minutes taken at the Chancellery at the time. The power Göring had gained under Hitler, like the entire Reich, was now to be put at risk.

On 12 January 1938 Göring turned 45. Nicolaus von Below writes: 'Hitler knew Göring's weakness for paintings, particularly the old masters, among whom he preferred Lukas Cranach. On this birthday however, Hitler presented him with a painting of the 19th century, as far as I recall "The Falconer" by Hans Makart. With this Hitler was addressing himself to Göring's passion for hunting. At home Göring was completely open and free from tension, even in Hitler's presence, quite in contrast to his appearances at the *Reichskanzlei*. In the context of his birthday his penchant for pomp, as compared to Hitler's simplicity, again came very much to the fore. I did not find Göring's pompous behaviour very nice, and sometimes even inappropriate. Hitler did not let anyone notice that he felt the same. He showed consideration for Göring's mentality and was pleased that the people liked Göring's manner and that he was popular.'

During the afternoon of his birthday Göring suddenly disappeared, which was unusual. He drove to the Reich War Ministry where, with Hitler, he was a witness at the wedding of von Blomberg with Eva Gruhn, which was only celebrated by a civil ceremony. In December 1937 at von Blomberg's request, Göring had arranged for a person who stood in the way of the marriage to be transferred abroad. Von Blomberg had not wanted his wedding to be reported in the press, but it was reported next day and was to have grave consequences.

21

The Road to Mauterndorf

A s Reichjägermeister, Göring's progressive hunting laws to protect game and ensure that hunting be conducted properly became models for other countries. He had laid down preserves in the Reinhardtswald, on the Darss peninsula in Pomerania and in the Rominter Heide. Bison and elk, wild sheep and horses, beavers and otters, ospreys, kites, capercaillies, ravens and black woodpeckers had been released in the Schorfheide. He had seven lions reared at the ministerial villa and at Carinhall, which were handed over to the Berlin zoo when they were older. He was a conservationist as well as a hunter.

In the autumn of 1937 he learned that his wife was expecting a child. Since in his marriage with Carin Göring a child had been denied him, he was beside himself with joy. It remains remarkable that a man whose wish in this respect was finally to be gratified was prepared at the same time to support Hitler's wild plans of aggression.

These began with an intrigue that was swiftly followed by another. Out of this grew first a Blomberg crisis, then a Fritsch crisis, and finally a Wehrmacht crisis from which Hitler emerged as Commander-in-Chief of the Wehrmacht, whereby his nominal command of the armed forces was converted to a direct command, with all the ensuing consequences.

The Blomberg crisis was merely a scandal, and the Fritsch crisis arose from a deliberate slander, which turned out to have been a conspiracy by Himmler and Heydrich against the Commander-in-Chief of the Army.

Göring's role in both cases was simple: he was the loyal paladin of his Führer who believed that he would inherit the Reich War Ministry which von Blomberg held. Command of the Army did not interest him; was he not Commander-in-Chief of the Luftwaffe?

Shortly after the marriage of von Blomberg and Eva Gruhn, a police file was unearthed, according to which the wife of the Field Marshal had had pictures of herself taken in the nude. This had brought her to the attention of the vice squad of the Berlin police. With this, von Blomberg's fate was sealed; his wife would have been expected to play a prominent role beside him in public affairs. Hitler was aghast at having been a witness to the wedding.

In the military hierarchy, von Blomberg's successor would have been General of Artillery von Fritsch. In order to prevent this, von Fritsch was falsely accused of being a homosexual. In Göring's presence, a confrontation took place in Hitler's apartment between the General and a man who accused him of having committed homosexual acts with him. A court-martial was held on von Fritsch at which Göring presided, and his interrogation of the accusing witness drove the latter into such a corner that he admitted that the accusation was false, and that the culprit had been a Major von Frisch of the Reichswehr. In the meantime, Hitler had dismissed von Blomberg and von Fritsch.

Von Blomberg recommended Göring to Hitler as his successor, and Göring demanded that he get the job. But Hitler, knowing that he was already heavily burdened by his other offices, would not hear of it. Göring is alleged to have interjected, that as Commander-in-Chief of the Luftwaffe he could not subordinate himself to a mere General as Commander-in-Chief of the Armed Forces, whereupon Hitler took over supreme command himself, since he was the only possible superior Göring respected.

At a stroke, in the great reshuffle at the end of February 1938, Hitler was now able to rid himself of all the generals who had disapproved of his plans.

Göring, who had long wished to be Air Marshal, was now given the highest rank, which von Blomberg had held until now, that of Field Marshal – which put him on the same level as Air Marshal Balbo in Italy. As Field Marshal he was also one rank higher than von Fritsch's successor, Colonel General von Brauchitsch. (Originally a Marshal had been the superviser of a Prince's retinue when travelling and on campaign, and from this developed the military rank of Field Marshal whose conferment, however, was not limited to times of war.) As Field Marshal, he was also the 'superviser' of all the Generals, the one who stood closest to the Prince who commanded the army. Hitler was now this Prince, this King, and Emperor, and Göring remained his loyal Marshal. The closer we observe Göring, the clearer the role as successor in which he had immersed himself emerges.

But he was also pleased to have himself photographed with Balbo during a sea trip to Tripoli in 1939, his Marshal's baton in his right hand, on his face a youthful smile. He was playing a new role as befitted his natural bent for acting. The era of National Socialism for him was a theatrical season, in which he rushed from one première to another in order to present himself in the lead to his audience, which for the time being still applauded him.

As the head of the Prussian State Theatre he was in a position to have himself put on stage in plays in which world history had become theatre, aided by the artistic director and actor Gustav Gründgens, whom Göring had meanwhile appointed Prussian State Councillor. In the spring of 1938 Gründgens produced Hans Rehberg's *The Seven Years War* and appeared in it as Frederick II. Paul Fechter wrote about the première in the *Berliner Tageblatt*: 'The rhythm of the language was harsh, loud – war determined the melody. Only one person walked through the bloody world tamed, almost taciturn – the King, played by Mr. Gründgens. He did not play "Old Fritz" as the Frederickus films show him, but portrayed an emotional ecstatic, a man who feels the remainder of his youth dwindling away in the war and holds himself and his nation together with an iron hand.' A Field Marshal, Göring was able to recognise himself in this figure.

When Gründgens produced Mozart's *The Magic Flute* a few weeks later at the Opera in Unter den Linden, he put on a fairy-tale full of naïve fantasies. The conductor was 30-year-old Herbert von Karajan. Naïve fantasies – this too was Göring. Out of them grew his dream since his exile in Innsbruck in 1923 to bring Austria finally under his rule, to see Mauterndorf Castle again. In these dreams he was in complete agreement with Hitler.

During the Blomberg–Fritsch crisis Nicolaus von Below had come to realise that 'with his ability to comprehend and his lightning quick reaction, Göring was able to influence Hitler. Sometimes we had the impression that it was Göring who ruled and not Hitler.'

He had not taken part in Schuschnigg's meeting with Hitler on the Obersalzberg on 12 February 1938, but when on 9 March Schuschnigg called for a plebiscite at short notice for the following Sunday, 13 March, which was to prove that the majority of Austrians supported him, Göring helped Hitler to make a quick decision.

On 11 March Prince Philip of Hesse, Göring's friend, flew to Rome with a letter that was intended to placate Mussolini. Göring had urged Hitler to send the letter by the hand of the Prince, who was married to the Italian Princess Mafalda.

In the morning of that day Göring held meetings at the Reich Ministry of Aviation. In the afternoon he began to telephone to Vienna. Since the German troops earmarked for the march into Austria needed to receive their orders before 7.30 p.m., the decision at government level in Vienna had to be taken by then. In Vienna, Austrian President Miklas was hesitating about appointing Minister Dr Seyß-Inquart, whom Hitler had recommended, as the new Chancellor. Göring was telephoning with urgency. The telephone minutes, which were to be preserved for history on his orders, show Göring as a man of energy who has to prod men of lesser energy in order to achieve the desired objective.

Since Göring's ultimatum expired at 7.30 p.m. without Seyß-Inquart having become Chancellor, the Wehrmacht received the order to march in on the morning of 12 March. This lead to Schuschnigg's declaring: 'We bow to force, since even in this fateful hour we are not prepared to spill blood ... God save Austria.' Göring thereupon dictated a telegram over the telephone to the German special ambassador Keppler who had replaced von Papen, which Seyß-Inquart was to send to Berlin: 'The provisional Austrian Government, which after the resignation of the Schuschnigg Government sees its duty in reinstating calm and order in Austria, urgently requests the German Government to support it in this endeavour and to help it to prevent bloodshed. For this purpose it asks the German Government to send German troops as quickly as possible.'

When Keppler asked whether Seyß-Inquart was to send the telegram from the office of the Chancellor, Göring said: 'Well please, just show him the telegram and tell him we ask – he does not even need to send the telegram, all he needs to say is : "I agree".' Keppler: *"Jawohl."* Göring: 'Call me on this, either at the Führer's or at my place. O.K. Do it right. Heil Hitler.'

That evening a great social event of the Berlin season, the 'Airmen's Ball', took place at 'Aviation House', the former building of the Prussian Diet. It was also attended by the diplomatic corps. Göring went there and told the Czech Ambassador Mastny on his word of honour, that his country now had no reason to be worried, and spoke of a 'family matter' that was taking place in Austria. Then Göring greeted the most important guests, including the British Ambassador Henderson, to whom he had a note passed during the performance by the ballet of the State Opera, saying that he would like to speak to him when the music was over. In this conversation Göring assured Henderson that the German troops would be withdrawn from Austria after the situation had stabilised and free elections without any pressures had taken place. Henderson informed his government in London which sent a note of protest to Berlin. Mussolini had given his assent to the German action.

On the morning of 12 March Hitler flew to Munich. At about 3 p.m. he entered the town of his birth, Braunau on the Inn, amidst the chiming of bells. In the evening he was in Linz where, to a delirious reception by the populace, he had a decree issued making Austria a state of the German Reich. On 15 March he spoke in Vienna from the balcony of the Neue Hofburg to the crowd on the Heldenplatz and announced before history the entry of his homeland into the German Reich. After the ball, Göring retired to Carinhall for the weekend, armed with full powers as Hitler's deputy.

On 16 March Hitler returned to Berlin. At Tempelhof airport Göring greeted him with wild enthusiasm. Göring was scheduled to go to Austria at the end of March to speak at election rallies, which were taking place because of the plebiscite on 10 April. These were mass meetings at which he, as Beauftragter of the four-year plan, would promise the Austrians new industries, autobahns, and power plants, but above all an end to unemployment. He promised the city of Linz a big steel plant, which was to be attached to the Reichswerke Hermann Göring. In order to connect the *Ostmark* (Eastern March), as Austria was now to be called, to the northern and north-western German industrial regions – to which Salzgitter and the Reichswerke also belonged – by water, he promised the building of the Main–Danube Canal.

He learned of Himmler's acts of violence and decreed the release of several thousand opponents of the Austrian National Socialists who had been arrested, condemned the suicides of Jews – primarily in Vienna – deploring the fact that a policeman could not be stationed behind every Jew to prevent him killing himself. That was his way of talking, and perhaps he did not realise how cynical he sounded.

But then he moved on, and others from the Reich, together with Austria's National Socialists, did what they had intended to do. Himmler and Bürckel, the new Gauleiter of Vienna whom Hitler had brought in from the Saar, ruled with an iron hand.

On this trip Göring also went to Mauterndorf in the Lungau. There lived Baroness Lilly, Ritter von Epenstein's widow and Göring's former fiancé Marianne, to whom he had not been officially engaged. He now returned to them with his soldiers as a field marshal. What goes on in the mind of a man who experiences events such as this?

On 10 April, 99.73 per cent of the Austrians – at least those that had not been arrested or who had fled – and 99.08 per cent of the *Reichsdeutsche* (after the annexation of Austria, all Germans stemming from Germany proper were called Reichsdeutsche to differentiate them from the 'newly acquired Germans') declared themselves to be in agreement with the incorporation of Austria and with Hitler's policies. Into the Reichstag of the Greater German Reich which, given the one-party system, had been re-elected in connection with the plebiscite, marched 814 deputies, who had nothing to say or to decide. Göring was again confirmed as their President.

Before Hitler left for Italy for a state visit on 3 May 1938, he drew up his will in which he named Göring as his successor in case of his death. As his deputy, Göring remained behind in Berlin. Since 21 April he had known that Hitler had prepared a military deployment against Czechoslovakia.

22

Luftwaffe as a Deterrent

T he intoxication of power which enshrouded Hitler after the annexation of Austria spurred him into taking military action against Czechoslovakia in order to try out the new Wehrmacht, supreme command of which he had taken over. Like the new Field Marshal Göring, he was convinced that in this year of 1938 Great Britain's rearmament was not yet sufficiently advanced for an intervention in Europe; in this they were both thinking primarily in terms of the Royal Air Force. The strength of the Luftwaffe should be enough to deter the British.

Furthermore, the situation in the Soviet Union, where Stalin was in the process of brutally 'cleansing' the Red Army of alleged opponents of his autocratic rule, favoured Hitler; as a military factor the Red Army was virtually non-existent for the time being.

But the German Army leadership as well as that of the Navy feared that military intervention in Austria could lead to a war that would revive the old alliance of 1914: Great Britain, France, and Russia.

When in mid May reports about German troop concentrations on the Czech border appeared in British and Czech newspapers, the President of Czechoslovakia ordered a partial mobilisation on the 20th.

The reports were denied by the German Government as being purely fictitious. It is possible that local exercises by the Army in Saxony, which were a part of its training programme, had given rise to these speculations. For example, on 10 May Motorised Machine-Gun Battalion No. 7 in Dresden was put on alert. After distribution of live ammunition the company commanders reported 'ready to march for deployment in combat'. The battalion, which was under the direct control of Army Command, was not deployed on the nearby frontier but remained in barracks.

On 21 May Hitler and Göring drove to Carinhall for a discussion about German fortifications in the east and west. Hitler assigned Göring to inspect the fortifications in the west, which would normally have been the prerogative of the Army. Before doing so Hitler had inspected the old installations on the bend of the River Warthe which dated from the days of the Reichswehr, adjudged them insufficient. After his inspection tour, Göring reported to Hitler that there were no fortifications at all between Aix-la-Chapelle and Basle, whereupon the builder of the autobahn, Dr Todt, was entrusted with the building of the Westwall (the Siegfried Line). The Army was only permitted to allow its pioneer staffs to decide what sort of bunkers should be built.

At first the Army leadership accepted this interference which had been initiated by Göring; the Luftwaffe was to organise a second zone of defence in the west, an 'air defence zone', behind the bunker emplacements. But now opposition began to be voiced by the Army, who felt that they had been tricked by Göring and the Luftwaffe. Nicolaus von Below writes that the Luftwaffe General Staff was worried at the time about Göring's orders to equip the air defence zone with AA and searchlight emplacements, for which trained soldiers and raw materials were lacking. 'Göring promised time and again that the Luftwaffe would receive priority in the four-year plan. But the actual practice was something quite different.'

On 28 May 1938, Hitler chaired a meeting of the Commanders-in-Chief at the Chancellery, and told them that the Prague government would never grant the Sudeten Germans the autonomy they demanded, so preparations for the attack on Czechoslovakia must be completed by 1 October 1938.

Next day Göring briefed his Luftwaffe officers on the new situation. Secrecy was strictly maintained. The German people went their way, carefree and unknowing in the fine weather, contented that no conflict had developed over Austria.

On 1 June Göring received a report that the Ju 88 dive-bomber had been test flown. This had originally been developed as a high-speed bomber, and in the spring of 1938 had reached a speed of 506 km/h over a distance of 1,000 kilometres. But the Luftwaffe leadership believed that it would only be viable as a dive-bomber if employed in conjunction with the Ju 87. As a dive-bomber the Ju 88 was 30 per cent heavier and slower, and had a range of only 800 kilometres; whereas in its originally intended role as a high-speed bomber its range was 1,500 kilometres. Göring had the Ju 88 cleared for series production, but this was frequently interrupted because serious deficiencies came to light.

On 2 June 1938 Göring became a father. The birth of Edda Göring turned his marriage to Emmy Göring into a family, which Göring clung to and which the Germans regarded almost as a guarantee the there would be no war. They believed that someone who could display such joy about this child Edda would never countenance the risk of war. The child was showered with presents.

In June 1938 Göring decreed 10-hour shifts in the aircraft factories to increase production. He used the occasion of a meeting with aircraft manufacturers at Carinhall on 8 July 1938 to bind them to greater efforts because a war against Czechoslovakia was in the offing, whereas a war against Britain and France was to be avoided. 'If we win the war, Germany will be the foremost power in the world,' he exclaimed to the industrialists. 'Then the markets of the world will belong to Germany, then the hour will come when Germany will be rich. But one has to risk something, one has to stake something.'

At Whitsun in 1938 Udet flew a new world speed record with the He 111 at the 100-kilometre range on the Baltic near Rostock. In his memoirs Ernst Heinkel comments on this: 'Every new record-breaking achievement from then on was unwittingly propagated in the political arena as a new German triumph, but seen as a threat in Britain and France, which could not be equalised by their own aircraft development which was still mainly running in the old ruts.'

On 22 June Ambassador Henderson visited the Görings at Carinhall. He liked little Edda, but Göring seemed to him to be 'depressed, more timid, and also less self assured' than he had ever seen him before. 'For the first time the Field Marshal did not indulge in any kind of bragging at all,' Henderson writes.

Göring was in poor physical condition again. He was suffering from a glandular upset and was bloated. But it is also possible that the new father was oppressed by the thought of a war which he was helping to prepare. Everything depended on keeping Britain and France out of the affair.

In mid July a secret study by the Luftwaffe leadership came to the conclusion that 400 fighters, 600 bombers, and 200 dive-bombers would be required for the assault on Czechoslovakia; 250 Ju 52s were to drop the 7th Parachute Division, which had been set up by General Student in Stendal, over Czechoslovakia.

July was the holiday month for the Germans, including those who belonged to the leadership hierarchy. But Emmy Göring went alone to Wenningstedt on the island of Sylt, her husband remaining in Berlin and Carinhall. Hitler was in Bayreuth, living at the 'Wahnfried' House and attending the Wagner operas. Nicolaus von Below gained the impression: 'that Hitler believed the Luftwaffe to be capable of far greater achievements than was the case. In the field of aircraft he had complete confidence in Göring and trusted his statements.'

Göring's most important job that summer was to maintain close contact with the ambassadors of the two Western Powers. For this, an invitation to Carinhall, which was felt to be a mark of favour, created a private atmosphere.

In mid August, the Chief of the French Air Force, General Vuillemin, came to Germany. He was shown the Messerschmitt, Junkers and Heinkel plants. During his visit to the new Heinkel plant at Oranienburg he also saw the air raid precautions which were operational. As Milch recalls, after Göring had asked Vuillemin what would happen if Germany were to resort to force against Czechoslovakia, he had a 'grandiose spectacle' staged. Vuillemin left Germany strongly impressed.

Lindbergh also came back again. He took part in the Lilienthal Aviation Congress in Munich, and Udet is alleged to have furnished him with 'secret' aircraft production figures. He reported that the Germans were turning out between 500 and 800 aircraft per month; the true figure was only 300, but he was believed in Washington and London.

Although Göring's bluff about the strength of his Luftwaffe was apparently succeeding in deterring intervention throughout the Sudetenland Crisis and during the haggling between Chamberlain and Hitler at the Obersalzberg and in Bad Godesberg during September 1938 – which led to the Munich Accord – Göring lived in constant fear that it could still come to a war with the Western Powers.

When the Chief of Staff of the Army, General Halder, succeeded General Beck in August because Beck had rejected a military operation against Czechoslovakia, Göring had no inkling that Halder and several other officers were planning to have Hitler arrested if he gave the order to attack.

On 28 September 1938, however, the Munich Conference of the 'big four' of those days took place (Chamberlain, Daladier, Mussolini, and Hitler), at which the cession of the Sudetenland was decided without consultation with the Czech Government.

Emmy Göring, who had gone to Munich with her husband, writes: 'Throughout the whole day and half the night I was waiting for my husband's report on the outcome. At last, towards 2 a.m. at night, he came to me brimming with joy: "We will have peace!" Peace – so the terrible fears in recent times had become superfluous. We were literally in high spirits for joy. A few minutes later I was down in the hall of the Hotel Vier Jahreszeiten. An army of journalists was blocking the phone booths. At every table there were celebrations, people were toasting one another. The owner of the hotel, Alfred Walterspiel, went from table to table in the most happy mood I had ever seen him in.' The French Ambassador François-Poncet sat at the Görings' table.

The German march into the Sudetenland, which began on 1 October, was now the second 'flower war' as the soldiers called it. The first had been the march into Austria. Göring had contributed to this outcome. Hitler was less happy. He would have preferred a war against Czechoslovakia in which he could have put his Wehrmacht to the test.

The Luftwaffe had played a decisive role without having to be deployed. When Chamberlain flew to Bad Godesberg on 22 September he carried a letter with him which Lindbergh had written at the request of the American Ambassador in London, Joseph Kennedy. This letter read: 'I believe that the German aircraft factories can produce 20,000 aircraft per year. Exact production figures at the moment are hard to determine. The most convincing reports I received are based on 500 to 800 aircraft per month. Germany now has the ability to destroy London, Paris, and Prague if it wishes to do so. England and France do not have enough aircraft for a counter-attack or for defence. A major European war would, so I believe, permit Communism to overrun Europe.

'I am convinced that it is wiser to permit Germany to expand in the east than to have England and France become involved in a war they are now unprepared for. For the first time in history a nation has the power to lay waste the famous cities in Europe or to spare them from this.' Seven days later the Munich Accord was signed.

In prison in Nuremberg in 1946, Göring said to Werner Bross, his defence counsel's assistant, who had mentioned the horrors Hitler had caused by his lack of restraint and scruples: 'Today I am of the opinion that it might have been best if the Führer had been the victim of a fatal automobile accident after the Munich Conference. He would then truly have gone down in German history as one of its greatest men.'

Göring would have been his successor. But which Göring?

23
'This is Rebellion'

When fighter pilot Adolf Galland returned to Germany from Spain in August 1938, having been replaced by Werner Mölders, he found, after fifteen months' absence, 'this peaceful Germany, beautiful with its order and cleanliness, its blooming cities, its mountains and hills, forests and lakes, and its people full of confidence and enthusiasm.'

Soon however he began to 'feel uneasy about so much order, discipline and single-mindedness'. He reported back to the Reich Ministry of Aviation, 'the colossal building in Leipziger Straße, on the corner of Wilhelmstraße, in Berlin' where there 'swarmed uncountable officers with red raspberry or white coloured stripes on their neatly fitting trousers'.

In July 1938 the number of unemployed had fallen to 218,328 as compared to 4,463,841 in July 1933. In the USA 10 million were unemployed, in Great Britain 1.7 million. Since more than half of Germany's unemployed were unemployable, bottle-necks in factory production occurred, and in October Göring was forced to employ women and issue an appeal to increase the number of work hours in order to be able to complete the four-year plan.

After the Munich Accord, Hitler demanded a five-fold increase of the Luftwaffe, which Göring promised although he knew that it was impossible to achieve. The officers of his General Staff were aghast at his kowtowing to Hitler, but in those days Göring believed that no foreign air fleet would ever be superior to his Luftwaffe. As Nicolaus von Below recalls: 'For him a war lay outside any realm of probability.'

This can also be deduced from Göring's favouring the fighter arm as opposed to AA defences or the building of air raid shelters. As von Below writes, Hitler had demanded highest priority for everything, 'despite the fact that Göring tried time and again to convince him that the fighter weapon was the best defence against enemy air attacks'. Hitler was reckoning on war; he wanted it. Göring could not see it and did not want it. After 1943, as von Below recalls, Hitler greatly reproached Göring because of the inadequate German air defence and pointed to his directives of 1938.

For the Reich Aviation Ministry, the 'five-fold increase' developed into a nightmare: 19,000 aircraft, of which slightly more than half were to be combat aircraft, meant 100 Wings. Supplying them with fuel meant importing more than 85 per cent of the world's output of aviation fuel. According to Milch's recollections, the final programme called for the production of 31,300 aircraft by April 1942, of which 7,700 were to be Ju 88 and He 177 which as yet did not exist. Udet's Technical Office intended to double aircraft production from 500 per month – which had finally been reached in November – to 1,000 per month by 1941.

All this shows that Göring actually did reckon on the 'peace in our time' fulsomely announced by Chamberlain on his return to London, though the term 'appeasement' would be associated with Chamberlain's name then and for ever.

Göring's hectic activities during the autumn were interrupted on 4 November 1938 by Edda's baptism at Carinhall. Reich Bishop Müller performed the ceremony. Hitler, a representative of the Luftwaffe, close relatives and friends, even Göring's housekeeper Cilly Wachowiak, acted as godparents.

Hitler did not stay long; his presence, as von Below recalls, caused nervousness at Carinhall. During the night he drove to Weimar where he made a speech in which he attacked Churchill and the Bolshevists.

Göring, who could not understand Hitler's aggressive attitude towards Britain which appears to have sprung up after the Munich Accord, must have sensed that his influence on the Führer was waning. He did everything in his power to fulfil Hitler's wishes, as his efforts in regard to the 'five-fold increase' of the Luftwaffe demonstrate.

On 9 November 1938 he was in Munich for the by now almost traditional 'march to the Feldherrnhalle' and was reminded of the serious injury he had suffered in 1923. In the afternoon, while he was at Hitler's apartment, news came that von Rath, whom Herschel Grünspan had shot in Paris, had died. (Grünspan was a 17-year-old German Jewish refugee who went to the German embassy in Paris with the intention of killing the ambassador. The young third secretary was sent to find out what he wanted, and was mortally wounded. Ironically, von Rath was no anti-Semite, and was in fact anti-Nazi.) In the evening Göring took part with Hitler in the gathering of comrades of the Party leadership in the old Munich city hall. Afterwards he immediately drove back to Berlin.

As to what happened next, he told Werner Bross in the Nuremberg Prison in 1946: 'The witness Körner, former State Secretary, knows that I first learned of the pogrom against the Jews on the morning of 10 November 1938. During the night my adjutant woke me up near Halle and pointed out a huge fire to me which lit up the clouds. But I did not yet know what this meant. It was only when driving through Berlin to my offices very early next morning that I saw the mess. I became spitting mad and had head-on confrontations with several gentlemen, primarily with Dr Goebbels. On 11 November, at noon, Dr Goebbels complained to the Führer about the serious altercations with me, more precisely, he snitched during his lunch with the Führer. I had really told those gentlemen off: For me the news of the pogrom was a punch in the face and I was in a towering rage! I myself had been buying from Jews to the end, mostly works of art.

'In the afternoon I then received a letter from the Führer in which he asked me to call on him. The Führer tried to mediate the differences between me and Dr Goebbels, who was also present, as it had always been his endeavour to mediate conflicts among his colleagues. Despite this, and against all ministerial protocol, he selected Goebbels as a member of the conference that had been convened for next day to settle finally the economic situation of the Jews in Germany by law.

'There Goebbels angered me mightily. Afterwards the Führer said to me when I was alone with him: "You must be more careful. People must not know of your pro-Jewish sentiments!" I alone was responsible for the meeting on 12 November 1938, just as for the subsequent measures taken by the specialist ministries, because as the Beauftragter of the four-year plan, I initiated their proposals and work!'

The pogrom immediately became known as the *Reichskristallnacht* (lit. Reich crystal night) because the rampaging SS smashed the windows and plundered Jewish shops and anything breakable in Jewish homes. Synagogues were burned down and Jewish people were beaten and killed. The terror had been instigated by Goebbels with the help of Heydrich and the SS, which also undertook its execution. Hitler, von Below writes, had been angry. 'I did not have any doubt that Hitler's surprise was not a show. He had known nothing. During the further course of the night Hitler had himself put through to Goebbels. It was a lengthy telephone conversation which he conducted alone from his living-room. After that Hitler did not appear again.

'The result was that Hitler was accused of having been the instigator. He knew this. Nevertheless he covered for the guilty, particularly since it soon became apparent that the instigator had been Goebbels.'

With this pogrom, Goebbels, the most avid enemy of the Jews in Hitler's entourage, had achieved a victory over the 'pro-Jewish' Göring. During the meeting which Hitler had ordered on 12 November, in the Reich Aviation Ministry, which lasted for four hours and at which the future discrimination against the Jews was discussed, sharp altercations between Göring and Goebbels took place. Göring was outraged at the material losses. He opposed reprisals that Goebbels proposed by making them look ridiculous.

From the minutes:

Goebbels: 'Furthermore I consider it to be necessary that the Jews be removed from public view where they are seen as a provocation. For example it is still possible today that a Jew can share a sleeping-compartment on a train with a German. The Reich Traffic Ministry must therefore issue a decree according to which special compartments are to be provided for Jews, and that if this compartment is full, the Jews have no right to a seat, and that the Jews, but only if all the Germans have seats, get a special compartment, and that on the other hand they are not intermingled with the Germans, and that if there are no seats, the Jews have to stand outside in the corridor.'

Göring: 'I think it is much more reasonable to give them their own compartments.'

Goebbels: 'But not if the train is overcrowded.'

Göring: 'Just a minute! There will be one Jewish car. If that is full the rest must stay at home.'

Goebbels: 'It should be considered whether it is not necessary to ban the Jews from going into the German forests. Today hordes of Jews are walking around in the Grunewald. This is a constant provocation, we have incidents all the time. What the Jews are doing is so inciting and provocative that fights constantly break out.'

Göring: 'O.K. We will put a certain part of the forest at the disposal of the Jews and Alpers (Forestry Official for Prussia) will take care that the various animals that damn well look very much like the Jews – the elk has a very curved nose – will be brought there and made to settle! Now please call in Herr Hilgard from the insurance company. He is waiting outside.

'There is a totally different situation in the case of glass insurance, which plays a very big role. Here by far the greater part of those damaged are Aryans. Namely, this is the ownership of the houses of which the preponderant part is in Aryan hands, whereas the Jew as a rule is only the tenant of the store.'

Goebbels: 'Then the Jew must pay for the damage.'

Göring: 'There is no sense in that. We do not have any raw materials. It's all foreign glass. It costs foreign currency. It drives you up the wall! This is rebellion. That is the legal term. It was not theft, not burglary, but quite evidently the masses rolled in and smashed things. Or disturbance ...'

Hilgard: 'For me it has to be self-evident that the honourable German businessman is not permitted to suffer ...'

Göring: 'Then its damn well up to you to take care that not so many window panes are broken! You are also a part of the people. Send your salesmen out. Have them enlighten people!'

At the end of the meeting the minutes state:

Göring: 'As a wording I will select, that for their dastardly crimes etc., the German Jews in their totality are sentenced to a collective contribution of one billion. That should hit the mark. The swine will not be so quick about committing a second murder.

'Otherwise I would like to state again: I would not wish to be a Jew in Germany.

'If the German Reich is to become involved in a foreign policy conflict in some foreseeable time, it is self-evident that we in Germany too will be thinking in the first instance of calling the Jews to a general accounting. Furthermore the Führer will now finally launch a foreign policy initiative abroad, initially with those powers who have raised the Jewish question in order then to actually come to a solution of the Madagascar question. He explained this to me on 9 November. There is no other alternative.' (Göring probably meant the afternoon meeting at Hitler's apartment in Munich during which the news of von Rath's death was received.)

'He also wants to show the other nations: "Why are you always talking about the Jews? – take them!" One can then also make a second proposal: "The rich Jews can buy a big territory in North America, Canada, or elsewhere for their co-religionists!"'

As much as Göring and his wife publicly and privately condemned the Reichskristallnacht, as Beauftragter of the four year plan, Göring had become involved in this 'dirty business', as he described it to Ambassador Ullrich von Hassel, by Goebbels' having instigated it and by Hitler having covered for Goebbels. This was to be the last time, he told von Hassel. When the Prussian Minister of Finance Popitz demanded of Göring that the culprits be punished, Göring replied: 'My dear Popitz, do you intend to punish the Führer?' Popitz believed that Göring was very upset about the excesses.

Roosevelt had recalled his ambassador. The tenuous threads that Göring had spun to the embassies of the Western Powers appeared to be tearing. He ordered Reich Minister Frick in a letter of 24 January 1939 to install in his ministry a central emigration office for Jews. Chief of this office was to be Heydrich, who was empowered to 'solve' the Jewish question by emigration and evacuation 'in the most favourable manner under the given circumstances'.

In his book *Failure of a Mission*, published in London in 1940, Henderson writes about the Görings: 'Of all the National Socialist Party leaders I found Hermann Göring to be the most sympathetic by far. In a crisis or a war he would be completely ruthless. He once told me that he really only admired Englishmen when they were pirates like Francis Drake, and he accused us of already being far too sophisticated. He himself was the typical freebooter, but did have some winsome character traits, and I must admit that I entertained some sympathy for him. I liked Frau Göring as much as him and possibly with greater moral justification. Göring always gave me to understand that he was Hitler's natural successor as Führer.'

After the Reichskristallnacht the German Ambassador in Rome, von Hassel, had suggested to Göring that he act against Hitler together with the Commander-in-Chief of the Army, von Brauchitsch, and dismiss him because of the pogrom.

On 16 May 1946 in his prison cell at Nuremberg Göring said to Werner Bross: 'Yes, it is sad that I did not take over the government in 1938.'

Göring had been the only Party leader, if one excludes Hitler, whom the people had actually respected, Henderson writes. Perhaps he wanted to defend his friendly stance towards Göring by this statement.

But Göring never even considered putting himself in the place of the man who had given him his power. He was able to serve him even when Hitler's actions, or those of people he covered for, went against his conscience. He had his power from Hitler, not from the people, who had no say in anything during the final year of peace.

24

War or Peace

At the beginning of 1939 a retiring element in Göring's conduct becomes noticeable. He withdraws from foreign politics, spends a brief time reorganising the Luftwaffe, and then avoids Berlin whenever possible. He goes hunting in the Rominter Heide and spends much time at Carinhall, where he undertakes a dieting cure in order to lose 60 pounds. At the end of February he leaves Carinhall with his wife on an extended vacation abroad. He knows that the next issue will be Poland, but he leaves the discussions with the Polish Ambassador Lipski and the government in Warsaw to Ribbentrop, who has now become Hitler's primary adviser on foreign policy.

He reorganises the Luftwaffe into three air fleets, and with effect from 1 February its command structure becomes combat ready. General Kesselring is given command of Air Fleet 1 (East), General Felmy of Air Fleet 2 (North), and General Sperrle of Air Fleet 3 (West). Colonel Jeschonnek, who is an enemy of Milch, becomes Chief of Staff. Milch again becomes Göring's deputy in the Reich Aviation Ministry. The most important new appointment, however, is that Udet is given the position of *Generalluftzeugmeister* (chief of all flying equipment) and has 24 departments reporting to him. With this, Udet has become the Luftwaffe General with the greatest work load, and the one who has to represent Göring's intentions with regard to the rearming of the Luftwaffe.

Udet is the wrong man for the job, but Göring wills it so. Milch would have been the right man, but Göring no longer likes him. He sees him as a rival for the leadership of the Luftwaffe, and one who would be better than he.

On 30 January Hitler had made a speech in the Reichstag, lauding Göring, Ribbentrop, and Mussolini, and warning the Jews not to plunge the nations again into a world war. Göring was in the chair when Hitler uttered the threat: 'Then the result will not be the Bolshivisation of the world and the victory of the Jews, but the destruction of the Jewish race in Europe.' With this Hitler had not only expressed what he was thinking, but also what he intended to do. The word 'war' had been uttered, and everything Hitler did from then on was directed towards this war which, however, need not necessarily become a world war.

Soon afterwards, Göring is alleged to have said in a conversation with Henderson, which the British Ambassador reported to Lord Halifax: 'Let people make as many mistakes as they like. I don't care.' Henderson added in his report: 'I believe that deep in his heart he would like to bring about decent conditions.

As the Field Marshal said to me this morning, tyrants who act against the will of the people have always come to a bad end.'

Beyond any doubt, the will of the German people was to live in peace, but Göring, who also wanted this, had also spoken of mistakes about which he no longer 'cared'.

The Görings sailed from Genoa to Tripoli in a German ship, accompanied by one of Carin Göring's sisters, a niece of Emmy Göring's, and Paul Körner. The passage was stormy. Marshal Balbo welcomed them on arrival and a photograph of the two Marshals, who had become friends, was taken. They stayed in Balbo's summer house by the sea. There were parties and an exercise during which live ammunition was fired. They rode on camels, froze in the summer house, and left again because Göring wanted to visit General Franco in Spain who was on the verge of winning the civil war. However, Göring had to cancel the visit and this angered him. They returned to Genoa and moved into a villa in San Remo, in which Göring could again turn to a personal passion, dealing in works of art. He bought and sold old paintings and antiques with the intention of making a fortune. He was afraid of war and wanted to enjoy life, but above all to regain his health on the Italian Riviera in the spring. He learned nothing of Hitler's preparations for the liquidation of 'rump Czechoslovakia'.

When on 10 March the government in Prague dismissed the pro-German Slovenian government under Tiso after unrest had broken out in the eastern sector of the country, Hitler saw the opportunity to annex Bohemia and Moravia to the Reich. On that day his adjutant to the Luftwaffe von Below asked whether he should inform Göring about the situation. Hitler declined with the remark that he did not want to unsettle Göring during his holiday in San Remo. It was the first time that he had refrained from asking Göring's advice on an important question. But as he told von Below, he also 'wanted to use Göring's stay in San Remo as a means of calming down excited emotions in Italy and other countries'.

On 12 March he ordered the Wehrmacht to march into Czechoslovakia on 15 March. It was not until 13 March, that von Below was permitted to call Göring back to Berlin, where he arrived by train on the 14th. There he was faced with a *fait accompli*, to which he submitted.

During a meeting with the Czech President Dr Hácha during the night of 14/15 March, Göring threatened to bomb Prague if he did not agree to the proposed invasion. Before Hácha gave in to the blackmail he fainted. Göring excitedly called for Hitler's personal physician, Dr Morell, who gave Hácha an injection. Göring left Hitler's office with the words: 'I hope nothing happens to him. It was a very strenuous day for such an old man.'

On the morning of 15 March the Wehrmacht marched into 'rump Czechoslovakia'. Slovakia became formally independent. On the evening of that day Hitler arrived at the Hradschin in Prague with Ribbentrop. Göring never went to Prague.

During Hitler's absence from Berlin, Göring spoke with the Polish Ambassador Lipski, who complained that he was no longer available for talks. Poland annexed the Olsa district which was part of Czechoslovakia. Hitler, taken by surprise, accepted this for the time being, but he was soon to use this annexation as grounds for making demands on Poland.

On 17 March Milch recommended that Göring use equipment taken over from the disbanded Czech air force to create a new Air Fleet 4 to cover the southeastern region. Air Force General Löhr, who had been taken over from Austria, was given this assignment. On 21 March Göring went back to San Remo to continue his interrupted vacation.

At the trial in Nuremberg Göring said that Hitler's coup in Prague had mostly taken place without him. Hitler had acted without asking his advice.

Göring knew now that he was no longer indispensable and he deplored the fact that his influence with Hitler was on the decline. But Chamberlain's government began to find Göring an interesting proposition now that Chamberlain no longer trusted Hitler, who had broken his word given at Munich. London believed that Göring was the only one left with whom serious negotiations could be conducted.

Under pressure, Lithuania ceded Memel, a Baltic port which had been lost to Germany by the Treaty of Versailles, and on 23 March Hitler sailed there in a warship of the Kriegsmarine. The Luftwaffe leadership was represented by Göring's deputy, Milch. The Polish Government was aghast, fearing that Hitler would raise the question of Gdansk and the Corridor. At the beginning of April Poland signed a treaty of alliance with Great Britain.

In mid April, before returning to Berlin from Italy to congratulate Hitler on his fiftieth birthday, Göring visited Ciano and Mussolini in Rome. On 7 April Mussolini's troops had occupied Albania. The little country was annexed to Italy.

Göring now believed that a war had become almost inevitable, but he hoped that by an alliance between Italy and Germany it could be postponed until 1942. By then the rearmament of the Wehrmacht was scheduled to be completed, and all the Luftwaffe's planning was based on this. The alliance was signed on 22 May 1939 in the new Chancellery which had been built by Albert Speer. There Ribbentrop, not Göring, was presented with the Order of the Annunciata by the King of Italy, which Ciano hung about the neck of the Reich Foreign Minister on a long gold chain. For Göring the sight was so sorrowful that his eyes filled with tears. It had been he who had negotiated with Mussolini for many years. He had to wait until May 1940 before he too received the order.

The alliance, known as 'the Pact of Steel', contained a clause of mutual assistance if one of the signatories were attacked. The 'axis Berlin–Rome', a verbatim invention of Mussolini's from 1938, had been given its steel frame.

On 3 April 1939, Hitler, without consulting Göring, had ordered the Wehrmacht to prepare 'Case White', the invasion of Poland which was to take place on 1 September. The three branches of the armed forces were required to furnish draft time schedules by the end of the month.

Göring returned from San Remo on the 18th. Tanned and 'cleansed', he immediately drove to the Chancellery for dinner with Hitler who told him that he had decided to settle the question of the Polish Corridor. When Göring asked what this meant, he was told that Gdansk had to become German and the question of the Corridor had to be solved. If these objectives could not be achieved by peaceful means, the Wehrmacht would have to be employed. Göring was dismayed. He told Hitler that world opinion would turn against the Reich for good. But he was forced to acknowledge to himself that, as with Prague, Hitler no longer needed his advice. Hitler replied that he had succeeded in all his undertakings so far and that Poland would not be an exception. Göring advised him to wait, but soon realised that he could achieve nothing against Hitler's determination, though he resolved to do everything he could to prevent the new conflict from breaking out.

'If the Führer would only leave things to me,' he said to his step-son Thomas von Kantzow who visited him during the summer, 'I would take care that Germany obtains its place in the sun and the next generation be able to live in peace – without war.' But Hitler wanted war with Poland, and he already saw a new ally in the Soviet Union.

When Hitler received the Commanders-in-Chief of the three branches of the Wehrmacht at his birthday reception on the morning of 20 April, he told them that the coming years would be dangerous. Until 1942 or 1943 Germany would still have an advantage in armaments, but these would then begin to decline. Therefore the fight would have to take place up to 1942 in order to gain as much as possible. He was now at the height of his power and he still had much to do which he did not wish to leave to his successor. Göring, the designated successor, was forced to listen to this.

On 25 April Göring ordered the Luftwaffe to prepare itself for new operations. Before setting off for Italy again in order to continue his vacation, he ensured that the French Government was warned about Hitler's intentions via the French air attaché in Berlin, Paul Stehlin. On 2 May he had his adjutant Bodenschatz explain to Stehlin Hitler's latest speech of 29 April, in which Poland had been attacked and the Soviet Union not mentioned at all. This time there would not be a war on two fronts. Whether this was a manœuvre by Göring designed as a deterrent or only the firm resolve to warn the two Western Powers of Hitler's intentions, which Göring believed were 'crazy', is a moot point. In any case, he did not want a war in the west, even if Hitler wanted to have his war in the east.

In a study dated 20 May, the Luftwaffe leadership declared: 'Equipment, state of training, and strength of Air Fleet 2 (responsible under General Felmy for the North) cannot bring about a rapid military decision against Britain in 1939.'

On 22 May Göring was present at the signing of the 'Pact of Steel' in Berlin, but in the secret meeting Hitler held on 23 May with the Commanders-in-Chief of the Wehrmacht branches he had himself represented by Milch. After Hitler's presentation, in which he had said that the overall situation in Europe was very tense and that the CinCs needed to be prepared at all times in case a war broke out against Germany's will, Milch asked whether he should inform Göring about the content of the presentation, he received the answer: 'No, I will do that myself.' In the hand-written minutes prepared by Hitler's adjutant to the Wehrmacht, Schmundt, Göring is listed as a participant, but this was not correct; he was not in Berlin at the time.

At Carinhall on 27 May Göring spoke to Henderson who informed London the following day: 'I had the impression that Göring was glad to see me. While Göring is hardly better than the other Party bigwigs, I am nevertheless sure he does not want war, and he hates Ribbentrop.'

After the occupation of Prague Göring also had private matters to attend to that were related to his fear of war. He took care that Ilse Ballin and her sister, who had tended his wounds in their house and hidden him from pursuit after the failed putsch in Munich in 1923, were able to emigrate to Argentina and take their possessions with them. He also arranged for an exit permit for Baroness Lilly von Epenstein who went to relatives in Chicago. Before leaving, the Baroness came to see him in Berlin and transferred ownership of Veldenstein Castle to Göring and his daughter Edda. Mauterndorf was only to be theirs after her death. However, in the summer she returned to Germany and died of a heart attack on 1 September 1939.

Göring now owned Veldenstein Castle, a Biedermeier house within the ruins of the castle, in which he had grown up as a child. In 1939 Mauterndorf became his as well, the legacy of Jewish Ritter von Epenstein, whose mistress his mother had been for so many years. He had much to lose if a world war were to break out. But had not Hitler assured him at the end of May that it would be crazy if he were to stumble into a world war because of the lousy Polish Corridor? But was Hitler still credible for Göring? Could he assume that Hitler was telling him the truth after he had concealed the coup in Prague and the preparations for a war against Poland from him?

On 23 June, Göring presided over a meeting of the Reich Defence Council. The topic was the labour force, of which seven million men would have to be replaced if they were called up during mobilisation. Göring clearly and harshly told the meeting what drastic measures were to be taken in case of war. It was the job of the Reich Defence Council to prepare these measures.

The raw materials situation had become even more difficult. In mid June Udet reported: 'that a proper fulfilment of the existing requirements was no longer possible'. The Wehrmacht Supreme Command had set new quotas which showed that rearmament could not continue as before because of lack of raw materials.

On 3 July aircraft, weapons, and equipment were demonstrated to Hitler at the Luftwaffe proving ground at Rechlin on the Müritzsee in Mecklenburg. The Luftwaffe leadership, trying to draw Hitler's attention to the new developments for which the required raw materials were not available. The demonstration had already been tried out on Italian officers at the end of June. Since Göring, Milch and Udet had planned the new developments within a programme that was to last until 1943, it made sense to explain to Hitler that he could not count on them before then. In this they were not as successful as they had hoped. 'Therefore Hitler came away from the Rechlin demonstration with completely wrong conceptions, which later on led to unjustified complaints against the Luftwaffe,' Hitler's Luftwaffe adjutant von Below writes. After the demonstration he had told Hitler that all this had been 'pie in the sky'. But Hitler was convinced that he could risk a war with such an air force. Göring believed that 1943 had been meant as the year the war would begin, but Hitler was thinking of 1939. Like Göring he knew that according to the plans of 'Case White' he had to decide by 12 August 1939 whether deployment against Poland was to begin or not.

Much of what had been shown would not ready for combat even in 1943. The reasons for this are to be found in Udet and his Technical Office. The most technically advanced projects were blocked. This is particularly true of the jet aircraft He 176 which Heinkel's test pilot demonstrated. Ernst Heinkel writes: 'For the demonstration in Rechlin a flying field three kilometres away from the actual Rechlin airfield had been prepared. I was waiting with my people while Hitler first visited Rechlin airfield and watched the main demonstration. What impressed him most as I learned later, were the flights of the He 111 with their take-off boosters (two rockets), which drove the machine upwards so fast that a second machine taking off simultaneously in the normal manner was left 150 metres behind. Shortly thereafter Hitler's car appeared. I held my breath when Warsitz squeezed himself into his seat, when the spume of smoke shot out of the tail of the machine and immediately afterwards the little bird began rolling across the field. Would everything work? The take-off? The flight?

'At that moment the machine took off. The undercarriage folded in. Warsitz flew past us at about 700 to 800 metres altitude, turned, "took his foot off the gas", glided down towards the edge of the airfield, suddenly turned the power on again so that the machine elegantly shot upwards once more. Happy and relieved I turned towards the group around Hitler. I tried to read in their faces what impression they had gained from what they had just witnessed. However, I was unable to form a clear conclusion.' The world's first jet aircraft flew at 800–850 km/h.

The outbreak of the war put an end to continued development, Udet's Technical Office was no longer interested. The He 176 was turned over to the museum of aviation in Berlin, where it was to become the victim of an air raid.

A new era in aviation had dawned, but for the time being the Germans took no notice. Göring's reaction is described by Heinkel: 'Göring took Warsitz aside: "Well, Warsitz?" he said. "What do you think about the whole business?" "Herr Field Marshal," Warsitz replied, "I am convinced that in several years' time we will still have very few military aircraft with propellers and normal engines." Göring laid his fat hand on his shoulder and smiled good-naturedly: "You optimist!" he said and his voice held an incredulous, condescending tone. Göring asked some additional questions but did not go further into the real issue which was burning in Warsitz' and my heart. "Well, Herr Warsitz," was all he said, "since everything worked out so well today, I am going to give you 20,000 marks." He looked at Udet: "You know what I mean," he said, "from the special fund." Then he drove off.'

After a reception given by Hitler and Göring, Warsitz returned from Berlin with the impression that they had 'considered the whole thing as being only an impressive toy, but that nobody believed one could do something practical with it within a foreseeable time span.' The development of the twin jet fighter Me 262 was to be carried out by Messerschmitt according to Udet's wishes, but at the time of the Rechlin demonstration there was as yet no engine for that machine.

In the spring of 1939 the English translation of Göring's authorised biography by Gritzbach, *Hermann Göring – The Man and his Work*, had been published in London by Hurst & Blackett. In the introduction R. H. Bruce Lockhart wrote: 'He is indeed something more than a soldier. Today he is a very strong force for good or evil in European affairs. In a world, in which one must face reality – and this includes an honourable attempt at bridging the gap between British and Nazi mentality – it is conceivable that Göring would like to become a loyal friend. Under other circumstances he must be seen as a ruthless and capable enemy.'

On 2 July the Swedish industrialist Birger Dahlerus had been a guest at a dinner at the Constitutional Club in London which had been arranged by Charles Spencer, one of the leading members of the Conservative Party. After dinner Spencer read a manuscript which dealt with the situation. During the discussion, the idea of a meeting with Göring – which Dahlerus had suggested – was discussed.

Dahlerus had had access to Göring since 1934, which was known to the gathering. Everybody agreed that there might be a chance of explaining Britain's real position to the Germans and disabusing the German government of its erroneous belief that it could go on unopposed with the kind of actions it had taken in 1938. Dahlerus promised to go to Berlin immediately and attempt to see Göring.

He writes: 'After I had arrived in Berlin on Wednesday 5 July, I was promised that I would be received by Göring next day at 1600 at Carinhall.'

On that 6 July Hitler left Berlin in his new aircraft, the four-engined Focke-Wulf 200 'Condor' to fly to Munich. From there he drove to the Obersalzberg to take a holiday. But at Carinhall too Dahlerus could see nothing to suggest that a war was threatening. A garden party for hundreds of guests from the world of theatre and film had been scheduled to begin at 5 o'clock. 'I was received by several officers from Göring's Luftwaffe regiment,' Dahlerus writes, 'who were dressed in pure white uniforms with white patent-leather shoes. With their rich gold embroidery, these uniforms reminded one to some extent of the Rococo with its tendency towards exaggeration and luxury. It was an environment in which no serious mood was in any way discernible.'

Dahlerus had last been at Carinhall in 1935 when it had consisted of a small Nordic blockhouse with walls of rough beams. Now he had come to a very large, two-storied building in the old German style, with a central section and two long wings. In the cellar was a cinema that could seat 100 people, there were several kitchens, and a German beer hall. Göring's office was of gigantic dimensions. The walls were covered with paintings by old masters.

For Dahlerus the old blockhouse had turned into a luxurious castle, which was obviously still being added to, since on his arrival he saw many workmen. From them he learned that the building was planned to be twice as large. The meeting with Göring lasted until 6 o'clock. The guests had to wait. Göring had them informed that he had more important things to attend to and that they had to be patient. Göring questioned Dahlerus. Wasn't Britain bluffing and wasn't the reason behind the whole affair its hostile and jealous attitude towards Germany. Dahlerus suggested that he have these questions answered by three of the men who had been at the dinner on 2 July. They were in Copenhagen at the moment and could come to Berlin. Göring agreed. Dahlerus drove back to Berlin. Spencer and his two companions arrived in the capital on 7 July. In the afternoon Göring called Dahlerus at the Esplanade Hotel to know whether the Englishmen had arrived and if so whether they had answered the questions he had posed.

'I answered in the affirmative and reported the answers the English had given in general terms.' Thereupon Göring invited the three Englishmen and Dahlerus to visit the Reich Aviation Ministry. A Luftwaffe general took them in tow.

'The Englishmen left Berlin on 8 July and I drove to Carinhall to report the result of our talks to Göring. He told me that he had spoken with Hitler about my suggestion of a meeting in Sweden. Hitler had agreed in principle, but had stressed as a specific condition, that such a conference would have to take place under such conditions that the meeting between leading personalities of both sides for the purpose of discussing the European situation would not become known under any circumstances. With this answer I returned to Berlin and flew on to Stockholm the same day.'

On 9 July the summer holidays had begun in Germany. The Görings sailed westwards on inland waterways in the yacht *Carin II*. In Essen they visited Fritz Thyssen, who asked whether it was true that Hitler was already negotiating with the Soviet Union. He could hardly credit that it was intended to conclude a pact with the 'Reds'. This would open all doors to Bolshevism and would be a tragedy for Germany. Göring tried to calm his friend down. All the Führer was trying to do by means of the negotiations was to prevent a new world war.

Göring's cruise on the canals and rivers was overshadowed by his fear that Hitler would put the country at risk. He loved Germany and he refused to imagine that his homeland could come to an end. He also knew that his Luftwaffe was not capable of successfully waging a European war that went beyond a war restricted to Poland, and he had watched with mistrust Hitler's attempt to approach the Soviet Union.

In Dessau he had visited the Junkers works, where production of the He 111 bomber had been cut back. Delays again occurred in the production of the Ju 88 dive-bomber. A 'bomber gap' was foreseeable in 1940.

On 21 July he arrived in Hamburg. At the Hotel Atlantic he met Birger Dahlerus who had come from London. The Swedish industrialist brought the assurance of his English friends that they would meet Göring at Trolle-Ljungby Castle near Kristianstad in southern Sweden. Göring said that Hitler had agreed.

On 22 July Dahlerus was Göring's grandstand guest at a parade put on by Dr Ley's organisation 'Strength through Joy'. Afterwards the new Strength through Joy passenger ship *Dr Ley* was commissioned in the harbour. It was to be used for holiday cruises, but it had been built in such a way that it could also serve as a hospital ship. Not liking Dr Ley, Göring took no part in this event, so Dahlerus had to meet Ley aboard the ship without him.

That day Udet came to see Göring to apologise for the fact that the Ju 88 dive-bomber was having technical difficulties, as Göring had been able to ascertain in Dessau. But Udet believed that by April 1941 there could be 2,357 Ju 88s available and by April 1943 even the required 5,000.

Göring continued his vacation in the yacht. Hitler arrived in Bayreuth on 24 July for the Richard Wagner Festival, which was to be his last. On 2 August the closing performance was *Götterdämmerung*.

On 25 July Hitler had learned that military missions from London and Paris were on their way to Moscow. The trip was being made by ship and therefore would take longer than by air, so that Hitler did not have to address himself to this problem immediately and could stay in Bayreuth for the performance of *Götterdämmerung*.

At the end of July Göring had sent the expert economist Dr Wohlfart from the administration of the four-year plan to London to conduct secret negotiations. He spoke about the situation with Horace Wilson from the Foreign Office. On 4 August Chamberlain adjourned Parliament for two weeks and during that time received the German Ambassador von Dirksen. On 6 August Foreign State Secretary Freiherr von Weizsäcker noted in his diary that there had been a secret feeler by Chamberlain about a compromise on condition that the German side would agree to a dialogue.

This dialogue had already been agreed: Göring's secretary Fräulein Grundtmannn had telegraphed Dahlerus in Stockholm on 2 August and asked when the meeting in Sönke-Nissen-Koog would take place. On 5 August Fräulein Grundtmann sent the following telegram to Dahlerus at Göring's request: 'Can make following time available for meeting in the koog: 1000 to 1600. G.' Göring used his long-time secretary for this correspondence, whose name, like his own, began with a 'G'.

For the following day, he called Milch, Udet, and Jeschonnek to his yacht for a very important armaments meeting. On this 6 August, a Sunday, Göring demanded of them that they build up an 'offensive air force' with 32 new bomber Wings (4,330 aircraft, including 2,460 Ju 88 dive-bombers) by April 1943. The consequences of this was that cut-backs had to be made in other types of aircraft. The three officers had the impression that with this Göring intended to turn the whole Luftwaffe planning since 1933 on its head. They were given the assurance by Göring that there would be no war with Britain now. But by 1943, the Luftwaffe would have to be prepared.

Then he boarded his special train to go to Bredstedt near Husum in order to meet with Dahlerus and the seven English industrialists at Sönke-Nissen-Koog on the morning of 7 August.

25
Final Attempts

'I did not want a war nor did I bring one about; I did everything to avoid it by means of negotiations. After it had broken out, I did everything to ensure victory. Since the three greatest world powers fought against us together with many other nations, we finally succumbed to the overwhelming superiority. I stand by what I have done.' These words by Göring during his closing statement at the Nuremberg war crimes trial in 1946, also include the balance sheet of his attempts to maintain the peace in August 1939. He believed at the time that Poland would never risk a war against Hitler's Greater German Reich if Britain and France did not want one. But in the event of war, he was not prepared to push Hitler aside, who had concluded the pact with Stalin. The war began against his will. It was Hitler's war, which could only end when Hitler no longer existed.

Göring's attempts to prevent the war have already been described in the first two chapters, and the hopes and defeats of this, the second man in Hitler's Reich, have become apparent. In the end he may probably have realised that he – like so many others – was merely being manipulated by Hitler when he was sent to negotiate with emissaries from England via the good offices of Birger Dahlerus.

When shortly after 9 a.m. on 3 September 1939 consular official Paul Otto Schmidt brought Hitler and Ribbentrop the written declaration of war by the British Government unless Germany stopped its aggression against Poland by 11 a.m. and withdrew its troops immediately, he heard Hitler's dismayed reaction: 'So they have declared war against us after all.' Göring came to the Chancellery later and said to Schmidt: 'If we lose this war, then so help us God.' But which God would help them?

Of the war upon which he was now embarking, he had heard of the comment made on 31 August 1939 by his friend Fritz Thyssen, who had gone to Paris: '*Finis Germaniae*.' When Göring telegraphed him to come back, saying that nothing would happen to him, Thyssen telegraphed in reply: 'I prefer to await the end of National Socialism here.'

Emmy Göring writes that her husband had been simultaneously enraged, angry and despairing. He had exclaimed that the war would be terrible, more horrible than anyone could imagine. His was no longer a 'deterrent air force'; that political aspect of the Luftwaffe was over and done with. But it was still the strongest air force in the world, with 4,093 combat aircraft of which 3,646 were ready for action. These consisted of 1,176 bombers, 408 twin-engined and 771 single-engined fighters, and 552 Ju 52 transport aircraft.

Paul Deichmann writes: 'According to a statistic of the Office of the Quarter-master General, at the outbreak of the war there were lacking 139 pilots for single-seat fighters (10.8 per cent of requirement); 54 crews for twin-seater fighters (13.2 per cent); 36 Stuka crews (12 per cent); 61 short-range (17.8 per cent); and 11 long-range (3.2 per cent) reconnaissance crews. This deficit was mainly the result of losses during training.'

Included in these losses was an incident that occurred on 15 August at the training ground at Neuhammer in Silesia. Units of 76 Stuka Wing were to demon-strate to Luftwaffe generals a close formation dive-bombing attack by the new Ju 87B which was powered by the new 1,150hp Jumo 211D engine. Twenty-seven aircraft took off from Cottbus despite the fact that there was heavy cloud over Neuhammer. Thirteen Stukas, their sirens screaming, plunged into the ground; 26 airmen died. The tragedy of Neuhammer was the writing on the wall.

The campaign against Poland which began at dawn on 1 September with strikes by the Luftwaffe against air bases and ground targets – in so far as the fog hanging low over the frontier permitted – was the first Blitzkrieg of the war. The young Panzer forces created by Guderian, and Göring's bombers and fighters, blasted their way through and destroyed the Polish armies. Joint action between the air force and the army had scarcely been practised beforehand. Now it worked like a charm.

The Luftwaffe lost 189 air crew killed and 285 aircraft, mostly during low-level attacks against Polish anti-aircraft batteries. Göring granted the widows of the fallen 1,000 Reichsmarks in compensation, which was given in the form of savings books. He continued this practice until the end of the war.

Göring used a special train with the code-name 'Asia' which was so luxuri-ously equipped that it was more like a court train from the days of the Kaisers. (Later on and even today it is still sometimes used, like Hitler's special train 'Amerika'. Göring's train was used by the Chief of the State Council of the German Democratic Republic. Hitler's train is at the disposal of the Chancellor of the Federal Republic.)

By the end of the campaign 50 per cent of bomb stocks had been expended. The British had assumed that the war would begin with an air attack on London. But no German aircraft appeared in the sky. British aircraft dropped leaflets but no bombs. One British aircraft was shot down.

On 10 September Göring sent his step-son, Thomas von Kantzow, who was staying at Carinhall, to Dahlerus in Stockholm with two letters from British pris-oners of war, which Dahlerus passed on to the British Ambassador in Sweden.

On 6 September Hitler had rejected a bombing attack on the British fleet which was at anchor in Scapa Flow. On 9 September he demanded of Göring, von Brauchitsch, and Keitel that under no circumstances were the French to be provoked.

On 26 September Hitler returned to Berlin, and Dahlerus flew to Berlin from Stockholm. Göring took him to see Hitler who told Dahlerus that the British could have peace. But he named conditions. Poland was beaten (Warsaw capitulated on 27 September), but a 'rump Poland' could continue to exist. Naturally, Poland would have to cede the former German eastern territories. In addition a guarantee of the German border in the west was required. Göring told Dahlerus that he was prepared to conduct peace negotiations with Britain immediately, in a neutral country, and that these should take place between military personnel. He was considering the Chief of the Imperial General Staff, Field Marshal Ironside. Hitler added that Britain would have to be quick. The Russians, who had invaded eastern Poland on 17 September, now had a say in the matter.

On the evening of 28 September Dahlerus, for whom all doors had been opened, had a meeting with Sir Alexander Cadogan, the highest ranking official in the Foreign Office. On 29 September he had a meeting with Frank K. Roberts, the Foreign Office's expert on Germany, and subsequently with Chamberlain, Halifax, and Cadogan.

During these talks in London, which lasted until the end of September, the British pinned their hopes on Göring whom they thought could bring about conditions from which a credible German foreign policy might emerge. For his part Dahlerus suggested that negotiated peace terms be confirmed by a plebiscite.

At the end of September Dahlerus was back in Berlin.

At the beginning of October discussions in London about peace plans must have taken place, because on 2 October the American Ambassador Kennedy telegraphed Secretary of State Cordell Hull that he had spoken to Churchill, who, as an exponent of the hard line, was considering an armistice. In the British file FO 371–22 985 (Germany, German aims, future policy, etc.) for the period 3–4 October 1939, 45 pages have been denied public access until the year 2015.

In the Reichstag on 6 October Hitler addressed an appeal to Britain for peace. On 9 October Dahlerus was back in Berlin and next day went with Göring to see Hitler. Dahlerus told them that Britain was prepared to negotiate peace terms, provided the subject was not only Poland but also the destruction of all weapons of aggression and a plebiscite in Germany. Hitler agreed.

Dahlerus went to the Hague with German proposals, and armed with a letter from Göring authorising him as a negotiator: 'I know that the other side also has complete confidence in you in recognition of the fact that you have always acted out of altruistic motives. You know that you enjoy my confidence to the same degree.'

In this letter, however, Göring fully supports Hitler: 'If Britain wishes peace, it can easily find a platform for this in the speech given by the Führer. I truly admired the Führer in his speech, particularly if one considers how strong the German position is today and that the Führer stands at the head of a large victorious army. If despite this we and in particular the Führer have expressed such a strong desire for peace, then it is above all from the conviction that at the moment there are no winners or losers among the three major powers Germany, Britain, and France, and furthermore that after years of war and battle, the problems will still be the same that they are today, so that exactly the same questions will have to be discussed, only with the terrible difference that there will then be millions of dead on both sides.' He ended by assuring Dahlerus that he would always be welcome.

Göring's phrasing in this letter concerning a war with heavy losses in the west and millions of dead is in accordance with the opinion of the German military leadership at the time, which was thinking of the blood-bath of the Great War. In Colonel General Ritter von Leeb's memos to von Brauchitsch and Halder it is similarly expressed.

In the Hague, Dahlerus passed the letter and the proposals to the British Ambassador who sent them to London. No negotiator from London came to see Dahlerus. On 12 October in the Commons, Chamberlain rejected Hitler's appeal for peace.

Göring still did not give up. On 14 October he suggested that King Gustav V of Sweden arrange for a meeting of senior officers. On 18 October the Scandinavian heads of state met in Stockholm. The main point of discussion was a mediation which the King desired but to which the current Swedish Prime Minister was opposed.

On 14 October General Halder, Chief of Staff of the Army, had a meeting with his Commander-in-Chief, von Brauchitsch, who saw three possible developments of the situation: attack, wait and see, basic changes. The latter could be interpreted in many ways. According to usage in German military circles at the time, what was meant was a change at the head of the Reich.

Hopes were placed in Göring that he would at least keep Hitler from an offensive in the west. On 16 October Göring learned from Hitler that he was willing to fight. That day the Luftwaffe flew a sortie against British battleships in the Firth of Forth near Edinburgh. Attacks against ships in British ports were still prohibited.

On 19 and 30 October, Göring, in his capacity as Chairman of the Reich Defence Council and Beauftragter of the four-year plan, signed decrees setting out the economic restructuring in the new eastern territories of the Reich. Since 12 October, 'rump Poland' had been renamed the *Generalgouvernement*, whose *Generalgouverneur*, Dr Hans Frank, a former Reich Minister, had his seat in

Krakow. Before war began he had been called up to the 19th Potsdam Infantry Regiment as a sergeant of reserves. From there, Hitler sent him to Poland.

At Göring's request Dahlerus again travelled to the Hague on 26 October in an endeavour to get the negotiations with London moving; unsuccessful, he flew back to Stockholm. There his memorandum of 31 October was prepared which listed possibilities for peace negotiations in great detail. He had it agreed by his government and handed it over to a British diplomat. But in London the Foreign Office insisted that Göring form a government that was able to negotiate. On 30 November the Russo–Finnish war broke out. Dahlerus went to see Göring, this time as advocate of the Finns, who had been attacked.

On 9 December Chamberlain and Halifax gave up all hope that they could win Göring over to a change in Germany. On 28 December Dahlerus was in London where Sir Alexander Cadogan told him that Hitler had to go and that the Germans had to realise that the policies of their government were leading the country to inevitable ruin.

A deliberately arranged indiscretion in the press hit Dahlerus. With this his role as an intermediary was over. Göring, deeply disappointed about the failure of his activities with Dahlerus, now had no further option.

When in early November he undertook the military preparations for the offensive in the west, which was scheduled to begin on the 9th, he appeared to be nervous and distraught. The offensive was postponed. A cold winter set in early, during which only the Luftwaffe and the Kriegsmarine were still waging war.

Göring kept his ties to Dahlerus until the end of the war. In the epilogue of his book on Dahlerus, *The Final Attempt* (new edition 1973), Walter Siemers comes to the conclusion: 'For his unique, idealistic action Dahlerus received small thanks, but much ingratitude and many disadvantages. In Sweden he was attacked as a National Socialist, and in Germany he was labelled a 'British agent', mainly at the instigation of Ribbentrop, Himmler, and Goebbels. It was only in Great Britain and the USA that he received the objective recognition that his attempts to prevent the outbreak of the Second World War merit.'

Göring's Sweden that he loved now moved out of his reach. In Nuremberg he said that it had been due to him that Sweden had not been occupied by German troops in 1940 like Denmark and Norway. After his capture in 1945 he also said that he could have escaped to Sweden but had not done so because of his family.

On 8 November Hitler escaped from an assassination attempt because he cut short his speech to the *Alte Kämpfer* (original Party members) in the Bürgerbräukeller in Munich. Göring would have become Hitler's successor as Chamberlain and Halifax had wished. He had not gone along to Munich because he could no longer stand the beery atmosphere and the memories of 1923 in the Bürgerbräukeller.

Emmy Göring writes that her husband had saved Hitler's life, because he had called adjutant Schaub in the Bürgerbräukeller and had him put a note on the rostrum. The note had said: 'Hermann Göring asks the Führer to cut short the speech immediately and to return to Berlin by the quickest possible means. There is really an important reason.' Thereupon Hitler had delivered some brief closing remarks and left the hall ahead of time. From his special train he had informed Göring that he was on the way to Berlin. Emmy Göring describes the 'important reason' to have been a visit to the Field Marshal by a man who lived abroad under a false name and had briefly come to Berlin to present Hitler with a 'sensational invention'. Since he had to leave again the following morning, it had been very urgent. There is no question but that Schaub placed several notes on the rostrum to urge Hitler to cut short his speech because the special train was to leave shortly. However this may be, Hitler survived. Göring did not become his successor, so was unable to pursue a different policy in his stead.

And so ended the year 1939. Hopes that had been placed in Göring were not fulfilled. There was a war on and Hitler charged Göring with ensuring that it could be sustained for five years.

26
Not Only Triumphs

At the beginning of 1940 Göring learned from Hitler that the Luftwaffe was to form a special staff to plan operations against Norway. Because of the Russo–Finnish war, Hitler had had himself briefed on Norway in December 1939. The issue for him was the Swedish iron ore which was brought to Germany by ship via Narvik. Any danger to the sea lanes around Norway must be prevented at all costs; furthermore, a victory by the Soviet Union over Finland would bring the Soviets to Lapland close to the Swedish iron mines in Kiruna.

Hitler did not know that the British Government was also thinking about this, and was planning an operation to occupy Norway in April 1940. Hitler was still intending to launch an offensive in the west, but had postponed the start three times. On 10 January 1940 he set the date for 17 January. Belgium, Holland and France were to be overwhelmed. From Belgium and Holland the Luftwaffe would then attack England and defend the Reich.

An event that occurred on 11 January put an end to these plans. It concerned the Luftwaffe and therefore Göring.

An aircraft flying from Münster to Cologne ran out of fuel and landed in Belgium near Mechelen. On board was a courier carrying the attack orders for a paratroop division that was to be deployed in Belgium on 17 January. The officer tried to burn the papers but was only partially successful. The Belgians immediately passed the alarming news of the Germans' intentions to the French.

Hitler had Göring and Jeschonnek report to him. He strongly admonished Göring. The enemy now knew not only of the planned assault, but also the fact that a violation of Belgian territory had been planned. Since the courier had been ordered to go to Cologne by land, but had let himself be taken along in the aircraft for greater comfort, Göring's authority as commander of the Luftwaffe had been called into question.

Emmy Göring went for advice to a clairvoyant she had consulted several times previously in order to learn if the papers had been destroyed by the flames to the degree of illegibility. The clairvoyant, a Dr Heermanns in Kassel, described the incident on the telephone as he saw it: The papers were for the most part illegible, and after his return the pilot also stated that it had been as the clairvoyant had described it. The courier committed suicide in Belgium. On 11 January, Hitler issued 'Basic Order No 1' to the Wehrmacht, according to which no officer was to be told more of a secret matter than the minimum necessary to perform his job. This order was hung in all military offices until the end of the war.

The attack had to be postponed yet again. A new plan was drawn up, the Manstein Plan, which produced the astonishingly rapid success in the west. Hitler now showed his lack of confidence in Göring by taking the planning for the Norway operation, which was already being prepared under the code-name 'Oyster', away from the Luftwaffe, and on 23 January ordered all future planning of military operations to be conducted by the OKW (Oberkommando der Wehrmacht = Armed Forces Supreme Command). Göring's self-confidence was shaken, and he vowed that he would now become 'Commanding General of his Luftwaffe'. The Commander of Air Fleet 2, General Felmy, was replaced by General Kesselring.

At Carinhall, which had now become his headquarters, Göring discussed operations with the Chiefs of the Air Fleets during February and March. As 'economic dictator' he had to take care of the plans for the incorporation of the territories that were yet to be conquered in the West. As Beauftragter of the four-year plan he had all the necessary powers.

During these weeks Göring suffered from a swelling in his hip joint caused by the wound he had suffered on 9 November 1923.

Carinhall was still being extended. After Göring's sixtieth birthday, it was to revert to the state, which was paying for it, as the 'Hermann-Göring Museum'. Here Göring intended to keep his collections, antiques and paintings, which the people could then admire.

On 9 February he held a meeting of the armaments producers at Carinhall, at which he decreed that all armed forces projects that were not decisive for the war were to be cancelled. Curiously enough, he now saw the war as lasting only until 1941, despite the fact that Hitler had ordered him to plan for a war lasting five years. An exception was made for the production of synthetic fuel. And so it came about that Milch cancelled work on the Jumo 004 jet engine, the fuselage for the twin-engined jet fighter Me 262, and the anti-aircraft rocket.

On 17 March Hitler appointed the engineer Dr Todt, who had built the auto-bahns and the Siegfried Line, Reich Minister for Arms and Ammunition. With this Todt was also given responsibility for arming the Army. On 5 March Göring had already been hit by another proof of Hitler's mistrust. During a discussion of 'Weserübung', the plan to occupy Norway, he learned that he was not to be permitted to lead the operation. The OKW under General Jodl was to be respon-sible. He reacted with anger, complained that he had not been consulted, and attempted to have the plan changed. Allegedly the main issue was the inclusion of Sweden, which Göring harshly rejected. In February he had had his step-son Thomas von Kantzow tell the Swedish king that Germany would respect the neutrality of his country. Sweden was left out of the plan.

During the first days of March, President Roosevelt's special ambassador Sumner Welles, who was visiting the belligerents in Europe, came to Berlin from Rome where he had met Mussolini. He was received at Carinhall on 3 March. He was shown the paintings, the game in the Schorfheide, and a young lion which had the run of the house. Like his wife, Göring was very nice, writes interpreter Paul Schmidt, but not a good host, because he let the Under Secretary leave without having invited him to dinner.

Sumner Welles, who was very reticent in his talk with Göring, gained the impression that he, before all the other National Socialist leaders he had spoken to in Berlin, was able to judge the relations between the USA and Germany clearly. He also asked him about the persecution of the Jews in Poland, whereupon Göring pointed to the Indians in America who had been persecuted by the whites. Then Göring dropped the subject.

When he first saw Göring, Welles had assumed that he was wearing make-up. But he became increasingly pale and the American reported home that Göring was a sick man.

After Sumner Welles had left, Hitler had a meeting at the Brenner Pass with Mussolini who assured him that he would join him against France. Göring learned of this at the Chancellery on 19 March, but he remained sceptical. His relationship with the Italian leadership was strained, not only because he still had not received the Order of the Annunciata, but he mistrusted Italian loyalty to the alliance once the war became really serious.

During these weeks he attempted to exercise a moderating influence on the cruelties being committed in Poland against Jews who were being herded into the ghettos. At Carinhall on 12 February he advised Himmler, who had been given full powers to 'Germanise' the eastern territories which had been won back, to interrupt the 'evacuation actions' because of the reports that were appearing in the foreign press, and reminded him of the need to strengthen Germany's war potential. On 23 March he banned all further transport of Jews from the Warthegau to the Generalgouvernement, but the ban only became effective in May. By then, Himmler's *Volksdeutsche Mittelstelle* (agency for ethnic Germans from abroad) had more or less concluded the resettlement of Germans and Balts returning from Russia and the Baltic States that had been agreed with the Soviet Government. Thousands came by ship or overland in caravans to the new Gau Danzig–West Prussia and Gau Warthegau, from which Poles and Jews had been evacuated to the Generalgouvernement. Many of these people fell victim to the harsh winter weather and cruel treatment.

The foreign press were not alone in learning of this; the German Army in the west knew about it, and when the German Commander-in-Chief in the east, General Blaskowitz, complained, he was dismissed by Hitler in February.

For the Luftwaffe 'Weserübung', which began on 9 April, was to be mainly a transportation assignment. Göring deployed 1,008 aircraft, half of which were transport planes. So it came about that during the Norway campaign the Kriegsmarine was to suffer heavy losses, because the bombing of military targets had not been planned. Norway was to be spared air attacks such as in Poland. Hitler wanted a bloodless occupation of Denmark and Norway. In Denmark this succeeded, but not in Norway. Copenhagen was intimidated by a fly-past of bombers. In Norway there was a short campaign, in which the Luftwaffe with its transports and about four hundred bombers played a decisive role.

The British undertook a landing operation on Norway's coasts only hours after the Germans had arrived, but their troops were heavily bombed and were soon forced to withdraw. British military historians describe the ill-organised operation as catastrophic.

The only exception was at Narvik where General Dietl's landing force came under heavy pressure. Hitler lost his nerve and wanted to send Dietl's mountain troops into internment in Sweden. Göring too was nervous, fearing for the prestige of his Luftwaffe. Milch was sent to Norway to organise a new Air Fleet consisting of about 600 fighters, bombers, and reconnaissance aircraft and to lead the air operations. He kept his nerve and did not allow himself to be influenced by setbacks at Narvik. Göring is alleged to have sent him 'idiotic' telegrams from Berlin. With the exception of Narvik, Norway was in German hands on 27 April, and on 4 May Milch was awarded the Knight's Cross by Göring in Berlin. Now the campaign in the west was in the offing and he needed his State Secretary for the new task.

In mid April Göring ordered General Intendant Gründgens to produce Mussolini and Forzano's play *Cavour*, a historical pictorial broadsheet, in three weeks' time at the State Playhouse. Count Cavour had created the Italian national state and was recognised as the man Bismarck had taken as his role model; a man as hard as iron, a statesman whose self-sufficiency was impervious to any form of corrupt influence. Gründgens had intended to play Cavour, but he was dissuaded, and Werner Krauß played the role under his direction. There were two reasons for this unusual interference in the repertoire by Göring: he wanted to recognise himself on his stage, mirrored in Cavour, before the beginning of the decisive offensive in the west; and it was intended as an admonition to Mussolini not to leave Germany in the lurch now, as he had done when the Nazis invaded Poland. The première took place on 9 May because Göring wanted to impress on himself the similarity of Cavour's situation to his own on this eve of the attack in the west; perhaps because what he now faced seemed more difficult than anything he had yet accomplished.

He had deployed the largest air force in history for the attack next morning, 10 May: 1,016 fighters, 1,482 bombers and Stukas, 42 fighter-bombers, and 248 twin-engined fighters. In addition there was an airborne division, special forces, and a huge air transport park. With this air armada, which had been created in only a few years, he had to defeat 1,151 enemy fighters, but fewer bombers than the Luftwaffe deployed. For the Army, air superiority over the battlefield and close support of the ground fighting were all important.

In London on this 10 May Chamberlain resigned and was succeeded by Winston Churchill who had initiated the Norwegian operation which had been a fiasco. With Churchill as the opponent, it would be all or nothing for Göring. He had experienced Churchill's indomitability when, until the end of 1939, he had still had contacts with Chamberlain and his entourage via Dahlerus.

Until 15 May Göring remained in his headquarters with Milch at Wildpark near Potsdam. His special train 'Asia' stood by near the extensive bunker system under the Ehrenpforten Hill. Milch flew to the front daily to report on the situation.

In the morning Hitler had moved into his command post in the Eifel. During the night of 16 May Göring followed him there in his special train which was preceded by another carrying the automobiles and the AA guns. Near the village of Trimbs west of Coblenz, near a tunnel in which the train would shelter during the night, he found Hitler's 'Cliff Nest'. A photograph taken of him there shows him in a stance that makes one think of Cavour on the stage: he is standing next to his car like an iron statue, self-contained, eyes screwed up, on his blouse the *Pour le Mérite* and Knight's Cross, and the armband 'Fighter Wing Richthofen'. He is wearing the new aviator's cap which makes him appear younger, in his mouth the long, old-fashioned Bavarian pipe, whose porcelain bowl he holds in his left hand. He would keep this pipe with him until the end of his days.

By now the Luftwaffe had long since gained control of the air, for which it had fought since 10 May. On the first day it had attacked 70 air fields, and eliminated fort Eben Emael in Liège with nine gliders towed by Ju 52 aircraft. In Rotterdam 4,000 of General Student's paratroopers had landed and heavy fighting had taken place in the city centre on both sides of the Meuse, and German bombers intervened while negotiations about the surrender of the Dutch in the city were already being conducted. Radio contact was inadequate and the first wave of 57 He 111s could not be prevented from dropping 97 tonnes of bombs on a triangular area some 2 kilometres long. The second wave was contacted before dropping its bombs. Some 814 of the city's inhabitants died in this bombing attack, and Rotterdam became a portent of aerial warfare. On 10 May three He 111s had already bombed a German city by mistake. They were to have attacked an air field near Dijon, but they hit Fribourg in the Breisgau. The bombs fell on a barracks and a kindergarten and caused casualties, some fatal. Goebbels put the blame for the attack on the French. Göring was distraught. In these initial days aerial warfare had shown its double face: civilian targets would be included. On 14 May Holland surrendered, having seen what happened in Rotterdam.

After their breakthrough on the Meuse, in which they had received strong air support, the Panzer divisions reached the Channel coast on 23 May; 6th Panzer Division was only fifteen kilometres from Dunkirk towards which the British Expeditionary Force was retreating. Göring called Hitler and suggested that he leave the destruction of the encircled BEF to the Luftwaffe. This chimed with Hitler's intentions to spare the Panzer divisions and redeploy them for the final battle against the French. He wanted to end the fighting as quickly as possible in order to prevent the French from consolidating fresh forces in southern France. He also feared heavy losses if the Army were forced to attack 300,000 encircled British and French. During the Great War he had fought on the blood-soaked earth of Flanders. Göring believed he could carry out an operation against an enemy on the ground with the Luftwaffe alone. The leadership of the Army were aghast when on 24 May Hitler, in agreement with Colonel General von Rundstedt, issued his 'stop order' from the latter's command post.

With this the encircled enemy had been given the possibility of reaching Dunkirk, which the Panzers could have denied them. Göring charged Kesselring's Air Fleet 2 with the destruction of the port facilities and the annihilation of the BEF. He had doubts about being able to do this, but Göring had given Hitler his word. The latter was already occupied with the new offensive which was to be launched against the French armies on 5 June.

And so the British were able to begin their Operation 'Dynamo' from Dunkirk on 27 May, which was successfully concluded on 4 June. Under the protection of their new Spitfire fighters, which were equal to the Messerschmitt 109, and with the help of mostly small ships and boats, 224,000 British and 114,000 other Allied soldiers were evacuated to England. The equipment was left behind, but an army had been saved.

It had become apparent that the Luftwaffe was unable to fulfil Göring's order of destruction, and not only because of poor weather and air fields that were too distant. The interdiction by air of such an embarkation, mostly carried out during the hours of the night, was just too difficult. It has been said that Hitler did not want to humiliate the British whom he still thought might support him in the execution of his plans for expansion in the east. Göring however, had no further illusions about Britain since Churchill had become Prime Minister.

During the battle of Dunkirk Göring was in Amsterdam with Udet. He then returned to Berlin in his special train. On 5 June he was back again in the west when Milch, who had flown to Dunkirk, reported to him what he had seen: the mass of the British army had escaped, an achievement that could hardly be surpassed. When Göring asked what was to be done, Milch suggested that the Luftwaffe and Kriegsmarine begin the invasion of the island immediately. 'If we leave the British in peace for four weeks it will be too late,' he said. Göring replied that this could not be done.

At Nuremberg he told Werner Bross: 'I had only one paratroop division, which I had had to develop on the sly, because I had not been able to assert my demand for four paratroop divisions against the requirements of the Army before the war. Had I had these four divisions at the time of Dunkirk, I would immediately have gone across to England.'

Shortly before the end of the battles in France, Italy entered the war on Germany's side. An Italian air attaché joined Göring's staff and watched him go hunting from his special train. Göring had had a forestry official come from Carinhall with a roebuck, which he missed however, because he had fallen asleep in his hunting-chair. This took place after 21 June, the day when the armistice was signed in the forest of Compiègne.

Behind Hitler, Göring boarded the coach which had been selected by Marshal Foch in 1918 for the reception of the German armistice delegation. Now it was the French who were asking for a ceasefire. This was Göring's greatest triumph of the war and he was thinking of the peace which must now follow. He was convinced that Britain too could be forced to make peace. His Luftwaffe held the island in a vice from the North Cape to the Bay of Biscay, but it had paid a heavy price. From about 3,600 aircraft, it had lost 1,200 in action and 300 in accidents. About 1,000 aircraft had been heavily damaged.

Paul Deichmann writes: 'The losses of airmen had an even far heavier effect. The 2,415 dead and missing were mainly bomber and transport crews, among them many instructor crews from the training schools. The losses of older, fully trained and experienced crews was disproportionately high. The numerical loss could just barely be made up by the training schools, but at a cost of curtailed duration and depth of training.'

Göring visited Paris, thought of buying paintings there and becoming engaged in the art trade, then went to Berlin to greet Hitler at the Anhalter station on 6 July. He was moved when he drove to the Chancellery behind Hitler's car. The streets were strewn with flowers, the people cheered. They believed the war had been won and was over.

On 19 July Göring called the session of the Reichstag to order. Hitler gave a speech, in which he promoted him to Reichsmarschall and awarded him the Grand Cross of the Iron Cross. From the Luftwaffe, Kesselring, Sperrle, and Milch were made Field Marshals, Major General Jeschonnek, Göring's Chief of Staff, became a General of the Air Force.

Reichsmarschall Göring: had he ever dreamt of this?

Five days later, on 24 July, he was approached by Dr Albert Plesman, the director of the Dutch airline KLM, in which Göring's nephew Peter Göring had been a pilot. This was another Dahlerus who wanted to mediate between Germany and England. Göring agreed but first wanted to seek Hitler's opinion, who was on holiday at the Obersalzberg.

In August Dr Plesman's attempts to mediate failed. Since the end of June the Royal Air Force was appearing over Germany and had begun dropping bombs on German cities. Soon Göring was to be asked by Berliners when driving through the city and stopping to learn what the mood was, why he was not allowing London be bombed.

27
Defeat and Resignation

When 47-year-old Hermann Göring received the commanders of the air fleets and the commanding generals of the air force at Carinhall on 21 July 1940, to notify them that within a few days he would need their proposals on how to gain control of the air over Britain, he was wearing the new uniform of the Reichsmarschall. Its colour was grey-blue, the collar – bordered by gold braid – had gold-embroidered crossed batons on its left badge, and on its right a Reich eagle embroidered in gold on silver brocade. The Luftwaffe eagle had been retained on the peaked cap. Over the *Pour le Mérite* and Knight's Cross, Göring wore the Gold Cross of the Iron Cross. The last person to have worn this high decoration had been Hindenburg. The title of Reichsmarschall had last been bestowed on the victor over the Turks, Prince Eugene of Savoy (formerly the hereditary title of the von Pappenheim family), and Göring was his direct successor to the title. There was no command connected to the title, but a monthly salary of 20,000 Reichsmarks which Göring could use to buy works of art.

On 16 July Hitler had signed Directive No. 16 on the continuation of the war, in which he spoke of 'preparations for a landing operation against England, if necessary'. The subordinate clause had been added because Hitler still appeared to be counting on concessions being offered by the government of the isolated islands of Great Britain, whereas Göring's appreciation of the British was more realistic. He did not want to go to their island; preferring rather to lead the Luftwaffe via Gibraltar and the Canary Islands to the Azores in order to cut off British supplies by sea.

In Directive No. 16 three weeks had been set for the destruction of the Royal Air Force, this to be completed by mid August. After that the Kriegsmarine and the Army were to establish three bridgeheads on the other side of the Channel.

The British were reckoning on a German invasion and had six combat divisions ready in July; German Intelligence under Admiral Canaris made it fourteen. In 1805–6 Napoleon had been the last person to threaten the island, with his deployment at Boulogne, which he then broke off. But in 1940 the Luftwaffe, operating from France, Belgium and Holland, was to pave the way for the cross-Channel assault.

'The fuel supply of the Me 109E was sufficient for 95 minutes flying,' writes Paul Deichmann, who as Chief of VII Fliegerkorps was preparing the coming air battle over the Channel. 'If one deducted 15 minutes for warm-up, take-off, reserve, and landing, there were 80 minutes left for the tactical assignment. In this time-span in free flight from the bases in the Pas-de-Calais, they could just barely fly 10 minutes or 60 kilometres beyond the northern border of London, or fight for 20 to 25 minutes in the London area before reaching their home base with their last drop of fuel. This applied to free flight. When the fighters were deployed as cover for the much slower bombers, tactical flying time was reduced by a further 10 to 15 minutes due to rendezvous and forming formation. For all practical purposes therefore, during daylight attacks the radius of operation of the German bomber arm shrunk to that of the fighters, and the area they could reach with bombs during the day came to only one tenth of the British island. What this meant for the battle against the British air force and its industrial potential can best be seen from the fact that none of the airfields north of London were endangered, and out of 25 aircraft and engine plants only seven lay in the endangered area, some of them in the London area which was enormously protected by fighters, AA, and barrage balloons. Eighteen of these factories could continue production by day and night, because during the day they could not be approached and at night they were hardly to be found. The best that could be achieved was a temporary and local air superiority in the area defined by the restricted radius of action of our fighters. And this meant that we first had decisively to weaken the British fighter arm which had shown itself to be so surprisingly effective at Dunkirk.'

The Army had already begun their preparations for the invasion. On 11 July, ten days before Göring's meeting with his commanders, General Halder noted in his war diary: 'Internal situation England: Dissonance Churchill–Halifax. Churchill has prevailed: "War to the end". English war: Airborne troops ready by 15.8.: 400 transports à 20 men with machine-guns = 8,000. 110 gliders à 1 group of 12. England now has about 600 aircraft, we 600. Time required to defeat the British air force about 14 to 28 days.' The Kriegsmarine was more hesitant. Admiral Raeder tried to dissuade Hitler from the invasion.

On 13 July Halder was at Hitler's Berghof to give a presentation on the execution of the invasion of England. 'What occupies the Führer most', he noted, 'is why Britain still does not want to take the road to peace. Like us he sees the answer to this question in that Britain still places a small hope in Russia. He is therefore reckoning that it will be necessary to bring Britain to peace by force. However, he does not like doing this. Reason: if we destroy Britain militarily, the British world empire will fall apart. Germany will not profit from this, however. We would achieve something with German blood, from which only Japan, America, and others would profit.'

It could not have escaped Göring's attention that Hitler was now looking towards Russia, which is why he held back. If Hitler really saw Russia as being the next opponent, it would be senseless to wear down the Luftwaffe in a battle with the Royal Air Force. Russia, and Göring knew this from many talks with Hitler, meant Lebensraum, and this was the true war aim of the man who had now become so powerful in Europe.

Before Hitler signed Directive No. 17, which said that the Luftwaffe was to 'defeat the British air force as soon as possible with all available forces', and which set 5 August as the starting date for the increased air war, the Luftwaffe formations which had been concentrated in northern France had not received any attack orders. Hitler's adjutant to the Luftwaffe von Below writes: 'I learned from Jeschonnek that he had sent his attack orders with all the details to the Reichsmarschall, but he had been keeping them in his safe for days and had not passed them on. I realised that the many talks Hitler had had with the Reichsmarschall during the last four weeks had mainly dealt with a continuation of the war in the east. This had led Göring to the conclusion that nothing further was to be undertaken against England. He was preparing himself for the year 1941 and the attack against Russia. In any case, it was a surprise for him when he now received Directive No. 17 and had to have the troops informed.'

The day before issuing Directive No. 17 Hitler had categorically told Raeder, von Brauchitsch and Halder: 'Britain's hope is Russia and America. If hope of Russia is eliminated, America is also gone. Russia factor Britain counts on most. Something must have happened in London! The British were really very low, now they are back on their feet. Bugged conversations. However, if Russia is beaten, then Britain's last hope is erased. Then Germany is the master of Europe and the Balkans. Decision: In the course of this struggle, Russia must be done away with. Spring 1941. The quicker we destroy Russia the better. Operation only makes sense if we destroy the state in one go. Just gaining some ground is not enough. Standing still during the winter cause for concern.' Halder made these notes in his war diary.

At the Berghof Raeder had mentioned 13 September as the earliest date of readiness for Operation 'Sea Lion' (invasion of England). Hitler was no longer concerned with Britain but with Russia. But first the attempt was to be made to destroy the Royal Air Force. That was a job for Göring who, as Air Marshal, was now being given his 'air-worthiness' test.

On 3 August the formations received their attack orders from Carinhall. The air offensive was to begin on the day that the meteorologists were able to predict three consecutive days of good flying weather. Göring chose the code-word 'Eagle Day' for the first blow against airfields. In connection with this the chain of radar stations, which were equipped with the latest technology, were to be eliminated. The German radar stations were inferior as a result of errors made in 1939.

Hitler admonished Göring for his shilly-shallying about issuing the code-word, but the Reichsmarschall offered poor flying weather as an excuse. He travelled to

Paris in his special train and took up a position near a tunnel in the Calais area. At this time he was taking about 30 Paracodeine pain-killing tablets a day; whenever he had to speak to Hitler by telephone he took two to calm his nerves.

Air Fleets 2, 3, and 5 (Norway), which he finally deployed with the code-word 'Eagle Day' on 12 and 13 August, had 702 single-seat fighters, 227 twin-engined fighters, 316 Stukas, and about 1,000 bombers. The Royal Air Force had about 250 bombers, but 576 single-seat fighters (Hurricanes and Spitfires), and 160 two- and three-seat fighters.

Paul Deichmann writes: 'The ratio in single-seat fighters, which were decisive for the obtaining of air superiority or command of the air, was therefore 1:1, although the British also had the important advantage of "home ground". This statement can in no way detract from the combat achievement of the British fighter pilots, but it must be stated in order to correct the erroneous picture of the conditions and events of the air battle which predominates even in most of the German publications. In those days in the summer of 1940 the David versus Goliath legend played an important role in the psychological conduct of the fighting. It awakened the spirit to fight of the British in the island and in the Empire, it appealed in the USA to the willingness to take sides – isolationism and neutrality or not – for the underdog, little David. And it also affected in a curious manner the evaluation of the situation by the German leadership.'

The British had succeeded in breaking the German radio code. As Group Captain Frederick Winterbotham writes, from mid July 1940 their 'Ultra' equipment was deciphering all Göring's radio traffic to his commanders on the Channel coast and in Norway.

'On 8 August Göring announced Operation "Eagle" in his order of the day. Within a matter of hours this radio message was in the hands of our Chief of Staff and the Prime Minister. Dowding had been informed directly. The text read: "Reichsmarschall Göring to all units of Air Fleets 2, 3, and 5. Operation Eagle Day: within only a few days you will sweep the British air force from the sky. Heil Hitler!" When on 13 August, "Eagle Day", the air offensive against England began, Dowding – informed in time about the German strategy by "Ultra" – would not be drawn but continued to deploy only small fighter formations, and by continuous attacks prevent the German bomber formations from conducting precision bombing. Since the German fighters did not dare to leave their charges in order to hunt the British enemy independently, our small formations, and even individual fighters, succeeded time and again in penetrating the German bomber formations. Without any doubt it was solely due to Dowding's tactics that we survived the offensive against our air bases. When Fighter Command had been being built up, nobody had reckoned with the help "Ultra" was to provide. "Ultra's" disclosures gave him a valuable picture of Göring's strategy of attack.

'Göring appeared to be highly dissatisfied. In a radio message he demanded an explanation from his commanders as to why the Royal Air Force had not yet been eliminated and ordered them to a conference at his headquarters. At this time Göring was already fighting for his reputation. He knew that in the eyes of the German officer caste he was but a political upstart, who had no general staff training whatsoever and could only draw on his experience as a fighter pilot during the First World War.'

The conference took place at Carinhall. Göring had again withdrawn there.

The decoding of German radio signals put the British in a favourable position of which the Germans had no inkling. Even leaving that aside, the defence by the Royal Air Force was extraordinarily favoured by the radar system that had been built along the coast. In radio directional finding the British had a head start that could not be made good during the rest of the war. The Luftwaffe formations flying in over the Channel were detected by radar even before they reached the British islands. Fighting on 'inner lines', the British fighters – even though suffering from an overall numerical inferiority – were able to make concentrated attacks against the Luftwaffe's bomber formations depending on the timing of their attacks and their actual targets. Already during the initial days it had become apparent that the Stukas deployed against the ports on the south coast had suffered such high losses, that their further participation had to be dispensed with.

The air battle that Göring had wished to have decided in fourteen days continued in the skies over southern England. Winterbotham writes:

'On 30 or 31 August Göring must have blown his top: he again took over personal command of his air fleets and by his radio messages (from Carinhall) gave us timely warnings of new German mass attacks. At this time, the situation of the RAF was desperate. We knew that we were facing a catastrophe if the Luftwaffe were able to continue the power of its attacks of the preceding fourteen days for another one or two weeks. However, the Luftwaffe was also suffering heavily. According to "Ultra" it was no longer able to replace the aircraft lost. Its supply and repair services were simply no longer able to cope with a battle of such attrition. Now the Wings only disposed of barely 50 per cent of their original attack strength. The Luftwaffe had been dealt a heavy blow and its morale had gone down. In this situation, Göring made a serious mistake! Had he continued his attacks against our air bases in southern England for another fortnight he would probably have eliminated our remaining fighter aircraft. At 1100 on 5 September, however, he ordered his Air Fleet Commander Kesselring to attack the London docks with 300 bombers. Thanks to "Ultra", Göring's attack order was in the Prime Minister's hands and those of Fighter Command within minutes. The shifting of the attack from our seriously damaged air bases to the country's capital caused lively discussions: Was this to be the death blow for England? Did Göring really believe that the RAF was finished? Or was he only seeking revenge for a British bombing attack against Berlin which had given the lie to the Reichmarschall's promise that no British aircraft would ever reach the German capital.

'5 September was a clear, sunny day. Churchill was standing on the roof of the Air Ministry in Whitehall. The afternoon sun lit up the waves of enemy bombers as, high above the Thames, they headed for the docks. Despite the RAF fighters that were trailing their condensation trails high in the sky, the Germans broke through and hit us hard. Black and white clouds of smoke rose over the docks. For the first time London suffered under the German "Blitz". This was to be our death blow and Göring's hand was guiding it. None the less, it was to our advantage when he was personally in command, because Göring obviously had unlimited confidence in the security of the Enigma encoding machine which he made use of to an extravagant degree. The German attack against the London docks had saved the last RAF fighters from destruction.'

On 4 September Hitler had given a speech in the Berlin Sports Palace in which he had threatened to 'erase' the cities in Britain. What prompted this had been the largely ineffective bombings of greater Berlin by the RAF. On 5 September he lifted all previous restrictions on the bombing of military and economic targets in London by day or night.

In the afternoon of 7 September Göring arrived at the observation post of Air Fleet 2 at Cap Gris Nez near Calais. When the German bombers flew towards London above the heads of the officers, he declared into the microphone of a war correspondent: 'I have personally taken over command of the Luftwaffe in the war against Britain.' Over the thrumming of the engines of 1,000 bombers he promised the German people: 'a gigantic blow of retaliation against the capital of the British Empire'.

Winterbotham's dramatic description of the situation prior to the target switch to London, however, is cooled down somewhat by the facts. From 1 September Air Marshal Dowding had begun to bring up his reserves which had been stationed in the areas beyond the range of the Luftwaffe. Between 5 and 15 September he was able to reinforce his fighter squadrons to such an extent that he had 360 aircraft available. On 17 September Hitler postponed the invasion operation 'Sea Lion' for an indefinite period. Towards the end of September the weather deteriorated. German losses mounted.

The Luftwaffe did not posses any heavy four-engined strategic bombers. It was not equipped to fight a forceful, operational air war. Göring changed his tactics: daylight attacks were reduced to only small formations of Ju 88 and fighter-bombers (Messerschmitt 109), the main attacks were shifted to the nights. The 'Battle of Britain', whose objective had been to gain control of the air over

England, was irrevocably lost to the Germans during these days in August and September, a defeat similar to what the Battle of the Marne had been for the Kaiser's army in 1914.

After his 40th air victory, over the Thames estuary on 24 September, fighter ace Galland was ordered to report to the Chancellery where Hitler decorated him with the oak leaf cluster to the Knight's Cross, the third soldier of the Wehrmacht after Dietl and Mölders to receive this award. 'I made no bones about my admiration for the enemy we were dealing with over England,' Galland writes. 'He nodded repeatedly and said my description confirmed his own opinion. He too had the greatest respect for the Anglo-Saxon race. He regretted that despite some initially auspicious beginnings he had not succeeded in bringing the British and the German people together.'

From Berlin Galland flew to East Prussia on 26 September to see Göring who had now taken up quarters in the Rominter Heide. 'In the *Reichsjägerhof* built of massive logs and covered by a gigantic straw roof, Göring came to meet me dressed in his hunter's outfit of sleeveless green suede vest under which he wore a silk blouse with long puffed sleeves, his high hunting-boots and, belted around his huge loins, a hunting-knife in the form of a Germanic long-sword. He was in the best of spirits. The trouble we had had during our last meeting (on the Channel), the worries his Luftwaffe was causing him in the air battle over England, seemed to have been wafted away. It was rutting time and the stags were belling outside in the heather. Every evening the day's bag was solemnly laid out between bonfires and burning torches according to a ritual he had devised. Besides his congratulations, he had prepared a very special honour for me. He gave me permission to shoot one of the royal stags that were normally exclusively reserved for him. It was a so-called *Reichsjägermeister* stag, each one of which he knew intimately, which had names, over which he watched, and from which he only parted with great reluctance. "I have promised Mölders", Göring said, "to keep you here for at least three days. You have plenty of time."

'Next morning at 10 o'clock I had shot my stag. But Göring stuck to the promise he had given Mölders and did not let me go. In the afternoon he was given the latest reports from Air Fleets 2 and 3. They were disastrous. During an attack that had just been carried out against London unusually high losses had occurred. Göring was shattered. He simply could not understand how the increasingly serious losses of bombers were coming about. Once again I assured him that despite the heavy losses we were inflicting on the British fighters, a decrease in their numbers and fighting ability could not be detected.'

In early October Göring had the daylight attacks discontinued. Now only night attacks 'against England', as it said in the song which Greater German Radio kept broadcasting, were permitted to be flown. Göring was a beaten man.

He lost interest in waging war, probably in the whole war itself which he knew Hitler intended expanding to the east. He still held several meetings in order to further aircraft production. Production of the Ju 88 was still causing problems. Monthly production figures for the fighter arm remained low. In order to be able to again take up daylight attacks against Britain in the spring, 1,000 long-range fighters were required. These were to be an improved version of the twin-engined Messerschmitt 110. But Messerschmitt had designed a new aircraft, the Messerschmitt 210, which Udet sent into mass production without flying trials. The new design was terribly dangerous to fly and the series was stopped. Göring left it up to Udet to solve the technical problems, which the latter was unable to do. Milch was to take care of air raid shelters, but not to cause any nervousness. Göring believed it would be better to build aircraft than to use the capacity for building bunkers as Hitler demanded, However, as Hitler explained to him, aircraft production was only to be given priority again after the victory over the Soviet Union in 1941.

As he told Werner Bross at Nuremberg in 1946, Göring had unsuccessfully tried to prevent Hitler from attacking the Soviet Union. For all of three hours (in August 1940) he had argued with Hitler, and as Bross writes, while reporting this Göring hammered the table with his fists. However, against his own better insight he gave in, as he did on the matter of air armament for the approaching war on two fronts.

In October he was at the Ritz Hotel in Paris. The headquarters of the Luftwaffe General Staff was at Le Déluge near La Boissière. He rode back and forth between Paris and Le Déluge. Working in the General Staff's special train 'Robinson I', he organised the AA defence of Berlin against the increasing British air attacks. From the Ritz he went to the Louvre and stood before the old paintings deeply moved, but he also bought paintings and sculptures.

In the Jeu de Paume museum works of art formerly belonging to Jews were on display, which Reichsleiter Rosenberg's special staff had been collecting. They were auctioned off and the money paid into a 'Jewish art fund' which the NSDAP controlled because, as Hitler had ordered Rosenberg, it had spent so much money on anti-Jewish propaganda during the 'time of struggle'.

During the ensuing war years, Göring found enough time by such means to acquire one of the most valuable art collections in the world with the help of museum directors and art dealers. He claimed that at auctions he always paid in French francs, but this was French money that was being printed for the German occupation forces. In addition he had the – thanks to the many conquests – increasing foreign currency reserves of the Reichsbank at his disposal. Hitler, who was having art bought for his museum in Linz, was Göring's biggest competitor in this. He enjoyed the privilege of first choice, which he had Posse, director of the museum in Dresden, exercise, but Göring claimed that it was he who had the better taste.

At the end of October he told Milch that he would shortly go on an eight weeks' holiday and that Milch would have to deputise for him as Commander-in-Chief of the Luftwaffe.

On 4 November, during a situation briefing at the Chancellery, he had, for the first time, to listen to sharp criticism of the Luftwaffe by Hitler. Spain's entry into the Berlin–Rome axis had become doubtful because of the failures over England. Furthermore Hitler chided Göring that the number of air victories had been exaggerated; he claimed he had more accurate figures.

Next day Göring left for the Rominter Heide in his special train 'Asia'. It appeared as if he were escaping there to recover his inner peace after his defeats. But he could not hide. He learned of the devastating air raid on Coventry, and of new heavy losses of his bomber formations which moved him to tears. At the Reichsjägerhof he was untroubled by air raid alarms. The British were not yet able to get there, it was too far away for them.

When the Soviet Foreign Minister Molotov came to Berlin, Göring dined with him but without any enthusiasm. Hitler and Ribbentrop conducted the negotiations with Molotov, Göring was not invited. After Molotov's visit Hitler firmly decided to wage war against the Soviet Union in the spring. In Rominten Göring was visited by Milch and Jeschonnek. The topic was aid by the Luftwaffe to the Italians, who had deployed in Albania in order to attack Greece but were suffering defeats. Now the war had also extended to the Balkans.

The British occupied Crete.

In early January, Hitler ordered the Luftwaffe to include Italy in its zone of operations in order to fight the British in the Mediterranean, and soon afterwards a secondary theatre of war was opened in North Africa for which the Luftwaffe was also in demand.

In the new year Göring granted his fighter pilots who had flown over England a skiing holiday. He was able to think of such a thing in the remoteness of the Rominter Heide.

On 13 January 1941 he held a meeting at the Ministry of Aviation with Milch, Jeschonnek and his adjutant to Hitler Bodenschatz, during which he indicated that a war against the Soviet Union could occur. Jeschonnek immediately flew to headquarters at Le Déluge to brief his staff officers on the plans for Operation 'Barbarossa'.

On 1 February Göring returned to Le Déluge from his holiday and again took over command of the Luftwaffe. He now wanted to learn the state of the Soviet Union's air armament, and on 1 March he sent an engineer colonel from the Aviation Ministry to this country which Hitler intended to conquer. When the repre-

sentative came back in mid March he reported to Göring about new aircraft factories and airfields he had seen. When Göring told Hitler about them, the latter said
that that only confirmed him in his intention to attack Russia as soon as possible
in order to eliminate this threat.

Göring's worries remained. He could no longer imagine how this war was to
end. But he hid his doubts from his subordinates.

In March Milch had a meeting with Göring at Carinhall during which he
pointed out the secret figures on American armament potential. Göring told him
they had one year's grace to free their back in the east before the Americans would
enter the war. Milch replied that a summer campaign against Russia would hardly
be sufficient. 'If we hit hard enough,' Göring rejoined, 'Russia will collapse like a
house of cards, because the Communist system in Russia is more than detested by
the masses.' Then Milch heard Göring laud Hitler. 'All we others, we smaller
people, can only march along behind him, filled with a boundless confidence in
him. Then nothing can happen to us.' He was now propagating this slogan, but
he himself did not believe in it. He had to obey, like Milch and the others. He no
longer had any choice and he had already deeply entangled himself in the preparations for the exploitation of the east.

The Reichsmarschall had lost his influence with Hitler because of his defeat in
the Battle of Britain. He was never to regain it, not even through his obedience.
As Reichsmarschall he let himself be used by Hitler in whatever manner the latter
wished. And Hitler knew what he had in this Reichsmarschall.

Göring's personality had been broken against Britain. What was now in the
offing was a long, dreary road to the rubbish tip of history.

28
Downfall

After the defeat of France Hitler had made Albert Speer General Building Inspector for the Reich capital. Among the new buildings planned was a Soldiers' Hall, designed by Wilhelm Kreis, which was to extend from Potsdamer Straße to Bendler Straße, where a new building for the Supreme Command of the Army was planned. Göring had seen these plans and, no longer keen on his Aviation Ministry, engaged Speer to design a new building. Speer suggested that a *Reichsmarschallamt* (Marshal's Office) be erected opposite the Soldiers' Hall, on the border of the Tiergarten, where Göring could unite his many offices. After the German campaign in the Balkans, the model was shown to Göring on 5 May 1941. Albert Speer writes:

'The plan for Göring's building featured many stair-wells, galleries and halls which took up more room than the actual working space. The central part of the area reserved for presentation was a grandiose stair gallery. The whole thing was purely for show. In my personal development this building marked a decisive step away from the intended neo-classicism, as could perhaps still be seen in the New Chancellery, to a tumultuous and *nouveau riche* display architecture. This part, with its 240-metre long façade on the *Große Straße* was connected to an equally long wing on the Tiergarten side that contained the festive halls Göring had demanded, which were simultaneously to serve as his living-quarters. I put the sleeping-apartment in the top storey. Using air raid protection as an excuse, I intended to pile four metres of earth on the roof so that even large trees could have taken root. Forty metres above the Tiergarten, an 11,800 square metre park with swimming-pool and tennis-court would have come into being, in addition to fountains, water basins, columnar arcades, pergolas and refreshment rooms, and finally a summer theatre seating 240 people – everything above the roofs of Berlin. Göring was overwhelmed and began to go into raptures about the garden-parties he would give there: "I will illuminate the large cupola with Bengal lights and from there put on big fire-work displays for my guests."' Excluding cellars, Göring's building would have occupied 580,000 cubic metres of space, as compared with only 400,000 for Hitler's New Chancellery. Göring intended to commission a statue of Speer from the sculptor Breker for this 'largest staircase in the world'.

Only a few weeks before, the British had bombed inner Berlin. The State Opera House, the university, the State Library, and the Crown Prince's palace had been hit. Von Below writes: 'The Opera burned out completely. Hitler was very angry about this attack. There was a serious altercation between him and Göring. I heard Hitler's reproaches because of the useless Ju 88, with which the bomber formations were not at all satisfied. They wanted to have the He 111 back. Göring did not deny the weaknesses of the current Ju 88, but intimated that the man responsible at Junkers, Koppenberg, had reported that the new machines coming off the production lines no longer had these weaknesses, and that the machines for 1942 would be delivered with a more powerful engine. Göring always knew how to calm Hitler down. Hitler immediately ordered Speer to rebuild the Opera House.'

Speer had taken Göring's measure and the model had been designed to impress him. But the project was to remain a fanciful arabesque for a megalomaniac; the client's decline in power would ensure that the extreme exhibitionism of the design – roof garden fantasies and all – would never be realised.

Göring was to direct his last operation as Commander-in-Chief of the Luftwaffe after Rudolf Hess, Hitler's deputy in the Party, on his own initiative had flown to Scotland on 10 May 1941, thinking that he could persuade the British to make peace. Göring learned of the affair at Veldenstein Castle, which he was having rebuilt as his headquarters in the Reich. With Udet he drove to the Obersalzberg and was a witness to Hitler's rage about this independent action by his former private secretary. He telephoned to Galland in France, ordering his Wing to take off immediately to intercept Hess' Messerschmitt 110. 'You are to prevent this excursion,' Göring told him. 'The Führer's deputy who has gone mad is flying to England in an Messerschmitt 110. He must be brought down at all costs.' Galland knew all about Hess' capabilities as a pilot, and could only order a symbolic take-off. Later he wrote: 'Here at the last possible moment someone attempted to pull the emergency brake on a train rushing over the wrong points.'

When Hitler asked Göring who should take over Hess' duties, Göring said: 'Anyone except Bormann.' But Hitler did name Bormann as Hess' successor, without however giving him the grandiose title of Deputy to the Führer.

On 20 May 1941 the bloody airborne invasion of Crete by paratroops and mountain troops began, supervised by Göring personally. The island was finally captured from the British, but the losses among General Student's paratroops were so high, that for the time being airborne troops were *hors de combat*, so much so that they were unavailable to the Army when the invasion of Russia took place the following year.

Göring had a meeting at Veldenstein Castle with General Kammhuber, commander of the night-fighter squadrons. Leonard Mosley noted down what Kammhuber reported about this: 'He noticed that the Reichsmarschall now looked far more sickly, his face was fiery red, he had deep rings under his eyes, and he appeared to be exhausted. After dinner they stepped out into the court-yard of the castle. Göring drew deep breaths of fresh air and spread his arms as if he could not get enough. All the while he looked as if something were bothering him and Kammhuber assumed that the smoke rising from the brewery on the Pegnitz below the castle was making breathing more difficult for him.' They then went into Göring's office where there was a big map of Europe. Göring told him that the campaign against Britain was no longer important; the Führer was of the opinion that the time had come to attack Russia. To Göring's question as to how many squadrons Kammhuber could deploy for the protection of East Germany against Russian air attack, Kammhuber replied that he did not have a single aircraft available for operations in the east.

Leonard Mosley writes: 'Göring looked at him in anger and said that he had not wanted this war against Russia. He was against it. As far as he was concerned it was the worst thing one could do. The war was economically wrong, politically wrong, and militarily wrong. He did not want to have anything to do with the matter, or with the entire war! He wished to be left in peace. And with this, Göring turned away and disappeared somewhere in the castle.'

At Nuremberg, Göring was to state: 'I repeat that for strategic and political considerations I was against a German attack at this time. However, I never had any moral scruples.' During his interrogation by Soviet officers on 17 June 1945 he said: 'I was always against a war with Russia ... I did not consider a war against the USSR to be expedient.'

Göring was one of forty senior officers who took part in the briefing at the Chancellery on 14 June 1941, following which they had dinner with Hitler. On 15 June he called his Luftwaffe commanders and their chiefs of staff to Carin-hall. Milch noted in his diary that the atmosphere was depressed and that Göring did not look very confident. According to Hitler's directives, the Luft-waffe had to 'free such strong forces for the campaign in the East that a rapid progression of the ground operations could be reckoned with', whereby 'attacks against Britain, in particular her supply' should not be permitted 'to be discontinued'. The Luftwaffe now had to fight a war on two fronts, against Britain and Russia. For the time being the Army was spared this, if one discounts North Africa.

The war that now began in the east was a war solely of Hitler's making. And, as with the invasion of Poland in 1939, Göring had been unable to prevent it. Two days before 22 June 1941, he told his wife that he had said to Hitler: 'Then you alone must accept the responsibility.' Hitler had replied: 'Yes I do, Göring; this is my war alone.'

In the early hours of 22 June 1941, Luftwaffe bombers attacked Soviet airfields and destroyed many aircraft before the invading army began its advance. Paul Deichmann writes: 'The purpose of these attacks was to create so much confusion on the Russian fighter bases that take-off by their formations would at least be delayed. Success was complete. When the mass of the bomber formations, which had taken off at the break of dawn, reached the enemy airfields, no Russian formation had as yet taken off. Command of the air had been achieved by the evening of 22 June. Within 24 hours, 1,817 Russian aircraft had been destroyed, of which 1,498 had been destroyed on the ground and 322 shot down by fighters and AA. Göring refused to believe these figures and had special units investigate the airfields the Army had captured in the meantime. They recorded the wreckage of 2,000 Russian aircraft.'

The Luftwaffe began the war against the Soviet Union with 2,770 first-line aircraft. In 1940 it had had 2,600 available for the air battle against Britain.

From the summer of 1940 Generalluftzeugmeister Ernst Udet had come under more and more drastic criticism by Göring's deputy Erhard Milch, who accused him of having presented sixteen different aircraft production programmes since the beginning of the war in 1939, none of which had been executed or taken seriously by anybody, and whose only purpose had been that invoices could be sent to the Luftwaffe. Udet defended himself by pointing to a directive issued after the victory over France, which had down-graded his air armament to the fifth level of priority in the Wehrmacht's armaments programme.

Göring had stayed on in Carinhall for several days after the attack on the Soviet Union had begun, and it was not until the end of June that he went to the new Luftwaffe headquarters which was housed in special trains at Goldap and far to the south in the Johannisburger Heide. The Reichsjägerhof Rominten, where Göring liked to stay, lay near Goldap. Führer headquarters *Wolfsschanze* (wolf's lair) near Rastenburg and the headquarters of the Army command on the Mauersee were within easy reach by train. But Göring kept his distance from the Wolfsschanze, where offices had been provided for him.

There, on 29 June 1941, Hitler signed a power of attorney which according to the conditions of the time made Göring's succession to Hitler legal: 'Based on the law concerning the successor of the Führer and Reichskanzler of 13 December 1934, and under repeal of all former decrees, I appoint Reichsmarschall of the Großdeutsche Reich Hermann Göring as my successor.'

The high number of aircraft shot down and the rapid advance of the army now reminded Göring of the campaign in France and he again became optimistic. But something held him back from visiting the country in which these military victories were being won. During his interrogation by Soviet officers four years later, he only mentioned Vinnitsa when they asked him which Soviet cities he had seen.

In July 1941 at Hitler's headquarters it was thought that the campaign had been won: Smolensk, only four hundred kilometres from Moscow, had been taken. Hitler was in triumphant mood: once again it appeared that he had been right. At last he could carry out what he had described in *Mein Kampf*: the seizure of land in the east. Already in his mind he was dividing Russia up. Göring's only wish was to have the forests of Bialystok, in which he had hunted in former times, made a part of East Prussia. This was agreed. The powers of the Beauftragter of the four-year plan were now extended to the conquered territories in the east, and Göring signed the decrees which dealt with their exploitation.

Behind the advancing armies the special forces of the SD (*Sicherheitsdienst* = Security Service, i.e., the extermination squads of the SS), had meanwhile begun their atrocities against Jews. When at the end of July Hitler believed that he had already destroyed the Russian empire west of the Urals, he felt powerful enough to 'settle accounts' with Jews who were within his grasp. He verbally ordered Göring to issue a power of attorney for Heydrich, Chief of the Security Police and the SD. It was signed by Göring on 31 July 1941. The wording of the typewritten document ran:

'Reichsmarschall of the Greater German Reich
Beauftragter of the Four-Year Plan
Chairman of the Council of Ministers for the Defence of the Reich
to the Chief of the Security Police and the SD SS-Gruppenführer Heydrich,'

and the assignment read:

'In extension of the assignment already given to you by the decree of 24.1.1939 to bring the Jewish question to the best possible solution in accordance with the existing situation through emigration or evacuation, I hereby empower you to make all necessary organisational, factual and material preparations for a total solution of the Jewish question within the German sphere of influence in Europe.'

'In so far as this touches on the responsibilities of other central institutions, they are to be involved. Furthermore I charge you to shortly present me with an encompassing draft covering the organisational, factual and material preparatory measures for the execution of the desired final solution of the Jewish question.

Signed: Göring'

The carefully disguised decree with the terms *Gesamtlösung* (total solution) and *Endlösung* (final solution) – the latter appears here for the first time –

made Göring Hitler's accomplice in the extermination of Jews, which Hitler, in his speech before the Reichstag on 30 January 1933, had forecast in the event of a war.

By the signature under this letter to Heydrich, Hitler had confirmed his successor whom he had so recently designated in a formal document. In case he himself were eliminated, Göring was to continue with what had now been ordered in writing. Heydrich had to present 'shortly' how all this was to be done. This took half a year, until the Wannsee conference on 20 January 1942. By then however, things were looking quite different with regard to victory in the east.

In August 1941 Goebbels came to the Führer's headquarters. He wanted to evacuate the 70,000 Jews living in Berlin to the east. As Hitler's adjutant to the Luftwaffe von Below writes: 'Hitler was not yet willing to do this. As we learned, he only agreed that Jews should be obliged to wear a distinguishing sign. A police decree published in the *Reichsgesetzblatt* (Reich Law Gazette) on 1 September 1941 ordered that from now on all Jews had to display prominently a yellow Star of David on their clothing. This problem was only to be fundamentally solved after the end of the campaign in Russia, "in the most generous manner". I only realised the unbelievable cynicism of this remark after the war.'

In the summer of 1941 Höß was called from Auschwitz by Himmler, who ordered him to make preparations for the mass killing of Jews in his camp. With this, the secret murder machine had been set in motion. A Prussian officer, now Reichsmarschall, had signed a decree on 1 July 1941, which threw open the gates to the field in which the appalling Heydrich would be free to roam. Göring would soon take care that Jewish workers were granted reprieves because he needed them for the war economy. But the Rubicon had been crossed.

On one occasion towards the end of this pitiless Russian summer he opposed Hitler who, in September, demanded that he bomb Moscow and Leningrad with formations brought in from all the theatres of war. These cities and their inhabitants must be destroyed.

His liaison officer General Bodenschatz describes Göring's reaction: 'He began in a very polite tone and said that the Führer's intention was certainly worth studying. He had, however, to say right at the outset that it would be extremely difficult to carry out the operation. When Hitler angrily asked why, he became more bold and said that it would be madness to withdraw the Luftwaffe from all the other theatres of war for a single operation. What would then happen with the attacks against London? Had the Führer not said that they were to be continued with undiminished strength? It would be dangerous to interrupt them now, because the British would be granted a breathing-spell. They would reopen their factories, take up the production of new aircraft, and within a short time the RAF would be just as strong as the Luftwaffe.' Leonard Mosley writes: 'Hitler had listened to Göring with a stony face. All the friendliness he had shown the Reichsmarschall had disappeared. Suddenly he interrupted and screamed, he knew why Göring was opposing his plan: the Luftwaffe was afraid. He had already suspected this in the attacks against England, and now he knew that he had been right. The Luftwaffe was made up of cowards, It did not want to attack Leningrad because it was afraid of the AA batteries deployed there.' Bodenschatz continues: 'Göring could have told him what everyone present knew, that AA defence in Leningrad was nowhere near as strong as in London, where our pilots had been in action for months. Instead he only said: "It is impossible, my Führer, it cannot be done." For a moment Hitler looked at him with icy eyes, then turned his back on him and took no further notice of him during the rest of the meeting.' It was now that Göring began to fear Hitler.

During this summer a catastrophe in the Luftwaffe leadership began to make itself felt, which had been caused by Ernst Udet's shortcomings and his personal inability to master the office of Generalluftzeugmeister. Ernst Heinkel writes: 'Hitler put pressure on Göring to give Milch power to install management controls in the Technical Office. Göring – fighting for his own prestige with Hitler – agreed. Milch, aware of his abilities and convinced that he could master developments, did not let his chance slip.' Milch uncovered failures by Udet and discovered that production figures had been falsified. Heinkel: 'He gained Hitler's confidence for ever by an achievement that was extraordinary, even though his many enemies cast it in doubt. Supply of aircraft to the eastern front was about to collapse in the summer of 1941. The fought-out formations were finished. They had lost hundreds of aircraft through crashes on poor airfields and through lack of spare parts. Milch flew to the eastern front with repair columns, repaired everything that had been left lying along the way, and by this act of brute force was able to again provide aircraft. This was just one of those "heroic orders" which were later on to become the norm and only blinded vision to hopeless reality. In Hitler's eyes the deed made Milch seem the coming man.'

'One altercation followed upon the last. In August 1941 Udet was already a completely broken man. For brief moments he still hoped that Göring would stand by him, because Göring feared Milch's ambition. But Göring was only looking to cover for himself. He looked for compromises. He did not support Udet. On the other hand, he shied away from openly removing Udet from office and putting Milch in his place, which would have been the natural solution. "You have to stay on. You have to work together with Milch," he said several times. "If I relieve you, the whole world will notice that something is wrong."

'At the end of August, Udet was again on the point of collapse. Göring talked him into going to his hunting preserve in the Rominter Heide for recuperation where he would not hear anything about aircraft or Milch for a few weeks. "I can no longer hunt," Udet – driven by the previously unimagined violence of the war which was only now developing in all its horror – had already confided to me. "I cannot shoot an animal any more. I cannot stand the sight of blood any more." He said the same to Göring. Göring admonished him: "Then recuperate by some other means. Go for walks. Only get your mind off things. I do the same."

'On 25 August Udet took sick leave. During his absence Milch took over the Technical Office for all practical purposes. When Udet returned to Berlin, still ill and tormented by pangs of conscience, his office had been reshuffled, his most trusted people removed.'

When Ernst Udet shot himself in his house in Stallupöner Allee in Berlin-Westend on the morning of 17 November 1941, he left a message of farewell for Göring: 'Iron One, you have abandoned me,' he had written in red chalk on the grey wall above his bed. Beneath this he asked Göring why he had delivered him into the hand of 'the Jews Milch and von Gablentz'. 'It was impossible for me to work with the Jew Milch,' he had written in a letter found in his safe.

Udet's suicide touched Milch deeply, but for Göring it was a catastrophe. He had lost his best friend. Udet was given a state funeral. Göring dictated the press communiqué to his personal physician Dr von Ondarza: 'Generalluftzeugmeister Colonel General Udet suffered such a bad accident while trying out a new weapon that he died of his injuries on the way to the hospital. The Führer has ordered a state funeral for the officer who died in such a tragic manner in the fulfilment of his duties.' After this press release, which was read in American newspapers, Carl Zuckmayer wrote his play *The Devil's General*.

Other tragedies, not fictitious ones as in the play, followed. On the day of Udet's funeral, Colonel Mölders died when an He 111 whose engine developed a fault, collided with a factory chimney near Breslau. He himself was not at the controls. Mölders, like all the other famous Luftwaffe holders of the Knight's Cross, had been ordered by Göring to attend Udet's funeral .

Galland became Mölders' successor as General of Fighter Forces and Milch took over Udet's position.

Göring ordered a military court investigation against Udet's most important colleagues, but because it began to draw attention to his own indifference towards air armament over the preceding years, it was soon cancelled.

The German advance failed in December 1941 before Moscow. Hitler declared war on the USA, which had been attacked by the Japanese at Pearl Harbor.

Ernst Heinkel writes: 'From the moment that it became clear that the war in the Soviet Union was losing itself in infinity, and simultaneously the entry into the war by the USA became a reality, the Luftwaffe found itself irrevocably on a lost battlefield, and its reprieve from the gallows would last only until the resources of the Soviet Union and, above all, the USA, were converted to an overwhelming air superiority. It is senseless to search for a thousand and one reasons for the downfall of the Luftwaffe after the fact. Even if all the leadership errors had been avoided, even if the best possible technical-industrial organisation had replaced the chaos that continued to develop after Udet's death, even if the oft discussed switch to a purely defensive weapon with a sky full of fighters had materialised, nothing in the end could have changed the natural disproportion of power. And this disproportion would only have been temporarily affected if the Luftwaffe leadership had recognised in time the potential of the new jet principle on which I had been working since 1936, instead of losing its way in illusions, short-sightedness, and rivalries. Such a technical head start in the area of air power would only have been of a temporary nature, given the state of general technical development in the world. In the situation in which Germany was, it would only have secured a brief reprieve, nothing more.'

Herbert Molloy Mason writes: 'No effort however great could make up for the failures in the planning and development of the preceding years. Germany took up the battle with the Soviet Union without the strategic bomber, the presence of which General Wever had considered to be a precondition for a victory over the Russians. Production of the He 177 was started up again, but the machine still suffered from the configuration of its power plant (on each wing the twin engines were coupled) which kept catching fire. Testing of this faulty design continued to cause the deaths of new crews.'

Udet and Mölders were buried in the Berlin Invaliden Cemetery, not far from the grave of Manfred von Richthofen. Göring called out his 'Now rise up to Valhalla!' at their graveside. Then he went to France to lay a wreath on the grave of his nephew, Peter Göring, who had fallen on 13 November while flying with Galland's Schlageter Fighter Wing. Galland writes: 'At the military cemetery at Abbeville, where already many comrades from the Schlageter Wing lay who had fallen in the Battle of Britain and the air defence of the Channel, I saw the Reichsmarschall again, who laid a wreath on the grave of his nephew. Just as he had named me as Mölders' successor at Mölders' open grave, here, while standing at Peter's grave, he announced my promotion to colonel in the name of the Führer and Supreme Commander of the Wehrmacht. For this he took two small gold stars from his pocket.'

'He seemed to be in a hurry and wanted to say good-bye. Christmas was approaching. And during this season of the year he was used to making his purchases in Paris in a very generous manner. But I succeeded in having him drive to Audembert with Colonel Oesau and myself. There the Wing had been paraded. This 5th of December 1941 was a noteworthy day in the history of the Wing. Through the stereotyped phrases which rolled so easily from his lips when he wanted them to, Göring's speech had contained a hearty and comradely tone which left a strong impression.'

29
Drama

On the stage of the theatre on the Gänsemarkt in Berlin now stood Mephisto, whom Gründgens played as 'a tragic embodiment of diabolical spirit in a blue-grey overcoat with long blond locks,' as one newspaper reported. He directed both parts of *Faust* with Paul Hartmann – whom he considered to be the most masculine of all German actors – in the role of Faust.

Göring also wore a blue-grey overcoat – the colours of the Luftwaffe.

'Out of my inbred animosity, later increased to the highest degree by outer circumstances, against anything blown up, anything "titanic", any exhibitionistic rooting around in one's soul,' as Gründgens wrote, he had achieved something: 'Action from line to line, movement from step to step – drama.' This drama was called Hitler's war. Action followed upon action, there was no escape, and in this third year of the war, Mephisto was the fallen angel who gambles with God knowing that he will lose.

It was the last flight of the artistic director and actor that the Görings were to watch from the Kaiser's box, blinded by their own artificial world in which they themselves lived out their own theatrics. Even if this is more true for the Reichsmarschall than for Emmy Göring, who knew little of what her husband was actually up to, she still suffered with him, accepted that he balanced his disturbed inner equilibrium by taking Paracodeine, watched him become addicted again, stuffing himself full of the tiny tablets that contained morphine. She was to write later: 'Göring, who recognised his position more clearly from year to year, but who could not give it up, both out of loyalty as well as from the motivation to help and to save, goes down in the history of this terrible war as a decidedly tragic figure.' And she writes about the 'psychological torment of a woman who each day experiences a man internally torn by unimaginable battles and monstrous pains of conscience, without the woman being able to help through intimately private discussions'.

Albert Speer took a harsher view: 'Basically, Göring was not blind to reality. Occasionally I was able to hear him make realistic comments on the situation. He acted more like a bankrupt who until the final moment wants to cheat himself while cheating everybody else.'

Fortune had treated Göring very lavishly, and now misfortune arrived on the same scale. He lost the power that had fallen to him, not all at once but step by step, just like the country he had believed he was serving when he made Hitler his idol.

At the end of January 1942 Hitler had sent him to Rome to demand troops for the Eastern Front from Mussolini.

After Dr Todt's death in an air crash, Hitler did not consult him, who had been the man's boss, when he appointed Speer as Todt's successor in February. On top of that, Speer was permitted to take armaments, for which Göring had previously been responsible as Beauftragter of the four-year plan, out of his hands, and Gauleiter Sauckel was given plenipotentiary powers to conscript workers in the occupied territories and deport them to Germany.

Until now all this had been part of the economics dictator Göring's empire, as had been the 'centralised planning' of raw materials allocation which he lost next. Nominally he was still in charge, but now he was obliged to stand aside and watch others, possibly more capable than he, take into their hands armaments and war economy, and uncover the mistakes for which he had been responsible.

To compensate he took things into his hands that were beautiful and valuable: diamonds, pearls, jewellery. He pulled these from his pocket during meetings or had an adjutant bring them to him. While he talked, he toyed with them. He was Midas counting his treasures which continuously flowed to him. Speer says that he loved to wear a green velvet dressing-gown when receiving guests, or a toga, as others reported.

At first he had objected to having his power eroded, but eventually he gave in. He saw his subordinates, whom he believed he had bound to himself for ever, begin to abandon him. 'Göring, who without doubt had initially advanced the four-year plan with great energy,' Speer writes, 'was generally seen in 1942 as being lethargic and decidedly averse to work. Increasingly he gave an impression of instability, he indiscriminately seized upon too many ideas, was erratic, and mostly unrealistic. It was an open secret that Göring was having industry pay for his huge expenses, and I had the impression that he feared a reduction of this income if his reputation were to diminish.'

But this did not happen. For his purchases, which he made himself or through agents in Paris, Amsterdam, and Rome, to complete his private collection – which he intended to will to the nation on his 60th birthday in 1953 – Göring continued to expect donations.

Visitors on official business recounted that they had been obliged to witness how at first he had been euphoric, had then fallen into a trance and then fallen asleep. By now the constantly changing euphoric and apathetic moods had become part of his persona. The Germans learned nothing of this. In 1942 they were being hit by the bombing attacks of the Royal Air Force, to which Göring's Luftwaffe and AA had no effective counter. In 1939 he had said he was prepared to be called 'Lehmann' if enemy bombers reached Berlin or other cities in the Reich. This had been corrupted to 'Meier', and now the Germans referred to Göring as 'Meier'.

Hitler showered him with reproaches which Göring took seriously, fearful that he would lose command of the Luftwaffe. Since December 1941 Hitler had been Commander-in-Chief of the Army and was waging his war in Russia where Göring rarely accompanied him. In the summer of 1942 he appeared at the Führer's headquarters in Vinnitsa, a large health resort on the River Bug, from where Hitler was directing the advances on the Caucasus and Stalingrad, but he escaped as soon as possible and went to the opera.

In April Göring had been back to Italy again. He visited Sicily where his VII Fliegerkorps was stationed and fighting over the Mediterranean. 'Actually he was scheduled to be taken from Reggio di Calabria to Messina in a speedboat,' writes Paul Deichmann, commander of the Fliegerkorps, 'but since there were heavy seas running, the Italians did not want to subject their corpulent guest to the dangers of Scylla and Charybdis in a mere nutshell so they laid on a special trip by one of the large ferries. When he sailed into Messina the crews of the naval vessels were paraded on deck. Despite this, the Reichsmarschall considered this sort of transportation beneath his dignity.' Outwardly Göring was still trying to convey something of the old splendour that had once surrounded him, but even he was beginning to realise that he was no longer being taken seriously. He still asserted himself, but much of it sounded like gallows humour.

In May an espionage ring had been uncovered in the Ministry of Aviation, a 'Red chapel' which had been providing information to Moscow. Their leader was a Luftwaffe lieutenant, Harold Schulze-Boysen, a grandson of Admiral Tirpitz, who worked in the Forschungsamt.

On 6 September 1942, as Beauftragter of the four-year plan, Göring chaired a meeting of functionaries from the occupied territories. After making some sarcastic remarks about the situation in the west, he turned his attention to the east: 'Now I have to tell you something so that I can soothe your feelings and so that you can look with high hopes to the future as far as the nourishment of your Wehrmacht is concerned. On the drive here I have just read from the land of the Don Cossacks – that is where your troops are just now – how a war correspondent arrived there with the troops. An old Cossack. Everything very proper. Now let us look at what they have to eat: "When the Panzer Grenadiers waved to the inhabitants from their vehicles they soon lost all their shyness and came with eggs, milk, butter, wheat bread, honey, and the first apples and offered these gifts of welcome to the troops in the armoured vehicles. They fetched sweet cream and cooked meat. There was sour milk as well and the Cossacks cut the white bread into big chunks and gave it to their guests, the German soldiers. These now learned how to eat this meat in the Cossack manner by piercing the chunks of meat on their forks and passing the chunks through the big bowls of cream."

'Well gentlemen, with the Wehrmacht being supplied in such a fashion nothing more need be said except this: for the time being the Wehrmacht is only to be issued with things that are seen as extras, chocolate and such things. I hope that we will soon be in possession of the smoke-drying plants and that we can pull in the rich fish preserves of the Sea of Asov and the Caspian Sea to a major extent. General Wagner, as far as the caviar is concerned we will go halves, half for the Wehrmacht and half for the home front – naturally only after we are there.'

(Interjection by State Secretary Backe of the Ministry of Agriculture: 'He can't have that much!')

'Yes he can, he can have half, if he conquers it. On this we hold that the additional delicacy can be eaten by the one who conquers the territory.

'Gentlemen, I would like to add something further here. I have an extraordinary workload and have to carry an extraordinary amount of responsibility. I have no time to read letters and memoranda. I only have time to ascertain by a short report from Backe whether demands are being met. If not, then we will have to meet again at a different level.'

When the German mountain troops became bogged down in the Caucasus, Göring said that these mountains were little different from the Grunewald (park) in Berlin. But in November he suddenly found himself at the different level with which he had threatened the functionaries in September. He himself had to accept responsibility for something, and he was prepared to do so.

When Sixth Army was encircled at Stalingrad on 6 November, Hitler forbade General Paulus to break out because Göring had solemnly declared that he would personally guarantee supply of Sixth Army by air. When Chief of Staff Zeitzler expressed doubts about this during the briefing, Göring declared that it was up the Luftwaffe to make the necessary calculations. But the Luftwaffe general staff had already calculated that supply of the pocket by air was impossible.

On 12 December Göring sent out invitations for the re-opening of the destroyed State Opera House in Unter den Linden. The performance was the *Meistersinger of Nürnberg*. Speer sat beside Göring in the Kaiser's box, which after the reconstruction was now called the Führer's box.

Ten days later Paul Deichmann, who had come to the Führer's headquarters in East Prussia with an Italian delegation, went to see Göring. Deichmann writes: 'Göring had ordered me to report to him at the Reichsjägerhof near Rominten, the former imperial hunting-lodge, after my briefing with Hitler. But I learned that he was still in the quarters that were reserved for him at the Wolfsschanze. When I approached his office I heard someone inside howling like a wolf. Nevertheless, the SS officer on guard at the door let me pass. Göring was seated at his desk, his head in his hands, and was making these noises. General Bodenschatz who was with him whispered to me that news had just been received that the airfields of

Tazinskaya and Morosowskaya, which were indispensable for the supply of Stalingrad by air, were probably lost. From time to time Göring muttered a few unintelligible words amidst sighs. A conversation did not come about. The scene was like one in the theatre. I fled.'

At the end of 1942 Göring told Speer, who had come to see him at the Wolfsschanze: 'We will be lucky if Germany retains its borders of 1933 after this war.' Speer writes: 'I had the impression that, despite the impudence with which he constantly and resoundingly kept echoing what Hitler said, he saw defeat approaching.'

On 14 January 1943 Hitler charged Field Marshal Milch with the task of supplying Sixth Army, but although his special task force was able to increase the number of supply flights, the last pocket was forced to surrender on 2 February. The Luftwaffe had lost 488 aircraft and 800 crewmen.

At Nuremberg Göring told Werner Bross: 'When later on bomber aircraft were lacking in the fight against Britain the Führer reproached me. But then I clearly told him (here Göring lifted his voice as if he were standing before Hitler at this moment and he spoke sharply and angrily): "You will have to go and look at Stalingrad. That is where my bombers are lying shattered in the fields".'

On 30 January 1943, from Aviation House in Berlin, he gave his last radio broadcast. It was heard in the ruins of Stalingrad by the remnant of Sixth Army, who had endured so much and now had to listen to their own funeral oration. 'Even in centuries to come people will speak of Stalingrad and the German heroes who fulfilled their duty for the Fatherland even unto death,' he shouted into the microphone in brittle, metallic tones.

This speech was really Göring's funeral oration for the Third Reich, ten years after his appointment as Reich Minister in Hitler's cabinet, and only a few days after the announcement by Roosevelt and Churchill in Casablanca of the demand for an unconditional surrender, the only condition under which the Germans could have peace.

In May 1943 Hitler decreed that all radio speeches by ministers must first be vetted by him. Göring was not prepared to accept this, and from now on he was silent.

30
Collapse

When American bomber fleets began their daytime attacks, starting with a raid on Wilhelmshaven on 27 January 1943, the air war entered a new phase. Hitler reproached Göring that his fighter arm was unable to prevent these attacks. But had not Göring warned Hitler against the war, and expressed his misgivings about coping with the Allied air forces? He had foreseen much of what was now to break over the Third Reich.

On 18 February in the Berlin Sports Palace Goebbels gave his speech on 'total war' during which the 'politically best trained audience' that one 'could find in Germany', as he told Speer after the event, 'applauded at all the right places'. After the funeral oration Göring had given on 30 January, Goebbels' speech was the reply from the death house of the NSDAP. Emissaries of the Minister for Propaganda had collected prominent artists for this event. Gründgens had learned about it beforehand and managed to extricate himself for one day from clutches that were degrading for a Prussian State Councillor. Goebbels ordered him to be found so that he could be stamped as one of his satraps through the newsreels, as he succeeded in doing with Heinrich George.

When in the evening after the political spectacle in the Sports Palace Goebbels was entertaining anxious Party comrades in his ministerial villa, Speer and Milch suggested that he re-activate the 'Ministerial Council for the Defence of the Reich' whose chairman Göring was. Goebbels immediately agreed. By doing this he could force Göring, whom he believed was gradually distancing himself, back into the collective responsibility. Göring had objected when Goebbels had had restaurants closed down, including the 'Horcher' where for many years Göring had been wont to feast with officers of the Luftwaffe. Göring kept it open, but Goebbels arranged for its windows to be broken. Göring had then withdrawn to the solitude of the Obersalzberg.

Speer was prepared to act as go-between: 'Here there was a constitutional organisation available, endowed with full powers, even the right to enact laws without Hitler's participation. With its help the positions of power that had been usurped by Bormann and Lammers could have been broken up. Bormann and Lammers would have had to submit to this authority, whose possibilities had remained untapped as a consequence of Göring's indolence.'

On 28 February Speer visited the Reichsmarschall on the Obersalzberg, and Göring appeared to be flattered that someone had remembered him. On 2 March he received Goebbels for a private talk. There was no longer any time to recall the past. Both Hitler's paladins were worried about the Führer's health, of whom Göring said that in three and a half years of war he had aged by fifteen years; Hitler had to be freed for his duties as military leader, although he was convinced that it was already too late. He also suggested that Himmler be taken into the Reich Council for Defence.

Goebbels was concerned to make Göring understand that he could not abdicate. In his diary he noted that Göring knew what would happen if 'we' were now to show weakness. 'He has no illusions about this. On the Jewish question, for example, we have taken a position from which there is no longer any escape.' With this, he nailed Göring to co-responsibility. 'This is a good thing. Experience shows that a movement and a people that have burned their bridges behind them fight better than those who still have the possibility to retreat.' Göring the ego-optimist was brought back into the circle of those responsible for the persecution and extermination of the Jews by means of these commitments, which were also shared memories.

Subsequently Göring went to Italy, Goebbels back to Berlin, which had just suffered a heavy air attack in which 700 inhabitants died and 35,000 were made homeless. But the conspiracy of the paladins came to nothing. When Goebbels and Speer went to see Hitler in his headquarters at Vinnitsa on 9 March, they had to listen to the Führer's criticism of the absent Göring: he was a dreamer, his liaison officer, General Bodenschatz, an ice-cold cynic. To this enraged Hitler neither Goebbels nor Speer dared to disclose their intention to re-activate the Reich Council for Defence under Göring.

On 20 March in Berlin Hitler carpeted Göring, whom he had called back from Rome, because of an air raid on Nuremberg. In the course of this he also spoke about the unsuitability of the Luftwaffe generals. The only thing that Göring could do if he wished to regain Hitler's confidence would be to start taking control of the Luftwaffe. At the end of 1942 he had been forced to relinquish part of the human reserves he had been holding back for the air war. Twenty-two Luftwaffe field divisions were set up, which could be employed at the fronts. Although the Army wanted to use these troops to make up decimated divisions, Göring was able to assert that they remained in the Luftwaffe and under his command. Now they had to wage a war for which they had not been trained, and they suffered casualties in proportion.

He had also set up the Panzer Division 'Hermann Göring', which was classed as a guard formation. It was now deployed in Tunisia and later on fought in Italy before being brought to the Eastern Front. The Divisional Commander was Beppo Schmid, an old confidant of Göring's.

In the spring and summer of 1943 Göring spread fear among his pilots, above all the fighter pilots in Italy, whom he accused of cowardice in the face of the enemy. At the same time he was worried about his Reichswerke Hermann Göring enterprises which were beginning to receive attention from enemy bombers. Developed when he was Beauftragter of the four-year plan, these now included 176 factories, 69 mines and metallurgical companies, 156 trading companies, 46 transport companies, and fifteen building firms.

He still found time to increase his art collection, which had already made him the richest man in Germany. Art treasures continued to flow to him from the occupied countries. In March 1943 he received 6 million marks from Bormann from the Reichs Fund for his activities in the art trade. There was still much that could be purchased abroad.

For the continuing extension of Carinhall, which became the main repository for the art treasures, he demanded 2 million Marks from Finance Minister Count Schwerin von Krosigk, who reluctantly had to give them to him – after having drawn his attention to the perilous state of affairs at home. Göring sensed that all was lost, but he continued to play King Midas even on the brink of the pit. In April Hitler's adjutant to the Luftwaffe, von Below, gained the impression that the Führer no longer wanted anything to do with Göring.

The American 'Flying Fortresses' were now reaching Italy and the German fighters could make scarcely any impression against their heavy armour and armament. On 11 June Göring sent a telegram to Luftflotte 2 in Italy: 'All fighter pilots in Italy are to be told that they are the most miserable fighters that I have ever commanded. If by chance they sight the enemy they are beaten off without achieving any success. Until further notice I forbid any leave so that I do not have to be ashamed of these miserable wretches here at home. Göring.'

Göring's General of Fighter Pilots Galland had flown the first Messerschmitt jet fighter Me 262 in the spring. In this aircraft he saw the possibility of decisively beating the bomber fleets, by which he meant inflicting such high losses that the pilots would lose their will to continue.

Between 25 July and 3 August Hamburg was largely destroyed by night attacks by British and daylight attacks by American bombers. During the raid, metal foil was dropped which blinded the radar equipment. Some 35,000 people were killed, including 5,000 children. Göring blamed his Chief of Staff Jeschonnek for the lack of defence against these annihilating streams of bombers. On 19 August Jeschonnek shot himself.

'To me Jeschonnek's death appeared to be symbolic of the condition of the Luftwaffe and the constant overtaxing of this branch of the Wehrmacht,' writes von Below. 'It was no longer capable of carrying out major assignments.'

After Jeschonnek's suicide Göring held a meeting with his closest associates at the Wolfsschanze. General Korten had become the new Chief of Staff. Galland writes: 'Göring summarised the results. After its offensive phase, the Luftwaffe must now go on the defensive in the west. It was now the most important task of the Luftwaffe not only to protect the life and property of the German people living in the cities threatened by bombs, but also to preserve the armaments potential of the Reich.' Galland goes on to report that never before or afterwards had he experienced such unanimity among the circle of those responsible for the leadership. 'It was as if under the impression of the catastrophe of Hamburg, everybody had given up any personal or departmental ambitions. There were no conflicts between General Staff and production, no rivalries between bombers and fighters. Göring too appeared to be carried away by this atmosphere. He left us alone for a time in order to report to the Führer bunker and to obtain the necessary powers for the immediate start-up of the measures envisaged.' At this time Galland got the impression that Göring now recognised how wrong the course the Luftwaffe was steering had been. 'To regain command of the air over the Reich and to secure it was the unanimous decision. And given the present situation of the development of the air war, this could only be achieved by the fighters. For me there could be no doubt that Göring would support us with all the weight of his authority.'

Then he saw the door open, Göring come in, eyes staring straight ahead, pass through their midst, and disappear into his adjoining office.

'After a while Peltz and I were ordered to report to him. The picture we saw was shattering. Göring was in a state of total collapse. His head buried beneath his arms on the table, he moaned unintelligible words. Embarrassed, we stood there for a moment. Then he sat up straight and said we were witnesses to the most despairing moment of his life. The Führer had withdrawn his confidence from him. All his recommendations, with which he had hoped to achieve a radical change in the situation of the air war, had been denied. The Führer had declared that he had been disappointed by the Luftwaffe far too often. The Luftwaffe had failed totally. He would now give it a final opportunity to rehabilitate itself by re-opening reinforced attacks against England. Terror could only be broken by counter-terror. This was how the Führer had dealt with his internal enemies. He, Göring, had recognised his error. The Führer was always right. As an initial measure, the Führer had ordered the creation of a Leader of the Air Attack against England. Göring stood up: "Colonel Peltz," he cried. "I hereby appoint you as Leader of the Air Attack against England."'

'The "Attack Leader England" went to work with lots of energy. With new tactics and new aircraft (Ju 188 and He 177) he was later able to revive the attacks against England. According to the Führer's order, all efforts by the Luftwaffe were to be subordinated to this task. Despite this, the new offensive was never able to achieve any strategic importance.'

After the Allied landing in Sicily in September, Italy had left the alliance with Germany.

Göring took off his medals. He is alleged to have said, when the bombing of German cities became more and more terrible: 'The German people suffer these air raids as a punishment by God.'

Once, from Carinhall, he tried personally to direct the deployment of fighters against incoming American bombers. He sent the fighters in the wrong direction. He visited the airfields and told his pilots: 'Don't leave me in the lurch,' and showed himself to the inhabitants of the cities that had been bombed.

On 26 November Hitler was shown the newest aircraft at the airfield at Insterburg in East Prussia. For the first time he saw the Me 262, called Messerschmitt to him and asked whether this jet aircraft could also be built as a bomber. Of this, von Below, who was standing behind Hitler writes: 'Messerschmitt answered this question in the affirmative and said the machine could carry two bombs of 250kg each. To this Hitler only replied: "This is the high-speed bomber."'

Hitler was thinking in terms of attacking the Allied bombers on their airfields, and may also have been considering the possibility of Allied landings in France. This twin-jet fighter-bomber could reach any altitude flown by the enemy bombers, or deal with enemy landings in low-level attacks, and its high speed would reduce turn-round time considerably. Hitler therefore remained obdurate when Göring tried to change his decision a few days after it had been reached. He did not take the defence of the Reich into consideration, for which the aircraft – with which the Luftwaffe would again have been able to gain stature with the German people being bombed in their cities – had originally been intended. Even though the Me 262 was soon to be produced in greater numbers, in 1944 its rapid conversion to a twin-jet fighter-bomber proved impossible.

Towards the end of 1943 Göring gave in to the fate that he had once chosen and that he had tried to change later on. He was always proud of the fact that he had stood beside Hitler, not below him, and he knew that it had been this position which had earned him the respect and even the love of the Germans during those years. Although he now knew that Hitler's road was leading to disaster, he wanted to remain the most obedient Reichsmarschall of the Greater German Reich, Hitler's loyal paladin, even into the hell that was opening at his feet. He had sworn loyalty to Hitler when they were both on their way to power. Now all that was left to him was to remain loyal against the day when he could finally assume the succession he had awaited so long. As Speer said later, in a Germany under Göring instead of Hitler, National Socialism would 'have become flat'. Under Göring National Socialism might not even have been possible. But these are fruitless speculations.

31

The Day of Judgement Approaches

When Göring celebrated his 51st birthday on 12 January 1944 he received the by now almost statutory gifts. Of the 200 crates of art treasures being stored in the monastery at Monte Cassino, where they had been evacuated before sending them to the Vatican, his Panzer Division 'Hermann Göring' sent him fifteen. These art treasures had mainly been brought to the monastery from Naples.

Göring refused these gifts, and even wanted the men responsible to be punished. The crates were taken to caves near Alt-Aussee in the Alps to protect them from air raids. Göring now also began to shelter valuables from his country estates and castles in air-raid bunkers. They piled up in the corridors of the subterranean Luftwaffe headquarters which he had had built under the Ehrenpforten hill near Potsdam, and where the coffins of the two Prussian kings from the Garnisonskirche had been kept since April 1943.

The city of Berlin, which in 1942 had given him a painting by Tintoretto worth almost a quarter of a million marks as a birthday present, in 1944 now sent a painting from the school of Antonio Moro which had cost about ten per cent of the Tintoretto. The Berliners were suffering under terrible bombing attacks which probably explains why they had become somewhat less generous.

Göring now owned five Rembrandts, and paintings by Rubens, Velasquez, Fragonard, Frans Hals, van Dyck, van Eyck, Boucher, Goya and the two Cranachs. In contrast to Hitler, who kept his paintings packed away in crates, Göring surrounded himself with his. He wanted to be able see them for as long as possible.

At Carinhall he had 217 large albums of photographs of his paintings and art treasures, the documentation of his mania as a collector. He was no longer interested in the model train set which was housed in the attic and shown to guests on rare occasions. But he pointed with pride to the paintings which hung on the walls. The collection was managed by the art dealer Hofer, who was Göring's main buyer, and by the librarian Gisela Limberger.

Napoleon had had works of art from all the countries he conquered brought to the Louvre in Paris. Göring purchased works of art or accepted them as gifts. Over them he still had power, in them he could submerge his ego, even his tormented soul, thereby maintaining the power that had long been taken away from him in other areas. He was able to see himself as the master of works of art. This was his final exercise of power. He was worried that air raids might destroy his acquisitions, as they were destroying the churches and cities of his country, but the bombs spared Carinhall, Veldenstein, and the Obersalzberg, and presumably Göring thought that he and his treasures were held in respect by the enemy.

Unbelievably, as late as 1944 he was still enlarging Veldenstein where he was staying more and more frequently and for longer periods. As a child he had learned obedience there, even if he had not liked it, but now he was having to submit to a man who was destroying the Reich. Sick in body and soul, his mood swung wildly from the euphoria induced by his regular ingestion of Paracodeine to its ensuing lethargy. One minute he was reprimanding his subordinates and the next was begging their forgiveness.

The destruction wrought by the Allied air forces did not succeed in turning the population against their leaders; rather, the more brutal the air war became, the more stoically it was suffered.

On 20 February 1944 the 'big week' offensive by the Allied air forces began, in which the aircraft industry and therefore the Luftwaffe were to be annihilated in preparation for the invasion in Normandy.

On 24 February Göring retired to Veldenstein Castle for a three weeks' holiday. With a small staff, he stayed in the Biedermeier house, telephoned his generals, alternately threatening them, and praising them if the fighters succeeded in shooting down greater numbers than before during the air raids on Berlin and Nuremberg. On 4 March Milch and Saur, Speer's deputy, came to see him in order to report that together they had installed the 'fighter staff' based on the model of the 'Ruhr staff', which had proved itself in the repair of traffic installations in the bombed-out Ruhr. The 'fighter staff' was to provide many new aircraft which were to be built in subterranean production plants. Göring was critical; in his view the industry was going underground much too slowly.

On the night of 24/25 March during his holiday, British flying officers broke out of the prisoner-of-war camp 'Stalag Luft III' near Sagan in Silesia. Without informing Göring, Hitler ordered that if any of them were caught they were to be shot. On 29 March Göring resumed his duties as Commander-in-Chief of the Luftwaffe. During his trial at Nuremberg he said: 'I was not present when the Führer issued the order. When I learned about it I objected most violently, but it was already too late. I myself saw this as the most weighty event of the whole war.' The shootings continued until 13 April. Of the 75 British flying officers who had broken out, 50 were murdered. When Göring learned about it after his return from vacation he confronted Hitler, but it was too late to countermand the order. This business had provided him with reason for breaking with Hitler, but he was no longer capable of doing it. Emmy Göring writes that her husband had been with her at Berchtesgaden on the day after her birthday when he learned about the shootings, and had been incensed. He had been very worried about his pilots who were prisoners of war in England.

Hitler probably went over Göring's head when he issued the order because he feared that Göring would finally refuse to obey him. He would have lost prestige if he had been forced to throw Göring out of office for insubordination. Despite all the conflicts he had had with Göring, he placed much value in having Göring remain what he had always been for the Germans and for their enemies.

At the beginning of April Hitler ordered a new Führer headquarters to be built near Waldenburg in Silesia, which used up as many tonnes of concrete and steel as the yearly allotment for public air-raid shelters throughout the whole Reich. Silesia had not yet had to suffer any air raids. Soon afterwards construction of air raid shelters by the state was discontinued. Now the people must take care of themselves.

Later someone wrote that before the Allied landings the world in which Hitler had been relentlessly asserting his will had been unreal. It may have seemed so, but in fact it had been atrociously real, and every measure he had taken was to have its dire consequences for his people.

Göring was at Veldendstein when he learned of the invasion of Normandy on 6 June. He immediately went to Kleßheim Castle near Salzburg for a situation briefing. On the initial day of the invasion his Luftwaffe was ineffectual; the Allies recorded only thirty attacks by German fighters and bombers involving 319 aircraft. The Me 262, Hitler's high-speed bomber, was still being tested. The jet aircraft could not be employed as a fighter because Hitler had forbidden it.

On 7 June Göring ordered all aircraft earmarked for the defence of the Reich to be transferred to France, but this didn't happen partly because of technical deficiencies and partly because of Allied air superiority.

In June there was a shortage of aircraft fuel because the hydrogenation plants which produced it had been bombed in May. Göring had no answer when Hitler asked him during a briefing at the Berghof, whether he and his Luftwaffe had hedged their bets with the enemy.

On 12 June the bombardment of London and southern England with the 'flying bomb' began; this was the *Vergeltungswaffe* V–1 (retaliatory weapon), which the Luftwaffe had developed at Peenemünde. There too Wernher von Braun had developed for the Army the V–2, a rocket packed with explosives, from which later on the space rockets of the Americans and the Russians were to emerge.

On 20 June air armament was transferred to Speer. Field Marshal Milch lost his office as Generalluftzeugmeister, but stayed on as Inspector-General of the Luftwaffe. Hitler did not wish for any sensational changes that might come to the notice of the enemy. The Technical Office, now called 'Technical Air Armament', fell to Colonel Diesing, who belonged to Göring's small leadership staff at the Veldenstein. Göring saw that the appointment of a new state secretary for aviation would be futile; the little that could still be done he wanted to do himself.

The army conspirators who intended to assassinate Hitler in July 1944 had included Göring and Himmler among their victims; Göring because he was the Führer's successor, Himmler because he was the chief of the police, the SS, and the concentration camps.

Colonel Count Stauffenberg saw an opportunity for the attempt on 11 July when he gave a presentation at Hitler's Berghof. However, since only Göring was present, he decided on a postponement. Four days later he was back again at the Berghof, but again not all the intended victims were present. The conspirators decided to do away with Hitler without waiting any longer for Göring and Himmler to take part in a briefing. When on 20 July Stauffenberg placed the bomb in the Wolfsschanze, Göring was at the Reichsjägerhof in the Rominter Heide. There it was time to pack, because the Soviet armies were approaching the borders of East Prussia. In the assassination attempt Göring's Chief of Staff General Korten was killed and his friend, General Bodenschatz, was wounded.

Together with Mussolini, who had arrived for a visit with a delegation after the assassination attempt, Göring inspected the devastated briefing barrack. Then they had tea in a large group, during which an enraged Göring accused Foreign Minister Ribbentrop of having brought the war 'down on the necks of the Germans' in 1939, while he had tried to prevent it with the help of Dahlerus. Losing control, Göring called the Foreign Minister 'you champagne salesman' and addressed him as 'Ribbentrop', whereupon the latter replied that his name was 'von Ribbentrop'. In 1933, when he had taken up office as Prussian Minister of the Interior, Göring had been given a file which revealed that Ribbentrop had purchased the title of nobility from an impoverished relative in 1931.

In the evening the Reichsmarschall called the commanders of his air fleets and ordered them to hang anybody who came to them as a 'representative of the new government'. If Hitler had been killed, Göring would have succeeded him. However, Himmler later said that he would have prevented this happening.

On 23 July Göring surprised Hitler by suggesting that the normal military salute (bringing the right hand up to the edge of the cap) be replaced throughout the Wehrmacht by the 'German salute' (i.e., the raised right arm while saying 'Heil Hitler!'). This unmilitary salute was then decreed by Hitler.

Having made this suggestion Göring said he had an infection of the throat and was going to Carinhall on sick leave. He spent the month of August there. Galland writes: 'He had withdrawn "for reasons of health". The real reason was probably his collapse under the reproaches that had been heaped against him and his Luftwaffe. Until the final moment he had tried to conceal the true situation from the top leadership. Now nothing could be explained away or hidden. Now the naked facts of the air war were speaking their unambiguous language. Göring could no longer be counted upon.'

In August the withdrawal from France began, which saw terrible scenes of disorganisation and despair in the Luftwaffe. Göring's pride was deeply hurt by this. The Luftwaffe had fought bravely and he had been proud of his men, proud too that the Luftwaffe had not been involved in the July plot. Now he could no longer protect his troops from the derision and scorn of the other branches of the Wehrmacht. It was being assumed that Eisenhower's forces would soon appear on the Rhine, but this did not happen.

On 4 September, Göring had six regiments of paratroops that were still in training placed at the disposal of the newly appointed Commander-in-Chief West, Field Marshal von Rundstedt, and in addition several thousand men from convalescent air and ground crews. From these Colonel General Student formed First Paratroop Army which was used to close a gap in the front.

Inspector-General of Fighters, General Galland, took care of the fighter pilot reserves, which he had suggested that Göring build up. Pilots were being trained and their numbers were growing. Göring had to accept the charges that he wanted to save his pilots from a hero's death, and maybe in his innermost soul he was actually thinking of this, because the war was lost and its ending appeared imminent.

At the end of August Gustaf Gründgens visited Carinhall and brought more bad news. In 1943 Gründgens had volunteered for the Luftwaffe and Göring had let him serve with the training unit of one of his regiments at Utrecht where he had attained the rank of sergeant. Gründgens had wanted to get away from the Gestapo whom he feared because of his unconventional private activities which Göring had covered. During his military service, Gründgens had continued to fulfil the duties of General Artistic Director part-time and in Luftwaffe uniform. In the spring of 1944 Göring had brought him back to Berlin permanently so that he could put on Schiller's *Die Räuber*. He had given him Schloß Bellevue as his residence. *Die Räuber*, with Gründgens in the role of Franz Moor, was the last Gründgens production in a Berlin tormented by air bombardment. Mephisto had turned into Franz, the villain, who on the stage of the playhouse on the Gänsemarkt, spoke of the day of judgement: 'Suddenly a monstrous peal of thunder hit upon my slumbering ear, and lo and behold, it appeared to me as if I saw rising up in fiery flames the whole horizon, and mountains and cities and woods melting away like wax in a furnace – and the naked plain began to move and disgorge skulls and ribs and jawbones and thighs, which drew together into human shape and flowed along enormously, a living stream.' This was to be his farewell message to the Berliners and to Göring who had held his protecting hand over the Prussian State Theatre.

The devastating news Gründgens now had for Göring came from the Ministry of Propaganda: all German theatres were being closed down, the staffs being sent to war or into the armaments factories. Göring learned of this through his General

Director, not from Goebbels who had initiated the decree. Gründgens hoped that an exception would be made in the case of the Prussian State Theatres, because they were under Göring's control. But, as in many other areas, Göring had become powerless here too. All he could do was to ensure that those actors who were not fit for service at the front were allowed to give recitations. And so his theatrical dream empire, in which great German theatre had been developed, collapsed as well.

After he re-assumed his duties in September, he kept his distance from Hitler in the Wolfsschanze. His new Chief of Staff, General Kreige, fell into disfavour there. In September Hitler wanted to transfer the leadership of the Luftwaffe to Colonel General Ritter von Greim who declined, however, because Göring was to remain in nominal overall command. To his Luftwaffe adjutant Hitler said he could not let Göring drop, his achievements were unique and it might be that he would need him again.

In mid September a major airborne landing on the lower Rhine in Holland, with which the Allies had intended to open their way to the Ruhr, failed, and it now looked as if the war would continue for some time. Hitler now had the offensive in the Ardennes (the Battle of the Bulge) prepared, for which he would need Göring's and Galland's fighter reserves.

For the *Endkampf* (final battle) which was now approaching, the Paratroop–Panzer Corps 'Hermann Göring' was formed at Modlin in Poland in September 1944. Like the Corps 'Großdeutschland', 'Feldherrnhalle' and XXIV Panzer Corps under General Nehring, it was only to be employed independently and so was given strong formations that included Panzer Division 'Hermann Göring' and Paratroop–Panzer Grenadier Division 2 'Hermann Göring'. These 'HG' formations, put at the disposal of the Army, had evolved from the 'Regiment Hermann Göring' which had been taken into the Luftwaffe on 24 September 1935 from the Prussian State Police. On 1 March 1941 this had been converted to the reinforced Regiment (mot) 'Hermann Göring'; in July 1942 to the Brigade 'Hermann Göring'; in October 1942 to the Panzer Division 'Hermann Göring'. The addition of 'Paratroop' to the designation had nothing to do with the state of training. There were no paratroops in these formations.

At Göring's personal disposal and for his protection was the Guard Battalion 'Hermann Göring', which developed into the 'Bodyguard Regiment Hermann Göring'. It was then split up, so that towards the end of 1944 a new 'Bodyguard Battalion Hermann Göring' on which he could depend had to be formed. At the end of April 1945 it supervised the demolition of his estate in the Schorfheide and the mausoleum.

Panzer Corps 'Hermann Göring' was among the units under General Reinhardt which successfully beat back the first break-through by the Red Army into East

Prussia; a Soviet Guard Army was stopped and forced to retreat. The fighting that took place between Surdauen and Schirwindt and between the Rominter Heide – where Göring's Reichsjägerhof was – and Ebenrode was particularly heavy.

Goldap was taken by the enemy. In the reoccupied village of Nemmersdorf the troops of Panzer Corps 'Hermann Göring' found horribly disfigured corpses of civilians which the Russians had left behind. The horrors committed by the Red Army in Nemmersdorf were publicised in the German *Wochenschau* (news of the week) and the press, so that everyone would know what could happen to civilians in the east. An officer of the Luftwaffe wrote about the horror of Nemmersdorf: 'The women surprised in the village, including some nuns, were herded together by the Russians, raped and badly beaten. Then the women were knifed or shot in the most beastly manner.'

Göring had had his refuge the Reichsjägerhof evacuated. The furniture had, as on former occasions, been donated to people who had been bombed out, mainly to actors in Berlin.

Before the Red Army could reach the Reichsjägerhof, Göring had a *Kette* (lit. a chain; tactical sub-unit of a Staffel, the Staffel being comprised of nine aircraft and equivalent to an RAF squadron or half a USAAF squadron) of three Fw 190s take off from the forward airfield at Gerdauen to destroy it with bombs. The Russians should find only ruins. On their return he greeted the pilots, shook their hands as he had often done on the return from sorties against the enemy, and awarded each of them the Iron Cross, First Class. The young pilots asked him about the state of the war, to which he replied that the war was lost, that there were no miracle weapons. The pilots were impressed. For them it was the first time that a senior officer had admitted that the war was lost, and Göring was no less than Commander-in-Chief of the Luftwaffe!

That a Panzer Corps 'Hermann Göring' fought in the Rominter Heide is but one of those coincidences of war, but it still has a symbolic implication. Göring's hunting preserve had become a battlefield, on which 'HG' – as the Panzer Corps was commonly known – was to have the final say.

In October 1944 Hitler was finally prepared to have the Me 262 used as a fighter. It had proved unsuccessful as a fighter-bomber or as a high-speed bomber because it lacked a bombsight that could be synchronised to the aircraft's high speed, so that the bombs missed their target by a wide margin. Jagdgeschwader 7 was supplied with the jet fighters.

As late as September 1944 Göring had lobbied for use of the He 162 as a *Volksjäger* (lit. people's fighter, i.e., as in *Volkssturm*, a desperate, suicidal, last-ditch measure, which bears resemblance to the Japanese Kamikaze attacks) which were easy and cheap to mass produce. In this jet aircraft, young, barely trained pilots were to hurl themselves against the Allied bomber streams.

In October 1944 Göring held a staff meeting at Berlin-Wannsee, during which he reprimanded his commanders and even heaped abuse on them. He had the speech recorded and sent to the airfields where the personnel had to listen to it. This led to growing opposition and bitterness within the Luftwaffe.

On 30 October he again visited Peenemünde on the Baltic island of Usedom to see the AA rocket *Wasserfall* (waterfall). This was optically steered and had a range of 26 kilometres and a ceiling of 18 kilometres. Development work had not yet been completed. As yet one had achieved a speed of 600m/sec. He found many representatives of the Ministry of Munitions and the Luftwaffe present. He was greeted by General Dornberger, the Army chief of the research station. 'He had changed so much that his appearance (compared with the spring of 1939) was unrecognisable to me,' Dornberger writes. 'Bright red, soft, morocco leather riding-boots with silver spurs were the first thing to attract the eye. Göring was wearing an amply cut thick fur coat of Australian opossum, the fur outwards. When this heavy man walking unsteadily on his small feet came towards me, the coat undone, I saw his airman's light grey uniform, the *Pour le Mérite*, and the Grand Cross of the Iron Cross. An airman's almost white, light grey cap and the interim staff to the marshal's baton completed the fantastic dress. Platinum rings with huge, deep red rubies, which sparkled in their clarity, shone on his soft, podgy hands. His formerly energetic face was flaccid, apathetic and terribly bloated. Light but unsteady eyes looked at me. I had the impression of a hedonist totally disinterested in events, lacking all energy and satiated.'

During the display the decision was to be taken on which types of AA rocket developmental work was to continue. For Göring this was so much theatrics. He knew that it was too late. The explanation of the equipment took place in a barrack of corrugated iron. 'He pretended to be studying the drawings on the walls,' Dornberger writes, 'but he was no longer looking at them. He was totally disinterested. I walked along beside him. About every five minutes his eyes started to turn until one could only see the whites. He staggered, reached into the pocket of his coat, and swallowed a small, round, rose red pill. Instantly he straightened and appeared to be quite normal again. After five minutes the same process.'

Eventually Göring said: 'I heard all this three-quarters of a year ago. Show me something new.'

When he climbed the stairs to the roof of the small tracking building of the 'Waterfall' project, he pulled a heavy revolver out of its holster, threw it up into the air several times and caught it again. His adjutant took the weapon away from him with the remark that it was loaded and not on safety.

Those rockets that were fired disappeared into the grey clouds in a matter of seconds; the electro-optical steering device was obviously still not functioning.

Göring's reaction was: 'If that is all you have to show me you can go to hell. I saw all this a year ago with exactly the same results.' .

He was then shown an A4, i.e., the V-2. Dornberger wrote: 'He acted like an excited child. Time and again he looked through the binoculars. Then finally smoke rose in the woods. The thrumming of the small first stage motor became audible and with a roll of thunder the rocket rose vertically into the sky. Then the turning curve came and the missile disappeared in the clouds in an easterly direction. Laughing, Göring turned around. His gigantic coat flowed around me. He pressed me to him and said: "This is great. This is something for the first Party convention after the war."'

Next he drove to the Luftwaffe's testing facilities at Peenemünde West, to see Ruhrstahl AG's Dr Kramer give a demonstration of a small wire-guided anti-aircraft rocket (the X4) which could be fired from an aircraft. 'Herr Reichsmarschall, I must have your decision today,' Kramer told him, 'so that the X4 will be given top priority. I must have this decision, otherwise we cannot complete the development work.' Göring answered with a resigned smile: 'What sense is there in my making a commitment to you? By the time I get back, some department in my general staff will most likely have revoked my decision. I have nothing to say in my own shop any more.'

In this autumn of the Third Reich, his Luftwaffe now virtually defeated, Göring wanted to get to the front and in September 1944 he told Hitler that he felt that his place was with First Paratroop Army in the west, but Hitler forbade this. He did not want his successor to be killed or taken prisoner.

In November 1944 General Koller became Göring's Chief of Staff; a quiet, composed officer, he was to accompany him to the end. Carinhall became Göring's last military headquarters. He had his wife and Edda with him. In February 1945 Hitler was to tell Goebbels that the Görings' influence had been detrimental; Emmy was not a National Socialist, and Hermann not a revolutionary but a bourgeois. That same month forty twin-engined Me 262 jet aircraft finally flew under command of Major Walter Nowotny, who did not return from a sortie. The formation was dissolved.

On 11 November 1944 Göring ordered all the highly decorated formation leaders of the Luftwaffe to attend a 'court day' at the air war school at Berlin-Gatow. The 'discussion' had been scheduled to last two days. Johannes Steinhoff writes: 'An illustrious get-together of men who were known to the nation as "heroes", whose pictures were untiringly put before the people in magazines, dime novels, and newsreels by the propaganda machine. Good-looking, mostly very young men. The autumn sun was reflected by their decorations which they wore about their necks or on their chests. They had been carefully selected – the most highly decorated in the Luftwaffe – and the Generals of the bombers, fighters, and reconnaissance formations.

'I was standing next to Lützow and the General of Fighters (Galland). The latter wore his blouse in a fashionable version, namely buttoned up at the neck. However, he was not wearing any medals.' Steinhoff goes on to describe Göring's appearance: 'He was wearing a dove blue uniform (the Reichsmarschall's privilege) with wide white silk lapels and – to my disappointment – long trousers. The fat man pressed himself between the arms of an easy chair and "let himself down". Then he immediately opened his wide energetic mouth and began to fill the room with his sonorous trumpet-like voice.'

'"Gentlemen, this meeting is an Areopagus, but certainly not an ostracism. What I expect from you, who are my most brave and successful, is that you critically evaluate everything in our service which – in your opinion – is not in order, needs to be improved. However, your criticism has to exclude the very top, your Commander-in-Chief. There is nothing to be discussed there, because: *habemus papam*. You are to help me recover the reputation of the Luftwaffe. The German nation expects that, because we have failed, failed unbelievably ..."'

Steinhoff describes Göring's appearance: 'His cheeks were rosy and the eyes, which appeared to be too small in the large plane of the wide face, began to glow. It had always been this man's mouth that had intrigued me, this energetic, huge mouth over the brutal chin. The lips were narrow and pulled in at the angles of the mouth. The mouth of a man of will, but at the same time a sensual, hedonistic mouth.'

After Göring's introductory remarks the officers were left to themselves. Given that they were not permitted to criticise the Reichsmarschall, there were only ideologically coloured discussions which ended in a 'declaration of faith in National Socialism' being signed. Since the officers believed that they were flying for Germany, not for a Party or a Weltanschauung, with few exceptions they considered the whole meeting to have been superfluous. At the end Galland passed a note to Colonel Steinhoff: 'Under pressure from the Führer, the Reichsmarschall has given permission to form the first turbine fighter squadron. Do you want to lead it?' Steinhoff wrote on the note: 'Thank you very much.'

On 12 November 1944 Galland was able to report that the fighter weapon was ready for action again. Training had been conducted for its deployment in the defence of the Reich. The result of the build-up of the fighter reserves was eighteen fighter Wings with 3,700 aircraft and pilots. The Luftwaffe had never been so strong before.

However, it was not destined for the defence of the Reich. On 20 November the Wings were transferred to the Ardennes. 'At this moment', Galland writes, 'for me any sense in continuing the battle broke down.' Hitler's final military idea, the decisive defeat of the Allied armies by a major offensive in the west, in order to gain a free hand against the eastern enemy, began under strictest secrecy on 16

December 1944 in murky weather which kept the Allied air forces grounded. On 24 December the sky cleared.

'The fighter arm received its death blow during the Ardennes offensive,' Galland writes. 'Under unfamiliar circumstances, with a lack of training and battle experience, the numerical strength of our fighters could not unfold at all. During transfer, on the ground, and in big air battles, particularly during the Christmas holidays, they were decimated and finally annihilated.

'The end of the chapter was the so-called Operation "Bodenplatte" (base plate). During the early hours of the final year of the war, on the morning of 1 January 1945, all our fighters took off at low level, partially guided by night-fighters and bombers, for an encompassing and carefully prepared attack on Allied airfields in northern France, Belgium, and Holland. By this action the enemy air forces were to be knocked out in one blow. Had the weather been good, the major action would have taken place sooner.

'In this act of desperation we sacrificed our last remaining substance.'

Since for reasons of secrecy the V1 restricted zones with their AA had not been informed, many fighters were shot down by their own side. Galland mentions 300 fighters, including 59 formation leaders.

On New Year's Day 1945 Göring appeared at the Führer's new headquarters *Adlerhorst* (eagle's nest) near Ziegenberg Castle in Hesse. The Ardennes offensive had failed, the sacrifice of his fighters had been for naught.

That evening it was not a fighter pilot, but a Stuka pilot who had destroyed Soviet tanks on the Eastern Front, who received the highest decoration for bravery from Hitler, the golden oak leaves with swords and diamonds to the Knight's Cross: Major Rudel.

After the award, Göring noted that Dönitz, Keitel, and Jodl – who were present – also wanted this medal, which was only awarded once, for their people as well. He said to Rudel: 'Do you see how jealous of me the others are and how difficult my overall situation is.' He had said 'me', not 'we' or 'you'. That is how self-centred he remained to the end.

Hitler had ordered Rudel not to fly again, but the Major succeeded in getting Hitler to change his mind. To Rudel Göring said that it was the last thing in the world he would have believed, that Rudel could make the Führer change his mind. When had he ever succeeded in doing this? It was a moment of truth for Göring, but the truth often has only a short life.

32

The Last Long Journey

I n the new year Göring had the night vision device 'Uhu', also known as the
Y-instrument, which had been installed in a few tanks during the summer of
1944, mounted on the windscreen of his Mercedes. With the aid of its infra-
red rays his driver could see the road at night up to 150 metres ahead and therefore drive at high speed. The Reichsmarschall sitting next to him had only the
black night before him.

When he celebrated his 52nd birthday at Carinhall, on 12 January 1945, there
were no festivities. No one from industry or commerce, from the destroyed cities
and provinces of Germany, sent him any valuable gifts. The only thing he received
was an unannounced visit by Erhard Milch who was living in his hunting-lodge
on Lake Stechlin. Milch wanted to patch things up with Göring. He asked
whether he had any new use for him. But Göring intended to make Bruno
Loerzer, the man who had introduced him to military aviation, the new Inspector-
General. The uninvited guest was asked to stay to dinner. Göring said: 'For the
Göring family good food has always been important. Now is not the time to fast.
We will all soon be given the *coup de grâce*.' He also gave a toast: 'Heil Hitler!
God protect Germany!'

Afterwards he went to see Hitler who was still at the 'Eagle's Nest' in order to
receive his heartiest, as von Below recalls, felicitations. It was the day on which
the great offensive by the Red Army began on the Vistula, which was to continue
until it ebbed away on the Oder not far from Carinhall.

On 16 January Hitler returned to the Chancellery, and Göring attended most
of the briefings he held there. On that same day at Carinhall, Göring as Reichsmarschall of the Greater German Reich, signed a decree by which the Luftwaffe
was to be given an NS Leadership Staff (Nazi political commissars). This institu-
tion had existed for some time at the OKW, the Army and the Kriegsmarine, but
Göring had refused to compromise his Luftwaffe by having it politically indoctri-
nated; he had taken for granted that it had always been National Socialist. Nor
did he want it to have to work with Martin Bormann's Party office as the other
branches of the Wehrmacht had been ordered to do.

But now he submitted to this yoke as well. It no longer meant anything to him.
He made the chief of the NS Leadership Staff of the Luftwaffe responsible for
ensuring that all the troops had a 'uniform fixed ideological orientation' and taking
care of their 'military-spiritual welfare'. But he also had to report to Göring on the
condition and morale of the troops. An officer from the NS Leadership Staff was

to join his own personal staff. The decree reached the various offices of the Luftwaffe only after the inevitable delays imposed by the chaotic situation. The last counter-signatures by responsible officers were not received until mid March.

By January Göring had long been aware that there was trouble afoot in the Luftwaffe. He had learned of deliberate delays by workshop personnel in the repair of combat aircraft on the front line airfields, but above all he had to fear a conspiracy by the fighter pilots. He had dismissed Galland, but had not found a successor. Himmler was making conspicuous efforts in the direction of senior officers of the Luftwaffe, his SS was just in the process of testing an AA rocket that could take off vertically.

On 13 January Colonels Lützow and Steinhoff had flown from Berlin-Gatow to Lodz, which was called Litzmannstadt, in order to meet the commander of the Air Fleets on the Eastern Front, Colonel General Ritter von Greim, who was the senior fighter pilot from the Great War. This was most unusual, even though they had discussed it with General Koller. They wanted von Greim to go to Hitler over Göring's head. They asked von Greim, who was badly worried about the Soviet offensive on the Vistula, whether he would be prepared to take over the Luftwaffe in the Reichsmarschall's stead. Von Greim told them that Hitler had already considered this possibility in September 1944. Now it was too late. Steinhoff recalls his words: 'I cannot become a traitor,' von Greim said. 'Not I. And above all not against Hermann Göring'.

He sent them back to the Reich to talk to General Koller, who – as Steinhoff writes – saw himself reminded of the events of 20 July 1944 and wanted to prevent a catastrophe. Koller therefore urged Göring to meet the five conspirators: Colonels Lützow, Trautloft, Neumann, Rödel and Steinhoff.

Göring met them at 'Aviation House' in Berlin. Colonel Lützow, their spokesman, presented him with a memorandum. Steinhoff writes that at first it seemed as if Göring were prepared to listen, but after Lützow had presumed to interrupt him, Göring had hit back. In his situation he could not afford a mutiny by his fighter pilots. 'Now I want to tell you what I think of this whole affair!' he screamed at his highly decorated officers. 'What you are offering me here, gentlemen, is high treason, is mutiny!' Pushing his armchair back, red in the face, he then shouted: 'You Lützow, you ... I will have you shot!' But it did not come to that. Göring transferred Lützow to an air staff in northern Italy and forbade him to return to the Reich. Galland was made to leave Berlin, but remain on call at any time. It was only now that Galland's dismissal was announced to the fighter squadrons. Colonel Gollob became his successor.

Now the Luftwaffe had also had its conspirators, but Göring, who confronted them, was able to handle this threat, which had also been a danger to him personally.

Galland was promoted to lieutenant-general, and Göring gave him a new assignment. He was to form the Luftwaffe's first jet fighter squadron at the airfield at Munich-Riem and was permitted to select his pilots personally. It was a suicide mission. Galland writes: 'He was specially recommending the obstinate and refractory commodores and commanders whom he had dismissed, at their head the "mutiny leader" Lützow.' Since Galland did not like the new General of Fighter Pilots, Gollob, he was thankful that he was to report directly to Göring. 'The ring began to close,' he writes. 'I had begun this war as a first lieutenant and squadron leader. I was to end it as a lieutenant-general and squadron leader! A fighter formation that as far as its reporting lines was concerned, hung in the air! A few chosen ones from the German fighter pilot élite as pilots! Jet fighters, of which we were firmly convinced that there was nothing better in the world at the time!'

Shortly before the end of the war Göring had managed to end the struggle about the use of the Me 262 as a fighter or a fighter-bomber. But although Göring considered the courage and desperation shown by Galland's jet pilots to be honourable and worthy of the fighter arm to which he had belonged since 1915, their deployment was to remain a mere foot-note in the history of the war.

Under Galland the Me 262s were flown by the best-known fighter pilots: Lützow, Steinhoff, Hohagen, Krupinski, Barkhorn, Bär, Herget, Bob, Eichel-Streiber. Lützow was killed, Steinhoff badly wounded. While all this was taking place, Generals of the Luftwaffe for whom there was no further use were being retired.

On 27 January 1945 during a briefing at the Chancellery, Göring had an argument with Hitler, to which he referred when talking to Werner Bross at Nuremberg in 1946. Hitler wanted to re-activate old officers on retirement and have them fight as simple soldiers or non-commissioned officers. They were to lose their former ranks if they were unable to lead the appropriate formations. Göring utterly repudiated this latter idea. He believed that it would be dishonourable if an honestly acquired rank were taken away from an officer. If a general were really incapable of commanding a company, one could put him on guard duty, but he would then stand guard as a general. 'The Führer then wanted to reassure me', Göring told Bross, 'that the pay would remain the same. That made me terribly angry. I told the Führer: "Then if I were one of these officers I would throw the money at your feet!" My stand on 27 January 1945 was the final reason for the Führer to withdraw his confidence in me entirely.'

This minute episode in the Götterdämmerung of the Third Reich coincided with the arrival of Marshal Zhukov's Army Group on the Oder. On 30 January, Hitler ordered the evacuation of all women and children from Carinhall.

On 31 January Emmy Göring bade farewell to her husband who remained behind at Carinhall. A Soviet attack was expected imminently, but in fact did not take place for the time being. Without once looking back she left the country estate in the Schorfheide. At Anhalter station Göring's special train was waiting, in which she took Berliners with her to Munich. On the morning of 1 February she was glad to see that the house on the Obersalzberg was still standing. With her were her daughter Edda and women from her and Göring's families.

At Carinhall the thunder of the guns from the nearby Eastern Front could be heard. The art treasures were carted away. The other belongings were to follow them to southern Germany or be buried in the Schorfheide.

From the briefing of 27 January Göring knew that Hitler was thinking about a final refuge in the Alps. On the Obersalzberg there were extensive tunnels and bunkers in which Martin Bormann had stored supplies.

On 3 February the *New York Times* reported that the fighting in Germany would continue even after the fall of Berlin. For this the Berlin government had prepared the Alpine region as a national redoubt. But there was never to be a militarily prepared Alpine fortress. It remained a phantom by which, however, General Eisenhower allowed himself to be deceived.

Around Carinhall Göring collected remnants of his replacement regiment 'Hermann Göring', which had been stationed at Utrecht and in which Gründgens had been a sergeant. In 1944 it had had to be transferred to West Prussia and as Paratroop-Panzer-Replacement and Training-Brigade 'Hermann Göring', was rushed to the fortress of Graudenz, which was able to hold out until March. From elements of this formation, which had remained behind the lines, two further regiments were formed near Carinhall on 28 January and 15 February. On 14 March they were united into a brigade at Joachimsthal on the border of the Schorfheide. From 17 March it belonged to the 9th Paratroop Division which was being made ready for combat again.

With the troops of these formations Göring had not only been able to protect himself to some extent from the enemy close by on the Oder, but also against his internal enemies. He knew that Goebbels was now one of his most bitter opponents, of whom there were many. Goebbels used every meeting with Hitler to blame the Reichsmarschall for the catastrophic air situation, the destruction of the cities, the downfall of the Third Reich. Repeatedly Goebbels demanded of Hitler to bring Göring before the *Volksgerichtshof* (Nazi Supreme Court, whose President Roland Freisler became notorious for his brutality in court and death sentences for the most minor offences) in order to have him thrown into the dustbin of history. But Hitler had no intention of offering the world such a spectacle.

Goebbels recommended giving Dönitz (Admiral, initially Commander of U-Boats, later Commander-in-Chief of the Navy, finally named successor as Chancellor in Hitler's will) command of the Luftwaffe, which Hitler rejected, because all the Großadmiral knew anything about was U-Boats. But Goebbels was also concerned with discrediting Göring as Hitler's successor so that he could take on the role, even if he no longer had any great expectations. He believed that in this he would achieve a far weightier place in history than by anything he had done so far.

On 13 and 14 February Dresden became the victim of three Anglo–American air attacks. The AA guns had been withdrawn in January to be deployed in the Endkampf in the west. There was not a single sortie by a Luftwaffe aircraft for the defence of the city against the bomber streams. Only a courier aircraft which happened to be flying to Berlin via Dresden was shot down by Allied fighters. Two days previously the conference at Yalta had ended, at which the future of Europe had been decided.

The air war over Germany had become a one-sided affair conducted by the superior opponents of Göring's Luftwaffe. There was nothing left for him to do except to take trips to the front. Maybe he was seeking death. When Hitler learned about this, he forbade him to undertake these dangerous excursions.

Göring went hunting in the Schorfheide and began to shoot his bison which he did not want to leave to the Russians. Speer visited him at Carinhall in mid February. He writes: 'Surely Göring had long been corrupted and nerve-racked. But at the same time he numbered among the few who from the day war broke out saw the turning-point Hitler had created by this war realistically and without illusions. If Göring, as the second man in the State, together with Keitel, Jodl, Dönitz, Guderian, and myself, had ultimately demanded of Hitler that he tell us his ideas on how he intended to end the war, Hitler would have been forced to declare himself. He had always shied away from conflicts of a personal nature, but now he could even less afford to abandon the fiction of a united leadership.'

'On this evening at Carinhall I came close to Göring as a person for the first and only time. By his fireside Göring had a vintage Rothschild-Lafite served and then ordered the servant to leave us alone.

'I openly described my disappointment in Hitler. Just as openly Göring told me that he understood my feelings only too well and that he had often felt the same. Nevertheless, it was easier for me, because I had joined Hitler late in the game and could therefore more easily give him up. He was tied to Hitler much more closely, many years of shared experiences and worries had bound them together – he could no longer get away.'

With this, Göring had also admitted a personal failing. He had courage, but faced by Hitler he remained a coward even now. While he knew that courage to oppose Hitler at this late date would no longer have been of any use, he also no longer had anything to give to the fatherland, which as Reichsmarschall he was duty bound to defend.

When the war had begun Göring had exclaimed: 'If we lose this war, then so help us God.' Now the day was here, but where was the God who could grant grace?

Göring still appeared to be hoping for some sort of grace, otherwise he would long have taken the cyanide he always carried with him. The appropriate time would have been after the destruction of Dresden.

At the beginning of March the *Joachimsthaler Zeitung* reported that the Reichsmarschall had shot a bison and given it to a caravan of refugees that were heading westwards on the road. Goebbels ran to Hitler with the newspaper in a final endeavour to get Göring replaced. But Hitler continued to hold on to Göring.

In mid March Göring's troops around Carinhall were ready for combat. The 9th Paratroop Division was sent to the Oder front, except one battalion which was kept behind at Carinhall.

At the end of March Hitler permitted Göring to go to Berchtesgaden with two special trains loaded with furniture and antiques. On the Obersalzberg he saw his family again and received General Galland at the beginning of April, who had flown from Brandenburg-Briest to Munich-Riem on 31 March with his formation of Me 262s, the first combat-ready jet aircraft of the war. The JV 44, as the formation was known, needed only 42 minutes to fly a distance of approximately 500 kilometres. The fighter pilots had been furious at the original concept of using the Me 262 as a low-level bomber against airfields in Britain; they had considered this idea to be senseless. Now Galland heard Göring – who greeted him in a friendly manner – say that Galland's predictions about the wrong use of the Me 262 as a bomber had been correct. Göring wanted to make his peace with Galland.

Göring's stay on the Obersalzberg was mainly concerned with the storage of his art treasures which were to be safeguarded from bombs. He could no longer count on being allowed to keep them, even if he were to survive the war, of which he was none too sure. One of his special trains was plundered later; it had been left standing on the track at Berchtesgaden.

Göring bade farewell to his wife and daughter and returned to Carinhall with his personal physician Dr von Ondarza and his adjutant Bernd von Brauchitsch. His servant Kropp, on whom he depended, was also still with him. From Carinhall he telegraphed his wife on their tenth wedding anniversary. The telegram ended with the words: 'May God protect Germany and us.'

To Colonel Rudel, who came to see him at Carinhall, he said: 'I am wondering when we will have to set fire to this dump.' Engineers had prepared the demolition of the buildings and the subterranean mausoleum. With Göring there were still General Konrad and Major Freigang, an officer from the General Staff. The command staff of the Luftwaffe with General Koller was in the bunker under the Ehrenpfortenberg near Potsdam and in barracks nearby.

On 16 April the Red Army began the battle on the Oder, and by the 20th the Germans had lost it. There were now Soviet and Polish troops south of the Schorfheide. The paratroops that had been deployed around Carinhall had been annihilated near Eberswalde. Göring shot his last four bison whom he had called to him by their names. He then bade farewell to his hunting staff and drove, without looking back, to Berlin in order to congratulate Hitler on his 56th birthday.

In Berlin he also took part in the briefing in the Führer's bunker, accompanied by General Christian, who was General Koller's representative to Hitler. He had had a new uniform made for himself, which appeared to be 'American' to the participants in the briefing. It was made of plain brown-grey cloth and had lapels of cloth with the gold embroidered Reichsmarschall's eagle.

This light uniform was intended for the Army's forthcoming summer campaign, and was already being issued to the troops; it was not in any way an American uniform. Göring was wearing it in order to be less conspicuous during his final journey through Germany on which he was about to embark. At the briefing he once again sat opposite Hitler, who had not yet decided whether he would seek death in Berlin or on the Obersalzberg. Several generals advised him to move headquarters to Berchtesgaden. Göring said that there remained only one road leading there that was free of the enemy.

Martin Bormann had already prepared the flight to Salzburg: ten Ju 352s were waiting in and around Berlin to fly the Führer's headquarters out.

The Obersalzberg appeared to be set for the final act of the Götterdämmerung. That evening Hitler's and Göring's dentist, Dr Blaschke, asked his technical assistant Frau Heusermann to fly to Salzburg with him, but she refused, because she did not want to die in Hitler's company. Nine of the ten Ju 352s arrived at Salzburg. One crashed in the Osterzgebirge near Börnersdorf.

When Göring bade farewell to Hitler it would have been natural to talk about the succession, but Göring told him that he had urgent duties to attend to in southern Germany and would probably manage to leave Berlin by car that same day. Albert Speer recalls that Hitler had looked at Göring without seeing him. At that moment he was probably emotionally upset by his own decision to stay in Berlin and risk his life. He had given Göring his hand with a few meaningless words. Luftwaffe adjutant Colonel von Below writes that Hitler had taken no further notice of Göring. It had been 'an unpleasant moment'. But on this 20th day of April he had the impression 'that Hitler had not yet decided whether he should leave Berlin or stay. In the evening we gathered in Hitler's small living-room for a drink.'

On this day American and English bomber formations attacked Berlin as 'a birthday present for Hitler', as the sorties were called. The last all clear was not sounded until 2.30 a.m. on the 21st. This was the reason why on his drive to Luft-waffe Headquarters near Potsdam Göring had to seek refuge in air-raid shelters several times, and in the process lost touch with his Mercedes. His adjutant von Brauchitsch went searching for him.

Dr von Ondarza who stayed close to Göring as his physician reports that he had been given a friendly reception by the Berliners in the air-raid shelters: 'He himself was very jovial and cracked jokes, particularly about his notorious state-ment that he would allow himself to be called Meier if ... Messengers were even sent from neighbouring bunkers to ask him to drop in. He even went there and was still quite popular with the Berliners.'

Göring's motorcade reached Luftwaffe Headquarters at about 2.20 a.m. General Koller, who telephoned von Brauchitsch there, asked to have a word with the Reichsmarschall. He urged haste because otherwise the passage of the Elbe before daybreak would not be possible. But at 3 a.m. Göring left with his motorcade without having talked to Koller. Göring's driver had mounted the 'Uhu' equipment in the windscreen.

Via Brandenburg and Belzig they came to Wittenberg, crossed the Elbe there, and continued on to Dresden, which was a heap of rubble. They drove through the Osterzgebirge to Teplitz and Pilsen. At Bayerisch-Eisenstein they re-entered the Altreich, out of which Hitler and Göring had made the Greater German Reich.

They then drove along the Ostmarkstraße and the left bank of the Inn, past Braunau, where the man Göring had remained loyal to for so long and who had brought destruction to the Germans had been born. In the evening they were at Berchtesgaden and on the winding road to the Obersalzberg.

The spring weather was as warm as summer, the land through which Göring drove was blossoming. In the south it began to rain, a fruitful spring rain. Göring drove over the last north–south road still free in his country, pursued by low-flying aircraft, past burning houses and shot-up cars. He was not alone with his motor-cade; many others were seeking escape.

From captured documents Göring had known since March where the lines of demarcation would be set. He now drove to the future American zone of occupation. He felt himself to be responsible for his adjutants and employees who were with him and he was glad that none of his people had had an acci-dent or been hit on the way. It is possible that he recalled the drive he had taken from Berlin to southern Germany with Carin Göring shortly before her death. At the time he had wanted to show her how beautiful this Germany was, to which she had followed him from Sweden. What had become of Germany since 1931! And during these fourteen years, how great had been his luck, his achievements, and his guilt.

He had had a look of desperation in his eyes when they saw each other again on the Obersalzberg, Emmy Göring writes. She wanted to learn from him whether Hitler was still hoping for something, but in this condition she could no longer ask him any questions.

Since Hitler had said the evening before that he would leave it up to fate whether he stayed in Belin or flew to the Obersalzberg, Göring had to reckon that Hitler would follow him to Berchtesgaden. The end in the Alpine Fortress, as it was called, could only be mass suicide, immolation, the plunge of the last remaining Goths into the crater of Vesuvius. For Göring, together with his wife and daughter Edda, whom he called 'Eddalein'.

The Obersalzberg was guarded by the SS. Göring had come without military escort. He had no guards to protect him and his family. Göring did not know that Reich Leader SS, Himmler, had been thinking of saving his own life since 13 April, when he began talks with Count Bernadotte, President of the Swedish Red Cross.

On the morning after Göring's arrival it began to snow in the Alps. Winter returned to the Obersalzberg. In Berlin on this 22nd day of April 1945 'historic events' were taking place, 'the most decisive ones of this whole war,' as General Christian told General Koller, Chief of Staff of the Luftwaffe, on the telephone that evening from the Führer's bunker.

Göring wanted to drive to Linz early next morning. There the Reichswerke which bore his name were still producing tanks for the Eastern Front in Austria. It is also possible that he wanted to check on the subterranean vaults near Altaussee and elsewhere in the mountains where his art treasures lay.

At about 10 p.m. General Koller called Göring's house via a directional beam in the Thuringian Forest. The connection was poor; Colonel von Brauchitsch answered the phone. 'He to whom we always must report does not want to get out of there. I have to get out,' said Koller. Brauchitsch replied: 'Göring wants you to come here.' 'I have to talk to Jodl first,' Koller said. Then the connection was broken off.

33
Captivity

One week before Hitler's suicide in Berlin, Göring was finally given the opportunity to dissolve his relationship of manic loyalty to this man and to act independently. It had always been typical of Göring that he had not dared to act without Hitler's agreement.

The Göring–Hitler relationship assumes a childish-naïve cast in this final moment of their dubious feelings of affinity. On Göring's part it must have been an exaggerated pact of loyalty between men; if not, no understanding or explanation seems possible, particularly at this remove.

Göring had no intention whatsoever of poisoning himself and his family with cyanide, of escaping from the responsibility he had borne. It did not befit him to slink away, even though he knew that he no longer had any support among the Generals of the Wehrmacht, of whom several blamed him for having been too cowardly to face up to Hitler in time – but what would 'in time' mean in this context? – and 'disempower' the dictator. The events of 23 April 1945 were to show that Göring did not want to play the coward, but they also prove that, in the attempt finally to do something off his own bat, he lacked the courage to split off from Hitler completely.

Only after Hitler was dead did Göring again feel himself to be the free man that he had once been. Before then he had been in fact Hitler's prisoner – and not only morally.

On 22 April Carinhall was still intact, because General Koller telephoned several times to officers there. The subject was the attack by Corps Steiner which was to break through to Berlin from the north. This was an illusion of Hitler's. At noon it dissolved. During the afternoon briefing Hitler's collapse took place. He gave up, intended to stay in Berlin, and shoot himself at the last moment. He said that Göring would become his successor and that he would negotiate. However, it was not clear from these sentences, as stenographer Hergesell reports, whether Hitler meant this as a direct order, or as a directive that would only come into force after his death.

When Göring was informed about the events in the Führer bunker by General Koller on the morning of 23 April, the latter gave him the following version of Hitler's statements about the Reichsmarschall, which he had received from General Jodl: 'He said he could not fight for physical reasons. He would not personally fight anyway because he would be in danger of falling into enemy hands wounded. We all tried our best to talk him out of it and recommended that the troops from the west be deployed for combat in the east. To this he said that everything was falling apart anyway. He could not do this, the Reichsmarschall should do it later. To a remark made by someone in the circle, that no soldier would fight for the Reichsmarschall, Hitler had said: "What do you mean fight! There is nothing much left to fight with, and when it becomes a question of negotiating, the Reichsmarschall is better at this than I am.'"

When Koller arrived, Reich Leader Bouhler was with Göring. Bouhler was a friend. General Koller had also reported to Göring that shortly before his take-off from Berlin-Gatow the news had been received that the Russians in the city had broken through to Alexanderplatz. From there it was not very far to the Chancellery; for Soviet tanks, a matter of minutes. Therefore Hitler's suicide could only be delayed for a short while.

The considerations Göring now made were based on this information. He had Reich Minister Lammers, the head of the Chancellery, called to him from Berchtesgaden, and asked him whether Hitler's will of 29 June 1941 was still valid. Göring allegedly fetched it from his safe. Lammers answered the question in the affirmative and added that if Hitler had decreed anything different he would have known about it. Without him, he could not have made it legal.

In the will it said: 'If I am to be restricted in my freedom to act or be incapacitated for any reason, then Reichsmarschall Hermann Göring will be my deputy respectively successor in all offices of the State, the Party, and the Wehrmacht.'

According to the report by General Koller, there could no longer be any talk of Hitler's freedom to act. It had to be assumed that he had given up. Despite this, Göring did not want to act without Hitler's agreement, if he could still obtain it.

The only strange thing was that during the farewell on 20 April Hitler had not said what he was to do if the Chancellery could no longer be held. But had not Hitler let him drive to southern Germany? A Göring, if he intended to continue to live, could not just retire to private life on the Obersalzberg like a mere general. Together with Reich Minister Lammers, Göring now dictated a message to Hitler:

'HQ. 23.4.45

My Führer,

Do you agree that after your decision to remain in the command post in the fortress, I, according to your decree of 26.6.41, immediately assume overall leadership of the Reich as your deputy, with full power to act internally and externally? Should there be no answer by 2200, I will assume that you have been deprived of your freedom to act. I will then consider the conditions of your decree as having been met and act for the welfare of the people and the fatherland.

What I feel for you in these, the most difficult hours of my life, is known to you and I cannot express it in words. God protect you and let you come here as soon as possible despite everything.

Your faithful
Hermann Göring'

Lammers had counselled leaving out the deadline of 2200, but Göring insisted. The signal was picked up by 'Ultra' and the Allies knew thereby that Hitler was finished. Göring sent similar signals to Ribbentrop and Keitel, who were asked to come to him if there were no answer from the Führer's bunker by midnight.

Emmy Göring writes: 'With bitter derision and in deepest despair his lips now uttered: "Now finally I am to have Germany given into my hands, now after everything is destroyed and it is too late!"'

Göring actually did believe he could still get tolerable conditions if he immediately contacted Churchill, Eisenhower, and Truman. But he did not delude himself that he would get off scot-free. He reckoned on being handed over, and asked his wife if she were prepared to 'bear everything, really everything, for the sake of Germany'. She answered the question in the affirmative. To this he replied: 'I wanted to hear this yes. And now I will act, as soon as the answer comes in.' At about 5 p.m. he received it:

'23.4.45
Radio message
Top secret – Chief only – only via officers.
The decree of 29.6.41 only comes into effect on my explicit agreement. There can be no talk of lack of freedom to act. I forbid you to take any steps in the direction you have indicated. Adolf Hitler.

Heil Hitler
signed. Martin Bormann'

Göring reacted immediately. He sent signals to Ribbentrop and Keitel: 'Führer informs me that he still has freedom to act. I repeal telegrams of today noon. Heil Hitler. Hermann Göring.' He did not know that Bormann, who had sent him the signal, had also sent a second one to the Obersalzberg. In it SS leaders Frank and von Bredow were directed to arrest Göring immediately for high treason.

Hitler's adjutant to the Luftwaffe von Below learned from Hitler that afternoon in the bunker: 'his decision was made to relieve Göring of all of his offices and have him taken into "honourable confinement" on the Obersalzberg. There can be no doubt that with this decree Hitler succumbed to Bormann's blandishments. Bormann also sent the necessary telexes to the Obersalzberg. That evening

I again spoke with Hitler privately about Göring and detected that he did have some understanding for Göring's stance. However, he held the opinion that Göring, as "the second man in the State", should only act according to his directives. According to these there was no room for negotiations with the enemy. Hitler directed me to order Colonel General Ritter von Greim to come to Berlin. Hitler intended to appoint him as Göring's successor.'

It is possible that Bormann, who did not want to die with Hitler, attempted to get him to fly out of Berlin at the last possible moment in order to take care of things on the Obersalzberg. He was not successful, but at least he had eliminated Göring.

On the evening of 23 April thirty SS men appeared. Göring was arrested and confined to quarters. He was then permitted to have dinner with his wife. On 24 April they again ate together, but only at lunch and under SS guard. After this Emmy Göring was permitted to bid farewell to her husband because, as an elderly SS man told her, they were now to be totally separated.

Bormann had decreed that Göring's SS guard would pay with their heads if he were to escape or be freed.

On the morning of 25 April an air raid on the Obersalzberg began which caused heavy damages but little loss of human life. The SS sent the Görings and the people with them in the house into the old air-raid shelter that had been built before the war. Since it was not safe enough, a large new tunnel had been dug for Göring in 1943–4, which was to have a link to Bormann's tunnel, something which Göring rejected. During a break in the attack they were ordered into the new tunnel by the SS men who feared for their lives in the old shelter.

However, they all survived. When, without the Reichsmarschall, they stepped out into the open in the afternoon, the Obersalzberg looked no different from the destroyed cities. Göring's country house was also heavily damaged. Emmy Göring managed to save a few items. They spent the night in the tunnel again.

Göring had asked SS leader Frank, who commanded their guard, to send Hitler a telegram: 'If Adolf Hitler believes me to be disloyal, then he should have me shot. But he should finally set my wife and the people who are with us free.' Emmy Göring asked Frank to add something to the message: 'If Adolf Hitler believes it to be possible that my husband did not keep faith with him, then he should have Edda and me shot as well.'

She did not know that Frank had a signal from Bormann in his pocket: 'The situation in Berlin is becoming ever more tense. Should Berlin fall and we go down with the capital, then the traitors of 23 April must be liquidated. Men, do your duty! Your lives and your honour are at stake!'

The signal which Göring had asked Frank to send was never sent. For the SS officer everything was clear. But Berlin was far away. Here on the Obersalzberg one had to concern one's self with how best to escape the destruction signalled by the air raid.

On 23 April General Koller had also been arrested by the SS in Berchtesgaden. But he was needed again. He received an order from the Chancellery to repair to Hitler immediately. He flew to Berlin, but could get no farther. He did not want to enter the witches' cauldron, and he had the feeling that he must do something for the arrested Reichsmarschall.

On this 25 April, Hitler relieved Göring of all of his offices. He even dismissed him as Reichsjägermeister, as Bormann said, who butted into a telephone call from General Krebs in the bunker to General Keitel.

On 27 April the Reich transmitter Hamburg, which was still in German hands, announced: 'Berlin, 27 April. Reichsmarschall Hermann Göring has been taken ill by his long-standing chronic heart condition, which has now entered an acute stage. At a time when the efforts of all forces are required, he has therefore himself requested to be relieved of the command of the Luftwaffe and all duties connected thereto. The Führer has granted this request. The Führer has appointed Colonel General Ritter von Greim as the new Commander-in-Chief of the Luftwaffe while simultaneously promoting him to Field Marshal.'

Anyone still able to receive this news would have gained the impression that Göring's death was imminent, even if, given the situation at this moment, the explanation of his abdication for reasons of health sounded ridiculous. But the bulletin had been so worded that it conveniently kept open the possibility of announcing his death from a heart attack if this were expedient. This was not quite in line with Bormann's directive to Frank; it was intended that Göring be shot after Hitler's death.

While this bulletin was being broadcast, the Görings were on the road with their SS guard. The Reichsmarschall had suggested to his guards that they move from the Obersalzberg, which had become inhospitable, to his Mauterndorf Castle in the Lungau. Before they left, Göring's entourage, including two adjutants, were taken to Kleßheim Castle near Salzburg. They too were to be shot when Hitler's death was reported. Emmy Göring hated Mauterndorf, which was always icy cold and which was supposed to be haunted .

There they now settled in. The officers of the SS guard ate with them at the same table, Göring acting as host. He probably wondered why nobody from his Luftwaffe had come to set him free.

On 30 April General Koller ordered a unit of air signals troops to help Göring get rid of his SS guards. Paul Deichmann and the staff of his Fliegerkorps I were near Linz. The Linz Gauleiter, Eigruber, told him that he was under suspicion of intending to free Göring, the traitor who intended to go over to the enemy, as he put it. Deichmann assured him that this was not so. He writes: 'The Reichsmarschall and his family and entourage were being held in a most generous manner at Mauterndorf Castle about sixteen kilometres away from my command post.'

In the evening of 1 May the radio announced Hitler's death. Emmy Göring was in bed with heart pains and sciatica, when Göring came to her with this news. She writes: 'Suddenly there was an uncanny calm around us. You have to say something now, I thought to myself. But everything inside me had been burned out.' Her husband reproached himself: 'And now I can no longer justify myself. I cannot tell him to his face that he has wronged me and that I was always loyal to him.' Since Emmy Göring feared that her husband was losing his mind, she tried to distract him, said she did not feel well, had strong heart pains. He remained seated by her bed and calmed down.

Then his two adjutants came from Kleßheim Castle with the rest of his entourage. Göring telephoned Field Marshal Kesselring, who had been given command of the territories remaining to the Reich in the south, and asked him to transmit a signal to Großadmiral Dönitz saying that the Reichsmarschall would expect to take part in the cease-fire negotiations. Kesselring had the message passed to Dönitz in Flensburg. There was no reply.

Shortly after the announcement of Hitler's death, however, Kesselring had received another call from Mauterndorf Castle. SS Standartenführer Brause, Göring's guard, asked him if he still had to execute Hitler's order, to shoot Göring, his family, and his staff, including two General Staff officers and a physician.

Former General Paul Deichmann writes: 'Kesselring forbade this and ordered him to move out with his command and leave Göring and entourage to themselves. He could no longer do any damage.

'While the SS command was secretly packing and marching off, Göring was in the castle gardens. At this moment one of my air signals units marched passed the castle park. Göring, who could not see any guards, waved to the soldiers. They recognised him, came into the park and crowded around him shaking hands. I learned of this event from Field Marshal Kesselring, whom I met on the air base at Zeltweg.

'Why high, and obviously the highest, Party officers had assumed that I could free Göring and his entourage is unclear to me. It may be that it was only a precaution, because as commander of the Luftwaffe in the area in which Mauterndorf Castle lay, in which Göring was, I disposed of strong forces. It is also possible that someone from Göring's entourage had attempted to contact me. However, a political battle for power in this war situation would have been a crime. My intervention – while Hitler was still alive – would most probably have meant the deaths of Göring, his family, and his entourage, because the SS command had the appropriate orders.'

Göring had regained his freedom. He stayed at Mauterndorf from where he sent his adjutant von Brauchitsch with a white flag and letters to negotiate with the Americans. In the letter to General Eisenhower he said that he knew that cease-fire negotiations were being conducted with the Dönitz government, but felt it would be expedient if in addition a direct contact between Eisenhower and himself were to be established on the basis of 'Marshal to Marshal'.

General Koller had had a country villa, 'Fischhorn Castle', near Zell-am-See, requisitioned for the Görings, the owner having refused to take Göring in.

When after much searching Colonel von Brauchitsch finally found some American troops, he told them that Göring was waiting for them at Fischhorn Castle. But it was not until 8 May that Göring left Mauterndorf to drive to Fischhorn Castle with his entourage.

En route he became entangled in the flood of German soldiers who were trying to make their way home. In Radstatt his car got stuck in the mob and he and his wife were recognised and joyfully greeted by the soldiers who crowded round his car and seemed glad that 'Hermann' was still alive. Many believed now that things would not turn out so badly.

An American lieutenant found him and together they went on to Fischhorn Castle. There he was greeted by the American Brigadier General Stack with a handshake and an invitation to dinner.

The Görings and their entourage were assigned rooms on the second floor of the villa, the Americans lived on the ground floor and the third floor. Emmy Göring persuaded her husband to go to dinner alone; she was at the end of her tether. Edda was put to bed on a couch. When she wanted to darken the windows, an American soldier told her she did not need to, the war was over, at which she wept. Next morning the Reichsmarschall had breakfast with General Stack, who had told him at dinner that General Eisenhower had granted Göring a safe conduct, which was not true.

Now Göring had to take leave of his family and companions. He was driven to General Spaatz's headquarters of American Seventh Army at Kitzbühel; Spaatz had been one of the signatories to the capitulation by the German armed forces in Berlin-Karlshorst. Göring was allowed to hold a press conference in the garden of a hotel. He had again exchanged his Reichsmarschall's uniform for the brown-grey field uniform he had worn before. He had much to tell the war correspondents, photographers, and film people. From him they learned about his captivity. When champagne was served, Göring must have had the impression that he was being offered the respect due a soldier, because he had done the same during the Great War in France with enemy pilots that had been shot down.

But this was something different.

Next day General Eisenhower was aghast when he learned of this press conference of Göring's, and ordered him to be taken out of circulation and brought to Augsburg for interrogation. On arrival the Americans took away his medals, the marshal's baton, the epaulettes, and the large diamond ring he wore on his finger. He was now a prisoner of war, like the three German generals with whom he was quartered in the same house. He did not like this at all; as Reichsmarschall he had expected better treatment. After all, the Generals were of a lower rank than he.

34
'The Can'

I n the modern housing area outside destroyed Augsburg, where Göring, his
adjutant Colonel von Brauchitsch and Major Klaas were held together with
several hundred prisoners from the Party, the state and the armed forces,
the interrogations began. But in Göring's case these were conducted in such a
manner that he was scarcely aware that he was being interrogated. In the
course of long conversations, during which no notes were taken, the Reichsmarschall willingly gave answers to more than six hundred questions. These
included important information about the Japanese, with whom the Allies were
still at war.

Göring asserted that he had never signed a death sentence or sent anyone to
a concentration camp except as a matter of military necessity. He declared that he
had not been in agreement with the anti-Jewish measures, had never condoned
the methods applied in connection with them, and that there was no excuse for
them. He showed one of the interrogation officers the stubs of cheques which his
wife had sent to a Jewish tailor in the Theresienstadt concentration camp on a
monthly basis, and explained that Theresienstadt had not been as bad as its reputation.

Whenever he became taciturn, the interrogation officers addressed him as
'Herr Reichsmarschall', upon which he always livened up. He felt as though he
were an English peer, a duke, who had to reckon with being banned from the
realm. During the talks he sometimes recalled Marshal Pétain, whom the
Germans had interned with all honours in Sigmaringen Castle. (In December
1944 Pétain had sent Göring a personal letter from there – from 'Marshal to
Marshal', as he wrote – in order to get rid of a 'personal companion' who had
been assigned to him and who was in contact with the Gestapo. This companion
wore a Luftwaffe uniform, but had never been in action. He had caused Pétain's
personal priest to be removed. Göring had the companion relieved.) But if he
were expecting one, no St. Helena was in store for Göring.

The reports of the interrogation officers underline Göring's vanity. He had
been clever, but not wise. He had seen himself as a European who had never
attacked a foreign statesman in times of peace and who had defended the
authority of the state against the Party. After the Battle of Britain his star had
declined.

During captivity he knew how to make himself popular by virtue of his
extensive knowledge of people. The camp commandant, a Major Kubala, was

an American of Hungarian descent. He was quite unpleasant, but Göring was able to get along with him. He even managed to get permission for his servant Robert Kropp, who had been allowed to stay with him, to drive to Fischhorn Castle in one of the three cars remaining to him in order to fetch clothing. In return for this favour, Göring gave Kubala an Italian painting of the Madonna which Kropp had brought with him. Göring said that he had bought the painting, which had formerly belonged to the Rothschilds, legally at an auction in Paris. The Major handed the painting in and it was valued at 300,000 dollars.

Kropp probably also brought the cyanide capsules with which Hitler's loyal followers had been supplied. Göring, always immoderate, kept three times the requisite dose with him in captivity and was able to determine the moment when he would make an end. Emmy noticed that Kropp was in a great hurry. He appeared to be distracted and when he took his leave said that everything was just too horrible.

On 19 May 1945 General Patch, commander of Seventh Army, received Major Kubala's report on the twenty-hour interrogation of Göring. He said that Göring was not at all the comic figure so often portrayed by the newspapers. He was neither stupid nor a Shakespearian fool, but rather cool and calculating. One should not underestimate this man. He proudly claimed that he had planned the landing of his paratroops on Crete and had drafted plans for the capture of Gibraltar. He was responsible for the build-up of the Luftwaffe but denied having had anything to do with the racial laws, the concentration camps, the SS or atrocities committed in Germany or abroad.

To quote from the report: 'Behind his clever and often witty remarks one senses that he seizes every opportunity to have himself appear in the best possible light. At all times Göring is an actor who does not disappoint his audience.'

The interrogation officers were concerned about the fate of his art collection. Göring was prepared to give truthful answers. He said that the paintings and Gobelin tapestries had been paid for. From the art treasures collected in the Jeu de Paume museum in Paris he had purchased at auctions valuables that had been taken from their Jewish owners. He was prepared to give them back. Göring said that the major part of these works of art were at Berchtesgaden in freight cars. He had not had time to store them in air-raid shelters before being arrested on 23 April. He gave the name of his art consultant Hofer, who could provide information on everything. A transcript of these statements was made. Leonard Mosley writes: 'All the paintings he mentioned were found (with the exception of those he had left in Berlin and which had fallen into the hands of the Russians). To celebrate their recovery Göring was invited to a second cocktail party in the officers' mess. This time the champagne had come from the freight cars which the Americans had found together with the paintings.'

On 21 May Göring and Kropp were flown to Luxemburg in a four-seater aircraft, a 'Piper Cub'. He was now allowed to keep only one adjutant with him, but since he needed the services of Kropp, he left both aides behind.

At the airport Göring said before take-off, that as an old fighter pilot from the Great War he knew that this aircraft was not dependable and refused to get in. Only after the senior American officer present, a colonel, told him in front of the approximately two hundred Americans who had not wanted to miss this spectacle, that he could guarantee a safe arrival did Göring get into the aircraft. Before that he gave a military salute which was not returned. The Colonel had addressed him as 'Herr Reichsmarschall' for the last time.

On the flight he was accompanied by a major from the military secret service, who reported later that he had housed Göring and his servant in the run-down Palace Hotel at the Luxembourg spa of Mondorf, which the Americans called 'the can'. Göring had been assigned a small room, a dungeon with a camp-bed, a chair, and a table, whereupon he said to the major: Now I see what the biggest mistake of my life was: that I did not take the same path as Adolf Hitler.'

But he still had the wherewithal for doing away with himself at any time because when he was searched only one of the three capsules had been found – in a tin of Nescafé. The large quantity of Paracodeine tablets he had with him and which he was still using were taken away. A medical officer named Kelley analysed them and found that they contained only a small amount of Paracodeine. At this time Göring's daily dose was one hundred tablets, which amounted to 150–200 milligrams of morphine. 'They could not have decisively influenced his mental abilities at any time,' Kelley wrote.

When he was taken to Mondorf Göring weighed 280 pounds.

At the beginning of June his servant Kropp had to leave him, and a German prisoner of war took over his duties. At Mondorf Göring again met many acquaintances, both friends and enemies: the Americans had thrown the top brass of the Third Reich and the armed forces into this 'can'.

On 20 June Emmy Göring with Edda and her female companions left Fischhorn Castle because all Germans had been banned from Austria. They found refuge in the Biedermeier house at Veldenstein Castle which had been plundered and was standing empty. The women stuffed straw into sacks for bedding and borrowed bed frames from a hotel in Neustadt. An American guard took up quarters in the manager's house. They too were now prisoners.

In August Göring learned that he was to be put before an international tribunal in Nuremberg as the 'No. 1 war criminal'. He had feared that he would be handed over to the Soviet Union, from which interrogation officers had come to question him in Mondorf. Among them was Lew Besymenskij who had acted as interpreter during the capitulation in Berlin-Karlshorst. Göring was nervous because he assumed that the five officers, including a woman, would take him back to Russia with them. Asked when it had become clear to him that Germany had lost the war, he replied: 'Doubts about the outcome of the war came to me with the landing of the Allied armies in the west. The break-through of Russian troops on the Vistula and the simultaneous attack by Allied troops in the west were the first serious signal for me.' Later, in court at Nuremberg, he said that in mid to end January 1945 he had no longer had any hopes. He told the Russians about the fighters with jet propulsion that were armed with six cannon and 24 rockets. With these it could have become possible to prevent the air attacks against Germany.

About Himmler he said: 'When my reputation began to decline, the authority of this person, who had occupied the next position after me, began to rise. I was seen as a conservative. The more radical Hitler and his policies became, the more he needed radical men. When Himmler was entrusted with command of Army Group Vistula, we all thought that the whole world had gone mad. Himmler was anxious to take my place, ensured me of his friendship but worked against me. I told him that I felt amicable towards him, but I was actually on my guard.'

To the question about Himmler's fate, Göring answered: 'If he is really dead, then I have no doubt that in that other world he will be a devil and not an angel.'

Asked about his role as crown prince, he answered: 'When twelve to eighteen months ago my poor relationship with the Führer became known, the head of the Chancellery asked the Führer whether I would still remain his successor. Hitler replied that he would not name Göring if he were to have to appoint a successor now, but since this had been done and had also been fixed in the minds of the people, he would not alter his decision.'

In August Göring went on a diet in order to look well when the court of the victors over the vanquished would assemble in Nuremberg.

In the end, he was to become 'the first man' he would so much have liked to have been long ago. He was also prepared to accept responsibility for everything he had done. In this he stood apart from many who had been thrown into the 'can' with him.

He could not imagine Hitler standing before this court. But he, Göring, was prepared to accept responsibility in Hitler's stead.

In September he was transferred to the prison at the Nuremberg palace of justice. The American director of the prison, Colonel Andrus, had already been a strict warder of the 'can' prisoners.

Albert Speer, who had been interrogated elsewhere, met Göring again at Nuremberg: 'From across the way, from the opening in the door of his cell, Göring looked over and shook his head. There was an uncanny silence. Göring constantly walked up and down in his cell.'

35
Poison

Göring spent the last months of his life in his one-man cell in the prison at Nuremberg, or in the courtroom. At first he was allowed to eat with the twenty other accused, but Colonel Andrus then ordered him to be segregated at meal-times to prevent his exerting influence on his co-prisoners. Once a day he was allowed to exercise in one of the courtyards. He was permitted lengthy sessions with his defence counsel Dr Stahmer and his assistant Werner Bross, was given access to documents that bore his signature, and was allowed to prepare documents setting out the events that had witnessed his rise and fall. He was permitted to write and receive letters. He autographed photographs of himself taken during his time of power and luxury. He had turned 53, but again looked younger. To those of his fellow-prisoners who had known him then, he appeared to be the Göring of 1933.

At the end he left a letter for Colonel Andrus telling him that whenever he entered the courtroom he had a capsule of cyanide concealed in his boot, Hitler's legacy to anyone he had deemed worthy of joining him in suicide. Göring had a second capsule concealed in a jar of Nivea Cream.

Unprepared, the prison authorities at Nuremberg had not instituted the meticulous security measures and rules that obtained at Spandau where several of Göring's companions in crime were confined after the trial.

At Nuremberg there was the renewed confrontation with the horrors of the past, horrors in documents and testimony by witnesses, which finally also drove Göring into self-tormenting doubts about the measure of his guilt, even though he had intended to make full use of this 'show' – as he called the trial – in which he had the right to play the leading role.

The American forensic psychologist G. M. Gilbert, whom Göring called his 'Santa Claus', was available to him for discussions until the very end. In *Nuremberg Diary*, Gilbert recorded the questions he had put to Göring and the replies he had received. Did he tell Gilbert what he really thought? The notes are not a transcript, but they reflect the opinions of a man who has settled his account with life, but is fighting for his life, nevertheless, and for his reputation in the memory of those who were his contemporaries in Germany. He had nothing to expect from them at the time. They were beaten, worn out, enmeshed in events – either guilty or blameless – for the like of which there had been no precedent in the history of the world. Göring had contributed to making these events come about. Next to Hitler he had been the man who had shone most brightly in the deceptive light, and who had fallen all the more deeply into the abyss of disaster. Why should they take pity on him, the enemies and friends, who had also lived and suffered because of him!

In the courtroom he saw many acquaintances again, who like himself now had to forget the acclamation of the masses which had lifted them above the masses and swept them into offices in which they had either failed or prevailed. The nation to which they belonged had become unworthy in the eyes of the world. Although the Nuremberg Tribunal left no doubt about this, it still differentiated in assessing individual degrees of guilt and thereby contributed much to the discovery of the truth.

Göring's comments as recorded by Gilbert are redolent of arrogance and cynicism, but also with shock and tormenting self doubts. Göring's IQ was the third highest among the accused after Schacht and Seyß-Inquart, as Gilbert discovered, and the verbal duels the 'No. 1 war criminal' fought in court with the American prosecutor Robert Jackson were even admired by his enemies. For a time he succeeded in forming a 'Göring faction' among the accused in which he once again proved to himself the power of leadership he possessed. But it was all vain in the face of the realisation that there was to be no escape for him – not into lifelong banishment as Reichsmarschall, not into an old age in which he could look back on his life, all passion spent.

When the trial began he was still dreaming that fifty years after his death the marble tomb his nation was holding ready for him would be his due. But when he saw what the Third Reich had left as its legacy, he lost this illusion as well. Despite this, he saw his secure place in history. He would live on, in places and in contexts he could no longer choose, but which somehow existed, nevertheless, no longer admired by anyone, burdened with guilt, hated and marked by what he had done or failed to do.

He objected violently to the accusation that he had contributed to bringing about the war, which he had wanted to prevent – at least against the Western Powers – and for which he had undertaken much. But he did accept responsibility for everything that he had done. His cross-examinations by the judges were shattering, but this did not prevent his rebelling against those who had to judge him, because the verdict was beyond any question.

Albert Speer had accused him of wanting to take them all, the rest of the defendants, along on his ride to Walhall. 'Rise up to Valhalla!' Göring had called to his dead pilot comrades Udet and Mölders in the Berlin Invaliden Cemetery. Walhall was Valhalla, the hall of honour of the ancient Germans, in which the warriors were to meet again, those men who had held high the shield of honour while they fought and suffered.

But Göring had not only been a soldier, he had also been Hitler's 'crown prince', who had lost his 'inheritance', been thrown out of the Party, dismissed from all his offices when the ride to hell was nearing its end. This made him unique among Hitler's paladins, but also in the history of the Third Reich, as well as among the legacies his nation now had to carry, and in the eyes of the world in which he was still living.

His idea of himself had been something totally different, but now he had been overtaken by his own past. In his closing statement before the tribunal he accepted everything for which he believed he had been responsible, but rejected anything over and above this, even though it had been proven by testimony.

When the verdict was announced, 'death by hanging', a technical defect in the apparatus with which he listened to the translations from English prevented his understanding it. He raised his arms to draw the court's attention to the defect.

He was permitted to say farewell to his wife, who had been taken from Velden-stein to the penitentiary at Straubing, where her daughter Edda had soon joined her. She was now at liberty again and was living in a hut near Hermann's child-hood home, Dr Ritter von Epenstein's Biedermeier house on the Franconian castle mount of Veldenstein. He was able to indicate to Emmy that he would not let himself be hanged.

On the next to last evening before his death he asked to have his dinner with the prison chaplain, the American vicar Captain Henry F. Gerecke, and to receive the consolations of the Lutheran Church. The chaplain refused both requests, because he believed that during the trial Göring had proved that he was not a repentant sinner. Earlier he had reminded Göring of his daughter Edda; surely he wanted to see her again in heaven? But even this appeal had failed to elicit an admission of guilt.

All that was now left to Göring was to deceive his guards, who on the eve of the execution were watching him through the spyhole in the cell door to prevent any attempt to evade the gallows. But he succeeded. He was able to slip the cyanide capsule into his mouth while wiping his face and, barely two hours later, on the way to the gallows, to bite down on it.

And so Hitler's fate overtook him after all, but he cheated the executioner who was waiting to hang him as the first of those that had been sentenced to death.

When the four officers from Great Britain, France, the USA and the Soviet Union inspected the corpses, Göring's body was on a stretcher beside those who had been hanged. Someone had put the noose he had evaded around his neck.

On 16 October 1946 the corpses were taken to Munich and burned in a crema-torium. The ashes were strewn in a roadside ditch where no one would find them.

These things took place and were then forgotten for many years. But they have been brought back from forgetfulness, because on this earth there is nothing that does not leave some trace.

And there is no mercy without repentance.

Epilogue

Charles Dickens said that if story tellers were only to tell the hundredth part of what life itself produces in the way of strange entanglements and coincidental events, their audiences and readers would accuse them of serving them with nothing but improbabilities. In this regard, a modern reader without experience of those long past decades might find this story of Hermann Göring's life and death too improbable, too contradictory to be true; a wild invention of the times, portraying a figure who could not have had any reality in fact.

But one must accept that he did exist. Without Hitler, he would have become a rich industrialist who played a role in aviation. With Hitler, he became a historic figure. He possessed the undeniable privilege and disadvantage of the soldier and officer, in that he had to obey unconditionally. As a Marshal of the Reich, however, he could have put service to this Reich ahead of his loyalty to Hitler. Had he done so, he would have gone down in history in a different way.

But his undoing – and that of the German people – was to put devotion and loyalty ahead of his own insights and experiences, to submit the weight of his own personality to a man who himself was not loyal to it or to his nation. But since Hitler had made him powerful and rich, he could not find the courage to oppose him openly, even though he often did so in his thoughts.

When in February 1943, after Stalingrad, Göring again started taking the drugs he had done without for ten years, his deputy Erhard Milch wrote in his diary: 'It was my impression that he was afraid of Hitler.'

This fear showed itself in two ways. Göring was actually afraid of this man, but he was also afraid of what this man was doing. This probably led to the 'heroic cynicism' behind which Göring hid in order not to become a danger to Hitler. And it also included the masquerades he enjoyed; the theatrical appearances in varying costumes with which he tried to impress his visitors who, however, found them foolish. They remind one of a Condottiere from the Italian Renaissance, or closer to home, of Mussolini's art of disguise. He was not ashamed of tears, which he showed openly, and he often wept in the presence of others when his feelings had been wounded.

Although his knowledge of art was not inconsiderable, there were forgeries among his collection of paintings of which he was unaware. He himself was a work of art of the Third Reich which often resorted to forgeries.

Any work of art, any artistic creation, falls outside the normal parameters, be an epoch ever so destructive and empty of sense. It attracts attention, and Göring did not lack for attention from the people. Behind the dignitary and paladin they saw the man, which was something very rare during the Führer's nightmare regime. And if they did not see the man, they were at least able to imagine that he must be hidden somewhere behind the mask.

'My strength was my tolerance,' Göring told his counsel's assistant in 1946. This too was a part of his bragging, but it does contain a kernel of truth if one considers what tolerance meant in a state that was not tolerant.

Since Göring was powerful, was able to give or lend power, he had friends. But even before he attained power, he was sought after. Friends from early days said later that his eyes were unforgettable, that they held something convincing and compelling. There must have been an aura about him that transcended his position and power. He was generous and liked to give presents.

In the many offices that had been heaped upon him, he seldom worked hard unless it were absolutely necessary; he believed in delegation. As Minister and Minister President he demanded memoranda of no more than two pages, otherwise they would tend to go unread; he would never read more than four pages. His reading material for recreation consisted of Edgar Wallace and Karl May, but also of works of history in which he searched for a reflection of himself.

From family background, upbringing, and as an officer decorated with the *Pour le Mérite*, he occupied a unique position among the potentates of the Third Reich. This also applies to his social position. The hopes placed in him that he would prove to be a guarantor of Prussian tradition were vain. From the heritage of Prussia he had only selected 'always on duty' for himself, but he spurned the morality connected with this sense of duty when he gave himself over to National Socialism. He knew life's difficulties and tried to be just, but at the same time he withdrew himself and lived in dream worlds where he was able to clothe in very down-to-earth fashion. In this context his mania for pomp made him assume the pretensions of a parvenu.

In the end, 24 hours before his death by potassium cyanide, he wrote a proclamation to the German nation. The American army newspaper *Stars and Stripes* had announced that it would be published, but this never took place. It is alleged to have disappeared in the American archives held at Alexandria in Virginia. But who would have heeded the Reichsmarschall at that stage?

For 600 years, since 1192, the Reich Marshals von Pappenheim were Quartermasters General of the Reich Army as well as being the supreme military judges and the men responsible for the road, transport, and health services of the army. The Reichsmarschall of the Third Reich Hermann Göring cannot be compared to them in any way.

He received many medals, for which the soldier's city of Potsdam gave him a shrine in which to keep them. In his day he received almost everything that was available to an ambitious and vain man, who felt himself duty bound by the tradition of his family to serve the state. But this is also where he failed. He was equal to many things, but not to the maxim of a morality which he nevertheless carried within him.

Bibliography

Abshagen, Karl Heinz. *Canaris: Patriot und Weltbürger* (*Canaris: Patriot and Citizen of the World*). Stuttgart, 1949

Below, Nicolaus von. *Als Hitlers Adjutant 1937–45* (*Hitler's Adjutant 1937–45*). Mainz, 1980

Bethell, Nicholas. *The War Hitler won*: *September 1939*. London, 1972

Bross, Werner. *Gespräche mit Hermann Göring während des Nürnberger Prozesses* (*Conversations with Hermann Göring during the Nuremberg Trial*). Flensburg and Hamburg, 1950

Burckhardt, Carl Jakob. *Memorabilien* (*Memorabilia*). Munich, 1978

Burmester, Dirks. *Alarmstart* (*Emergency Take-off*). St. Michael, Austria, 1982

Dahlerus, Birger. *Der letzte Versuch* (*The Final Attempt*). 2nd edn, Munich, 1973

Deichmann, Paul. *Der Chef im Hintergrund. Ein Leben als Soldat von der preußischen Armee bis zur Bundeswehr* (*The Chief in the Background. Life as a Soldier from the Prussian Army to the Bundeswehr*). Oldenburg–Munich–Hamburg, 1979

Dimitroff, Georg. *Held von Leipzig. Eine Dokumentation auf zwei Schallplatten mit Originalaufnahmen des Reichssenders Leipzig von 1933 anläßlich des Reichstagsbrandprozesses* (*Hero of Leipzig. A documentation on two records with original recordings from 1933 by Reich Radio Station Leipzig on the occasion of the Reichstag arson trial*). Litera DDR, n.d.

Dornberger, Walter. *Peenemünde – Die Geschichte der V-Waffen* (*Peenemünde – History of the V Weapons*). Esslingen am Neckar, 1981

Fraenkel, Heinrich, and Manvell, Roger. *Hermann Göring*, Hanover, 1964

Galland, Adolf. *Die Ersten und die Letzen. Jagdflieger im Zweiten Weltkrieg* (*The First and the Last. Fighter Pilot in the Second World War*). (Paperback), Munich, 1982

Gilbert, G. M. *Nürnberger Tagebuch* (*Nuremberg Diary*). (Paperback), Frankfurt am Main, 1962

Goebbels, Joseph (ed and trans by Louis P. Lochner). *The Goebbels Diaries*. New York, 1971

— (ed and intro by Professor Hugh Trevor Roper). *The Goebbels Diaries: Final Entries, 1945*. New York, 1979

Goertz, Heinrich. *Gustaf Gründgens*. Reinbek bei Hamburg, 1982

Göring, Emmy. *An der Seite meines Mannes* (*By My Husband's Side*). Preußisch Oldendorf, 1980

Gritzbach, Erich: *Hermann Göring: The Man and his Work*. (English trans of the authorised German version). London, 1939

Guderian, Heinz. *Erinnerungen eines Soldaten (Recollections of a Soldier)*. Heidelberg, 1951

Halder, Colonel General (ed Hans-Adolf Jacobsen with Alfred Philipp). *Kriegstagebuch (War Diary)*. vols. 1–3, Stuttgart, 1962

Heinkel, Ernst, with Jürgen Thorwald. *Stürmisches Leben (A Stormy Life)*. Biography, (Paperback), Munich 1977

Hoegner, Wilhelm. *Flucht vor Hitler (Escape from Hitler)*. Munich, 1977

Ilsemann, Sigurd von. *Der Kaiser in Holland (The Kaiser in Holland)*. Munich, 1968

Irving, David. *Hitler und seine Feldherren (Hitler and his Commanders)*. Frankfurt am Main–Berlin–Vienna, 1975

— *Tragödie der Deutschen Luftwaffe. Aus den Akten und Erinnerungen von Feldmarschall Milch (Tragedy of the Luftwaffe. From the Files and Recollections of Field Marshal Milch)*. (Paperback), Frankfurt am Main–Berlin–Vienna, 1975

— *The War Path. Hitler's Germany 1933–1939*. London, 1978

Jablonski, Edward. *Airwar*. New York, 1979

Kehrig, Manfred. *Stalingrad – Analyse und Dokumentation einer Schlacht (Stalingrad – Analysis and Documentation of a Battle)*. Struttgart, 1974

Kesselring, Albert. *Soldat bis zum letzten Tag (Soldier to the Final Day)*. Bonn, 1953

Koller, Karl. *Der letzte Monat (The Final Month)*. Mannheim, 1949

Kordt, Erich. *Wahn und Wirklichkeit. Die Außenpolitik des Dritten Reiches. Versuch einer Darstellung (Mania and Reality. The Foreign Policy of the Third Reich ... Attempt at a Portrayal)*. Stuttgart, 1947

Kuntze, Paul H. *Das neue Volksbuch von den Kolonien (The New Handbook on the Colonies)*. Leipzig, 1941

Maser, Werner. *Adolf Hitler. Das Ende der Führer-Legende (Adolf Hitler. The End of the Führer Legend)*, Düsseldorf–Vienna, 1980

Mason, Herbert Molloy. *Die Luftwaffe*. Vienna–Berlin, 1973

Mosley, Leonard. *Göring*. (Paperback), Bergisch Gladbach, 1977

— *Lindbergh. A Biography*. New York, 1976

Nauroth, Holger. *Die Deutsche Luftwaffe vom Nordkap bis Tobruk 1939–1945 (The Luftwaffe from the North Cape to Tobruk, 1939–1945)*, in pictures, Friedberg, n.d.

Paul, Wolfgang. *Der Heimatkrieg 1939 bis 1945 (War on the Home Front, 1939 to 1945)*. Elzlingen am Neckar, 1980

— *Brennpunkt. Geschichte der 6. Panzerdivision 1937–1945 (Focal Points.*

History of 6th Panzer Division 1937–1945). 2nd edn, Osnabrück, 1983

— *Das Feldlager. Jugend zwischen Langemarck und Stalingrad* (*The Field Camp. Youth between Langemarck and Stalingrad*). 2nd edn, Esslingen am Neckar, 1979

— *Das Potsdamer Infanterieregiment 9. Preußische Tradition in Krieg und Frieden* (*Potsdam Infantry Regiment 9. Prussian Tradition in War and Peace*). Osnabrück, 1983

— *Der Endkampf um Deutschland, 1945* (*The final Battle for Germany, 1945*). 2nd edn, Elzlingen am Neckar, 1978

Plehwe, Friedrich-Karl von. *Reichskanzler Kurt von Schleicher* (*Reich Chancellor Kurt von Schleicher*). Esslingen am Neckar, 1983

Reinhard, Colonel (ret.). *1918–19. Die Wehen der Republik* (*1918–19. Birth Pangs of the Republic*). Berlin, 1933

Rieckhoff, Herbert-Joachim. *Trumpf oder Bluff?* (*Trump or Bluff?*). Zurich, 1945

Ruge, Wolfgang. *Hindenburg*, Berlin, 1980

Schmückle, Gerd. *Ohne Pauken und Trompeten* (*Without Fanfares*). Stuttgart, 1982

Schramm, Wilhelm Ritter von. *Geheimdienste im Zweiten Weltkrieg. Organisationen – Methoden – Erfolge* (*Secret Services in the Second World War. Organisations – Methods – Successes*). 4th edn, Munich, 1983

Simon, Heiner. *Wohin mit Nadescha?* (*Where to with Nadescha?*). Heilbronn, 1983

Speer, Albert. *Erinnerungen* (*Recollections*). Frankfurt am Main – Berlin, 1969

— *Technik und Macht* (*Technology and Power*). ed. Adelebert Reif, Esslingen am Neckar, 1979

Sommerfeldt, Martin Henry. *Ich war dabei. Die Verschwörung der Dämonen, 1933–1939* (*I was there. Conspiracy of the Demons, 1933–1939*). Darmstadt, 1949

Steinhoff, Johannes. *In letzter Stunde* (*In The Final Hour*). (Paperback), Munich, 1974

Tessin, Georg. *Verbände und Truppen der deutschen Wehrmacht und Waffen-SS im Zweiten Weltkrieg, 1939–1945* (*Formations and Troops of the Wehrmacht and the Waffen-SS, 1939–1945*). vol. 1, *The Branches, an Overview*. Edited from documents in the Federal and Military Archives, and published in co-operation with Brün Meyer with the support of the Federal Archives and the Committee for Military Research, Osnabrück, 1977

Wilamowitz-Moellendorf, Fanny Gräfin von. *Carin Göring*, 556.–620. thousand. Berlin, 1941

Winterbotham, Group Captain F. W. *Aktion Ultra* (*The Ultra Secret*), Frankfurt am Main– Berlin–Vienna, 1976

Wehrwissenschaftliche Rundschau, vol. 17 (1967): *Die Vernehmung des Reichs-marschalls Göring durch die Sowjets am 17. Juni 1945 (Interrogation of Reichsmarschall Göring by the Soviets on 17 June 1945)*, trans and commentary by Wilhelm Arenz

Zeitschrift für Politik, vol. XIX (1972): *Britisch-Deutsche Friedenskontakte in den ersten Monaten des Zweiten Weltkrieges. Eine Dokumentation über die Vermittlungsversuche von Birger Dahlerus (British-German peace contacts during the initial months of the Second World War. A documentation of Birger Dahlerus' attempts at mediation)*, by Bernd Martin

War Diary of the Supreme Command of the Wehrmacht (Wehrmacht Operations Staff), vol. IV, 1 Jan 1944 – 22 May 1945

State Archives, Berlin

Federal and Military Archives, Freiburg im Breisgau

Private publications and unpublished sources

Private archives of Wolfgang Paul, Berlin-Grunewald

Index